GERMAN MEN OF LETTERS
VOLUME VI

Literary Essays

GERMAN
MEN OF LETTERS
VOLUME VI

Literary Essays

edited by
ALEX NATAN
and
BRIAN KEITH-SMITH

OSWALD WOLFF
London

ISBN 0 85496 011 2

MADE AND PRINTED IN GREAT BRITAIN BY
THE GARDEN CITY PRESS LIMITED
LETCHWORTH, HERTFORDSHIRE
SG6 1JS

CONTENTS

Preface

Volume VI of the series *German Men of Letters* had been planned and mostly written before the death of its Editor Alex Natan in January 1971. Mr. Brian Keith-Smith took over as Associate Editor by arrangement with Mrs. Wolff and Mr. Natan's executor Mr. Graham Davies. Mr. Natan's introduction was available in first draft and has been reproduced with only a few minor corrections. Choice of authors and contributors was made by Mr. Natan; the editing of the contributions was carried out by Mr. Keith-Smith.

Tribute to Alex Natan

(1906–1971)

"Misfortune is a favourable opportunity like any other. Every ass can meet with misfortune. The whole ingenuity consists in knowing how to make the most of it." These lines from Frank Wedekind's *Marquis von Keith* could epitomise the career of Alex Natan who died after months of failing health in January 1971 following an operation the previous summer. Heinz Alex Natan was born in 1906 into a middle-class business family in Berlin, completed a *Realgymnasium* education there, went on to study Law, History and Political Science at the Universities of Berlin, Heidelberg, Munich and Leipzig, and wrote a doctoral thesis on *South West Africa as Mandate 'C' of the League of Nations* in 1930.

Alongside his distinguished academic training Alex had found time and energy to become a member of the German Olympic athletic team in 1928, and captained his country's athletic team against Switzerland in 1929. He represented Germany in several international meetings, was Secretary of the Berlin Rugby Union and in charge of the Junior Rugby League. While studying at Heidelberg he took an important part in organising the new University Institute for Physical Education.

He took up work as a free-lance journalist, private tutor, and secretary to a professor, and in 1932 became sports and film editor of the Berlin liberal newspaper *Die Welt am Montag* until it was suppressed by the Nazis the following year. He also wrote a *History of Political Persecution at German Universities since 1670* and a novel on sports not published due to the political situation at the time. Actively involved in the struggle against the rise of the Nazi party, he was forced to leave Germany as early as 1933, and on return in 1934 from Britain for a holiday was arrested, but he managed to escape.

He settled in Britain until he was forcibly interned in Canada in 1940 as an enemy alien. He had taken up advanced studies in Political Science and Sociology as a research student at the London School of Economics, and became a Research Assistant there during 1936. In 1937 he toured public schools, training establishments and sports clubs lecturing on the most recent

9

techniques in Physical Training, and started out on a teaching career first at Rendcomb College and later at Clayesmore College. 1939 he spent lecturing in Scotland and wrote a government report on the "State of Health and Physical Education in Scotland". During internment Alex became among other things spokesman for the sewing department, camp librarian and group leader and also worked on a sociological and psychological study "Community Behind Barbed Wire".

Returning to England, Alex took up a post as teacher of history and German literature at King's School Worcester, where he remained until his retirement in 1967. The final years of his life he spent in a London flat and travelling in Germany and Switzerland. To the very end he was writing and planning numerous publications and welcoming old friends and personalities in the British German-speaking world.

Bare facts tell little of the character and achievement of Alex Natan, yet if anyone knew how to make the most out of an upset life, he did. He relished life among the avant-garde of Berlin in the twenties, and despite his genius for adaptation to institutions and ways of life which he openly detested, one feels that he was never really happy outside an atmosphere of cultural experiment. On many occasions he simply did not have the right (English) qualifications and had to make his way by the sheer force of his industry and his wide intellectual knowledge. Alex, by nature a *brillant causeur,* felt obliged to immerse himself in publishing and writing in order to escape the restrictions that a small provincial English town was bound to make on such an ebullient and cosmopolitan character. It is to Worcester's credit that it offered a congenial enough home for over twenty years to someone who must have seemed an archetypal eccentric German teacher quite deliberately opposed to what he saw as a philistine English backwater. His publications alone bear witness to his range of knowledge and interests. Apart from reviewing countless books for German newspapers and periodicals, he wrote for them a number of articles on this country and the following books since 1945 :

Neues Deutschland (Basil Blackwell)
Britain Today (Bayerischer Schulbuch Verlag)
Prima Donna (Basilius Presse, Basel)
Primo Uomo (Basilius Presse, Basel)
The Operas of Richard Strauss (Basilius Presse, Basel)
Graue Eminenzen (Walter Verlag, Olten)

He edited the following :

German Men of Letters Volumes 1, 2, 3, 5 (Wolff, London)
Swiss Men of Letters (Wolff, London)
Silver Renaissance (Macmillans)

also several books on sport including *Stadium, Sport and Society*.

To those who knew him, Alex achieved a typically British aim : he became a most gifted all-rounder, a fact that cannot be appreciated from reading his books alone. For not only did he have a professional's knowledge of history, economics, politics and literature, he also had an astute critical knowledge of music and modern art. He was a connoisseur of opera and had many interesting stories to narrate about German stage productions and personalities. In his later years he was an active member of the cultural sub-committee for the 1972 Olympic Games in Munich, also a member of the Hamburg Shakespeare Prize committee. He took particular delight in having put forward as he put it "two rather different people" as candidates (Graham Greene and Harold Pinter) for this prize in successive years, even more when he could say : "as usual my horses have won !" An individualist who impressed so many people in so many different ways, it was Alex's fate to have had to accommodate himself time and again to systems for which he had scant respect. That he found the ingenuity to cope with such a life is not surprising, for he had a quick and warm-hearted sense of humour that broke out often into a sympathetic, even cherubic-looking smile.

Alex Natan will be remembered by English-speaking students of German for his editorship of the *German Men of Letters* series. He too was a German man of letters, but unlike most of the authors dealt with in this series, he belonged to a generation whose talents were either cut short by war or political suppression, or else were scattered abroad on to land that did not favour them. That he made his name was due to his innate and persistent energy coupled with a shrewd and cheerful humanity that knows no frontiers and turns even misfortune into a favourable opportunity.

B.K.-S.

Introduction

by ALEX NATAN

"Aufklärung"

During the eighteenth century the Age of the Baroque gave way to the Age of the Enlightenment with which the essays of this volume are concerned. It is curious that a man of Frederick II's literary circumspection should have failed to observe that during his long life and reign (1712–86), and in the German states, that remarkable revival of German language and letters called the "Aufklärung" had come to the fore. Like the Baroque, the Enlightenment was a European movement which transcended literature and the visual arts and embraced philosophy and rational criticism as well as music and the modern beginnings of mathematics and sciences. Enlightenment resulted from French rationalism and English empiricism. Rationalism recognised in Man's reason a regulating principle for the perception of matters of general validity. Empiricism deduced all perception from the experience of the mind. Professor Peter Gay, whose two-volume work on *The Enlightenment* cannot be recommended enough, sees the movement as a "recovery of nerve". According to him, with increasing secularisation Man gains a true picture of his environment and sees how free he is. This degree of freedom encourages him towards inquiry, criticism, reform, a readiness to take risks, an awareness of his self-dependence. "One might say that generally Candide's garden seemed the only solution for today. Eldorado belonged to the day after tomorrow" (*Times Literary Supplement*).

From its very beginning the German "Aufklärung" differed from the general European Enlightenment in that "it attached less importance to deductive Reason and more importance to 'instinct', sentiment and sensual impressions. The empirical to them was as significant as the rationalistic : 'Gemüt' (which is but approximately equivalent to our term 'Soul') became for them as sacred a word as 'Reason' became for the Western rationalists, Romanticism, although it originated in England, was a plant that prospered lavishly in German soil" (Harold Nicolson). Immanuel Kant gave this reply to the question "Was ist Aufklärung?" :

"Have the courage of making use of your own intelligence (*sapere aude*)".

The "Aufklärung" commenced with Leibniz, one of the most universal minds the Western world has produced. None of his contemporaries or successors could match the range of his seemingly unlimited learning, his profound curiosity, and the inexhaustible vitality of his intellect. Lessing became the embodiment of the "Aufklärung" and Kant finally its copestone and simultaneously one of the progenitors of German Idealism. From 1770 onward the emotional forces of "Sturm und Drang" began to turn against the one-sidedness of the "Aufklärung", and after 1785 German Classicism became the dominant expression in literature and art.

However, it would be wholly misleading to assume that these dates could fix precisely the limits of these trends in artistic development. All progress in history takes place as a gradual transition. It disposes of what is obsolete, and it crystallises what remains alive as a starting point for new ventures. Therefore in Germany during the "Aufklärung" poets and thinkers appeared side by side who came from diametrically opposite camps. The stern rationalist Gottsched lived at the same time as the amiable Wieland, the master of the Rococo mood. The critical Lichtenberg was a contemporary of Lenz and Klinger, advocates of unbridled irrational forces.

This co-existence was made possible by the impact of those forces from abroad which influenced noticeably Germany's intellectual and literary development. French Rationalism became already the dominating outlook on life in the age of Louis XIV. It was based upon the philosophical works of René Descartes (*Discours de la Méthode* 1637 and *Méditations sur la philosophie première* 1641) which are often held to be a significant point in the history of modern thought. The philosopher advanced a twofold proposition : the analysis of the brittle values of the past and the construction of a new edifice of thoughts emanating from a single principle. Therefore he confronted the faith of the Middle Ages with the self-assurance of the human mind, in which he perceived the only indubitable reality. For—so his argument ran—I may doubt everything except my own doubtings ("cogito ergo sum"). Thus Descartes became the proponent of a critical rationalism, which recognises the mathematical reason as the only authoritative form of perception. Upon this proposition modern science could base its impressive construction which Descartes' philosophy imagined as a sort of universal mathematics.

The arts and sciences of this epoch confirmed Descartes'

philosophy. Men appear in the dramas of Corneille, Racine and Molière, in the fables of La Fontaine, in the sermons of Bossuet, in the letters of Madame de Sévigné, who are conscious of their dignity as thinking human beings, who are able to subordinate their passions to their perception, who can smile at the confusion of the world by virtue of their reason, and who can put their thoughts in order and clarity. In the eighteenth century, in the age of Louis XV, Diderot, Bayle, Montesquieu, Voltaire confronted the flagging forces of the French feudal society with the challenging thought of a reasonable political order which would guarantee the liberty and equality of all human beings. They defined the dynamic power of reason as the supposition of a life worthy of Man and extended its sway over subjects which had hitherto been the preserve of religious faith. Germany's intellectual history, her literature and arts in the same period were remarkably stimulated by France's classical literature, by its Rationalism, by the clarity of French form and by the elegance of its style.

England's philosophy of Enlightenment too exercised considerable influence. Already Francis Bacon, later Hobbes, Locke and Hume had stressed that experience and the perception of the senses were the only source of knowledge, a conception which was in accordance with the sober appraisal of reality practised by the English. But popular enlightenment too supported this philosophy of life. Moralistic periodicals like the *Tatler, Spectator* and *Guardian* contributed much to the sharpening of judgement and to the rise of social criticism through their treatises, comments and genre-pictures. However, the Germans felt rather reluctant to accept the English tendency towards an epistemological scepticism and empiricism, just as philosophical materialism which became one of the important schools of French thought never appealed to the German thinkers of the eighteenth century.

Before the influence of the French and English Enlightenment were felt in Germany, Gottfried Wilhelm Leibniz had established the logic of truth and the logic of probability, which organised the descriptive natural sciences and history. Thus he restored the harmony between God and Man, between creator and creation which had been questioned since the days of the Renaissance.

The literature of the "Aufklärung" preferred, in accordance with its nature, the instructive forms of the didactic poem, of the satirical epigram, of the moralising fable and of the educating drama. At the same time the Baroque became the poetic source of the Rococo style. Here too Reason found itself triumphant. However it was a witty, ironical, sophisticated reason. It preached a graceful, sensuous hedonism, avoided seriousness and depth, dallied serenely with the superficiality of life, and cultivated the charming style of a gentlemanly art of living. "Virtue and pleasure are eternally akin" rejoiced one of their spokesmen Johann Ludwig Gleim.

The Rococo signified the dissolution of everything which seemed pathetic and exaggerated in a display of graceful movement. Particularly in France the Rococo became identified with an entire mode of life. There the nobility, discarding its social responsibility towards the people, surrendered wholly to a care-free attitude towards life, towards a sensuous and elegant enjoyment of life which found its adequate expression in the architecture of its castles and its wealthy towns. From France the Rococo entered Germany. Still today we admire its Chinese porcelain, its lacquer work, its tapestry, the figurines of Vienna, Meißen, Nymphenburg, Frankenthal, Sèvres, Worcester and Chelsea, the paintings of love pastiches and park scenes. The gods of pleasure and beauty descended to earth : Bacchus, Amor, Venus-Cythere. The Graces dallied in hidden grottoes or at murmuring brooks. Delightful girls danced merrily roundelays. A preying lover surprised his sleeping love in grove or wood. The paintings of Watteau, Fragonard, Boucher retained the magic of this graceful *joie de vivre*. A kindred mood is reflected in the portraits of Reynolds and Gainsborough, the architecture of Vanbrugh and the gardens of William Chambers in Britain.

In Germany this enjoyment of life was displayed in the buildings of the Brothers Asam, in Pöppelmann's "Zwinger" in Dresden, in Knobelsdorff's "Sanssouci" in Potsdam. Even today visitors cannot escape the illusion of listening there to the music of Gluck, Haydn, Mozart, to the discreet sounds of the harpsichord and to the stately movements of the minuet. However, it is just as well to point out there is nothing comparable in the poetry of German Rococo which can stand up to the perfection of Mozart or to the inspiration of a Balthasar Neumann and to the architecture of Dominikus Zimmerman and Fischer von Erlach.

The delicate, tender verses of the *poésie fugitive* became the outstanding literary form of the Rococo. This kind of lyrical poetry spread all over Europe and was called "Anacreontic" in Germany. For the Greek poet Anacreon—side by side with Horace, Theocritus and Catullus—was revered as father and master of such serene and light-hearted verse. The subject matter of the Anacreontics is narrow and skin-deep. Love, wine, conviviality, the seemingly superficial pleasures of life are unceasingly praised. Mortals disguised as shepherds make merry and fondle

* *

in an unrealistically idyllic landscape. Serious reflections were banned. Every poem was based upon wit and point, while the novel praised ironically rejection of all excess and sensible moderation in pleasure.

"The literary epoch into which I was born," wrote Goethe in his autobiographical *Dichtung und Wahrheit*, "developed from the preceding one through contradiction." This summary statement described the radical change which came to pass in Germany in the second half of the century. This "Sturm und Drang" was a clarion call against a mode of life which was mainly guided by motives of reason and expediency, and was ultimately doomed to produce a paralysis of everything intuitive or emotional. The "Aufklärung" was confronted with the first wave of Romanticism, Rationalism with Irrationalism, that is with the conviction that Man's existence in its deepest contents could not be comprehended by a process of rational thought but revealed itself in and through subjective feelings.

The first attack was mounted by the inclination towards "sensibility" in England. Richardson wrote his sentimental and enormously popular family novels. Edward Young gave widespread and much noticed expression to the protest against the prevailing *Zeitgeist*. His *Night Thoughts on Life, Death and Immortality* and his *Conjectures on Original Composition* vigorously pilloried the petrifaction of his times in reason and rational rules.

But it was France which produced the most effective outburst against the Enlightenment. There Rousseau dared to challenge tradition and civilisation. He voiced his conviction that Man's great achievements had also destroyed his happiness, created disorder and brought confusion everywhere. "Among the elements harmony prevails, among men chaos." Instead of trusting to reason as a reliable guide through life, Rousseau preached : "Le sentiment est plus que la raison." Considering feelings he was convinced that all men were equal, and regarding sentiments he believed they did not know of any social differences, of class distinctions, of prejudices. He demanded a return to Nature as being the original reason for all life. This did not mean a return into the woods to live there with the beasts but a return to a natural sentiment, to a more personalised life, "which did not rest on thoughts and opinions but on the depth of the unconscious ego, in personal feelings and in the dark urge of one's own volition."

Europe felt startled by Rousseau's writings. Thus "Sturm und Drang" became a youth movement, a rebellion of the younger

2—GMOL-6   *   *

against the older generation, an insurrection against Enlightenment and Regulations. Nature, emotion, passion were the slogans
of those angry, young men who proclaimed a new style of life in
drama. To be a "fine fellow, a guy who unhinges the world" was
their highest praise, freedom, political, moral and aesthetic
liberties their highest goal. But since they were deficient in
constancy, diligence and self-discipline, the literary result did not
correspond with their high-strung self-assertion. Perhaps this
particularly German situation explains Peter Gay's puzzling
remark in *The Enlightenment* Vol. II about the rehabilitation of
passions because "as the power of conscience had grown, the
passions had become safer." Certainly the Enlightenment seems
to have been less frightened of its own irrationality than any
previous period.

When the German classical period overtook one-sided
Rationalism and left also the unrestrained emotional outburst of
"Sturm und Drang" behind, embodying at the same time what was
valuable and lasting in both movements, it could rely for much
support on the work of Immanuel Kant. In his *Critique of Pure
Reason* Kant examined the sources and possibilities of rational
perception. He drew the limits of human thought. Religious conviction was outside the judgement of scientific reason, for "transcendental objects are to us no objects of our theoretical
knowledge". On the other hand Kant secured the reliability of
rational sciences through his philosophical examination as far as
they are confined to the contents of our experience in life.

If Kant stood as a towering beacon at the end of the
"Aufklärung", his *Critique of Practical Reason* drew also the
limits of emotional experience. Moral conduct may not rest upon
mere feelings, emotions or moods. It must be done for its own
sake and be based on the firm norm which exists as the
"categorical imperative" in our conscience. Man's dignity rests
on the assumption that he obeys this imperative without regard
to its consequences. To be able to do so gives him the conviction
of inner freedom and thus forms the nucleus of his humanity.

While Western philosophers followed their traditional course
of empiricism well into the nineteenth century, Germany's
philosophy found its own way in the idealistic systems of Kant, a
concomitant of inestimable value to the German classical movement. The German "Aufklärung" should not be regarded as a
passing phase or as an artificial imitation of foreign patterns in
literature and art. Rather, it proved to be a significant milestone
for German Idealism, to which it passed on many of its
fundamental impulses.

Gottfried Wilhelm Leibniz

Gottfried Wilhelm Leibniz

by JOHN COTTINGHAM

Introduction

OPEN almost any book on the thought of the seventeenth or eighteenth centuries and you are likely to find the name of Leibniz figuring prominently in the index. For Leibniz was a paradigm case of that now extinct species, the polymath. To say that his interests were wide-ranging is a gross understatement : for he brought his formidable intellect to bear on what, in our age of specialisation, seems an extraordinarily diverse series of disciplines. That a man who did his doctorate in Jurisprudence should become a philosopher of world rank is perhaps remarkable enough, but it is even more striking when we remember that, from the point of view of his career, the philosophical work was very much a sideline. In the service of the Duchy of Hanover Leibniz spent a great amount of his energies on historical research; as a diplomat and traveller he was an active participant on the European political scene.

Even if we say that Leibniz' chief claim to fame is as a philosopher, this is liable, if the term "Philosophy" is construed in its modern, academic sense, to give a misleadingly narrow impression. Leibniz excelled in every branch of Philosophy in the older and wider sense of the word, which included the mathematical and physical sciences as well as metaphysics and morals. For physicists and mathematicians, he is an important critic of the Newtonian theory of space and time, and has an assured place in history as inventor of the Infinitesimal Calculus; for logicians, he is the man who foresaw the crucial importance of modern symbolic techniques; for metaphysicians, he is the chief exponent of pluralism; for modern analytic philosophers, he is the thinker who developed the logical analysis of the proposition as the primary tool of philosophy; for Empiricists and Rationalists alike, he has a key place in the development of the Theory of Knowledge; for moral philosophers, he is a writer of depth on the perennial problems of causality and human freedom; and for theologians (and anti-theologians) his attempt to find a rational solution to the problem of evil is of definitive importance. Finally, Leibniz' place in the general development of European thought is pivotal : he can be seen, on the one hand, as the last and most impressive of the great seventeenth century systematic metaphysicians; and on the other, as the herald of the German "Aufklärung", or Enlightenment.

Outline of life and intellectual development

Gottfried Wilhelm von Leibniz was born at Leipzig, in Saxony, in 1646. He was of well-to-do academic stock, and his father (who died when Leibniz was six) was Professor of Moral Philosophy at the University of Leipzig. Though Leibniz was a remarkably precocious child, showing a prodigious zeal for acquiring knowledge, his early mastery of the Classics and his admission to the University at the age of fifteen were not as unheard of feats as they would be today. Leibniz was educated in what was still the predominant scholastic tradition of the German universities : Greek philosophy (as developed by the Scholastics of the Middle Ages), Logic and Law predominated. Latin was to remain the chief language in which the learned works published in his lifetime were written. In 1663, Leibniz defended his baccalaureate thesis on the Principle of Individuation (*Disputatio Metaphysica de principio individui*), and then went to Jena, where he studied Mathematics under Erhard Weigel.

Three years later, at the age of twenty, Leibniz produced his *De arte combinatoria*, in which he examined the possibility of translating logical combinations of ideas into a symbolic language. This idea is important for two reasons. First, it looks forward to the great development of symbolic logic in the twentieth century : the advantage of a symbolic calculus over ordinary language is, as Leibniz saw, that it enables propositions and chains of reasoning to be exhibited in a clear and unambiguous manner, thus conferring on philosophical reasoning some of the precision of mathematics. Second, the treatise contains the germ of what was to be an ongoing concern of Leibniz, the idea of a universal language (*characteristica universalis*), which would enable the entire corpus of human knowledge to be laid out as a systematic whole. "The characteristic art, of which I conceived the idea," Leibniz later wrote in 1677, "would contain the true organon of a general science of everything that is subject matter for human reasoning, but would be endowed throughout with the demonstrations of an evident calculus." [1] This quotation gives some idea both of the scope of Leibniz' imaginative powers and of his conception of knowledge as a unified system—an idea central to his philosophy.

In 1667, Leibniz presented his doctoral dissertation in Jurisprudence at the University of Altdorf (*De Casibus Perplexis in*

Jure). The work was apparently so well received that Leibniz was straightway offered a professorship at the University—this at age twenty-one. Leibniz' refusal of this offer—a key decision in his life—marks his rejection of an academic career in favour of the more active pursuits of the courtier and diplomat. The same year he entered the service of the Elector of Mainz.

The following years were to see Leibniz devoting his energies to European politics, which were at this time dominated by the aggressive policies of Louis XIV. To this period belong numerous memoranda on diplomatic questions, including pamphlets like the *Consilium Aegyptiacum*, prepared for the French king with the intention of diverting his expansionist schemes from Europe to the East.

In 1672, Leibniz' diplomatic activities took him to Paris, where he was to remain for four years. These years spent in the intellectual capital of Europe were a time of intense and fruitful intellectual stimulus for Leibniz. (Here too, he acquired the fluent, if somewhat quaint French in which much of his work, especially the more popular material, was subsequently to be written.) In Paris Leibniz met men like the great Cartesian philosopher Nicolas Malebranche, and the mathematician and theologian Arnauld, with whom he later corresponded at length. From Paris he visited London, in 1673, where he met Henry Oldenburg and the chemist Boyle, and was made a foreign corresponding member of the Royal Society. It was at the end of "the Paris years" that Leibniz made his famous discovery of the Infinitesimal Calculus. It is now agreed that Leibniz arrived at his results independently of Newton. (Neither man published his work in full until the 1680s, but at the end of the century Newton's friends were to raise the unpleasant charge of plagiarism, insinuating that Leibniz had seen an earlier letter of Newton's to Oldenburg, from which he had stolen the basic ideas.)

On his return to Germany in 1676, Leibniz stopped at the Hague, where he held his famous conversations with Spinoza. The relationship between the two giants is something of a mystery : though Leibniz himself mentions the meeting, there is no detailed account of what was said. Leibniz clearly had a great respect for Spinoza's work, and apparently got permission to copy some of his *Ethics* (then unpublished). Later however, he was to attack many aspects of Spinoza's system, and there is no doubt that the philosophical standpoints of the two men diverge widely, particularly on the nature of substance and on questions of religious belief.

The reason for Leibniz' return to Germany was that he had decided to accept the post of librarian to Johann Friedrich, Duke of Brunswick. He remained in the service of the Hanoverian house until his death, and spent great energy on researches into the origins and history of the ducal family. That the mature Leibniz still placed courtly service first in his order of priorities has been upsetting to scholars. Bertrand Russell refers scathingly to Leibniz' "undue deference to princes and lamentable waste of time in the endeavour to please them".[2] But to wish that Leibniz had chosen otherwise is to fail to respect the peculiarly versatile genius of the man. In fact, the years that followed Leibniz' return to Germany were among his most productive. In 1682 he founded in Leipzig a learned journal, the *Acta Eruditorum*, in which much of his more technical mathematical and philosophical work was to appear (e.g. the paper on Knowledge, Truth and Ideas, *Meditationes de cognitione veritate et ideis*, of 1684). He also wrote an enormous number of letters to learned friends abroad— men like Arnauld and the sceptic Bayle. In 1686 he wrote a short but major work, the *Discours de Métaphysique,* and in the early nineties a detailed criticism of Cartesian philosophy (*Animadversiones in partem generalem principiorum Cartesianorum*).[3]

Leibniz' enthusiasm for strengthening communication between scholars continued as he grew older, and he worked, unsuccessfully, for the foundation of learned societies in Dresden, Vienna and St. Petersburg. In 1700, he founded the Berlin Academy of Sciences, of which he was the first president. The "deference to princes" continued too. In fact Leibniz' success in Berlin was made easier as a result of his close friendship with Sophia Charlotte (later Queen of Prussia), the daughter of the Electress of Hanover. For a time Leibniz was Sophia's tutor, and the conversations he had with her concerning the Christian faith no doubt influenced the composition of the *Théodicée* ("A Vindication of God's Justice"), the largest work published in Leibniz' lifetime, which appeared in 1710. Nor did Leibniz' political interests abate : throughout his later years he worked, again unsuccessfully, for a reconciliation between the princes of Europe, and for a healing of the breach between Catholicism and Protestantism. All this time Leibniz continued working on Philosophy, and the *Monadologie,* a summary of his system, appeared in 1714, two years before his death.

Though Leibniz achieved considerable honours towards the end of his life (he was made an Imperial Privy Councillor at the Court of Vienna in 1712), he seems to have lost favour with the House of Hanover. He was left behind when the Elector Georg Ludwig (nephew of his original patron) acceded to the British throne, and he died in solitude in 1716. Neither the Court of Hanover, nor his own Berlin Academy, symbols of the courtly and scholarly worlds he had served so well, sent representatives to his funeral.

Leibniz' philosophy

To attempt a summary of the philosophy of Leibniz is at the same time a daunting and an attractive task. It is daunting because of the enormously prolific and diverse nature of his writings. The monumental task of editing his scattered correspondence (some 15,000 letters) and the numerous pamphlets and treatises, begun by the Prussian Academy of Sciences in 1923, and recently resumed by the German Academy in East Berlin in collaboration with Western scholars, is still far from finished. The attractiveness lies in the fact that the scattered limbs of Leibniz' writings seem to form a remarkably tightly-knit and systematic body of thought. In what follows, I shall endeavour to indicate the main structure of Leibniz' system under three principal headings, viz., Theory of Knowledge, Logic and Metaphysics, and Ethics and Religion.[4] The last section will lead us on to a brief consideration of the influence of Leibniz' extraordinary genius on subsequent European thought.

Theory of Knowledge

In a symposium entitled "Language and Philosophy", published in 1969, the editor speaks of "a recent counter-revolution in Philosophy which claims that empirical tradition from Locke down is false and the rationalistic tradition of Leibniz is sound".[5] To the English student, one side of the old philosophical debate referred to here will be much better known than the other. Indeed, his approach to philosophy is almost bound to be dominated by the tradition of British Empiricism, extending through the work of Berkeley and Hume to the present day, and widely regarded as having originated in the philosophy of John Locke. Accordingly, Locke's famous *Essay Concerning Human Understanding*, published in 1689, is likely to be much better known in this country than the detailed reply composed by Leibniz. Written during the period 1701–9, this reply was never completely finished, and was only published posthumously in 1765 under the title *Nouveaux Essais sur l'Entendement Humain*.[6]

Locke's principal thesis in the *Essay* is that all knowledge originates in experience. In essence, this is a denial of the Cartesian view that there are present in the human mind from birth certain *a priori* concepts, or "innate ideas". These innate ideas enable us, according to Descartes, to arrive, independently of experience, at certain necessary truths which are the logical foundation of all knowledge. Locke had advanced a number of arguments to show that the hypothesis of innate ideas was not proven, and was in any case quite redundant : everything that the theory purported to explain could quite well be accounted for on the simpler hypothesis that the mind is, at birth, a *tabula rasa*—a blank sheet. It is a consequence of Locke's view that sensory experience is the ultimate basis of our knowledge.

Leibniz' reply to Locke is impressive both in its detail and in its subtlety. He begins by making what looks like a concession : the senses are indeed necessary for the acquisition of knowledge. But they are not, Leibniz goes on to say, sufficient. Sense perception may elicit knowledge, but only in so far as it enables us to see what is already "hidden within us, but appearing at the instance of the senses like the sparks which come from the steel when it strikes the flint".[7] In order to support this view, Leibniz cites the propositions of Logic and Mathematics. These subjects deal with necessary and "eternal" truths—propositions whose verification is quite independent of experience. No number of instances or experiments can, for example, establish the truth of a Euclidian theorem : the proofs are purely deductive and *a priori*.

Locke (whose own explanation of necessary truths may be omitted here) had an obvious objection to explaining our knowledge of such propositions by positing innate ideas implanted or imprinted in the mind. He had argued that if the notion of ideas being "implanted" or "imprinted" meant anything, it must involve the mental awareness of the person concerned. Yet it is a plain fact that young children, for example, are quite *unaware* of the truth of such propositions.[8]

To this Leibniz replies that "we must not imagine that we can read the eternal laws of reason in the soul as in an open book".[9] The "eternal verities" are present in the mind not in a fully developed form, but as capacities or *"virtualités"*. To elucidate this, Leibniz suggestively compares the human mind to a sculptor's block of marble : not a uniform block indifferently suited to receive any shape the sculptor may choose to impose upon it, but a block already *veined* in a particular pattern, so that the sculptor only has to chip away and uncover the vein to reveal the shape underneath.[10] Thus knowledge arises, for Leibniz, out of a combination of sensory stimuli (the blows of the sculptor) and an innate set of "natural inclinations, dispositions, habits or powers" of the mind. He sums up his position by adding to the empiricist slogan "Nihil est in intellectu quod non prius fuerit in sensu" (there is nothing in the mind which was not previously in the senses) the crucial qualification : "Excipe : nisi ipse intellectus" (except the mind itself).[11]

The theory is not without its problems : it may be doubted, for example, whether the talk of "dispositions" and "powers" is not too vague to be of much explanatory force. But there is no doubt that in the scope and force of his arguments Leibniz is easily a match for Locke. Nor are the *New Essays* purely critical. There are many passages suggestive, if only in outline, of a Kantian approach to Epistemology; and it is interesting to see in the work of the distinguished contemporary philosopher Noam Chomsky a return to the idea of innate mental structures (in this case as a hypothesis to explain certain facts about the way language is learnt.)[12]

Always reconciliationist rather than polemical in character, Leibniz observes at one point in the *New Essays* that his theory is not really so far removed from that of Locke. For Locke in fact divided the ideas which are the basis of our knowledge into two classes : to the "ideas of sensation" (i.e. those of perceptual knowledge) he added the "ideas of reflection", which are in effect the product of internal operations of the mind. Despite this apparent convergence, however, Leibniz' development of his theory of knowledge reveals a fundamentally distinct approach from that of Locke. For Locke, the mind is essentially a passive receptor : "in the reception of simple Ideas the Understanding is for the most part passive".[13] The basic underlying picture is of the external world acting on the mind. To this Leibniz opposes an essentially active conception of the mind; indeed, there is a sense (as will emerge in due course) in which it is the external world that is contained or reflected in the mind of the individual.

Developing his idea of activity, Leibniz writes : "Activity is no more separable from the soul than from the body. . . . Now we believe that if the body is never at rest, neither will the soul that corresponds to it be without perception."[14] The doctrine that the mind is in a state of continual active perception sounds at first straightforwardly false. What, for instance, about periods of sleep? But *"perception"* for Leibniz is strictly a technical term : by it he means little more than the activity of a substance which somehow reflects the external world. "Perception" is thus sharply distinguished from the full self-conscious awareness of a mind, which Leibniz terms *"apperception"*. Now Leibniz' thesis is that the mind has a continuous and infinite series of "perceptions", though some, which he calls "petites perceptions" may be too confused and faint for us to be aware of.[15]

This strange thesis has been regarded by some as a precursor of the Freudian theory of the Subconscious. In fact, however, it is not so much a piece of explanatory psychology as a logical consequence of certain doctrines that lie at the very centre of Leibniz' philosophical system. For the continuous "perceptual" activity we have referred to is not for Leibniz a prerogative of minds, but of all created things. Each individual unit of substance or "monad" has within it "perceptions", or internalised representations of the entire universe. The ultimate constituents of the universe are thus essentially active : Leibniz uses the old term "entelechy" (though in a very different sense from that in which Aristotle had used it) as a fitting name for all created substances, in order to convey the active principle present in all of them, which makes them complete, self-sufficient and changing only as a result of internal action.[16] To explain this remarkable theory of the nature of the world, it is now necessary to turn to an examination of Leibniz' logical and metaphysical doctrines.

Logic and Metaphysics

The term "metaphysics" is more likely, nowadays, to raise eyebrows than to provoke awe. Modern Philosophy, it is widely believed, has no use for portentous-sounding but unverifiable pronouncements about the ultimate nature of reality. Yet Leibniz seems to fall right into the class of propounders of dubious "ultimate truths". He was indeed regarded by Kant as a paradigm case of the metaphysician. And the doctrine for which he is best known—that reality is composed of an infinite number of discrete "windowless" substances, the monads—seems conspicuously metaphysical in character.

There is no space here to discuss whether the general scepticism about metaphysics (largely the result of the fame achieved by the Logical Positivist movement of the thirties) is warranted. But something positive does need to be said about the sense in which Leibniz was a metaphysician, and about the nature of his claims. Leibniz, like Descartes and Spinoza, took over from Aristotle a concern for what is perhaps the central question of traditional Philosophy—the question "What is there in the world?" This enquiry boiled down for Aristotle, as for Leibniz, to an investigation of the nature of Substance. This is not such a lofty or obscure investigation as it sounds : for the most part, whenever we make any statement about the world we make a statement of the form "so and so is such and such"; that is, we ascribe some attribute to some subject. The question then arises as to the nature of these subjects : what *are* underlying entities or substances to which the attributes we apply are said to "belong"? As Leibniz expresses it (in somewhat scholastic jargon) : "Since actions and passions properly belong to individual substances, it will be necessary to explain what such a substance is."[17]

The enquiry, then, is closely bound up with the logical structure of ordinary statements (or propositions). Indeed for Bertrand Russell (whose first publication was a critique of Leibniz' philosophy) Leibniz' metaphysics is "almost entirely derived from his logic".[18] (By "logic" here, Russell meant the analysis of the proposition and its truth.) Russell's interpretation, as will emerge, puts too little emphasis on the place of God in Leibniz' system. But in approaching Leibniz' metaphysics, it is nonetheless helpful to start with an examination of his doctrines concerning the proposition.

Leibniz divided all true propositions into two classes, viz., truths of reason (*vérités de raison*) and truths of fact (*vérités de fait*). He defines these classes as follows :

"Truths of reason are those which are necessary and of which the opposite is impossible, and truths of fact are those which are contingent and of which the opposite is possible."[19]

This crucial distinction between propositions which have to be and those which happen to be true has played a vital part in modern Philosophy; though it is the work of Kant (centering on his dual distinction between the analytic and synthetic on the one hand, and the *a priori* and *a posteriori* on the other) that has been historically more influential. In fact however, Leibniz' *method* of drawing the distinction between his two types of proposition is reminiscent in many ways of Kant's later account of analyticity, even though the two philosophers differ widely as to precisely *where* the line is to be drawn. But Leibniz' account presents some special problems of its own.

The account of the truths of reason is simple enough. Leibniz derives these from his "Principle of Contradiction"—one of the two great principles on which he claimed our reasoning is founded.[20] This principle says simply that a proposition is true if its opposite (by which is meant its negation or contradictory) implies a contradiction. Thus, to call something a triangle but to deny that it was three-sided would be to contradict oneself : hence "all triangles are three-sided" is a truth of reason. Putting it another way, Leibniz says that the reasons for the truth of such propositions can be found through *analysis*, since they either are, or can be reduced by analysis to, "identical propositions". These identical propositions are what we should call tautologies—propositions of the form "A is A". To take the triangle example again, our proposition "all triangles are three-sided" can be converted by means of the definitional equivalence "triangle = three-sided figure" to the proposition "all three-sided figures are three-sided" : that is, it can be reduced by analysis to a tautology. Incidentally, it is interesting to note in this connection that Leibniz regarded the propositions of mathematics as essentially tautological,[21] thus going against the later analysis of Kant, but anticipating the view of many modern thinkers.

Leibniz' view of contingent propositions is more idiosyncratic and more complicated. The chief complication is the famous doctrine that for all true propositions the predicate is contained in the subject (*predicatum inest subjecto*).[22] Leibniz expressed this as follows (in a letter to Arnauld):

> "Always, in every true affirmative proposition, whether necessary or contingent, universal or particular, the concept of the predicate is in some way comprehended in that of the subject, *predicatum inest subjecto*; otherwise I know not what truth is."[23]

Now this is very strange. The notion of the subject "comprehending" or "containing" the predicate, though somewhat metaphorical, is perhaps intelligible enough, and was taken over by Kant. But for Kant, the feature of the predicate's being contained within the subject was confined to—indeed was the hallmark of—the *analytic* proposition. And this is what we should expect. If we take our old example—"All triangles are three-sided"—it seems plausible to say that the necessary truth of this proposition derives from the fact that the concept of three-sidedness is contained within the concept of triangularity; the one concept is logically bound up with the other.[24] But what of a particular contingent proposition, like "Mr. Heath won the 1970 election"? To say that the concept of winning the 1970 election is contained within the subject here seems to suggest that there is some *a priori* link between being Mr. Heath and winning the election. But this is precisely what one would want to deny : Mr. Heath did *in fact* win the election, but he *might* not have done. At this stage, the doctrine that, in *all* true propositions, the predicate is contained within the subject not only appears intuitively bizarre, but, worse, threatens to blur the very distinction between truths of reason and truths of fact that Leibniz is so anxious to articulate.

Before we discuss whether Leibniz was able to find a way out of this difficulty, let us go back and see how the doctrine of containedness described above ties in with Leibniz' enquiries about substance and his theory of monads. The connection is in fact explicitly made by Leibniz. In the *Discourse on Metaphysics,* after referring to the doctrine that the subject must always contain the predicate, Leibniz goes on to say :

> "This being so, we can say that the nature of an individual substance or of a complete being is to have a notion so complete

that it is sufficient to comprise and to allow the deduction from it of all the predicates of the subject. . . ."[25]

Leibniz then uses the example of Alexander the Great, and says that if one were able to perceive the "thisness" (or "haecceity") of Alexander, one would be able to see the foundation and reason of everything that can truly be said of him (e.g. that he would conquer Darius). Thus, every individual substance has "inside it", so to speak, everything that it has ever done or will do. We have now arrived at the metaphysical counterpart of the doctrine *"predicatum inest subjecto"*, namely the doctrine of the monad : the individual unit of substance, "laden with its past and pregnant with its future", containing once and for all everything that has ever happened or will ever happen to it.

From this "completeness" of the monads, it follows that they are "self-contained", or as Leibniz puts it, "changeless", in the sense that they do not need to be acted upon externally in order to change. In the famous Leibnizian metaphor, they are "windowless" —they work completely independently of each other.[26]

The theory of complete, self-contained individual substances that has now emerged presents Leibniz with two major problems. (1) How, if the monads are truly self-contained, is Leibniz to explain the apparent causal connections we observe around us—the fact that the things in our world seem to act and react upon one another in a regular fashion? (2) The second problem is the difficulty referred to already : how, if the monads are truly complete (contain once for all everything that will happen to them), is Leibniz to preserve the contingent character of the class of truths of fact? Significantly enough, the resolution of both these problems takes us straight into Leibnizian theology, and depends heavily on the existence of the Supreme Monad—God.

(1) Leibniz solves the problem of causal interaction by means of his theory of Pre-Established Harmony. God, in creating the universe, brought it about that all the monads should independently work together so as to form the most perfect whole. Thus, though no monad has windows, each monad is, as it were, a mirror of the universe. "This connection of all created things with every single one of them and their adaptation to every single one," writes Leibniz, "has the result that every single substance stands in relations which express all the others. Whence every single substance is a perpetual living mirror of the universe."[27]

A special case of the problem of the interaction of substances, which enables Leibniz to make full use of his principle of Pre-Established Harmony, is the problem of the relationship of Mind and Body. This problem—still of considerable interest to contemporary philosophers—was a legacy from the radical dualism of Descartes, under which Mind (*res cogitans*) and Matter (*res extensa*) were distinguished as two completely distinct and unrelated types of substance. This absolute distinction tends to be rejected in Leibniz' system; for there is a sense in which all the monads possess a germ of consciousness in so far as they individually mirror the whole universe. But in another sense, the monad which constitutes a given human soul is logically quite distinct from, and independent of, the set of monads that constitute the corresponding body. Leibniz' way out of this complex maze is to regard the body as a sort of automaton, which God (with complete foreknowledge of our intentions) has programmed in advance, according to the system of Pre-Established Harmony, to perform the acts willed by the soul.[28] This "solution" is perhaps unlikely to be very satisfying to the modern philosopher of Mind; but Leibniz clearly regarded it as an advance on the more fantastic "Occasionalism" of his predecessors, which had maintained that God perpetually and miraculously intervenes in nature in order to move our bodies in the ways in which our souls will them to move.[29]

(2) With regard to the second problem, Leibniz attempts to elucidate the status of contingent truth in his system by means of his famous Principle of Sufficient Reason. We have seen that necessary truths are true in virtue of the Principle of Contradiction. But there is also, Leibniz asserts, a Principle of Sufficient Reason. . . .

". . . by virtue of which we hold that no fact can be true or existing . . . without a sufficient reason for its being so and no different; albeit these reasons must most frequently remain unknown to us."[30]

The concluding qualification here has led some interpreters to construe the Principle of Sufficient Reason as a methodological postulate : as scientists we must assume that there is an explanation to be found somewhere for everything that occurs. This interpretation squares well with Leibniz' assertion of a Principle of Continuity—the principle that "Nature never makes leaps". But Leibniz means a great deal more than this by his Principle of Sufficient Reason. For Leibniz, everything that happens in the world originates in the creative act of the Supreme Monad. Contingent truth is thus considered in the light of God's original act of choice in creating our universe :

"Since in the divine ideas there is an infinity of possible universes of which only one can exist, the choice made by God must have a sufficient reason which determines him to the one rather than to the other. This reason can only be found in fitness, that is, in the degree of perfection contained in these worlds."[31]

Thus, God having chosen our world from all possible worlds as the most perfect, it follows that a "reason" for any event in the world can, in principle, be found in terms of the original selection made by God. Any given particular substance behaves in this way, rather than some other way, because of its place as a member of the total set of substances necessary to build the most perfect universe. As Leibniz puts it: "God, legislating for the whole, has considered every part, and particularly every monad."[32]

It does not of course follow from this that human scientists can, or will ever be able to, discover the sufficient reason for any particular contingent truth. An investigation of the reason for any particular event would, says Leibniz, involve us in a complex and infinite chain of causes.[33] It belongs only to God to perceive the sufficient reason behind every event. But what Leibniz does want to assert is that behind each event there is, whether we can discover it or not, a final cause—that is, a reason deriving from the ultimate purposes of God.

Now it may well be asked at this point whether Leibniz' principle of Sufficient Reason really does anything to elucidate the dubious status of contingent truth in his system. For the picture of the universe that begins to emerge is of one in which every true statement could (at least by an infinite intelligence) be deduced *a priori*, in which each single substance contains inside itself once for all the germ of all it will do. Does it not follow from this that every true proposition is in some sense necessary? Leibniz himself felt the pressure of this sort of difficulty, and felt it most acutely in the area of human action, where his metaphysical scheme raised the thorny problem of the Freedom of the Will. He writes, in connection with his theory of substance:

"It seems that this will destroy the difference between contingent and necessary truths, and that human liberty will have no more place, and that an absolute fate will reign over all our actions as well as over all the other events in the world."[34]

Although this written as early as 1686, Leibniz was to become increasingly concerned with the moral and theological problems arising out of his system. This is therefore a convenient place[35] for us to turn to an examination of these problems—but with a warning that the fresh heading is in many ways arbitrary: for, as will by now be clear, Leibniz' theistic beliefs have a place at the very core of his logical and metaphysical doctrines.

Ethics and Religion

Leibniz, as a defender of Christian theism, was committed to the doctrines of personal responsibility and desert, and therefore to finding a place in his philosophical system for human freedom. But, precisely because of the character of the rest of his system, this turns out to be a major task. The problem is this : if the monad that constitutes, for example, Julius Caesar has once and for all built into it, as it were, the attribute "crosser of the Rubicon" (this predicate being, like all the others, contained in the subject), how can it be said of Julius Caesar that he freely chose to cross the Rubicon? For, under Leibniz' schema, the decision was necessarily "part of him". Leibniz' answer (the example is his own) is that it was logically possible that Caesar should not have crossed the Rubicon; hence there was no necessity about his decision to cross the river; for "nothing is necessary of which the opposite is possible."[36] The suggestion here is clearly that "Caesar crossed the Rubicon" is a "truth of fact", not a "truth of reason" : to say "Caesar did not cross the Rubicon" is not to contradict oneself. But unfortunately this answer merely glosses over the difficulty. For if God chose the universe which was the best and most perfect of all possible universes, and Julius Caesar (together with all his attributes) is a   constituent of the universe that God in fact selected as being the most perfect, then it is hard to see how Caesar's decision was in any meaningful sense open, or "up to him". The mere possibility that God might have selected another universe in which there was a deutero-Caesar who did not cross the Rubicon is hardly enough to bestow any genuine freedom or avoidability on Julius Caesar's actual decision.[37]

Leibniz returned to these problems in detail in the longest work published in his lifetime, the *Théodicée*, which he subtitled "Essays on the Goodness of God, the Freedom of Man and the Origin of Evil." The contributions here to the problem of Freedom are interesting in that they anticipate the work of many modern "Reconciliationists"—philosophers who attempt to find a place for the notion of human freedom within the framework of a thoroughgoing scientific determinism. Leibniz himself, as a logical result of his system of monads and Pre-Established Harmony, is a convinced determinist : "All is certain and determined beforehand in man, as everywhere else," he writes, "and the human soul is a kind of spiritual automaton."[38] To hold that freedom was possible within this completely determined universe represented a clean break with the Cartesian insistence on the unlimited and undetermined power of human choice. "M. Descartes" writes Leibniz "demands a freedom which is not needed, by his insistence that the actions of the will of man are altogether undetermined, a thing which never happens."[39]

But attractive though his approach is, Leibniz has little success in showing what the freedom he tries to defend can consist in. The phrase "spiritual automaton" is worrying enough to the modern ear,[40] and at the end of the day it seems clear that an automaton in our sense is just what Man must be in Leibniz' system. Apart from reiterating his old (and inadequate) argument that only logical (or "absolute") necessity threatens freedom, Leibniz can do little more in its defence than point to "a marvellous spontaneity which in a certain sense makes the soul in its resolves independent of the physical influence of all other creatures."[41] Leibniz is clearly thinking here of the "self-containedness" of the monads—all of them working independently but in concert through the system of Pre-Established Harmony. But the "independence" on which Leibniz lays so much stress is specious. For although, as he says, "all that passes in the soul depends, in my system, only on the soul",[42] the character of each monad (i.e. the set of all its predicates) is still determined in advance, for all time, by the original selection of God; and this merely raises again the old problem of Caesar and his decision to cross the Rubicon.[43]

The other principal theme of the *Théodicée* is also reconciliationist in character. Leibniz' declared purpose in writing the work was to effect a reconciliation between Reason and Faith. In undertaking this task, he was attempting to present a detailed reply to the arguments of Pierre Bayle (1647–1706), whose *Dictionnaire historique et critique* (published in 1679) had achieved great popularity. Bayle had specifically attacked some of Leibniz' doctrines (e.g. that of Pre-Established Harmony, in the article *Rorarius*), and had also presented a devastating analysis of the problem posed for the Christian believer by the existence of evil in the world. For Bayle the difficulties were too acute to be argued away by reason, and only faith (through revelation) could prevent the conclusion that there exists in the universe, alongside of God, an active Principle of Evil.

The Problem of Evil, though particularly acute for an optimistic philosopher like Leibniz, is of course a perennial one for religious faith. It has been neatly summarised as follows[44] :

"Is God willing to prevent evil, but not able? then is he impotent. Is he able but not willing? then is he malevolent. Is he both able and willing? whence then is evil?"

Now whenever Leibniz' approach to this problem is mentioned, the grotesquely naive optimism of Pangloss, the buffoon of Voltaire's

Candide, springs automatically to mind. Indeed, the modern reader is likely to be much better acquainted with *Candide* than he is with the *Théodicée* which means that Leibniz' views on evil are too often judged on the basis of the caricature presented by Voltaire.[45] The label "optimist" too is unfortunate for Leibniz : the modern connotations of the term are likely to suggest a cheery and unreasoned attitude of "hoping for the best". But in fact Leibniz' "optimistic" treatment of the problem of evil is merely a corollary of his central philosophical thesis, already referred to above, that God created the best (*optimum*) of all possible worlds. That he did so follows logically, for Leibniz, from the defining characteristics of God :

> "Now this supreme wisdom, united to a goodness that is no less infinite, cannot but have chosen the best; . . . there would be something to correct in the actions of God if it were possible to do better . . . : so it may be said . . . that if there were not the best (optimum) among all possible worlds, God would not have created any."[46]

The argument, then, is purely *a priori* : it starts from the existence of a perfect God as its basic premise. Accordingly, it is essentially a believer's argument, and cannot be expected to have much impact on those who would wish to start from an empirical investigation of the actual evil in the world, and then see whether the results support the hypothesis of a Christian-type deity.

But even if we grant Leibniz his basic premise, the argument seems over brief. It is all very well to say that this *must* be the best of all possible worlds; but why, for instance, if God is omnipotent, could he not have created a world more or less like ours except for the absence of suffering? Leibniz has two answers to this. (1) The first is to point to the essential unity and connectedness of the universe :

> "The universe, whatever it may be, is all of one piece, like the ocean . . . thus, if the smallest evil that comes to pass in the world were missing in it, it would no longer be this world."[47]

Here Leibniz seems to be equivocating. Of course it is logically true that if any feature of our world were different it would not be precisely the same world. But it does not follow from this that God, if he is omnipotent, could not easily have created a world just slightly different. If Leibniz replies, as he seems to suggest in this passage, that the part cannot be changed without having repercussions for the whole, then this seems to detract from the omnipotence of God. God seems to become rather like Plato's

"Demiurge",[48] making the best he can of the available materials, but with external limitations as to what types of total combination can be achieved. Leibniz would no doubt meet this objection by pointing out that the limitations as to what combinations can be achieved are purely logical ones, and hence do not detract from the omnipotence of God. Only certain combinations of monads can logically exist together (are "compossible"). Furthermore, a certain amount of imperfection is necessary if anything besides God is to exist at all. Thus, even the most perfect universe possible will contain a residual amount of imperfection or "metaphysical evil". This evil is not willed directly by God : he wills it not "antecedently" but only "consequently"—as a necessary consequence of creating the best possible combination of imperfect substances.[49]

(2) Leibniz' second reply to the argument that an omnipotent benevolent God would have created a world without suffering is that we only suppose such a world would be better than ours as a result of a narrowly anthropocentric assessment of what counts as good. Leibniz is always insisting on how limited our knowledge of the universe is. He considers the possibility of life on other worlds, pointing out "how small a thing our Earth is in relation to all visible things, since it is only an appendix of one of them (the sun)."[50] This reply, characteristically Leibnizian in its stressing of the harmony of the whole, may perhaps be thought effective against a crudely utilitarian complaint that the universe is not framed so as to conduce automatically to the welfare of mankind. But the difficulty remains that the argument, despite Leibniz' earnest protestations, does seem to cast doubt on God's benevolence and concern for man. There is thus something in the direction of thought here that anticipates the Deistic movements of later in the century.

We have noted already that Leibniz' treatment of the problem of evil is distinctly *a priori* in character; and it is when Leibniz does turn to a consideration of actual evils to be found in the world that he is on his weakest ground. Typical is his famous concluding passage on the wickedness and unhappiness of Sextus Tarquinius : "The crime of Sextus serves for great things : it renders Rome free; thence will arise a great empire which will show noble examples to mankind."[51] This sort of approach to specific evils shows a glibness and insensitivity to individual suffering which makes Voltaire's strictures seem not entirely unfair :

"Houses came crashing down. Roofs toppled on their foundations and the foundations crumbled. Thirty thousand men women and children were crushed to death under the ruins. . . .

'What can be the "sufficient reason" for this phenomenon?' said Pangloss."[52]

Conclusion

In the passionate reaction of Voltaire, we can see something of the impact made by Leibniz' thought in the decades following his death. But the reaction was far from all hostile. The *Théodicée* has been described as "probably the most widely read book of the century, at least in Germany" and "in a sense the embodiment of the enlightenment".[53] For, although the eighteenth century is regarded as essentially an age of secularisation, the endless debates conducted by atheists and apologists alike were to follow, in many respects, the lines of argument which Leibniz had set forth.

But the influence of Leibniz went far beyond his contribution to the problems of Christian belief. Perhaps the best known figure of the German "Aufklärung" Christian Wolff (1679–1754) was widely regarded as the inheritor and developer of Leibniz' system. In fact this view of Wolff did more harm than good to Leibniz' reputation, for Wolff's philosophy undoubtedly falls far short of the subtlety and logical rigour of Leibniz' thought. But there is no question that the Wolffian emphasis on a unified metaphysical system, and a rationalistic, deductive schema of knowledge takes its impetus from Leibniz. And even the arch-enemy Voltaire later in his life was to acknowledge the pervasive influence of Leibniz' genius on European thought.[54]

Even the commonly applied title of "Father of the Enlightenment", however, fails to do justice to the extent of Leibniz' influence; for the repercussions of his thinking can be felt far beyond the end of the eighteenth century and even down to the present day. Mention has already been made of the anticipation of the importance of symbolic logic, of the mathematical discoveries, of the still influential contributions to the Theory of Knowledge. And, at the centre of Leibniz' logical doctrines, we have seen, in the account of the two types of proposition, the opening up of an area of analysis which is still being grappled with today. When all this has been said, there remains of course much of Leibniz' thought that is mainly of historical interest. The metaphysical pluralism of the Monadology, for example, will find few supporters among philosophers today. But even in this area commentators have discerned the seeds of more modern thinking. It has been argued that the concept of individual substances, "laden with their past and pregnant with their future" has been the inspiration behind the evolutionary cosmology of Bergson and, more recently, Teilhard de Chardin; Leibniz' doctrines concerning the monad have even been regarded as anticipating the genetic theories of modern Biology.[55] However fanciful these comparisons may seem, it probably remains true that the influence of Leibniz on Philosophy—in both the narrowest and the widest senses of the word—is still not yet exhausted. And that is perhaps the best tribute to the creative genius of the man.

NOTES

Abbreviations: N.E. *New Essays on the Human Understanding.*
D.M. *Discourse on Metaphysics.*
Mon. *Monadology.*
Th. *Theodicy.*
Other works are referred to by the author's or editor's name in CAPITALS, and are listed in full in the bibliography.

1. *Scientia Generalis Characteristica,* XV, translated in SCHRECKER.
2. RUSSELL, Ch. I, para. 1.
3. This work, together with the *Meditationes,* can be found in SCHRECKER.
4. The headings are not mutually exclusive: as will be seen, there are many areas of overlap. Nor are they exhaustive: in a study this size there is inevitably much of interest that has to be left out. (Those interested, for example, in Leibniz' doctrines on Space and Time should consult RUSSELL, Ch. X and RESCHER, Ch. VIII.)
5. HOOK, p. x.
6. The *New Essays on Human Understanding* constitute, with the exception of the *Théodicée,* the only extended piece of continuous philosophical writing produced by Leibniz.
7. *N.E.* Introduction (tr. LATTA, pp. 361–2).
8. LOCKE, Bk. I, Ch. 2, para. 5.
9. *N.E., ibid.* (LATTA, p. 364).
10. *Ibid.* (LATTA, p. 367).
11. *N.E.,* Bk. II, Ch. 1, para. 2.
12. See HOOK, part II.
13. LOCKE, Bk. II, Ch. 1, para 25.
14. *N.E.,* Bk. II, Ch. 1, para. 10.
15. *N.E.* Introduction (LATTA, pp. 370 ff.) cf. *Mon,* para. 21.
16. *Mon.* para. 17, 18.
17. *D.M.,* VIII. (trans. LUCAS & GRINT).
18. See RUSSELL, preface to second edition.
19. *Mon.* para. 33.
20. *Mon.* para. 31.
21. See *Mon.* paras. 34–5.
22. This needs qualification: Leibniz holds that the idea of existence

(which he regards as a predicate) is *not* contained in the subject. The exception to this is the concept of God, which Leibniz regards as necessarily involving that of existence. For the importance of these points, see COPLESTON, pp. 281 ff. and 324 ff, and RESCHER, Ch. I, and Ch. V.

23. Letter of July 1686 (MATSON, p. 63).

24. For the talk of "concepts", and a discussion of what precisely Leibniz means by "subject" and "predicate", see PARKINSON, Ch. I.

25. *D.M.* VIII.

26. *Mon.* para. 7.

27. *Mon.* para. 56.

28. *Th.,* Part I, 66.

29. *Ibid.* 61.

30. *Mon.* para. 32.

31. *Ibid.* 53, 4.

32. *Ibid.* 60.

33. *Ibid.* 36.

34. *D.M.* XIII. This is one of several passages in which Leibniz shows himself aware of the danger of a "general collapse into universal necessitarianism of the Spinozistic type" (RESCHER, p. 35).

35. Space does not permit a fuller discussion of the importance of the Principle of Sufficient Reason, and, in particular, of what Leibniz regarded as one of its logical consequences, the Principle of the *Identity of Indiscernibles*. This celebrated principle says that no two substances can be exactly alike in all respects and still be numerically distinct. See further RUSSELL, Ch. V. and PARKINSON, p. 130 ff. (for the question of whether the principle is necessary or contingent).

36. *D.M.* XIII.

37. Though our discussion is confined to human freedom, there are parallel problems for Leibniz about the free choice of God (e.g., was his decision to create the most perfect universe necessarily "part of him"?). See further RESCHER, p. 43 ff.

38. *Th.* Part I, 52.

39. *Th., Preliminary Dissertation on the Conformity of Faith and Reason,* para. 69.

40. How free, for instance, would we consider the actions of a robot programmed in advance, to take certain "decisions"? It is not clear what Leibniz himself meant by the term "automaton"; probably, he wished to convey little more than "self-moving thing".

41. *Th.* Part I, 59.

42. *Ibid.,* 64.

43. It is interesting to speculate on whether Leibniz was really satisfied with his defence of human freedom; for in a significant passage in the *Théodicée* he canvasses the possibility of justifying the institutions of praise, blame, reward and punishment *not* by reference to the free choice of the agent in question, but by reference to the effectiveness of the consequences of praise, etc. (Th. I, 68–70).

44. This is Hume's formulation of "Epicurus' old question", in his *Dialogues Concerning Natural Religion* (see HUME, part X). Written

some fifty years after the *Théodicée,* the *Dialogues* contain a superbly incisive critique of some of the arguments used by Leibniz.

45. Written in 1758, *Candide* was a bitter and very explicit attack on Leibnizian doctrine. All the catch phrases of Leibniz' system are there; although it has been suggested that Voltaire's target was chiefly the work of Leibniz' followers, in particular Christian Wolff. See Conclusion, p. 38.

46. *Th.*, Part 1, 8.

47. *Ibid.*, 9; cf. Part II, 119.

48. See Plato's *Timaeus,* 29d7 ff.; 69bl ff.

49. "Metaphysical evil" is the first and most important of the three categories into which Leibniz divides evil. (Metaphysical, physical, moral; *Th.*, p. 21). For "antecedent" and "consequent" will, see *Th. I*, pp. 22–3. See also, on these topics. COPLESTON, p. 330 ff.; RESCHER, Ch. XII.

50. *Th.* Part I, 19.

51. *Th.* Part III, 416.

52. VOLTAIRE, Ch. V, p. 33. Voltaire of course had in mind an actual incident, the Lisbon earthquake of 1755, which had been the subject of another bitter attack on "Optimism". (*Poem on the Disaster of Lisbon,* 1756)

53. MARTIN, p. 16.

54. See CASSIRER, Ch. I, p. 35 ff.

55. For these comparisons see VAN PEURSEN, Chs. III, V.

SELECT BIBLIOGRAPHY

1. Texts and Editions.

Sämtliche Schriften und Briefe. Edited by the *Deutsche Akademie der Wissenschaften,* (Darmstadt and Berlin, 1923–). Planned as the definitive critical edition, this project is still not completed.

Die philosophischen Schriften von G. W. Leibniz ed. C. I. Gerhardt, 7 vols. (Berlin: Weidmann, 1875–90).

The following works are available in English translation:

H. G. Alexander	*The Leibniz-Clarke Correspondence.* Manchester University Press, Manchester 1956.
E. M. Huggard	*G. W. Leibniz: Theodicy.* Routledge & Kegan Paul, London 1952. An abridged edition of this translation, edited by D. Allen, is available in the Library of Liberal Arts Series.
A. G. Langley	*New Essays concerning Human Understanding by G. W. Leibniz.* Open Court, La Salle, Ill. 1916.
R. Latta	*Leibniz: The Monadology and Other Philosophical Writings.* Oxford 1898; reprinted Oxford University Press, London 1925.
L. E. Loemker	*Gottfried Wilhelm Leibniz: Philosophical Papers and Letters.* D. Reidel, Dordrecht, Holland 1969.

H. T. Matson	*The Leibniz-Arnauld Correspondence.* Manchester University Press, Manchester 1967.
M. Morris	*The Philosophical Writings of G. W. Leibniz.* J. M. Dent, (Everyman) London 1934.
P. Lucas and L. Grint	*Leibniz: Discourse on Metaphysics.* Manchester University Press, Manchester 1952.
P. and A. M. Schrecker	*Leibniz: Monadology and Other Philosophical Essays.* Bobbs Merrill, New York 1965.

2. *Books on Leibniz.*

H. W. Carr	*Leibniz.* Ernest Benn, London 1929; reprinted: Dover, New York 1960.
H. W. B. Joseph	*Lectures on the Philosophy of Leibniz.* Clarendon, Oxford 1949.
G. Martin	*Leibniz: Logic and Metaphysics.* Tr. K. J. Northcott and P. G. Lucas. Manchester University Press, Manchester 1963
G. H. R. Parkinson	*Logic and Reality in Leibniz' Metaphysics.* Clarendon, Oxford 1965.
N. Rescher	*The Philosophy of Leibniz.* Prentice Hall, Englewood Cliffs 1967.
B. Russell	*A Critical Exposition of the Philosophy of Leibniz.* University of Cambridge Press, Cambridge 1900; Second edition George Allen & Unwin, London 1937
C. A. Van Peursen	*Leibniz.* Faber & Faber, London 1969.

3. *Other Books*

W. H. Barber	*Leibniz in France: From Arnauld to Voltaire, a study in French Reactions to Leibnizianism 1670–1760.* Clarendon, Oxford 1955
E. Cassirer	*The Philosophy of the Enlightenment.* Tr. F. C. A. Koelln and J. P. Pettegrove, Princeton University Press, Princeton 1951.
F. Copleston	*A History of Philosophy, Volume 4: Descartes to Leibniz.* Doubleday, New York 1963.
S. Hampshire	*The Age of Reason.* New American Library, New York 1956.
P. Hazard	*The European Mind, 1680–1715.* Tr. J. Lewis May. Hollis and Carter, London 1953. Available in Penguin Books (Pelican).
S. Hook (ed.)	*Language and Philosophy.* New York University Press, New York 1969.
David Hume	*Dialogues Concerning Natural Religion.* Ed. H. D. Aiken, Haeffner, New York 1948.
John Locke	*An Essay Concerning Human Understanding.* Ed. A. D. Woozley, Collins, London 1964. Abridged Fontana Books edition with introduction.
Voltaire	*Candide.* Tr. J. Butt. Penguin Books, reprinted 1970.

Johann Christoph Gottsched

Johann Christoph Gottsched

by G. L. JONES

Gottsched was born on February 2, 1700 in Juditten, near Königsberg, the son of a Protestant pastor. In 1714 he entered the University of Königsberg where he studied theology and philosophy. During these years he also began to write German verses under the influence and guidance of J. V. Pietsch, the Professor of Poetry in Königsberg. In order to avoid recruitment Gottsched fled in 1724 from Königsberg to Leipzig. In the "Pleissathen", as he frequently calls the city, he became in 1726 the "Senior" of the local literary society, the "Deutschübende-poetische Gesellschaft", later re-named "Die Deutsche Gesellschaft". In 1730 Gottsched was elected to the chair of Poetry in the University of Leipzig and four years later to the chair of Philosophy. After his marriage in 1735 to L. A. V. Kulmus, the daughter of a Danzig physician, Gottsched remained in Leipzig for the rest of his life, apart from a visit to Vienna in 1749 when both he and his wife were presented to Maria Theresia. In 1757 Gottsched was granted an audience on three occasions by Frederick the Great. His wife died in 1762 and Gottsched remarried in 1765; he died a year later on December 12, 1766.

THE engraving of Gottsched by J. M. Bernigeroth (1757) depicts him as the successful Leipzig professor surrounded by his books. Significantly, this man has not the appearance of the ascetic scholar who has sacrificed his physical and material well-being to the pursuit of learning. In fact, Gottsched looks well-fed and well-dressed. He has obviously endeavoured to obey in his own life that natural law which calls on man to perfect his whole being. He has educated his mind, it is true, but not at the expense of his body and his material welfare. This man exudes an air of confidence : here is no tormented soul, bewildered by the problems of existence in a hostile world, but rather the incarnation of that "satisfied citizen in the city of God", to whom he himself gave the name Ernst Wahrlieb Biedermann. This "serious lover of truth and virtue" describes himself as a happy subject in the realm of the great Creator of nature. He regards the world as one of the most densely populated cities in the kingdom of this perfectly wise and good monarch. This earthly city is inhabited by rational creatures, all of whom are subject to divine Providence which desires their ultimate happiness and perfection. In this city order, beauty and justice rule supreme and in it a man like Biedermann can feel secure and happy :

> "Aus allem diesem Erkenntnisse ist mir ein besonders vergnügter Zustand erwachsen. Alles was mir und andern widerfähret, scheint mir so gut zu seyn, dass es nicht besser erdacht werden könnte. Ich bin also niemahls unglücklich sondern allezeit glücklich, und wenn ich kurtz sagen soll, was ich bin, so werde ich antworten : Ein zufriedener Bürger in der Stadt Gottes."[1]

It is important to realise that these words were not written by a mature man at the end of a long life, full of varied experiences, but by a young man in his twenty-seventh year who had already discovered in Leipzig a physical and intellectual security which remained with him for the rest of his life. Even before his arrival in Leipzig (1724) the foundations of this sense of security had been laid. Gottsched appears to have been spared the growing pains of youth, which less than a decade earlier had overwhelmed another Leipzig student, Johann Christian Günther, who "fell ensnared in the nets of flesh and youth" and alienated from his father. From an early age Gottsched shunned vice and followed his father's guidance; this early love of virtue and his respect for paternal advice remained intact throughout the years of childhood and adolescence :

> Mein Zweck war schon von Kindheit an,
> So viel ich mich besinnen kann,
> Mit Ernst der Welt und Dir [Gott] zu dienen,
> Du weist, dass meiner jungen Brust,
> Die Reizung lasterhafter Lust
> Schon als ein süsses Gift geschienen :
> Was mancher höchst bemüht gesucht,
> Davor nahm ich sehr oft die Flucht.
>
> Dein Geist hat mich getreu regiert,
> Und mancher Tugend zugeführt,
> Die sonst der Jugend Trieb verfehlet.
> Dem dank ichs, nicht der eignen Kraft,
> Dass ich den Weg der Wissenschaft
> Auf meines Vaters Wink erwählet.
> Die erste Wohlthat Deiner Hand
> Hat mir den Führer zugewandt.
>
> Der lenkte mich von Jugend auf
> Von jener Bahn, wo sonst der Lauf
> Durch viele Lasterpfützen leitet :

Wenn junger Herzen Lüsternheit
In grosser Städte Wildigkeit
Mehr Böses lernt, als Kunst erbeutet.
Gott! vor Gefahren solcher Art,
Hat mich des Vaters Fleiss bewahrt.[2]

His flight from Königsberg to Leipzig in January 1724 to escape the Prussian recruiting officers can hardly be interpreted as a serious threat to his well-being. Indeed, he himself accepted it philosophically: "Voritzo bin ich zwar aus Königsberg gezogen; Doch wer aus Preussen zieht, der zieht nicht aus der Welt."[3] Once in Leipzig his academic success ensured for him a comfortable existence. His marriage to L. A. V. Kulmus, though not blessed with children, remained unclouded until his wife's illness and death in 1762. Their settled mode of existence was not even greatly affected by the Seven Years' War, which represented more of an inconvenience to them than a painful disruption. Publicly their happiness culminated in the private audience which Maria Theresia granted them in Vienna in 1749. It is clear from Gottsched's own account[4] of this audience that he was deeply moved by the honour bestowed on them and particularly on his wife, who was presented to the Austrian monarch as Germany's leading woman writer and scholar. Eight years later in 1757 Gottsched was received on three occasions by Frederick the Great. These audiences were the outward, visible proof of Gottsched's success; they must have deepened his conviction that he lived in the best of all possible worlds. Another important factor in the creation of this conviction was the political and social stability of Saxony which Gottsched attributed to the enlightened rule of its princes. In the poem *Wettstreit der Tugenden,* written in 1728 to celebrate the birthday of Friedrich August, Gottsched apostrophises Saxony as the land of peace and security, in which the horrors of the Thirty Years' War can be forgotten:

Hier wohnt der Unterthan in voller Sicherheit,
Ein ehrenvoller Greis vergisst der alten Zeiten,
Da Deutschland überall, in dreyssig rauhen Jahren,
Die Wuth des harten Mars ohn Unterlass erfahren.
Der Landmann baut sein Feld, der Winzer seinen Berg,
Der Künstler treibt beglückt und schliesst sein Tagewerk,
Die Jugend liebt und lacht, und scherzet mit Vergnügen,
Und sucht der Nymphen Herz nach Wunsche zu besiegen.[5]

Security, which was so much a part of Gottsched's life, is also a characteristic of his intellectual outlook. Although not entirely unaware of the dangers which attend on dogmatic certainty, he did not himself display any desire to revise in later life those philosophical views which he first accepted as true whilst still a student in Königsberg. By 1719 he had already escaped from the sea of doubts and confusions produced by lectures on various conflicting philosophical systems, and had discovered in the works of Leibniz and Christian Wolff "a safe harbour" and "firm land" :

> "Ich las dessen Theodicee mit unbeschreiblichem Vergnügen, weil ich hundert Skrupel darinn aufgelöset fand, die mich in allerley Materien beunruhiget hatten. Ich lernte aber zu gleicher Zeit auch Herrn Hofrath Wolfs Gedanken von Gott, der Welt und der Seele des Menschen kennen. Hier gieng mirs nun wie einem, der aus einem wilden Meere widerwärtiger Meynungen in einen sichern Hafen einläuft, und, nach vielem Wallen und Schwenken, endlich auf ein festes Land zu stehen kömmt."[6]

When in 1744 Gottsched came to translate Leibniz' *Théodicée* (1710), he described it in the preface as a book which had been "his favourite for the past twenty-four years". In this work Gottsched found a philosophical interpretation of the world and of man's place in it which was to form the basis of his entire thinking on literary matters. His account of the workings of the poetic mind, his theory of imitation of nature, his stress on rules in artistic composition, his insistence on the universality of good taste—all these things will not appear in their true light unless they are seen against the background of Gottsched's philosophical thinking. As in Gottsched's person the chairs of poetry and philosophy in Leipzig were united, so, too, in his works literature and philosophy are inextricably linked.

The certainty which Gottsched derived from his study of the *Théodicée*, stemmed from Leibniz' conviction that the existing universe is the best of all possible worlds both in a structural and a moral sense. Given the finite limits of time and space, God has combined in His creation the greatest possible harmony with the greatest possible variety; also He has ensured that the majority of His creatures will practise virtue and so attain happiness. The infinite Creator has, thus, endowed His creation with beauty and goodness. The key to this optimistic view of existence is to be found in "reason". God, who is supremely rational and good, has created man in His own image. Consequently, there is no qualitative difference between God and man, but only a quantitative one. God, Leibniz maintains, possesses reason as an ocean, of which man only has a few drops. However great the difference may be between the divine and the human, the basic affinity remains.

Thus, man by using his reason can attain knowledge of God, the world and himself. No longer is man at the mercy of Fate or Fortune, an inscrutable force ruling over a chaotic existence; in the light of reason he is firmly convinced that life is governed by Providence, a beneficent Being whose will he can not only accept with confidence but which he can also anticipate rationally by his own actions. If it were not for his reason, man would be overwhelmed by a sense of his own vanity when he surveyed the whole of creation. This point is given particular emphasis by Gottsched on the frontispiece to his *Erste Gründe der gesammten Weltweisheit* (1734). Here below the vignette of the spinning planets are the words :

> Hier starret Sinn und Witz, der Geist verliert sich gantz
> In aller Welten Heer, Pracht, Ordnung, Lauf und Glantz.
> O ! was ist hier der Mensch? Er wäre nichts zu nennen,
> Könnt er am Wercke nicht des Meisters Grösse kennen.[7]

It is by his reason that man not only approaches the divine but also distances himself from the bestial. If he is to become a virtuous being, then he must seek to govern the bestial side of his nature by his understanding and reason. The pursuit of the good demands the suppression of the senses and of the imagination, for as Wolff declared :

> "Je scharffsinniger demnach der Mensch ist und je gründlicher, je mehr ist er von den Thieren unterschieden : hingegen je mehr er an seinen Sinnen und Einbildungs-Krafft hanget, und daher der Sclaverey unterworffen ist, je näher kommet der den Thieren oder dem Viehe."[8]

Gottsched argues that the senses lead man into making false judgements, into failing to distinguish between the true and the false, and that the imagination distracts him by reawakening past physical desire and so interrupting rational considerations. Here in Gottsched's philosophical thinking is the source of his suspicion of the poetic imagination in so far as it is not governed by the writer's intellectual powers. In his various comments on poetry, stress invariably falls not on the imaginative but on the reasonable. Thus, the word "reasonable" appears in the title of Gottsched's first moral weekly, *Die vernünftigen Tadlerinnen* (1726–7) and also in his own translation of the motto from Horace to the *Critische Dichtkunst* (1730) : "Scribendi recte sapere est et principium et fons", "Vernunft und Klugheit sind die Quellen schöner Lieder !"[9]

Before we proceed to examine in greater detail the meaning of the term "reason", it is essential to understand the role which Gottsched assigns to learning, of which philosophy and literature are branches, in life. Already in *Die vernünftigen Tadlerinnen* (2/28) he rejects any suggestion that the pursuit of learning is an end in itself. Neither the man of war nor the man of learning, he maintains, is without obligations to his fellow human beings. The true hero should use his prowess not to indulge in war for its own sake but to defend his country; the truly learned man should use his gifts not to indulge in scholarship for its own sake but to further the virtue of the human race. Gottsched is really only interested in philosophy and literature in so far as both can contribute to the moral enlightenment of mankind. Consequently, he is never in danger of getting lost in vague speculations about metaphysical or aesthetic questions which have no practical application. His concern is constantly with the influence on life of philosophy and literature. The slight difference in emphasis between Wolff's and Gottsched's definitions of philosophy underlines this concern. Wolff places more stress initially on the intellectual aspects of the subject :

"Die Welt-Weissheit ist eine Wissenschaft aller möglichen Dinge, wie und warumb sie möglich sind."[10]

Gottsched, on the other hand, emphasises the practical aim of philosophy :

"Die Weltweisheit nenne ich die Wissenschaft von der Glückseligkeit des Menschen; in so weit wir sie, nach dem Maasse unsrer Unvollkommenheit, erlangen und ausüben können."[11]

This goal of happiness can, of course, only be achieved by the virtuous man. Philosophy defines the aim of life, literature communicates this aim to those who are not gifted enough intellectually to comprehend philosophical truths in a pure form. The literary writer sugars the pill of moral philosophy, thus making it palatable and attractive to those who would otherwise be deprived of its beneficial effect. It is from this point that the stress on moral didacticism in Gottsched's theory of literature must be grasped. Taken out of this wider context, Gottsched's demand that the first task, for example, of the tragedian should be to choose a moral precept will appear excessively ludicrous. This demand is not enjoined on the tragedian as such, but on every literary writer whose work is worthy of serious attention.

In posing the question : What is the meaning of "reason"? we are not inviting the reader to take part in a philosophical investigation the end of which is lost in the clouds of speculation, but rather to concentrate on the basic concept in Gottsched's understanding of life and literature. In the act of creation God uses His reason to link together the contingencies of the universe in such a way that the greatest possible structural and moral harmony will be produced. Divine reason is thus the source of overall order : in a physical sense it creates beauty and in a moral sense goodness. On a human level man not only uses his reason to perceive this beauty and goodness but also to imitate them in his own creative works. Although the events in this world are described as contingencies ("Zufälligkeiten"), in the sense that they are not subject to absolute necessity—i.e. other possible worlds could be created—they are not ordered fortuitously but rather according to a principle formulated by Leibniz and adopted by Gottsched, called "the principle of sufficient reason" ("Der Satz vom zureichenden Grunde"). According to this principle the events in the world are all linked together by a great chain of cause and effect. Human reason can by means of this principle comprehend the causal relationship between these events. In so far as the contingencies of the created world are based on this principle of sufficient reason, they are said to possess truth. Gottsched argues that man's experience of reality would be chaotic were it not for this principle :

> "Will man indessen zur Erläuterung etwas haben, dieses desto besser einzusehen : so bemerke man, dass man die Wahrheit von einem Traume nicht würde unterscheiden können, wenn dieser Satz des zureichenden Grundes nicht zum Probierstein angenommen würde. Im Traume geschieht fast alles ohne zureichenden Grund. Man ist bald hier, bald da; und man weis nicht warum? Wie man hin, oder weggekommen? Im Wachen aber, oder in der Wahrheit, hat alles seine Ursachen. Wer da kömmt, der weis, warum er kömmt; und so weiter. Dieser Satz kan also ein sicheres Merkmaal der Wahrheit abgeben."[12]

The contrast between truth and dream recurs throughout Gottsched's writings and casts considerable light on all the central issues in his theory of literature. Truth in the real world becomes in the fictional world the "semblance of truth" ("Wahrscheinlichkeit"). Because the world created by the writer is based on reality, its contingencies must still be governed by the principle of sufficient reason; without this principle an unreal world of fantasy would be produced which Gottsched calls "Schlaraffenland",[13] i.e. a land in which apple trees would bear pears, rose bushes would bring forth lilies, tulips would flower like narcissi or hyacinths, the stork would give birth to children, and women produce geese. Similar abortive creations of the poetic fantasy are, of course, mocked by Horace in the opening lines of his *De Arte Poetica,* the full Latin text of which Gottsched published as a preface to his *Dichtkunst* along with his own German translation of it. Horace also describes them as "aegri somnia" (1.7), an image Gottsched repeats when he attacks the lack of probability in *Orlando furioso:*

> "Genug von *Ariosts* Phantasien, die gewiss eher den Träumen eines Kranken, wie *Horaz* spricht, als der vernünftigen Dichtung eines Poeten ähnlich sehen : weil weder Wahrscheinlichkeit, noch Ordnung darinn anzutreffen ist."[14]

So important is this principle of sufficient reason to Gottsched that he even insists[15] that the poetic imagination should function in accordance with it. Imagination, which he defines simply as man's ability to recall past experiences and sensations, is thus virtually identified with reason. It is the rational man's experience of reality which provides the criterion by which probability in a work of literature is to be judged. The poet is thus denied any freedom in the creation of his imaginative world. Reason and reality invade the realm of the imagination and of fiction and impose on it extraneous criteria. Gottsched's various comments on the dramatic unities, which strike the modern reader as ludicrous, are simply the practical application of this refusal to allow the writer any autonomy. The physical needs of the rational spectator override the possibility of the creation of a dramatic illusion of time and space. It is highly significant that when Herder came to refute the restricting influences of the unities, he postulated as the dramatist's prime duty the creation of a dream in which the audience is obliged to believe imaginatively :

> ". . . und wäre es nicht eben jedes Genies, jedes Dichters, und des Dramatischen Dichters insonderheit Erste und Einzige Pflicht, dich in einen solchen Traum zu setzen? Und nun denke, welche Welten du verwirrest, wenn du dem Dichter deine Taschenuhr, oder dein Visitenzimmer vorzeigest, dass er dahin und darnach dich träumen lehre?"[16]

The real weakness in Gottched's argument is not that he demands probability in literature, but that his interpretation of probability is too narrowly selective.

This selectivity must be borne in mind in any attempt to understand what Gottsched means by the imitation of nature. In his thinking there is an obvious difference between nature and reality. He does not deny that man has dreams; i.e. he grants their real existence. What he does deny is that such states in man's experience possess any validity. In other words, dreams are real but not true. This distinction between reality and truth is exemplified in an early number of *Der Biedermann* (1727-9), Gottsched's second moral weekly. There he narrates an anecdote about Ptolemy, the son of Lagus, who in an effort to amuse his compatriots with something unusual, introduced into Egypt a pitchblack Bactrian camel and a man who was half-white and half-black. These two objects had anything but the desired effect on the Egyptians who were terrified by the camel and regarded the bi-coloured man as a monster. When Ptolemy noticed that his subjects were not interested in such rarities, he became so annoyed that he let the camel die of hunger and sold the bi-coloured man to a musician. Gottsched sees in the common sense of the Egyptians a trait which, he believes, is characteristic of the Germans :

"Mit diesen lobenswürdigen Egyptern kan ich meine werthesten Landesleuten auch vergleichen. Ich weiss, sie lieben was verständliches, ordentliches und vernünfftiges. Sie sehen die Natur vor was begreifliches an, und wollen auch dass Scribenten derselben nachfolgen sollen."[17]

Like dreams the camel and the bi-coloured man did exist, they were real, and yet they were disregarded because they lacked the intelligibility, order and rationality which the Germans not only look for in nature but also expect to find in literary imitations of nature. Thus, when Gottsched advocates the poet to imitate nature, he is not commending complete realism in literature. His theory of poetic imitation does not demand that the writer should hold a mirror up to nature in all her manifestations. Literature, for Gottsched, is not a reflection of every aspect of reality, however unintelligible, irrational, trivial, ugly, destructive and chaotic it may be. Such aspects of reality are excluded not simply because they are unworthy of the poet but more fundamentally because they represent but a small and uncharacteristic part of nature as a whole. Although there is a certain amount of ugliness, disorder and irrationality in the world, in general beauty, order and rationality predominate. In order to ensure that his readers will not misunderstand this vital distinction between reality and nature, Gottsched sometimes designates the object of poetic imitation "die schöne Natur". The clearest definition of this concept will be found in one of Gottsched's late works, *Handlexicon oder Kurzgefasstes Wörterbuch der schönen Wissenschaften und freyen Künste* (1760):

"*Natur, die schöne,* ist nicht das Wahre, welches wirklich ist, sondern das Wahre, das seyn kann, mit allen Vollkommenheiten, die sich zusammen schicken. . . . Die schöne Natur aber enthält alle Eigenschaften des Schönen und Guten in sich. Sie ergetzet

den Witz, indem sie ihm vollkommene Gegenstände zeiget; sie
vergnüget das Herz, indem sie solche liefert, welche ihm nützlich
sind."[18]

According to this definition "beautiful nature" has a dual effect on
the reader : it both delights and instructs him. It thus differs from
those aspects of reality, such as the black camel or the bi-coloured
man, which merely elicit amazement or wonderment. At this point
an important difference emerges between Gottsched's theory of the
effect of poetry and that found in the literature of the second half
of the seventeenth century. In the works of such writers as
Hofmannswaldau, Lohenstein and Zigler wonderment is produced
in three different ways : firstly, by descriptions of the exotic,
secondly, by a view of the world which stresses the inscrutability
of Fate, and thirdly, stylistically by the use of conceits. As far as
descriptions of foreign countries and peoples are concerned,
Gottsched comments that Siam, Peru, Ceylon and Japan have been
so filled with fictitious wonders that their inhabitants probably
regard the Germans as "one-eyed".[19] In the heroic novels of the
seventeenth century life is portrayed as a labyrinth, governed it is
true by a supernatural force, called fate, fortune, the gods or even
providence, but in which man is unable to detect any kind of
pattern until at the end of the novel the various strands of narrative
and the many characters are drawn together in a final triumph of
the beautiful and the good. Time and again in a novel like Zigler's
Asiatische Banise (1689) the reader is reminded of the inscrutability
of divine will :

> "Der Götter Gerechtigkeit ist unerforschlich, und also bemüht
> man sich nur vergebens, dem Geheimnisse des wundervollen
> Schicksals nachzugrübeln."[20]

The key word in this sentence is, of course, "wundervoll"; this
word or other compounds of "wunder-" will be found not only in
the heroic novel but also in the picaresque and more realistic
novels of the age. The lack of rational causality in life is reflected
in the episodic plots of such novels : here in place of a rational
order of events the hero is tossed by fortune from one experience
to another. We, the readers, are meant to wonder at the totally
unexpected relationship between events and characters and to be
filled with amazement in the same way as the characters in the
novels themselves listen in awe to the narration of various strange
tales. Seen from a less pleasant point of view the irrationality of
existence evokes not gasps of amazement but cries of horror. The
destruction of the beautiful, the violation of the innocent, the

defeat of the virtuous—all these things led many writers of the seventeenth century to describe life as a transient and nightmarish dream. In subjecting the real to the natural, the rationalists of the eighteenth century strove to wake man from this dream and to show him the wonderful not in terms of its inscrutability but of its rationality. For Gottsched what is wonderful is not that which contravenes nature, but nature itself :

> "Das beste und vernünftigste Wunderbare ist, wenn man auch bey Thieren und leblosen Dingen, nur die Wunder der Natur recht nachahmet, und allezeit dasjenige wählt, was die Natur am vortrefflichsten gemacht hat."[21]

The third source of wonderment in the German poetry of the seventeenth century is to be found in the highly metaphorical style of Hofmannswaldau, Lohenstein and their imitators. These "galant" writers sought to emulate the style of the Italian poet Marino (1569–1625), who himself had defined the aim of poetry as the creation of the "marvellous" :

> "È del poeta il fin la meraviglia
> (Parlo de l'eccellente e non del goffo) :
> Chi non sa far stupir, vada alla striglia."[22]

To achieve this end Marino exercised his wit in the invention of endless comparisons of an exotic and startling nature. One example from Hofmannswaldau will suffice to illustrate the essence of these "concetti", translated by Gottsched as "spitzfindige Einfälle". In the poem *Lob-rede an das liebwertheste frauen-zimmer* Hofmannswaldau states his aim quite bluntly in line 13 : "Die brüste sind mein zweck". In the remaining ninety-five lines, however, he bombards his subject with an amazing variety of conceits which range from the conventional marble, alabaster, roses and snow-balls to the "marvellous" lines :

"Sie sind ein runder sarg/ wo liebe liegt begraben/
  Ein ditrich/welcher auch des hertzens grund auffschleust/ . . .
Zwey fässer/welche sind mit julep-safft erfüllet/
  Lockvögel/derer thon ein freyes hertze bindt."[23]

So successful was Hofmannswaldau in the creation of the "marvellous" that he earned from his Silesian compatriot, Andreas Gryphius, the praise : "Biss Hoffmannswaldaus Mund die Sinnen mir entzücket/Der nichts denn Wunder spricht".[24] It is hardly surprising that Gottsched was extremely critical of Marinistic verse and demanded that the poet should employ his wit not to invent totally unexpected affinities between wholly disparate objects

but to discover actual similarities in different objects. Marino's
wonderful conceits which astound the reader, thus yield to Gottsched's reasonable similes and metaphors which both delight and
instruct him.

The distinction between truth and dream, nature and reality can
also be expressed in terms of the difference between the probable
and the possible. At one point in the *Dichtkunst* Gottsched appears
to free the poetic imagination from the shackles of reason and to
advise the poet not to restrict himself to the probable, i.e. the
created universe, but to base his imitation on the possible uncreated
worlds. Had Gottsched really granted the imagination this freedom,
his controversy with Bodmer and Breitinger would have been
avoided. For the Swiss critics the imagination has a dual function :
firstly, it is the "treasurer of the soul", in so far as it recalls the
probable, and secondly, it has the magic power to create the possible. In bestowing this power on the imagination, they widened
the scope of the wonderful and so were able to justify the poetic
practice of Milton and Klopstock. When Gottsched commended
the possible to his readers, he was not acknowledging the existence
of such an autonomous realm of the imagination but simply defending his own concept of conditional probability. He uses this concept
to defend deviations from truth in moral fables in which animals
and trees are endowed with human speech. Gottsched's insistence
on the probable in poetry is a result of his conviction that the
existing universe is the best of all possible worlds. There can be
no sound reason why the poet should turn to the other possible
worlds which of necessity are inferior both in a structural and
moral sense. To recognise the validity of the Swiss argument would
have meant for Gottsched the relinquishment of his own philosophical standpoint. When in 1740 Bodmer suggested that the
Germans were unable to appreciate Milton because their excessive
philosophising had rendered them incapable of enjoying the pleasures of the imagination, Gottsched retorted that this alleged weakness was in fact a reflection of the good taste of his compatriots :

"Es ist wahr, Deutschland hat seit zwanzig Jahren mehr, als
vorhin philosophiret. Die Vernunft ist unter unsern Landesleuten
sehr geläutert, der wilde Witz gebändiget, und die ausschweifende
Phantasie in ihre gebührende Grenzen eingeschränket worden.
Dadurch ist nun auch der Geschmack in den freyen Künsten um
ein vieles verbessert worden, und man hat Dinge zu verachten
angefangen, die man vorhin himmelhoch erhoben hatte. . . .
Was kann nun das philosophierende Deutschland dafür, dass ihm
Milton gleichfalls nicht schmecken will? Es sieht ohne Zweifel

auch in diesem Engländer den lohensteinischen und zieglerischen Schwulst, die ungeheure Einbildung, die hochtrabenden Ausdruckungen, und die unrichtige Urteilskraft herrschen."[25]

Gottsched objects to Milton's poetry because it directs attention away from the natural to the supernatural. The angels and devils of *Paradise Lost* have, he argues, no counterpart in nature; they seem to him to be an anachronism from an age whose superstitious belief in the occult had been destroyed by the rational insights of the eighteenth century. By the natural as the object of poetic imitation Gottsched means the human; the true poet is concerned above all else with man and his actions :

"Vor allen Dingen aber ist einem wahren Dichter eine gründliche Erkenntniss des Menschen nöthig, ja gantz unentbehrlich. Ein Poet ahmet hauptsächlich die Handlungen der Menschen nach. . . ."[26]

Racine's human interpretation of the tragic dilemma in *Iphigénie*, his refusal to have recourse to Euripides' *deus ex machina* must have been amongst the factors which influenced Gottsched to choose this play as the first which he translated from the French. Gottsched's interest in drama and epic is a reflection of the stress which he places on human actions in his theory of poetry. In comedy those actions which deviate from the normal behaviour of the rational man are exposed to satirical laughter. In tragedy the problem facing the rationalistic writer is more complicated. How can he harmonise tragic disorder with an optimistic view of the world? This problem, which Lessing endeavours to solve in *Emilia Galotti,* is avoided by Gottsched. His tragedies have more in common with stoical dramas of the seventeenth century than one might have expected from such an optimistic thinker. They are set in a world governed by inscrutable Fate and not by rational Providence; a world in which the highest virtue is steadfast acceptance of one's lot, as Cato indicates :

Ein andrer würde hier in tausend Aengsten seyn,
So sehr stimmt das Geschick mit unsern Feinden ein.
Der junge Scipio und Juba sind geschlagen;
Nur Cäsar triumphirt auf seinem Siegeswagen.
Bey uns hergegen, Prinz, gibt es mehr Muth als Glück :
Vieleicht hält dieser noch des Schicksals Hass zurück.
Getrost und standhaft seyn, das stärkt und lehrt die Herzen."[27]

Instead of trying to solve the problem of the evil which overtakes the virtuous man, in a way consistent with his philosophical opti-

mism, Gottsched argues in the *Weltweisheit* that such misfortune
provides the sufferer with an opportunity to practise the virtue
of fortitude.[28] Similarly, he understands by "catharsis" the purification of impatience in misfortune and the creation of a sense of
satisfaction and constancy. In stressing human nature as the main
object of poetic imitation, Gottsched not only excludes the supernatural but also assigns to purely descriptive nature poetry a position
of minor importance. In his notes on Horace he calls excessive
poetic descriptions boring and states unequivocally : "Dichten heisst
nicht bloss malen."[29] Later he criticises Brockes for his lack of
"taste" and "art". Without expanding on the differences between
poetry and painting, Gottsched has thus in a modest way antici-
pated Lessing's central thesis in *Laokoon*.

Gottsched's optimistic belief in man's ability to lead a virtuous
and happy life in society finds clear expression in the poem *Die
Donau* (1749). On the journey from Regensburg to Vienna the
ship passes through a mountainous region between Straubing and
Passau. At the sight of the mountains Gottsched is prompted to
muse, like Haller before him, on the happiness of those fortunate
begins who live in geographical isolation—they are untroubled by
the pursuit of beauty, wealth and ambition which makes court and
urban life so unpleasant :

> Beglücktes Gemsenvolk ! du weist nicht was die Stadt
> Für Noth und Angst bey ihrer Schönheit heget :
> Dir wird kein falsches Geld, zu deiner Quaal, gepräget,
> Das weder Werth noch Ansehn hat.
> Dich plagt kein Geiz; der Wucher ist verbannet.
> Die Ehrsucht quält dich nicht bey Hofe gross zu seyn :
> Du wirst ins Joch der Grossen, nicht gespannet,
> Und machst auch keinen Grossen klein.
> Ein Berg verstecket dich. Dein ganzes Weltgetümmel
> Ist Fels, die Donau und der Himmel.[30]

Immediately he expresses this thought, however, he corrects himself : such a conclusion must be erroneous; cut off from human
society, these mountain dwellers lack true knowledge of man and
God :

> So scheints : doch scheints auch nur. Wie elend lebt ein Mann,
> Den die Gesalt kaum lässt zu Menschen zählen?
> Wie viel gebricht ihm nicht, was sonder Gram und Quälen
> Uns die Gesellschaft liefern kann?
> Er lernt nicht sich, nicht andre Leute kennen.
> Sein Gott wird jeder Klotz, vor dem er thöricht kniet :

Den Heiligen weis er oft nicht zu nennen,
Den er mit dummer Ehrfurcht sieht.
Wie will er, als ein Christ, das höchste Wesen ehren,
Das niemand ihn will kennen lehren?[31]

Here again an unexpected affinity can be discovered between Gottsched's thought and that of Lessing. When Gleim, in a fit of misanthropy, declared his intention of becoming a hermit, he was reminded by Lessing that the company of human beings, however evil they may be, is infinitely better than isolation :

"Besser ist unter noch so bösen Menschen leben, als fern von allen Menschen ! Besser ist, sich vom Sturme in den ersten besten Hafen werfen lassen, als in einer Meerstille mitten auf der See verschmachten."[32]

Gottsched's image of man, the virtuous child of the rationalist philosophers, forms the basis of his attitude towards the Ancients and the French. To see in Gottsched a servile imitator and a blind neo-classicist, is to misunderstand his philosophical position. Gottsched advocates the imitation of the French, not because he is convinced of their innate superiority, but rather because he sees in them the modern custodians of "good taste", which they derived from the Romans who had in turn received it from the Greeks. This static concept of "good taste" is the literary expression of Gottsched's philosophical belief in the immutability of human nature. It is because the rational man has an unchanging view of literary excellence, regardless of the time and place in which he happens to live, that Gottsched can urge his compatriots to imitate the French neo-classicists :

"Die Natur des Menschen, und seiner Seelenkräfte ist noch eben dieselbe, als sie seit zweytausend Jahren gewesen : und folglich muss der Weg, poetisch zu gefallen, noch eben derselbe seyn, den die Alten dazu so glücklich erwählet haben."[33]

The French are worthy of imitation not because their literature is peculiarly French, but because it reveals those timeless poetic qualities of which Gottsched approves. The universal validity of the rules of "good taste" does not depend on the authority of those writers who possess it, be they Greek, Roman or French, but on the nature of the rules themselves. One is reminded in this context of Lessing's controversy with Goeze. Lessing's conviction that the truth of any statement is not dependent on the authority of the person who advances it but rather on the truth of the statement itself, is already foreshadowed by Gottsched, even though the latter is, in

fact, more respectful of authority. Both writers exemplify their
arguments by reference to Euclid. For Lessing (*Axiomata*, 1778)
a geometrical theorem is not true because it is found in Euclid, but
rather because its truth can be established geometrically. In other
words, a geometrical theorem is not true because Euclid taught it, but
he taught it because it is true. Gottsched, on the other hand, is
prepared to accept truths discovered by previous thinkers; he
argues that the prudent mathematician does not disregard the
validity of truths established by Euclid, but accepts them on the
latter's authority (see *Weltweisheit*. Vorrede). For a similar reason
Gottsched maintains that German writers should accept the rules
propounded by the Greeks. How can Germans be so presumptuous,
he asks, as to query the authority of a nation without whose
influence they themselves would still be numbered amongst the
barbarians? This respect for the Ancients is, however, ultimately
based on the conviction that their greatness depends not on their
nationality but on their regularity. This point is made with considerable emphasis in the *Ausführliche Redekunst* (1736):

> "Nichts ist in Wissenschaften und freyen Künsten vernünftig, als
> was auf gute Gründe gebauet ist. Diese sind aber nicht die
> Meynungen und Zeugnisse grosser Leute; nicht die Exempel
> derer, die hier oder dort für Redner gehalten werden; nicht das
> Neue oder Alte, in so weit es neu oder alt ist: sondern die
> unveränderliche Natur des Menschen, als mit welchem ein
> Redner zu thun hat . . . die Alten werden von uns nur darum
> zu Lehrern und Mustern angepriesen, weil sie ihre Regeln und
> Exempel nach dieser Vorschrift eingerichtet haben."[34]

It is paradoxical that Gottsched, who was so concerned to communicate to his compatriots an understanding of the universal rules
of "good taste", should also have been fired by a profound desire
to make German literature truly German. His cultural patriotism,
which is an important element in all his works, seems directly
opposed to his rejection of relativism in poetry. It is difficult to
understand how German literature could conform to universally
recognised, European standards, and at the same time retain its
own peculiar stamp. In a letter to Bodmer, written in 1739,
Gottsched explains that he would not even be averse to English
literature exerting some sort of beneficial effect on German
writers, provided that it did not increase to such an extent that,
like French literature, it threatened the very continuation of
national literature in Germany.[35] This concern with the preser-
vation of the peculiar characteristics of a national literature is
closely related to Gottsched's belief in Providence. He is convinced

that it is the duty not only of every individual but also of every nation to fulfil the role assigned to it by Providence. In aping French speech and manners, the Germans were, thus, showing themselves to be ungrateful to Providence and unworthy of their divine calling. The demand for a specifically German literature could best be met, so Gottsched believed, by encouraging German poets to write correctly in their mother tongue, by suggesting that tragic and epic poets should choose subjects from German history and that writers of comedy should expose the weaknesses of contemporary German manners, and by creating an awareness in Germans of their own literary tradition. Although by these measures Gottsched succeeded in purifying the language, in bringing literature closer to life, and in keeping alive a knowledge of the poetry of the seventeenth century, he did not, indeed he could not ever succeed in creating a literature which would be unmistakably German. Not until the basic philosophical assumptions of the rationalists had been refuted, could a critic like Herder explore the unique richness of the German language and its literature. Apart from the language and the German setting the literature written by Gottsched and by his followers hardly differs from neo-classical literature in other European countries.

The most unsatisfactory aspect of Gottsched's literary theory and practice resides in his failure to grasp the true nature of the relationship between content and form in a work of art. For Gottsched form is entirely subservient to content. What is important in literature is the moral precept; metre, rhythm, rhyme, stanza form, metaphor, all these things merely serve to communicate this precept to the reader; they do not stand in any close relationship to the content. In an early chapter of the *Dichtkunst* Gottsched explains how the moral truth : "Ungerechtigkeit und Gewaltthätigkeit wären abscheuliche Laster" (p. 161) can be clothed in Aesopian, comic, tragic and epic form. In other words, the content is much like a liquid which can be poured into bottles of various shapes and sizes and which is not bound inextricably to one form of expression. The main function of form is to lend clarity and order to the content. These qualities can be lost in two different ways : firstly, by obscurity, and secondly, by formlessness. The former he regards as a characteristic of Marinistic verse and of the poetry of Klopstock. In one of his poetic epistles Gottsched parodies this new obscurity in verses entitled *Der geistvolle Poet*, from which the following stanzas are taken :

> Welt ist, und auch der geistge Dichter :
> Natur wirkt allzeit wesenreich.

Sie rauscht im Meer; sie stralt durch Lichter,
Reimt im Poet, gleich stark am Zeug.
Als sich vermählte Nichts und Was:
Entsprang Luft, Feur und trocknes Nass;
Da lag schon zu des Reimers Bildung
Der Urgrund möglichster Vergüldung.

Sein Forschgewicht senkt der Poete
Aufs alten Chaos grundlos Meer.
Von seines Nachruhms Morgenröthe
Sieht er im Reime Zeitpunktsehr.
Mit Wechselernst schwänt seine Stimm;
Sein Geist, als Riesencherubim,
Trägt er sich gleich in Baustofschirbeln,
Fährt reitend doch in Schwefelwirbeln.[36]

That Gottsched ascribed this cult of the obscure, at least in part, to the Swiss critics is clear from his ironic comment on the verb "schwänt": "Für Schwanenlieder singen. Ein Machtwort: wie unterjochen, für unters Joch bringen."[37] He does not appreciate the reasons why a poet like Klopstock wishes to deviate from normal syntax; for him "Phöbus", the god of light, is the god of poetry. The formlessness produced by the alternation of lines of varying length is censured by Gottsched in Brockes and Haller. In a letter to Haller Gottsched comments as follows on the opening verses of *Über den Ursprung des Übels* (1734):

"Der Ursprung des Bösen hat mir sonderlich wol gefallen. Nur hätte ich gewünscht, dass alle Verse von einem Maasse und von einer Art der Abwechselung gewesen sein möchten. Leibnitz nennt eine gewisse Art der Fatalisten Vertheidiger einer faulen Philosophie. Wir pflegen hier in Meissen die Brockesischen regellosen Verse die Faulen zu nennen."[38]

The philosophical term "lazy reason" ("lógos äergos") is used by Leibniz (v. *Discours de métaphysique.* 4, *Théodicée.* Préface) to denote a misuse of reason by those who do not desire to act in anticipation of divine will but who wait passively for disaster to overtake them. It is characteristic of Gottsched that he applies a Leibnizian concept to literature. "Lazy poetry" is a reflection of the poet's failure to organise his material in a rational manner. Although critical of formlessness Gottsched is certainly not an advocate of excessive formalism. He does not favour the sonnet, for example, because it places inordinate formalistic demands on the poet; in such poems the writer is in danger of sacrificing the con-

tent to the form. When form does in fact free itself from content
and begin to lead an existence of its own, it is immediately attacked
by Gottsched. He is particularly critical of many formalistic
devices employed by poets in the seventeenth century. Thus, he
comments unfavourably on Paul Gerhardt's famous poem, *Befiehl
du deine Wege,* because it contains an acrostic. Gottsched's criticism echoes Addison's observation that "your laborious *German*
Wits will turn over a whole Dictionary for one of these ingenious
Devices."[39] In Gottsched's view the rational reader will never
delight in such formalistic artistry; he will derive maximum aesthetic pleasure from unobtrusive formal regularity which is designed to
lend greatest effect to the moral lesson. Much of the poetry written
in accordance with these demands for formal regularity and clarity
will inevitably strike the modern reader as pedestrian and prosaic.
Gotsched himself was not entirely unaware of this danger; in an
epithalamium written in 1749 he excuses his own lack of inspiration :

> Ach ! ruf ich, Göttin, irrst du nicht?
> Die Wahl an mir wird dich gereuen !
> Mein allzublödes Lobgedicht
> Wird dieses Helden Ruhm und deinen Trieb entweihen.
> Ein Dichter von zu scheuer Kunst,
> Ein Feind von Schwulst und finsterm Dunst,
> Bleibt in der Tiefe stehn, und kann nicht Helden loben.
> Geh ! feure kühne Sänger an,
> Die auf der wilden Geister Bahn,
> Wie Delphins Priesterinn, in dunklen Räthseln toben.[40]

In spite of this realisation, however, Gottsched's poetry, instead
of quickening the dry bones of moral philosophy, frequently
becomes affected by that very aridity which it sought to overcome.
In sacrificing form to content, Gottsched fails to endow the content with any compelling poetic qualities.

Nine months after Gottsched's death Abraham Gotthelf Kästner
read a paper to the "Royal German Society" in Göttingen in
which he appraises the Leipzig critic's contribution to German
literature. Kästner describes the task Gottsched performed in
purifying the German language and reforming its literature as
"Herculean". Having placed Gottsched's merits in their historical
context, he goes on to outline the main reason why Gottsched's
views were so quickly discredited :

> "Dieses scheint der Fehler zu seyn, der das meiste zu Gottscheds
> Falle beygetragen hat. Er blieb bey den Einsichten stehen, die er

sich in seinen jungen Jahren erworben hatte. Im Jahre 1730 da die kritische Dichtkunst zuerst heraus kam, gaben ihm diese Einsichten vielleicht einen Vorzug; allein diesen zu behalten, sollte er sie beständig erweitern, und selbst das nicht aus der Acht lassen, dass es in Künsten, die zum Putze der Gelehrsamkeit gehören, veränderliche Moden geben muss."[41]

That certainty which Gottsched discovered so early in his life proved in the course of time to be of dubious value. Rational conviction easily becomes pedantic dogmatism, unless it is tempered by self-criticism. Gottsched did not escape the danger which all "legislative" critics run : when he was confronted by creative works of literature of which he had given no account in his theoretical criticism, he was obliged to condemn them rather than confess his own inadequacy and modify his critical standpoint. Thus, he failed to appreciate the poetry of Klopstock and merely saw in it the revival of the Marinistic verse of the seventeenth century.

NOTES

1. On the basis of all this knowledge I have arrived at a state of particular happiness. Everything which happens to me and to others appears to me to be so good that it could not be conceived of as being better. I am, therefore, never unhappy but always happy, and if I am to say briefly what I am, then I will answer: a satisfied citizen in the city of God. *Der Biedermann.* Leipzig 1728, p. 3.

2. From childhood itself my aim, as far as I can remember, has been to serve in a serious manner the world and Thee [God], Thou knowest that the attraction of evil desire appeared already to my young breast as a sweet poison: what many sought after with all their power, I frequently eschewed.

Thy spirit has ruled me faithfully and guided me to many a virtue which youthful instinct usually misses. It is to Thy spirit and not to my own strength that I am indebted for choosing, on my father's advice, the path of learning. The first benefit of Thy hand provided me with my guide.

He it was who guided me from youth away from that course which usually leads through many sloughs of vice: when the lasciviousness of young hearts learns more of evil in the wildness of large towns than of art. God! my father's diligence has preserved me from such dangers. *Gedichte.* 2. Auflage. Leipzig 1751, 2. Theil, p. 238.

3. For the time being I have, it is true, left Königsberg;/Yet he who leaves Prussia does not leave the world. Ibid. 1. Theil, p. 495.

4. *Der Frau L. A. V. Gottschedinn sämmtliche kleinere Gedichte.* Hsg. J. C. Gottsched, Leipzig 1763.

5. Here the subject lives in complete saftey, a respected old-man can forget the old times when Germany felt everywhere, in thirty rough years, the anger of cruel Mars without respite. The farmer cultivates his field, the wine-grower his vine-yard, the artist pursues happily his daily work to its end, the young fall in love and laugh and delight in jocularity, and seek to conquer freely the nymphs' hearts. *Gedichte*. 2. Theil, p. 440

6. I read his Theodicy with indescribable pleasure, because in it I found the answers to a hundred scruples which had been worrying me in all kinds of subjects. However, at the same time I also became acquainted with Herr Hofrath Wolff's Thoughts on God, the World and the Soul of Man. On reading these works I felt like a man who sails into a safe harbour from the wild sea of conflicting opinions, and who, after much wandering and tossing, at last reaches firm land. *Erste Gründe der gesammten Weltweisheit*. Leipzig 1734 Vorrede.

7. Here sense and wit are overwhelmed, the mind loses itself completely in the number, splendour, order, course and brilliance of all the worlds. O! what is man here? He would be called nothing, if he could not recognise the Master's greatness in the creation. Ibid. Frontispiece.

8. Accordingly, the more perspicacious and the more thorough man is, the further is he removed from the animals: conversely, the more he is bound to his senses and his imagination, and is, therefore, subject to slavery, the nearer does he come to the animals and the beasts. *Vernünfftige Gedancken von Gott, Der Welt und der Seele des Menschen*. 4. Auflage, Frankfurt and Leipzig 1729 p. 554.

9. Reason and good sense are the sources of beautiful songs. *Versuch einer Critischen Dichtkunst*. 5. Auflage. Darmstadt 1962 p. 47.

10. Philosophy is a science of all possible things, how and why they are possible. *Vernünfftige Gedancken von den Kräften des menschlichen Verstandes*. 4. Auflage Halle 1725 p. 3.

11. Philosophy I call the science of the happiness of man; in so far as we can attain and practise it according to our imperfection. *Weltweisheit*. 2. Auflage Leipzig 1736 p. 4.

12. However, if an explanation is needed in order to make this point clearer: then let it be observed that one would be unable to distinguish truth from a dream if one did not accept as a criterion this principle of sufficient reason. In a dream almost everything happens without sufficient reason. In one moment one is here, in the next there; and one does not know why? How one arrived there or departed? In a state of wakefulness, however, or in truth everything has its causes. Whoever comes, knows why he is coming; and so on. This principle can, therefore, provide a sure criterion of truth. Ibid. p. 124.

13. Cloud-cuckoo land. *Herrn Gottfried Wilhelms, Freyherrn von Leibnitz, Theodicee*. 5. Auflage Hannover and Leipzig 1763 p. 572.

14. Enough of Ariosto's fantasies, which are certainly more like the dreams of a sick man, as Horace says, than the reasonable creation of a poet: because there is neither probability nor order in them. *Dichtkunst*. p. 211.

15. *Weltweisheit.* 6. Auflage Leipzig 1756 1. Theil p. 481.

16. . . . and would it not be the prime and sole duty of precisely every genius and every poet and in particular of the Dramatic poet, to place you into such a dream? And now consider what worlds you will confuse if you show the poet your pocket-watch or your guest-room and ask him to teach you to dream within their confines. *Sämtliche Werke.* Hsg. B. Suphan. Hildesheim 1967 Vol. 5 p. 228.

17. With these laudable Egyptians I can also compare my most worthy compatriots. I know that they love everything which is intelligible, orderly and reasonable. They regard nature as something comprehensible and desire also that writers should follow her. *Der Biedermann* p. 4.

18. *Nature, beautiful,* is not the truth which exists in reality but the truth which may exist, with all those perfections which harmonise together . . . However, beautiful nature contains within itself the qualities of the beautiful and the good. It delights the wit by showing it perfect objects; it pleases the heart by providing it with such as are useful to it. Leipzig 1760 col. 1153–4.

19. *Dichtkunst* p. 195.

20. The justice of the gods is inscrutable, and thus, one endeavours in vain to ponder over the mysteries of wonderful fate. München 1965 p. 230.

21. That miraculous is best and most rational which is based, even when imitating animals and inanimate things, solely on the wonders of nature, and always selects that which nature has made most excellently. *Dichtkunst* p. 195.

22. cit. Mirollo, J.V.: *The Poet of the Marvelous. Giambattista Marino.* New York and London 1963 p. 25. Mirollo gives the following translation: "The end of the poet is to arouse wonder (I speak of the excellent, not of the foolish): Let him who cannot arouse wonder go work in the stables."

23. They are a round coffin/in which love lies buried/
A skeleton-key/which opens even the recesses of the heart/ . . .
Two vessels/which are filled with Julep/
Decoy-birds/whose note binds a free heart.
Herrn von Hofmannswaldau und anderer Deutschen . . . Gedichte. Hsg. B. Neukirch Tübingen 1965 Anderer Theil p. 4.

24. Until Hofmannswaldau's mouth, which speaks nothing but wonders, enchants my senses. *Gesamtausgabe der deutschsprachigen Werke.* Hsg. M. Szyrocki and H. Powell. Tübingen 1964 vol. 3, pp. 141–2.

25. It is true, Germany has philosophised in the past twenty years more than ever before. Reason has been much purified amongst our compatriots; wild wit has been tamed, and excessive fantasy has been confined to its proper limits. In this way taste in the free arts has been improved considerably, and people have begun to despise things which they previously praised to the skies . . . . Now can philosophising Germany help it if it has no taste for Milton, either? Without doubt it sees in this Englishman Lohensteinian and Zieglerian bombast,

monstrous imagination, pretentious expressions and inaccurate judgment. *Beyträge zur Critischen Historie der Deutschen Sprache, Poesie und Beredsamkeit.* Leipzig 1732–44 24. Stück vol. 4 p. 661.

26. Above all things, however, it is necessary, indeed quite indispensable that a true poet should have a thorough knowledge of man. The main aim of the poet is to imitate the actions of men. *Dichtkunst* p. 107.

27. Any other man would be filled with a thousand fears here, so much does fate concur with our enemies. Young Scipio and Juba are defeated; only Caesar is triumphant on his victor's chariot. But for us, Prince, it is more a question of courage than of good fortune: perhaps our courage will yet check the hatred of fate. To be consoled and steadfast is what strengthens and teaches hearts. *Sterbender Cato.* Act 5 Scene 1. In: *Ausgewählte Werke* Hsg. J. Birke Berlin 1970 vol. 2 p. 38.

28. *Weltweisheit* 6. Auflage Leipzig 1756 2. Theil p. 26.

29. To write poetry is not simply to paint. *Dichtkunst* p. 12.

30. Favoured chamois-people! You know not what distress and fear the town, in spite of its beauty, harbours: no false money, which has neither value nor worth, is coigned to torment you. No greed plagues you; usury is banished. Ambition to be great at court does not worry you. You will not be yoked by the great, and neither do you belittle any great person. A mountain conceals you. Your whole world and its turmoil is rock, the Danube and the sky. *Neueste Gedichte auf verschiedene Vorfälle* Regensburg 1749 p. 42.

31. So it seems: yet it is but an illusion. How miserably lives a man whose physical appearance barely allows him to be regarded as a human being! How much does he not lack of those things which society can bestow on us without grief and torment! He gets to know neither himself nor other people. His god becomes every block before which he foolishly kneels: often he knows no name for the saint whom he so stupidly reveres. How can he wish to honour, as a Christian, the highest being if no one desires to make Him known to him? ibid.

32. It is better to live amongst men, however evil they may be, than to live far from all men! It is better to be thrown by the storm into the first harbour that appears, than to languish during a calm in the middle of the sea. *Gesammelte Werke.* Hsg. P. Rilla. Berlin 1954–8 vol. 9 p. 600.

33. The nature of man and of his intellectual powers is still exactly the same as it has been for the last two thousand years: and consequently, the way to give pleasure poetically must be still that which the Ancients were so felicitous in choosing. *Dichtkunst* p. XI.

34. Only that is rational in sciences and arts which is based on sound foundations. But the latter are not the opinions and testimonies of great people; not the examples of those who have a local fame as orators; not the new or the old, in so far as it is new or old: but the immutable nature of man, which is the concern of an orator . . . we only commend the Ancients as teachers and models because they have based their rules and examples on this precept. 4. Auflage Leipzig 1750 pp. 84–5.

35. Brief an Bodmer 11.5.1739 cit. Wolff, E.: *Gottscheds Stellung im deutschen Bildungsleben.* Kiel and Liepzig 1895 and 1897 p. 232.

36. World is, and also the spiritual poet: nature's effects are always rich in essence. She roars in the sea; she beams through lights, rhymes in the poet, of equal power. When Nothing and Something were wed: air, fire and dry wetness were produced; the original basis of the greatest possible gilding lay there already to be formed by the rhymester.

His exploratory weight the poet lowers into the bottomless sea of old Chaos. From the dawn of his posthumous fame he sees in the rhyme momentary honour. With changing seriousness his voice "swans"; his mind, like a gigantic cherubim, he bears himself at once in the debris of building material, travels riding still in sulphurous whirls. *Gedichte* 2. Theil p. 527.

37. For: to sing swan-songs. An emphatic expression like "under-yoke" for "to place under a yoke." ibid.

38. The Origin of Evil pleased me particularly. My only wish would have been that all the lines might have been in the same metre and of regular alternation. Leibniz designates certain kinds of fatalists defenders of a lazy philosophy. Here in Meissen we usually call Brockes' irregular lines lazy. E. Stäuble: *Albrecht von Haller Über den Ursprung des Übels.* Zürich 1953 p. 66.

39. *The Spectator.* London 1763 vol. 1 No. 60 p. 242.

40. Alas! I cry, goddess, aren't you mistaken? You will regret having chosen me! My all too ingenuous panegyric will profane this hero's fame and your inspiration. An artless poet, an enemy of bombast and obscurity, remains earthbound and cannot praise heroes. Go! fire bold singers who, on the course of wild spirits, rage like Delphi's priestess, in dark puzzles. *Gedichte* 2. Theil p. 86.

41. This appears to be the error which contributed most to Gottsched's downfall. He adhered to opinions which he had formed in his early years. In 1730, when the *Critische Dichtkunst* first appeared, these opinions may have given him a certain superiority; however, in order to retain this superiority he should have constantly added to them and should not have ignored even the fact that in those arts which adorn scholarship, there must be changing fashions. *Betrachtungen über Gottscheds Charakter.* In: *Neue Bibliothek der schönen Wisser-schaften und der freyen Künste.* Leipzig 1788 Bd. 6 St. 1 pp. 211–12.

SELECT BIBLIOGRAPHY

(a) Primary Sources
Until Joachim Birke began editing Gottsched's works in 1968, no standard edition was available. Apart from a few reprints most of Gottsched's works only exist as individual eighteenth-century editions. The Taylorian Institute, Oxford and the British Museum possess many such editions. Of the reprints the following are the most accessible: *Ausgewählte Werke.* Herausgegeben von Joachim Birke, (Berlin, 1968f).

At the time of writing four of the fourteen planned volumes have appeared.
Versuch einer Critischen Dichtkunst. Unveränderter photomechanischer.
Nachdruck der 4., vermehrten Auflage, Leipzig 1751 (Darmstadt, 1962).
Der Biedermann. Eine Auswahl (Leipzig, 1966) Insel-Bücherei Nr.
855.
Sterbender Cato. (Berlin and Stuttgart, 1882), Deutsche National-
Litteratur, Nr. 42; (Stuttgart, 1964), Reclams U-B 2097–97a.
Dicktkunst. Auswahl; Agis, König zu Sparta (Leipzig, 1935), Deutsche.
Literatur in Entwicklungsreihen. Reihe Aufklärung, Band 3.

(b) Secondary Sources

M. Bernays	*J. W. von Goethe. J. C. Gottsched.* Leipzig 1880.
S. Bing	*Die Nachahmungstheorie bei Gottsched und den Schweizern und ihre Beziehung zu der Dichtungstheorie der Zeit.* Inaugural-Dissertation, Köln. Würzburg 1934.
J. Birke	*Christian Wolffs Metaphysik und die zeitgenössische Literatur- und Musiktheorie: Gottsched, Scheibe, Mizler.* Berlin 1966.
F. Braitmaier	*Geschichte der Poetischen Theorie und Kritik von den Diskursen der Maler bis auf Lessing.* 2 Teile. Frauenfeld 1888 and 1889.
W. H. Bruford	*Theatre, Drama and Audience in Goethe's Germany.* London 1957.
F. Brüggemann	*Gottscheds Lebens- und Kunstreform in den zwanziger und dreissiger Jahren.* Entwicklungsreihe Aufklärung Bd. 3. Leipzig 1935.
K. O. Conrady	*Gottscheds Sterbender Cato.* In: von Wiese: *Das deutsche Drama.* Bd. 1. Düsseldorf 1958.
T. W. Danzel	*Gottsched und seine Zeit. Auszüge aus seinem Briefwechsel.* Leipzig 1855.
G. Schimansky	*Gottscheds deutsche Bildungsziele.* Königsberg and Berlin 1939.
G. Waniek.	*Gottsched und die deutsche Litteratur seiner Zeit.* Leipzig 1897.
E. M. Wilkinson	*Johann Elias Schlegel. A Pioneer in Aesthetics.* Oxford 1945.

Immanuel Kant

Immanuel Kant

by PAUL ROUBICZEK

Immanuel Kant was born on April 22, 1724 in Königsberg, the son of a saddler. One of his ancestors is said to have immigrated from Scotland, but this is not certain. His home was Lutheran and, through his mother, influenced by Pietism for which he always showed great respect, even after his school, where a similar attitude prevailed, had made him abhor all compulsion in religious matters. In 1740, when he was still very young, he entered the university of his home town, where he became established in 1755 as a "Privatdozent". The remuneration for this post was so small that, coming from a poor home, he had to continue earning his living—as he had done since 1746—mainly as a private tutor, an exhausting and sometimes humiliating activity about which he often bitterly complained. Despite many important publications and his unusual success as a widely known lecturer, it took fifteen years before his university in 1770 felt at long last obliged to appoint him as "ordentlicher Professor" to the chair of logic and metaphysics, obviously because other universities had offered him chairs. Only from then onwards, with his livelihood secure, was he able to concentrate on his first major work, the *Kritik der reinen Vernunft,* which, being a completely new departure in philosophical thought, took a long time to prepare and was only published in 1781. Afterwards his main works followed each other in quick succession: *Prolegomena* appeared in 1783, *Grundlegung zur Metaphysik der Sitten* in 1785, the thoroughly revised second edition of *Kritik der reinen Vernunft* in 1787, *Kritik der praktischen Vernunft* in 1788, *Kritik der Urteilskraft* in 1790.[1]

His life was uneventful; he never left Königsberg and its immediate surroundings; he did not marry (though he was very sociable and a circumspect and witty host). Nevertheless a crisis arose in 1794, when the reactionary successor of Frederick the Great, King Frederick William II, objected to his work *Die Religion innerhalb der Grenzen der bloßen Vernunft,* published in 1793, which was generally and mistakenly thought to be anti-Christian, and threatened him with "disagreeable measures". Kant did not recant but decided, after much heart-searching, that silence was justified to safeguard his teaching; he promised to refrain from further public discussion of "natural and revealed religion". In 1798, however, after the death of the king, he no longer felt obliged to remain silent, since he had given the promise to the king personally; he gave an account of the conflict in the introduction to *Der Streit der Fakultäten.* This was to be his last work; his powers now rapidly declined, and the following six years were a painful conclusion to an

73

admirable life. He had always been of frail health; finally his body and mind gave way, but he remained restless and conscious of his senility. Occasionally he was still able to write, and his last notes even seem to indicate a new development of his thought. He died on February 12, 1804, "vertrocknet wie eine Scherbe".[2]

"HABE Mut, dich deines eigenen Verstandes zu bedienen!"[3] This is the essence of Kant's *Beantwortung der Frage: Was ist Aufklärung?*, an essay in which he pays high tribute to this epoch. But in 1784 when this essay was written Kant, though still appreciating some general aspects of the "Aufklärung", had already rejected its philosophy so completely that Moses Mendelssohn, its great representative, called him "Alleszermalmer", the all-crushing. In fact, the date of the essay must not mislead us; Kant's activity is clearly divided into a pre-critical period lasting till 1769, which belongs to the "Aufklärung", and the subsequent critical period which transcends it.

This division means that, for a long time, Kant's thought remained in agreement with that of his age. Like most of the philosophers since the Age of Reason he was preoccupied with natural science; many of his early works were based on Newtonian physics; but he also went further and made an important original contribution to astronomy in *Allgemeine Naturgeschichte und Theorie des Himmels* (1755) which already showed the power of his mind; it was the first theory which tried to explain the origin of the stars in a purely scientific way. The French astronomer Laplace developed a similar theory some years later, without knowing of Kant, and the Kant-Laplace hypothesis, as it is usually called, provided the basis for further developments in the nineteenth century. Gradually, however, Kant's attention turned more and more to philosophy, but he still followed Leibniz and Christian Wolff; his deviations from their teachings are corrections of detail or enlargements, not a questioning of the foundations of this approach. Yet he also becomes increasingly aware of the shortcomings of this kind of rationalism.

One of the last works of his pre-critical period is a satire, *Träume eines Geistersehers, erläutert durch Träume der Metaphysik* (1766), particularly remarkable because of the rare occurrence that in it Kant's wit and sense of humour come to the fore. Chiefly it is an attack on the strange mysticism of Swedenborg but, as the title indicates, Kant is also beginning to doubt all metaphysical speculations, including his own. Soon afterwards, in the "great year" of 1769, he read David Hume and was, as he said, awakened by him from his "dogmatic slumber", and this initiated the

"Copernican revolution" in philosophy which is his lasting achievement.

Most philosophers throughout the ages have tried to create a metaphysical system—that is, to find an all-inclusive unitary explanation of the universe and man, based on a single fundamental concept. These attempts were particularly prominent during the "Aufklärung". Thus, on the one hand, Leibniz, Wolff and many others were idealists and made an abstract idea of God the basis of their systems; even the *Monadologie* which Leibniz later added was only a further elaboration of this idea. On the other hand, materialism, coming mainly from France, began to make itself felt. Kant now recognised that none of these systems could withstand philosophical scrutiny and that this also applied to all preceding ones, from Plato and Aristotle onwards; none could be accepted as a valid interpretation of the whole of existence. They only created confusion because they contradicted each other, with no criterion but individual inclination as a means of deciding between them. Parts of them remained valuable, but none survived intact. Kant therefore raised the question of whether it is at all possible to build a metaphysical system, and his answer was "Copernican" because it went far beyond similar attempts by some British philosophers—John Locke, Bishop Berkeley and even David Hume —who had embarked on this course before.

Kant's answer is based on two fundamental theses. The first is mainly elaborated in *Kritik der reinen Vernunft* (1781 and 1787) and in *Prolegomena zu einer jeden künftigen Metaphysik, die als Wissenschaft wird auftreten können* (1783); the second mainly in *Kritik der praktischen Vernunft* (1788) and in *Grundlegung zur Metaphysik der Sitten* (1785). The titles of the two subsidiary works are relevant because they can help to prevent a misunderstanding of the critiques : Kant is going to deny the possibility of any metaphysical system but not, as is often thought, the possibility of dealing with particular metaphysical problems; these he continues to investigate.

The first thesis concerns the theory of knowledge. According to Kant, we have no immediate, ultimate and therefore absolute knowledge of reality because our knowledge is dependent on the working of our mind, which is a kind of mechanism and imposes its own requirements upon our thinking. Since, to put it paradoxically, we cannot think without thinking, we have only a relative knowledge of reality; we know it as it appears to us and not as it is in itself. We are unable to create an all-inclusive metaphysical system, because we cannot possibly penetrate to the ultimate nature of the universe; we do not know what the universe would be like if it were grasped directly without the intervention of our thought; nor is there an external viewpoint from which we could compare the world with our thinking, and examine how they correspond. At the same time, Kant is the supreme realist; he never denies the existence of reality; for him, it does not exist in our minds alone, but also outside; our organs have to be stirred by it for us to have any experience and in order to become conscious of any appearances. Our knowledge is always determined by these two factors : by the laws of thinking contributed by our minds and by the impression which reality makes upon us. "Zum Erkenntnisse gehören nämlich zwei Stücke : erstlich der Begriff, dadurch überhaupt ein Gegenstand gedacht wird (die **Kategorie**), und zweitens die Anschauung, dadurch er gegeben wird . . . Ohne Sinnlichkeit würde uns kein Gegenstand gegeben, und ohne Verstand keiner gedacht werden. Gedanken ohne Inhalt sind leer, Anschauungen ohne Begriffe sind blind."[4]

The significance of this new start can be appreciated when we remember those theories concerning knowledge which paved the way for Kant and which he nevertheless rejected. Locke drew attention to the working of our minds, but assumed that the mind is simply a "white paper void of all characters, without any ideas" upon which reality imprints itself directly and reliably.[5] This obviously disregards the activity of thinking, and Locke involved himself in contradictions when he tried to explain thinking on this basis. Berkeley became aware of the fact that our perception must be taken into account when we want to judge our knowledge, but he overemphasised perception and went so far as to deny the independent existence of reality; for him, things only exist when they are perceived; their *esse* is *percipi*—a view which he could only hold because, as a kind of afterthought, he introduced the concept of God to restore the existence of things. Kant was evidently right in abandoning this complete idealism and in accepting what cannot be denied, namely both perception and reality. Hume saw the failure of all metaphysical systems, but went beyond their dismissal and developed a total scepticism which made him doubt everything which reason or our senses tell us. But can we ever really believe that we are unable to rely on anything and that none of our knowledge is truly valid? Kant is on safer ground when he restricts total doubt to metaphysical speculations and shows that our knowledge, though relative, can be relied upon within its legitimate sphere, in everyday experience as well as in science, and that well-founded knowledge is valid. By showing its conditions, limitations and scope, he alone does justice to our actual experience.

Kant's thesis is founded upon several basic concepts and claims which are essential for his argument. A discussion of a few of these may, by adding relevant details, help us to understand his teaching more fully.

One of these concepts has been referred to already—the concept "category"; it defines the nature of several related concepts as "reine Verstandesbegriffe . . . die Urteile als objektiv gültig bestimmen."[6] The most important maong these are *cause and effect,* leading to *causality* and *necessity; the one and the many;* and *substantia et accidens.* The way in which they are to be defined is perhaps best understood when we remember Hume's way of dealing with causality.

Kant comes to be concerned with the categories because he asks how it is that we can ever say "must" in the sphere of knowledge. We have to rely on experience, but our experience is limited; the claim that something must be as it is or happen as it does assumes a complete knowledge, and this knowledge we obviously do not possess. So far he agrees with Hume, but his conclusions are different. Hume rejects necessity altogether; he says that all statements containing "must" (such as that a cause must necessarily produce a predictable effect) are merely based on custom and habit and that the acceptance of strict causality is merely due to laziness of mind. He believes that all knowledge springs from our perception of reality, and his argument runs : perception, being limited, does not disclose necessity; causality is derived from perception; therefore causality cannot have necessity. Kant, however, accepts necessity. He agrees that perception has no necessity, but insists that causality has; he therefore draws the conclusion that causality is not based on perception. "Wenn aber gleich alle unsere Erkenntniss mit der Erfahrung anhebt, so entspringt sie darum doch nicht eben alle *aus* der Erfahrung."[7] Since Kant sees that knowledge has two sources—perception and the laws of thinking —he can base necessity (and all the other categories) on the latter, which is the contribution of our mind. We can say "must" because the laws of thinking apply, but only so far as they apply.

This shows Kant once more as the supreme realist. We obviously could not live our lives if, say, we had to admit that our table could suddenly jump into the air without any explicable cause. We have to rely on necessity, and both practical experience and science show that there are vast realms where this trust is justified. At the same time, the categories exemplify another of Kant's basic concepts, for they are, according to him, given *a priori,* before any experience; they precede it, and only because they do can we have experience which makes sense. Without them, our perception would remain blind. This is obvious in the processes which produce knowledge : perception makes us merely aware, for instance, of a sequence of events, not of their interconnection. But we look for causes—which are often hidden—because we are bound to presuppose their existence; and it is the discovery of them which enables us to grasp events.

This *a priori* knowledge also has another implication which is particularly important for Kant's rejection of metaphysics. This can be illustrated by his definitive refutation of the old proofs of the existence of God, which had still helped to make the abstract concept of God the basis of metaphysical systems in the "Aufklärung". In these proofs, thinking and logic are made the test of existence; because our thought forces us, say, to introduce causality and to assume that there was a beginning of the world in time, there must be a first cause which produced the world, and this cause must logically be God, for the first cause is independent of any further causation, while all others are effects of preceding causes. Kant shows that it is impossible to prove the existence of anything in this way, because all concepts given *a priori,* including the categories, have no meaning in themselves; they only acquire meaning by being applied. We have to know concrete examples in order to understand what a cause, a substance, or the one (and thus the first) and the many mean. Therefore existence, though grasped with the help of such concepts, is known only if experience supports them; purely logical proofs are invalid because the categories by themselves remain empty.

The *a priori* concepts, however, also include space and time, not as categories, but as "Anschauungsformen", as forms which make perception possible. This claim may be more difficult to accept : how could anything be known with greater certainty than our bodily existence and the ageing which leads to death? Of course, Kant does not say that space and time are mere illusions; they enable us to grasp reality and thus become part of our experience of reality. But it is still difficult to accept that they are contributions of our mind.

Kant takes great pains to make his claim convincing and tries to prove it in several ways. There is, he says, no experience of external reality without space and time; this reality must be perceived with their help; therefore, as we can say "must", they are contributed by the mind and precede all experience. This is supported by another argument. Of objects we can think that they exist or do not exist, but we can never think that there is no space and no time, and while we grasp external reality only so far as we grasp objects or events—that is, only so far as something exists or happens—we can think of space without objects and of time without events. Thus, while all other concepts denote certain things or events (even categories have to be applied to these), space and time include all objects and events. Moreover, space and time imply the concepts of infinity and eternity; but infinity and eternity are not given in experience.

Yet all these proofs, though convincing in themselves, have failed to make the impact one might have expected. But we can see, nevertheless, why this claim, too, ought to be accepted. The influence of natural science, as regards space, has meant for those who submit to it uncritically a reduction of awareness, because infinity, since it is not given in external reality and must therefore transcend it to become meaningful, is reduced to mere endlessness or vastness of space. But once we are unable to look beyond space, our whole lives are impoverished; we are robbed of a further, of the transcendental dimension. The same applies to the concept of time when it is seen as ultimately real. If there is nothing but the passage of time which can be measured, if we are unable to look beyond it, our lives are again robbed of the transcendental dimension. Eternity is replaced by the endlessness of the passage of time which is bound to remain meaningless. Thus, however, not only the religious idea of eternity loses all significance, but also the timeless experience of the "erfüllte Augenblick", the moment of complete fulfilment, realised so vividly by Goethe and other poets. It is no accident that those Existentialists who take time to be absolute face a complete void—"das Nichts", nothingness—in life and in death.

Kant's second thesis shows what this loss actually means, because it only becomes possible if the existence of a transcendental reality is admitted. This thesis is concerned with the foundation of moral knowledge and states that, although all external knowledge must remain relative, we have nevertheless a different kind of knowledge which is absolute—that which discloses good and evil and prescribes laws for our actions, regardless of whether or not our conscious knowledge agrees with these laws, or whether we accept or reject them. Kant is again not concerned with psychology, with individual processes of thought, but with the scope of knowledge. The relation of this knowledge to our thinking is different from that in external reality because we are ourselves embodiments of the absolute; if the absolute exists, we must partake in it. This does not mean that we are enabled to know ourselves wholly in a direct way; even to grasp what characterises us as individuals we still have to employ pure reason which makes direct knowledge impossible. But we also possess

practical reason (practical, because it refers to action) based on
conscience—that is, we hear within us the "still small voice" of the
absolute and can thus know what it demands. Though deprived
of absolute external knowledge, even with regard to our own
existence, we do know absolutely that we ought to do what is good.

To have established this distinction between two different kinds
of reason and ways of thinking is one of Kant's main merits. It
is most beautifully expressed in the famous conclusion of the *Kritik
der praktischen Vernunft* which also shows that he, once again,
bases his philosophy on our actual experience.

"Zwei Dinge erfüllen das Gemüth mit immer neuer und zuneh-
mender Bewunderung und Ehrfurcht, je öfter und anhaltender
sich das Nachdenken damit beschäftigt : Der bestirnte Himmel
über mir, und das moralische Gesetz in mir. Beide darf ich nicht
als in Dunkelheiten verhüllt, oder im Überschwenglichen, außer
meinem Gesichtskreise, suchen und bloß vermuten; ich sehe sie
vor mir und verknüpfe sie unmittelbar mit dem Bewußtsein
meiner Existenz. Das erste fängt von dem Platze an, den ich in
der äußern Sinnenwelt einnehme, und erweitert die Verknüpfung,
darin ich stehe, ins unabsehlich Große mit Welten über Welten
und Systemen von Systemen, überdem noch in grenzenlose
Zeiten ihrer periodischen Bewegung, deren Anfang und Fort-
dauer. Das zweite fängt von meinem unsichtbaren Selbst, meiner
Persönlichkeit, an, und stellt mich in einer Welt dar, die wahre
Unendlichkeit hat, aber nur dem Verstande spürbar ist, und mit
welcher (. . .) ich mich, nicht wie dort, in bloß zufälliger, sondern
allgemeiner und nothwendiger Verknüpfung erkenne. Der erstere
Anblick einer zahllosen Weltenmenge vernichtet gleichsam meine
Wichtigkeit, als eines thierischen Geschöpfs, das die Materie,
daraus es ward, dem Planeten (einem bloßen Punct im Weltall)
wieder zurückgeben muß, nachdem es eine kurze Zeit (man
weiß nicht wie) mit Lebenskraft versehen gewesen. Der zweite
erhebt dagegen meinen Werth, als einer Intelligenz, unendlich
durch meine Persönlichkeit, in welcher das moralische Gesetz mir
ein von der Thierheit und selbst von der ganzen Sinnenwelt
unabhängiges Leben offenbart."[8]

A word about Kant's style may be appropriate here. It is often
said that it is so involved and intricate as to make understanding of
him difficult, and to a certain extent this is true. We have to
remember that it was only late in the "Aufklärung", shortly before
Kant, that Wolff first used the German language in philosophical
works; Leibniz still used Latin and French. It is not surprising,
therefore, to find Kant strongly influenced by Latin constructions,

and these are not easily reproduced in German. But this should not deter anybody from reading Kant; his sentences, when disentangled, are always clear, and the reader is frequently rewarded by passages of great beauty, such as that just quoted, which he will never forget.

When Kant turns to the moral law itself, he recognises as its main characteristic that it establishes an unconditional obligation; he therefore tries to discover the law of thinking which enables us to say "must" in this context, the law which makes the moral "ought" absolute. This obligation, moreover, is always experienced as a particular demand, and so we need a criterion by which to judge whether the demand is really moral. Kant meets this need by formulating what he calls "der kategorische Imperativ". It has to be categorical because it is unconditional, not dependent on any further purpose, for the good must be done for its own sake. If we subordinated the good to another purpose, if we said, for instance, that we ought to do the good to achieve happiness, we would no longer be concerned with goodness, but with happiness, and this might necessitate using means which are not good. And it is an imperative because it does not refer to something which exists, but to future actions which are required.

The first version of the categorical imperative runs : "Handle nur nach derjenigen Maxime, von der du zugleich wollen kannst, daß sie ein allgemeines Gesetz werde."(9)

This version expresses clearly and precisely one of the fundamental experiences which we have when we become subject to an absolute moral demand; the commandment to love our neighbour, for instance, is meant to be a general law. It is also justifiable to make the imperative define a maxim, for moral actions are guided by principles and not only by impulses. A maxim, according to Kant, "ist das subjektive Prinzip des Wollens"(10)—that is, the principle which we accept—and the necessary task of the imperative is to ensure that we accept, not some arbitrarily chosen and possibly wrong principle, but the right one. Nevertheless this first version of the categorical imperative remains open to objections because it is purely formal and does not say anything about the nature of the actions we ought to choose. We can, after acting, judge by it what we have done, but ethics should teach us how to act and how to live, not merely how to judge ourselves. Kant obviously feels this himself and therefore attempts to support this version by another which introduces the concept of duty. This seems to make the demand more substantial, but in fact only throws into relief the merits and demerits of the first version.

Kant defines duty as "die Nothwendigkeit einer Handlung aus

6—GMOL-6 * *

Achtung vor dem Gesetz."[11] This shows why the concept is important; it ensures that one of the main requirements of any moral action is realised : "Bei dem, was moralisch gut sein soll, ist es nicht genug, daß es dem sittlichen Gesetz gemäß sei, sondern es muß auch um desselben willen geschehen."[12] Thus the emphasis is put on the motive—one of the main characteristics of Kant's ethics and, again, a realistic one. Evidently, an action is only good, in the moral sense of the word, if it is done for the right reason; if we try, say, to help a person in order to gain a material reward, our action may still appear to conform to the good, and it may be useful, but it is not really moral. Without the right motive "ist jene Gemäßheit nur sehr zufällig und mißlich, weil der unsittliche Grund zwar dann und wann gesetzmäßige, mehrmals aber gesetz-widrige Handlungen hervorbringen wird."[13]

But the concept of duty is also very general and much in need of further clarification. If the law to be obeyed is not sufficiently specified, duty may demand obedience to any law; moral quality then resides simply in being obedient. Such a misinterpretation has actually happened; Kant's concept has been interpreted as military duty. To accuse him of having this interpretation in mind is wrong; he was one of the first to give the desire for universal peace a concrete shape by developing, in his book *Vom ewigen Frieden*, the idea of a League of Nations. He never leaves any doubt that "law" in this context means the moral law. Yet, in the course of events, the lack of further definition was of consequence; "Kantian duty" has been used to add lustre to the Prussian army. The concept is important because, correctly understood, it points in the right direction, but it becomes extremely dangerous when it is misunder-stood, and, again, Kant's conception is too formal to prevent mis-understanding.

Yet his final version of the categorical imperative succeeds in defining the moral law fully. This time he says : "Handle so, daß du die Menschheit sowohl in deiner Person, als in der Person eines jeden anderen, jederzeit zugleich als Zweck, niemals bloß als Mittel brauchest."[14] This is the essence of all morality—that man is an end in himself, that the individual is of absolute value. This version is also particularly valuable because of two other points which it includes. On the one hand, Kant remains realistic; he says "never as a means only" because, in any society, man has up to a point to be used as a means—as a producer of goods or as a worker who keeps society functioning. But for this very reason it is important to be told that such needs should never override the main consideration—respect for man's humanity. On the other hand, Kant emphasises that this respect means that we must also respect the humanity within ourselves, and it is this emphasis which makes the apparently abstract concept "humanity" come to life and ensures that it can be experienced.

At the same time, however, part of his general argument remains open to doubt. Emerging from the "Aufklärung" and witnessing a faulty reaction against it, namely the rise of sentimentality, Kant distrusts feelings; although an admirer of Rousseau, he finds it necessary to combat both "Empfindsamkeit" and the rule of passion advocated by the "Sturm und Drang" movement. In this respect he is obviously right, but he fears that all feelings—with the sole exception of respect—are unreliable and misleading; he therefore wants them excluded altogether. This becomes evident in his radical rejection of inclinations. Again, his view is partly justified : inclinations tend to fluctuate and cannot simply be relied upon. Yet he wants to exclude them not only when they contradict the moral law, but also when the two coincide.

"Überdem gibt es manche so theilnehmend gestimmte Seelen, daß sie auch ohne einen anderen Bewegungsgrund der Eitelkeit oder des Eigennutzes ein inneres Vergnügen daran finden, Freude um sich zu verbreiten, und die sich an der Zufriedenheit anderer, sofern sie ihr Werk ist, ergötzen können. Aber ich behaupte, daß in solchem Falle dergleichen Handlung, so pflichtmäßig, so liebenswürdig sie auch ist, dennoch keinen wahren sittlichen Wert habe, . . . denn der Maxime fehlt der sittliche Gehalt, nämlich solche Handlungen nicht aus Neigung, sondern aus Pflicht zu tun."[15]

It is true that inclinations, being changeable, are often insufficient to ensure that we behave morally; but should they always be excluded? Duty has indeed frequently to struggle against inclination, but it seems more fully, more safely obeyed when it is supported by inclination. Perhaps we should even rejoice when duty and inclination happen to agree. (This is Schiller's argument; Kant's influence on him will be discussed later.)

This distrust of feeling explains why, instead of continuing the elaboration of ethics, Kant turns in a different direction and asks what metaphysical conclusions can be based on the moral law. His answers may seem to contradict his previous endeavours, but he succeeds in reconciling them with his rejection of metaphysical systems, because they are stated, not as concepts *a priori,* but as "Postulate". A postulate does not precede knowledge, but is added *a posteriori,* after knowledge has been achieved. It is a logical conclusion suggested by the moral law and known only through its moral consequences; it can be assumed to exist because it makes morality logically consistent, but cannot itself be known directly.

Kant establishes three such postulates : of man's immortality, of the freedom of the will, and of the existence of God. Of these, however, only that concerning freedom is an important further contribution to his theory of knowledge; the others point in the wrong direction.

There is obviously a contradiction between the working of pure and of practical reason. Pure reason is concerned with those laws of thinking which lead to necessity, and though it leaves gaps in the knowledge of necessity, these appear merely as accidents, as contingency, and cannot form the basis of the freedom of the will —that is, of man's freedom to choose, to decide and to act. Yet morality must imply man's ability to perform moral actions in external reality; moral laws and categorical imperatives would be meaningless if man were unable to obey them and to translate them into action. Nor, if he were not free, could he be held responsible for what he does. Therefore morality only makes sense if, despite the claims of pure reason, the existence of freedom is postulated. We have to accept the contradiction that necessity helps us to understand external reality, but that, nevertheless, we shall never understand morality unless we base it on freedom.

But Kant does not rest content with accepting this contradiction; he goes further. He tries to reconcile freedom with pure reason by showing that freedom belongs to another world which is accessible only to the intellect ("intelligible Freiheit") and, in order to support this rather weak point in his philosophy, he introduces the postulates of immortality and of the existence of God. These, however, really detract from his achievement. When he had set out to attack metaphysical systems, he had said : "Ich mußte das Wissen aufheben, um zum Glauben Platz zu bekommen";[16] he had wanted to show that only faith can answer such ultimate questions as that about God. Yet now he comes near to replacing faith by logically developed abstract concepts. He returns more and more to the ideas of his youth—a phenomenon not rare in old age—and almost re-establishes those aspects of the "Aufklärung" which he had outgrown or even destroyed. This becomes particularly obvious in his late work *Die Religion innerhalb der Grenzen der bloßen Vernunft* (1793) which is hardly more than a continuation of the "Aufklärung".

But before the decline of his powers—"um, wo möglich, meinem zunehmenden Alter die dazu noch einigermaßen günstige Zeit noch abzugewinnen"[17]—Kant had written his third critique, *Kritik der Urteilskraft* (1790), and this work represents a considerable further development of his philosophy.

Kant distinguishes between two kinds of judgment. The one we make when we subsume a particular phenomenon under a general law; he calls it "bestimmend" because it defines a particular phenomenon by what determines it, for instance the falling of a stone by causality, or an action as moral by the categorical imperative. With this kind of judgment he deals in the first two critiques. But there is also another which is creative because we start from a particular phenomenon and find a general quality which is a new discovery, for instance when we realise that a tree is beautiful. It is this second kind which Kant now explores.

As always, he tries to ascertain whether there is a concept *a priori* at work, and he discovers it here in the concept "Zweck" or "Zweckmäßigkeit". This concept of purpose or purposefulness is not a category because we are free to apply it or not; vast realms of experience are known without it. He calls it "ein regulatives Prinzip"; as such it is as relevant as the categories, however, for we can hardly avoid using it. Yet since we are not obliged to apply it, it gives a further example of freedom at work—another important addition to Kant's theory. He investigates the application of this concept mainly with regard to the teleological principle in biology and to aesthetics. Of particular importance is his discussion of beauty; three of the points he makes are essential.

He claims that beauty, since it is based on a concept *a priori*, must be an absolute experience of general validity. This is often doubted today, but again he is probably the true realist, for what could be more direct and beyond doubt than the impact due to the beauty of, say, a sunset or a Brandenburg concerto? According to Kant, we must not be misled by "das Angenehme", by what is merely agreeable or pretty; this is a purely subjective experience while beauty, though also partly subjective, is generally valid. Somebody speaking of beauty "urtheilt nicht bloß für sich, sondern für Jedermann."[18] But here a difficulty arises. Kant also recognises that beauty is something "was ohne Begriffe allgemein gefällt",[19] beauty obviously becomes real by whatever is beautiful and not by the application of a concept. Does it thereby become so vague as to lose its meaning? Yet here the underlying concept *a priori* comes to the rescue, in a paradoxical way : beauty is also "die bloße Form der Zweckmäßigkeit ohne allen Zweck."[20]

It would obviously be wrong to define beauty in terms of a purpose; it is an intrinsic value, an end in itself. But any work of art expresses a content, and it does so by a form or structure; it attempts to create a form which expresses the content as completely as possible, and the great work of art is one which achieves a perfect identity between the two. Without being subordinated to anything outside itself, it becomes perfect through its purposefulness. To support his explanation, Kant uses here a criterion which he never admitted before—the satisfaction of feeling; the whole critique is explicitly concerned with it. An astonishing enlargement of his philosophy! As he intended, this third critique fills many gaps previously left open; it does not deserve to be as much neglected as it usually is.

This new regard for feeling leads Kant to make another distinction which includes art as well as nature—that between "das Schöne" and "das Erhabene". In this context the beautiful is compatible with the vision of classicism and its emphasis on harmony, though Kant also emphasises the essential role of genius, this time coming near to the "Sturm und Drang" movement. Yet an overwhelming impression can also be produced by what is sublime—that is, by something not beautiful in the classic sense—but, on the contrary, "furchtbar", terrifying, destructive, "zweckwidrig". It is in such an experience that we most directly touch upon the transcendental: "Erhaben ist, was auch nur denken zu können, jeden Maßstab der Sinne übertrifft."[21] We are once more reminded of Schiller.

Kant's influence on German literature has undoubtedly been great; Schiller is only one instance of it. The most commonly held view is that it was disastrous—a strange misjudgment if ever there was one. Schiller's development alone would suffice to disprove it. One could say that Schiller was too much preoccupied with ideas, but this can equally well be said of the plays which he wrote before he embarked on the study of Kant. He pursued it during the ten years of study which followed *Don Carlos*, and it was to a large extent Kant's philosophy which enabled him to write the later plays which establish his greatness. He fully accepted Kant's theory of knowledge, wrestled with the conflict between duty and inclination, and was inspired by the idea of "das Erhabene", even if he interpreted it somewhat differently. Kant's influence led to the unfolding of Schiller's genius.

Goethe is rarely mentioned in this context, apart from his early rejection of Kant. Yet the basic attitudes of Kant and of the later Goethe are essentially the same, and, after Schiller had persuaded him that Kant was worthy of consideration, Goethe realised this more and more. "Kant hat unstreitig am meisten genützt, indem er die Grenzen zog, wieweit der menschliche Geist zu dringen fähig sei, und daß er die unauflöslichen Probleme liegen ließ."[22] This shows his agreement with the first critique, and he obviously also agrees with the other two when he says: "Man mußte es zuletzt am geratensten finden, aus dem gesamten Komplex der gesunden menschlichen Natur das Sittliche sowie das Schöne zu entwickeln."[23]

It is true that Kleist, by reading Kant, was thrown into a crisis which could well have been fatal, because his original trust in the power of reason was destroyed by Kant's claim that we do not possess absolute metaphysical knowledge. Yet it is difficult to imagine that Kleist would ever have become the great poet he was had he stuck to his naive rationalism, so reminiscent of the "Aufklärung". The crisis was also his awakening. In fact, although he tried hard to shake off the influence of Kant, his *Prinz Friedrich von Homburg* achieves, in a different manner, exactly what Kant had desired : formal military duty and rebellion against it are transformed and surpassed in such a way that, in the end, a free and truly sublime moral decision opens upon the transcendental. "Nun, o Unsterblichkeit, bist du ganz mein!"[24]

The German Romantics misunderstood Kant; since, for him, thinking forms a constitutive part of our knowledge of reality, many of them jumped to the conclusion that the mind actually creates reality. Thinking seemed to be freed from all fetters; it could be used to achieve whatever was desirable; they saw man as independent creator and supreme lawgiver and therefore believed themselves able to create the ideal world of their dreams. Nevertheless this misunderstanding did prove an enormous liberation for them; it produced the extraordinary enthusiasm which characterised the beginning of the Romantic movement and helped, above all else, to bring it into being.

Thus Kant's work really marks the end of the "Aufklärung"; despite the eventual weakening of his powers he had laid the foundations for very different new developments. Long before his death, the new age which bears his mark had begun.

NOTES

1. The English titles of the works referred to in this essay are, in the order in which they are mentioned:
Critique of Pure Reason.
Prolegomena to any future metaphysics which is to be a science.
Foundations of the Metaphysics of Morals.
Critique of Practical Reason.
Critique of Judgement (literally: *of the Power of Judgement*).
Religion within the Limits of Reason alone.
The Quarrel between the Faculties.
Answering the Question: What is Enlightenment?
General Theory and Natural History of the Heavens.
Dreams of a Spirit-Seer, illustrated by Dreams of Metaphysics.
Perpetual Peace.

2. Dried out like a potsherd. (See the moving contemporary biographies by his friends L. E. Borowski, R. B. Jachmann and E. A. C. Wasianski, Königsberg 1804, reprinted in Deutsche Bibliothek, Berlin, 1912).

3. Have the courage to make use of your own intelligence! (*Theorie-Werkausgabe* (TW), xi, 53).

4. Knowledge consists of two parts: first the concept through which an object is thought of at all (the category), and secondly the perception by which it is given. Without the power of sense no object would be given to us, without intellect no object would be thought. Thoughts without content are empty, perceptions without concepts are blind (TW iii, 145, 98).

5. *An Essay concerning Human Understanding*, Bk. ii, Ch. I, par. 2.

6. Purely intellectual concepts which define judgments as objectively valid (TW v, 193).

7. Although all our knowledge begins with experience, it does not therefore all spring from experience (TW iii, 45).

8. Two things fill the mind with ever new and increasing admiration and awe, the oftener and the more steadily we reflect on them: the starry heavens above and the moral law within. I have not to search for them and conjecture them as though they were veiled in darkness or were in the transcendent region beyond my horizon; I see them before me and connect them directly with the consciousness of my existence. The former begins from the place I occupy in the external world of sense, and enlarges my connexion therein to an unbounded extent with worlds upon worlds and systems of systems, and moreover into limitless times of their periodic motion, its beginning and continuance. The second begins from my invisible self, my personality, and exhibits me in a world which has true infinity, but which is traceable only by the understanding, and with which I discern that I am not in a merely contingent but in a universal and necessary connexion. The former view of a countless multitude of worlds annihilates as it were my importance as an animal creature, which after it has been for a short time provided with vital power (one knows not how) must again give back the matter of which it was formed to the planet it inhabits (a mere speck in the universe). The second on the contrary infinitely elevates my worth as an intelligence by my personality, in which the moral law reveals to me a life independent of animality and even of the whole sensible world (TW vii, 300).

9. Act only according to such a maxim that you can also will that it should become a general law (TW vii, 51).

10. Is the subjective principle of volition (TW vii, 51).

11. The necessity of acting from respect for the law (TW vii, 26).

12. In order that an action should be morally good, it is not enough that it conform to the moral law, but it must also be done for the sake of the law (TW vii, 14).

13. That conformity is only very contingent and uncertain; since a principle which is not moral, although it may now and then produce

actions conformable to the law, will also often produce actions which contradict it (TW vii, 14).

14. Act so, that you treat humanity, in your own person as well as in the person of any other, always at the same time as an end, never as means only (TW vii, 61).

15. There are many minds so sympathetically constituted that, without any other motive of vanity or self-interest, they find a pleasure in spreading joy around them, and can take delight in the satisfaction of others so far as it is their own work. But I maintain that in such a case an action of this kind, however proper, however amiable it may be, has nevertheless no true moral worth . . . for the maxim lacks the moral import, namely, that such actions be done from duty, not from inclination (TW vii, 24).

16. I have found it necessary to deny knowledge, in order to make room for faith (TW iii, 33).

17. In order to win, if possible, from my advancing age the time which is still, to some degree, favourable for me (TW ix, 241).

18. Does not judge only for himself, but for everybody (TW x, 290).

19. What universally pleases without concepts (TW x, 288).

20. The pure form of purposefulness without any purpose (TW x, 300).

21. The sublime is that which, even to be only thought of, transcends the measure of all the senses (TW x, 336).

22. Kant has undoubtedly been most useful in drawing the boundaries of how far the human mind can penetrate, and leaving the insoluble problems alone (to Eckermann, May 2, 1824).

23. So it was found in the end most advisable to develop, out of the whole complex of healthy human nature, the moral as well as the beautiful (to Carlyle, March 14, 1828).

24. Now, o immortality, you are entirely mine.

SELECT BIBLIOGRAPHY

Works:

The most recent and easily available edition of Kant's works is *Theorie-Werkausgabe,* herausgegeben von Wilhelm Weischedl, Suhrkamp-Verlag, Frankfurt am Main, 1968, 12 volumes, quoted as *TW*. Text and pagination are identical with the six-volume *Werke,* Insel Verlag, 1960.

Secondary Literature

N. Clark	*An Introduction to Kant's Philosophy.* London 1925.
F. Delekat	*Immanuel Kant, historisch-kritische Interpretation der Hauptschriften.* Heidelberg 1969.
A. C. Ewing	*A Short Commentary on Kant's Critique of Pure Reason.* London 1950.
F. Grayeff	*Kant's Theoretical Philosophy.* Manchester 1970.

R. Kayser	*Kant, eine Biographie.* Wien 1935.
J. Kemp	*The Philosophy of Kant.* Oxford 1968.
W. Klinke	*Kant for Everyman.* London 1951.
S. Körner	*Kant.* Pelican Books 1955.
A. D. Lindsay	*Kant.* London 1934.
T. Litt	*Kant und Herder als Deuter der geistigen Welt.* Heidelberg 1949.
H. J. Paton	*The Categorical Imperative, a study in Kant's moral philosophy.* London 1946.
P. Roubiczek	*The Misinterpretation of Man.* London 1947.
J. Watson	*The Philosophy of Kant Explained.* Glasgow 1908.
T. D. Weldon	*Kant's Critique of Pure Reason.* Oxford 1958.

Christoph Martin Wieland

Christoph Martin Wieland

by W. E. YUILL

Wieland was born on September 5, 1733 in Oberholzheim and brought up in the small imperial city of Biberach nearby, where his father had been appointed "Oberpfarrer". He soon exhausted the educational resources of Biberach and was sent to school at Klosterberge, near Magdeburg, and subsequently to the University of Tübingen (1750–2). His work attracted the attention of Johann Jakob Bodmer, the Swiss critic, who invited Wieland to his house in Zürich. He remained in the city, earning his living as a private tutor until 1759, when he moved to Berne. In 1760 he returned to Biberach as "Kanzleidirector" and in 1765 married Anna Dorothea von Hillenbrand of Augsburg, "ein unschuldiges, von der Welt unangestecktes, sanftes, fröhliches, gefälliges Geschöpf", who bore him fourteen children, of whom three sons and six daughters survived infancy. In 1769 Wieland was appointed Professor of Philosophy at Erfurt. In 1772 he took up a post as tutor to Karl August and Konstantin, the children of the dowager Duchess Anna Amalia of Weimar. He retired from this appointment on a generous pension in 1775 and devoted himself henceforth entirely to literary work. In 1797 he purchased a small estate at Oßmannstädt, near Weimar. His wife died in 1801, and in 1803 Wieland sold his property at Oßmannstädt and returned to Weimar. He lived a retired life there, but was presented to Napoleon when the Emperor was in Weimar on October 6, 1808. Wieland died on January 20, 1813 and was buried with his wife in Oßmannstädt.

O F the major German writers none more literally deserves the appellation "man of letters" than Wieland : not many were as precociously prolific—and few had an intellectual adolescence so protracted. When he was no more than nineteen he had already impressed a leading critic of the day—but it was another seven years or so before he came of age and found his authentic poetic voice. Wieland himself became aware of this development, and his own testimony has lent authority to the notion of a sudden conversion from "seraphic Christianity" to sensuality and scepticism. The change was, however, neither as radical nor as dramatic as it might seem from the evidence of his published works. The "great revolution" of which Wieland speaks was a process, initiated by certain personal experiences, which brought to the surface and into focus a variety of ideas already latent in his mind. The result was an emotional adjustment leading ultimately to a more balanced view of life.

Seen in retrospect the intellectual universe of Wieland's youth seems relatively simple and stable, dominated by orderly systems of faith or reason; human personality and behaviour could still be judged by unambiguous moral criteria; poetry, finding timeless models in the ancient classics, was still the hand-maiden of ethics and the Christian religion. Nevertheless, there was sufficient variety of opinion to stimulate a mind as agile and move a heart as tender as Wieland's. His intellectual grasp seems to have been more highly developed than his critical faculty : he assimilated without apparent distress the conflicting ideas of pietism, rationalism and sensualism, which represented the main intellectual cross-currents of his youth. The pietistic teachings of his home were reinforced by his schooling in Klosterberge, but it was in Klosterberge also that he came to love the pagan literatures of Greece and Rome and conceived in particular a life-long admiration for the practical wisdom of Xenophon's *Cyropaedia* and *Memorabilia*. He was even introduced by one of his teachers to that bible of the rationalists, Pierre Bayle's *Dictionnaire historique et critique*. A brief residence with his sceptically inclined relative in Erfurt, Professor Baumer, added to these models and influences a study of the rationalistic philosophy of Christian Wolff and an acquaintance with Cervantes' *Don Quixote*. The list of other writers and thinkers of whom Wieland claimed some knowledge at this time is long and varied : it includes Leibniz and Spinoza, Plato, Addison and Steele, Gottsched, Richardson and Brockes. Little wonder that, when he came as a seventeen-year-old student to the University of Tübingen, he could describe himself as "farouche and pedantic". Although he leaned towards the idealism of Plato he was at times exasperated by this "overwrought philosopher who seems aggrieved that we are in fact human beings" and he was subject to fits of typical youthful scepticism : "Ich lebe noch nicht neunzehn Jahre, und habe doch genugsam erfahren, wie unergründlich boshaft die Menschen sind . . ."[1]

A stabilising influence was provided by the poet's cousin, Sophie Gutermann, for whom he developed the kind of sentimental friendship that was characteristic of the age, a friendship that could very properly in his case be called platonic. Of Sophie he wrote to Bodmer, "Ihre Freundschaft, und endlich auch ihr obwohl kurzer Umgang machte mich plötzlich zu einem ganz andern Menschen . . . (ich) ward gesetzt, zärtlich, edel : ein Freund der Tugend und Religion."[2] Fifty years later Wieland could write to Sophie with evident sincerity, "nichts ist gewisser, als daß ich, wofern uns das

Schicksal nicht im Jahre 1750 zusammengebracht hätte, kein Dichter geworden wäre."[3]

It was Sophie who gave to Wieland's mind and sensibilities the impulse that propelled him into his "seraphic" phase. Even during this period of Platonic rapture, however, there are signs of that groping towards a balance of reason and emotion that was to form the central theme of his mature works:

"Ich glaube und bekenne, daß ich der Meinung Miltons sei, daß der Mensch minder zum Denken als zum Empfinden geschaffen sei. Ich glaube aber auch dagegen, daß alle unsere Gedanken zu Empfindungen und unsere Empfindungen zu Gedanken gemacht werden sollten; oder, die Wahrheiten sollen aus dem Herzen in den Verstand und aus diesem ins Herz übergehen. . . . Wenn das Herz nicht recht viel an allen Wahrheiten teilnimmt, so sind mir solche Wahreiten noch lange nicht so schätzbar als die schönen Irrtümer einiger Poeten, die das Herz mit süßen und guten Empfindungen füllen. Der Mensch ist eigentlich zur Freude geschaffen. Diese aber kann nicht dem Menschen anständig sein, wenn es nicht eine weise Freude ist, an der der Verstand Anteil nimmt.—Die wahre Weisheit ist die Kunst, sich und andere recht sehr glücklich und selig zu machen. Ich tadle und verachte daher die zwei Abwege von der Weisheit, da man, wie die meisten, entweder in die Tiefen zu Tieren taumelt, oder . . . in Wolken herumschwärmt."[4]

Wieland was not to realise the ideal thus fleetingly glimpsed until he had spent some years "in the clouds" and a rather briefer spell in the nether regions. Still under the heady influence of the Christian Platonism that inspired his *Lobgesang auf die Liebe* (1751) and *Die Natur der Dinge* (1752) he was received into Bodmer's house as a "second young Klopstock". He accepted the part with enthusiasm, laboured at his patriotic epic on Hermann and embarked on a Miltonic poem, *Der geprüfte Abraham* (1753). Poetry he regarded as "the songstress of God", or, in less elevated terms, the vehicle of "those useful truths most necessary to our happiness". He attacked as immoral Anacreon, Tibullus and their contemporary successors, Chaulieu, Gay, Prior and Uz:

"—Verächtliche Toren,
Denen die Tugend gering genug ist, dem witzigen Einfall,
Der beim Kelchglas entstand, geopfert zu werden!"[5]

Wieland entered with gusto into Bodmer's feud with Gottsched, wrote an exhaustive defence of his patron's *Noah* and threatened the Leipzig critics with a *Dunciad*. Lessing looked on the young enthusiast with a sardonic eye, while Friedrich Nicolai detected an element of sycophantic coquetry in Wieland's relationship with the patriarchal Bodmer : "Wieland's muse", he wrote, "is a young maiden acting the nun to please old Widow Bodmer." The alliance between the captious critic and the precocious poet could not long endure : in June 1754 Wieland left Bodmer's house to earn his living as a private tutor. But the time had not yet come for him to descend from the clouds. On the contrary, he became the admired protégé of a coterie of sentimentally pious matrons whose attentions no doubt comforted him for the loss of Sophie Gutermann, who had terminated their engagement about this time. The young tutor found himself involved in a series of uneasy skirmishes on the ill-defined frontier of the erotic and the platonic. "Man hielt mich in Zürich," he wrote later, "für einen Genius höherer Art, der nicht zur Sinnlichkeit herabsteigen konnte. Ich selbst lebte damals bloß in platonisierenden Morgenträumen."[6] He later looked back with some bitterness on these equivocal affairs, particularly on his relationship with a handsome and wealthy widow, Frau von Grebel-Lochmann, whom he accused of a "pious prudery" that drove him from "devout ecstasy to despair". By the middle of 1756 he had reached the point of emotional exhaustion and found himself "hot-tempered, touchy, fantastical, moody and morose". In years to come he regarded such "spiritual debauches" as an abuse of nature and remarked ironically, "that in the interests of my health I have tended subsequently not to practise this kind of exaggerated chastity".

The works of this period, *Briefe von Verstorbenen an hinterlassene Freunde* (1753), *Sympathien* (1754) and *Empfindungen eines Christen* (1757), show signs of Wieland's traffic with the mystical writings of Saint Theresa and reflect the influence of the morbidly edifying effusions of Edward Young, Elizabeth Rowe-Singer and Madame de la Motte-Guyon. These works are replete with radiant visions of the life to come, of which our present existence is only a pale shadow. Earthly joys and sorrows are but the preparation for immortality :

"Die Erde ist die Pflanzschule des Himmels. . . . Unser Richter ist selbst der Aufseher und Zeuge unsers Lebens. Und was ist dieses Leben als ein Stand der Prüfung und Vorbereitung, worin sich Alles auf eine andere Welt bezieht. . . ."[7]

In prose hymns on such topics as the Omnipresence of God and the Justice of the Almighty, Wieland indulged a propensity for preaching from the formal exercise of which he was debarred, he tells us, by a congenital weakness of the chest.

It was in this period of his life that Wieland was most guilty of a purely superficial sensibility and he has been much criticised as hypocritical but he probably deceived himself as much as anyone else. He was a protean character, quick to adopt the colouring of his environment. "Je ressemble pour mon malheur au Caméléon," he wrote to his friend Zimmermann, "je parois vert auprès des objets verts et jaune auprès des jaunes, mais je suis ni vert ni jaune, je suis transparent ou blanc." The fluency of his writing carried him along on a shallow flood of sentiment. His intellectual precocity had outstripped his judgement while his hitherto relatively sheltered existence had provided him with little in the way of emotionally testing experience. All the same, there are embedded in the rapturous or polemical writings of this period grains of a more pragmatic philosophy. Particularly significant are occasional references to the English philosopher, Lord Shaftesbury. It is hard to determine the date of Wieland's first acquaintance with Shaftesbury's writings or to assess precisely his undeniable influence on the poet. The works of Shaftesbury were by this time relatively well known in Germany and Wieland was in any case familiar with many of Shaftesbury's fore-runners and sources. There is passing mention of Shaftesbury in the *Sympathien*, where he is casually listed with Xenophon, Plutarch and Plato, but already in a lengthy digression of his anti-Gottschedian *Ankündigung einer Dunciade* (1755) Wieland had established that link between aesthetic and moral experience that is the essence of Shaftesbury's philosophy and constitutes what he calls the "sensus communis":

"Wir empfinden ebenso schnell ein lebhaftes Vergnügen über eine tugendhafte Tat als über den Anblick eines schönen Angesichts. Beides ist unsrer Seele natürlich, es wäre denn, daß unsre Empfindlichkeit durch eine stärkere Kraft gehemmt würde. Und diese beiden, einander so nahe verwandten Vermögen, die von einem vernünftigen Geschöpf unzertrennlich sind, machen endlich das aus, was man le Sens-commun heißt, die man nie anders als mit der Menschheit verlieren kann. . . . Da nun die Natur ein so festes Band zwischen dem Schönen und Guten geknüpft hat, so ist ganz natürlich, daß auch zwischen dem guten Geschmack und dem moralischen Gefühl eine genaue Verbindung sein muß. Das Schöne ist allein dazu bestimmt, uns das Gute angenehmer zu machen."[8]

Here already is the seed from which the "philosophy of the Graces" was later to flower. About the same time characteristic statements on the duality of man's nature and his capacity for

self-development begin to emerge, even in works with an ostensibly
transcendental orientation :

> "Aber dieses ist die große Bedingung, ohne deren Beobachtung
> es dem Allmächtigen selbst unmöglich ist, uns glücklich zu
> machen : wir müssen der Natur, die er uns gab, getreu bleiben.
> Damit wir glücklich wären, schuf er uns gut; verschlimmern
> wir uns, so machen wir selbst unser Unglück und zerstören sein
> Werk. Er schuf uns für die Wahrheit und Tugend. Dieses ist
> unsere Natur."[9] (*Hymne auf die Gerechtigkeit Gottes*, 1756)

Or :

> "Die ganze Vollkommenheit des Menschen besteht in Fähig-
> keiten, die gleichsam ineinandergewickelt im Schoße der Seele
> liegen und Zeit, glückliche Einflüsse und die treibende Wärme
> gemäßigter Gemütsbewegung nötig haben, um zur Wirklich-
> keit hervorzublühen."[10] (*Platonische Betrachtungen über den
> Menschen*, 1755)

Towards the end of his stay in Zürich Wieland was already
expressing disillusionment with the frustrating sentimentality of his
"seraglio" :

> "Il a été un temps que j'étais charmé de Young," he wrote on
> April 17, 1758 to Zimmermann. "Ce temps est passé. Je n'aime
> plus les contes de Fées, je ne trouve plus que tout le monde soit
> Caton, et je ne vais plus instruire les jeunes filles dans les
> mystères de la philosophie de Platon. Voilà bien des Change-
> ments, mais qui ont été amenés par des degrés presque imper-
> ceptibles."

He proclaims his new ideal : "Je vise au caractère du Virtuoso, que
Shaftesbury peint si admirablement dans tous ses écrits."

It will be observed that Wieland was not a highly original or
impulsive thinker. He had the habit of charting his intellectual
voyages by reference to the great variety of writers to which
erudition and unflagging industry gave him access. He was not
simply a plagiarist : what he sought was not ideas that he himself
lacked but confirmation of his own thoughts and experience as
well as models of conduct. Goethe said of Wieland's attachment
to Shaftesbury : "An einem solchen Manne fand nun unser Wieland
nicht einen Vorgänger, dem er folgen, nicht einen Genossen, mit
dem er arbeiten sollte, sondern einen wahrhaften älteren Zwillings-
bruder im Geiste, dem er vollkommen glich, ohne nach ihm
gebildet zu sein."[11] In characteristically eclectic fashion Wieland
linked the virtuoso, "the real fine gentleman" who through the

breadth of his culture becomes his own second creator, the moral artist of his own life, with the "Kalokagathia", the combination of the beautiful and the good in a man that is praised by Xenophon.

The first fruits of the poet's "descent from the clouds" of Platonic "Schwärmerei" were in fact associated with Xenophon. The epic *Cyrus* (1759), of which only five cantos were completed, draws a parallel between the ancient Persian conqueror praised by Xenophon and Frederick the Great. That Wieland could invoke Shaftesbury's "moral Venus" in connection with the Prussian monarch who was then engaged in his aggressive Seven Years War seems to indicate that his idealism had not been entirely dissipated —or that he was little acquainted with the real character and political aims of Frederick. At least the poem shows a healthy interest in the affairs of this world rather than the next, while in structure and style it is one of Wieland's most accomplished works. *Araspes und Panthea* (1760) is also based on Xenophon's *Cyropaedia*: it elaborates in the form of a dialogue novel an episode calculated to show a young man's capacity for self-deception in what he believes to be a platonic relationship. The relevance to Wieland's experience in Zürich is clear enough.

These two works give evidence of a more rational outlook and a firmer grasp of psychological factors than is apparent in the "seraphic" writings. Wieland's formal control of his material has also become much firmer, the approach more objective and the style less rhetorical. But the poet, at the age of twenty-seven, had still not achieved a lasting equilibrium. The circumstances of his return to Biberach—which included an unhappy love-affair and a wearisome dispute about his appointment as town clerk—deepened his disenchantment :

"Was am meisten beigetragen hat", he wrote to Zimmermann, "diese Verwandlung oder wenn Sie wollen, die Herstellung meiner ursprünglichen Gestalt, woraus die Magie des Enthusiasmus mich gedrängt hatte, zu bewirken, das ist hauptsächlich die Unzahl von Mißgeschick, Not und Plagen, die mich seit der Rückkehr in mein Vaterland verfolgt haben. Da fühlte ich das Nichts all der großen Worte, all der glänzenden Phantome, die in einer süßen Einsamkeit oder an der Seite einer Guyon oder Rowe so verführerische Reize haben für ein empfindbares Herz wie das meinige, und für eine Einbildungskraft, die um so tätiger war, da sie mich für alles, was den Sinnen abging, entschädigen mußte."[12]

Looking back on these experiences Wieland could see them as salutary : they produced the "great revolution", "durch welche

der Grund gelegt wurde, mich zu gleicher Zeit zu einem erträg-
lich brauchbaren Subjekt an der Spitze einer reichstädtischen
Kanzlei, zu einem Autor von *Idris* und *Agathon,* und (wie man
mir schmeichelt) zu einem ganz angenehmen Gesellschafter für
Leute, die etwas mehr als Cannibalen und Orang-Utangs sind, zu
machen."[13] An important part in this transformation was played
by the household of Graf Stadion at the "enchanted castle" of
Warthausen, near Biberach, which soon became for Wieland "the
centre of my world". Here he met once more the love of his youth,
Sophie Gutermann, now married to the count's agent, Georg von
La Roche. Warthausen was a miniature rococo court where
Wieland encountered an urbane atmosphere and an elegant style
of life very different from the pedantry of Zürich scholars or the
pietism of the "seraglio". He responded to his new environment
with typical alacrity, producing satricial and erotic verse tales that
are in startling contrast to the Platonic rhapsodies of Zürich. It
was in the main these *Komische Erzählungen* which gained Wieland the reputation of "lasciviousness" and which attracted a
degree of attention from censorious critics quite out of proportion
to their importance. They are bound to strike a modern reader
as absolutely innocuous. With his witty accounts of erotic escapades
amongst the Gods of Greece—some of which undoubtedly referred
to *affaires* at Warthausen—Wieland flattered the sophisticated
taste of Stadion but admitted that amongst his motives was also
a desire to avenge himself on the "prudes" of Zürich.

Accomplished as they are, the *Komische Erzählungen* (1765) are
merely peripheral to the main literary activities of the years that
Wieland spent in Biberach and Erfurt, which included—almost
incidentally—the translation of twenty-two plays of Shakespeare.
"The scales had fallen from my eyes", Wieland wrote. He at last
had a clear view of his own moral, intellectual and emotional
development : all that had gone before was in the nature of a pre-
lude. He set his seal on the German language as few writers before
him had done. He brought the tradition of the verse epic to a
triumphant climax—and initiated a new era in the prose narrative
with the first great psychological novel of modern German literature. He created a new literary style remarkable for its ingenuity,
flexibility and urbane irony. At last Wieland had found the great
theme that was to occupy him repeatedly for the remainder of his
life : man's search for wisdom in the specific sense of a proper
harmony and balance between spirituality and sensuality, reason
and instinct, thought and feeling. Three works, very different in
scale and idiom, may be regarded as major variations on this
theme : *Don Sylvio von Rosalva, Agathon* and *Musarion.*

The relevance of *Don Sylvio* (1764) to Wieland's experience is indicated in the sub-title : *Der Sieg der Natur über die Schwär-merei*. The novel is a burlesque satire which relates the adventures of a naive young nobleman and his down-to-earth retainer Pedrillo on their romantic quest for the hero's phantom love, whom he believes to have been transformed by fairies into a blue butterfly. In the course of the story Don Sylvio is cured of his belief in fairy-stories, achieves a sound view of his own nature and acknowledges the claims of the senses. The work is a latter-day *Don Quixote*, with the French fairy-tales of d'Aulnoy, Crébillon and Hamilton taking the place of medieval romances—and representing symboli-cally Wieland's defunct Platonism. The originality of the novel consists principally in a boisterously whimsical and ironic style, modelled on Fielding and Sterne, through which the narrator establishes a link with the fictive reader, conducting a dialogue with him, teasing and tantalising him and anticipating his reactions. In its playfulness and in the delicate piquancy with which the author handles erotic motifs, for example in the tale of Prince Biribinker, in the fluency and polish of its language, *Don Sylvio* is a revolutionary work in Germany and a superb specimen of rococo narrative by any standards.

Die Geschichte des Agathon (1766) is a more ambitious under-taking. It is, in a sense, Wieland's *Faust*. It shares with Goethe's drama the problem of the "two souls" in the hero's breast, but Wieland's approach is essentially pragmatic and psychological. *Agathon* undeniably lacks the fathomless profundities and the transcendental tendency of *Faust*. It moves within a social universe that is fundamentally rational and reflects a character less ambi-valent than Goethe's. There is no descent to "the Mothers" : the epiphanies that Agathon experiences in Delphi prove to be spurious. Nevertheless, the authentic perplexity with which Wieland approached his theme is indicated by the way in which he repeatedly returned to the novel in search of a satisfying conclusion : revised and extended versions appeared in 1773 and 1794.

The contemporary critic, Friedrich von Blanckenburg, whose *Versuch über den Roman* (1744) is largely based on *Agathon*, pointed out that the hero shared with Tom Jones a problematic quality and possessed a psychological veracity which differentiated him from wooden paragons of the Grandison type : "Bei Agathon sehen wir, *wie* er zu all den Eigenschaften gelangt, die ihn uns so schätzbar machen."[14] A typical philosophical propensity of the German "Bildungsroman" as compared with the graphic social realism of Fielding determines the setting of *Agathon* in the late Classical age of Greece. The novel is, however, essentially philosophical rather than historical. Wieland pays scant attention to accurate details of local colour. His aim was to stress the universality of the problems he depicts. The particular age he chose, apart from being one that appealed to him as exceptionally cultured, offered a rich variety of religious experience and philosophical belief without involving the author in acrimonious theological controversies of his own day, as, for example, Friedrich Nicolai's *Sebaldus Nothanker* had involved its author. The novel illustrates admirably Wieland's view of the ideal nature of literature :

> "(Die Dichtkunst) muß sich über die bloße Nachahmung der individuellen Natur, über die engen Begriffe einzelner Gesellschaften, über die unvollkommenen Modelle einzelner Kunstwerke erheben, aus den gesammelten Zügen des über die ganze Natur ausgegossenen Schönen sich ideale Formen bilden und aus diesen die Urbilder zusammensetzen, nach denen sie arbeitet."[15]

Although Agathon's career reflects fairly clearly the course of Wieland's personal development it does so in a way that is typical rather than characteristic. The ambition to synthesise and epitomise experience in this way may be regarded as a feature of literary Classicism.

We first encounter Agathon in a moment of failure and a mood of disillusion : a change of political fortune has driven him from Athens and deprived him of his patrimony. Seized and sold by pirates, he comes as a slave into the house of a wealthy hedonist Hippias, who, provoked by Agathon's prudish idealism, plans to have him seduced by the beautiful and cultured hetaira Danae. To the dismay of Hippias and somewhat to the surprise of the lady a heart-felt love develops between the couple. Hippias spitefully reveals Danae's past and Agathon departs in dudgeon for Sicily, where he embarks on a political career at the court of the tyrant Dionysius. During his association with Danae he had told her of his experiences as an acolyte in the temple at Delphi, where he had been shocked by the hypocritical deceits of the priests. Here, too, he was exposed to erotic advances by the priestess Pythia. In her jealousy Pythia had parted Agathon from Psyche, for whom he felt an ethereal love. After initial successes at the court of Syracuse Agathon falls victim to the intrigues of envious courtiers and is imprisoned. Spurning the help of the cynical Hippias he is finally liberated at the instigation of the sage Archytas, who brings Agathon to his estate at Taranto. Here Agathon again encounters Danae, repentant and regenerated by her love for Agathon, which is henceforth tempered to affectionate friendship. Agathon's ambivalent feelings for Psyche, which had so perplexed him, are explained when he discovers that she is his long-lost sister. The second version of the novel adds the "secret history" of Danae, tracing her development into a "schöne Seele"; the third is concluded in a somewhat inept manner by the story of Archytas and his Utopian settlement. It is a confession of failure that Wieland is obliged to abandon the hero whose evolving character he had described with such psychological truth and revert to a paragon figure in order to illustrate his ideal. However, the essence of Wieland's belief in human nature precluded the kind of transcendental conclusion that Goethe did not hesitate to use in the second part of his *Faust*. The doctrine of moderation which Wieland preaches allows no sensational climax to Agathon's career. The sum of his experience is expressed as follows:

". . . daß der Mensch—auf der einen Seite den Tieren des Feldes, auf der andern den höhern Wesen und der Gottheit selbst verwandt—zwar ebenso unfähig sei, ein bloßes Tier als ein bloßer Geist zu sein : aber daß er nur alsdann seiner Natur gemäß lebe, wenn er immer emporsteige; daß jede höhere Stufe der Weisheit und Tugend allezeit das richtige Maß sowohl der öffentlichen als der Privatglückseligkeit unter den Menschen gewesen, und daß diese einzige Erfahrungsweisheit, welche kein Zweifel zu entkräften fähig ist, alle Trugschlüsse der Hippiasse zerstäube und die Theorie der Lebensweisheit des Archytas unerschütterlich befestige."[16]

This conclusion may not appeal to the more sophisticated modern reader. It relies on postulates of the age of enlightenment, such as the confidence that we can recognise virtue when we see it in much the same intuitive way that we recognise physical beauty. It presupposes the power of reason to master sensual desires and to dictate right moral choices : "Denn moralisch gut zu sein," Wieland once wrote, "hängt lediglich davon ab, daß man es ernstlich sein wolle."[17] This comment epitomises what may indeed seem like a very naive optimism on Wieland's part. There is some truth in the criticism that he lacked a sense of fatality and underrated the power of the irrational to overthrow the sweet reasonableness which is his ideal. Nevertheless, within the limits of a rationalistic environment and generally sanguine temperament Wieland had at least an inkling of the problematic play of providential, personal and environmental forces in human destiny. He had given thought to the nature of evil and did not accept without question the assumption of the Enlightenment that all partial evil is universal good or that wickedness was bred invariably of ignorance and stupidity. He concerned himself repeatedly, for example in *Bonifazius Schleicher* (1776) and the novel *Peregrinus Proteus* (1791), with the questionable motives of the religious enthusiast and the whole problem of hypocrisy in matters of belief. Life has grown a good deal more complicated in its organisation than it was in Wieland's time or in the fourth century B.C. and more elaborate psychological systems have been devised to explain human behaviour. But human nature does not change fundamentally and in *Agathon* Wieland has expressed some quintessential truths about it.

Agathon is an important landmark in the history of the German novel. The modern reader may miss the realistic texture and the social relevance to which he has become accustomed, and the work certainly has its longueurs—it was written, after all, for a leisured public as much interested in philosophical discourse as in incident or characterisation. Nevertheless, the novel still has power to charm by its humour and irony and by the picture-squeness of many scenes as well as by the often rather portly elegance of Wieland's style.

The doctrine of harmony and the golden mean is compressed into less than 1500 lines in the idyll *Musarion* (1768). This poem— Goethe called it "das allervortrefflichste Ganze, das je erschienen ist"—is a gem of rococo art, pointedly witty and fashioned in flowing free verse with a kind of well-rounded grace that is reminiscent of a Dresden porcelain group. The plot is rudimentary and much like that of a stage comedy. Phanias, a young Athenian, having squandered most of his fortune, is disillusioned with the world and seeks the solitude of nature to live the simple life enjoined for different reasons by his mentors, Theophron the Pytha-gorean and Kleanth the Stoic. Musarion, a hetaira, whom Phanias has hitherto exasperated by his love-sick posturings, pursues him nevertheless into the arcadian wilderness in the hope of making him see reason. She contrives a situation in which Theophron, for all his high-flown idealism, reveals himself as a satyr and Kleanth forgets his ascetic doctrine in a gluttonous debauch. Phanias is inclined to repudiate the two systems of philosophy as discredited but Musarion teaches him to discriminate between the doctrines and their practitioners. Having taught him moderation in thought and in emotion she then surrenders gracefully to his renewed advances. In her combination of charm and tolerant wisdom Musarion embodies the "philosophy of the Graces".

"Die reizende Philosophie,
Die, was Natur und Schicksal uns gewährt,

Vergnügt genießt, und gern den Rest entbehrt;
. . . .
Nicht stets von Tugend spricht, noch, von ihr sprechend, glüht,
Doch, ohne Sold und aus Geschmack, sie übet;
Und, glücklich oder nicht, die Welt
"Für kein Elysium, für keine Hölle hält"[18]

It would be churlish to enquire too closely into the plausibility of this moral fiction. The charm of the piece is irresistible. Wieland plays smilingly with the conventions of the rococo mode—as they must be played with—ironising conventions that are in themselves ironical. The three scenes of which the tale consists are delicately stylised vignettes. The learned Classical allusions with which it is embroidered stand in humorous contrast to the slightness of the plot and the erotic playfulness of the main incidents. Everywhere we sense the presence of the narrator making his ironic points and sallies at the expense of readers as well as characters.

In such works Wieland embellished the austere features of the Enlightenment, warmed it with wit and made it real in terms of human experience. In doing so he helped to lay the foundations of German Classical humanism.

Wieland reveals a different aspect of his talent in the entertaining and less obviously didactic verse epics in which he handles with dexterity traditional themes of a highly imaginative kind. In *Idris und Zenide* (1768) and *Der neue Amadis* (1771) he breathed new life into old romances, reviving them for the taste of an enlightened public. Few poets can match Wieland as a metrical craftsman : with his verse epics he introduced into German a whole range of metrical forms from the Romance languages, anticipating the Romantic poets and often excelling them in virtuosity. He endowed German with a rich musicality, mastering "das Rauhe, Wiehernde und Unsingbare unserer Sprache". Among the verse romances one is supreme : "Solang Poesie Poesie, Gold Gold und Kristall Kristall bleiben wird," wrote Goethe, "so lang wird Wielands Oberon als ein Meisterstück poetischer Kunst geliebt und bewundert werden."[19] The skill with which Wieland welds together the tale of Huon of Bordeaux, Chaucer's *Merchant's Tale* and the Titania and Oberon episode from *A Midsummer Night's Dream* constitutes, as he claims, "die eigentümlichste Schönheit des Plans und der Komposition dieses Gedichts".[20] The quarrel of Oberon and Titania over the fidelity of human lovers is linked to the adventures of Huon, who has been sent by Charlemagne to the Holy Land on an impossibly hazardous quest. With the help of his squire Scherasmin and the supernatural assistance of Oberon, Huon achieves his mission and abducts the Sultan's beautiful daughter Rezia. Unfortunately, the couple are not proof against temptation and break the condition of chastity imposed by the fairy powers. Seldom can a moral lapse have been described with such urbanity and lapidary wit. On the ship bearing them back to Europe Huon and Rezia fall into each other's arms :

"Mit vollen Zügen schlürft sein nimmer satter Mund
Ein herzberauschendes wollüstiges Vergessen
Aus ihren Lippen ein; die Sehnsucht wird vermessen,
Und ach! an Hymens Statt krönt Amor ihren Bund."[21]

The enraged Oberon raises a tremendous tempest which abates only when the guilty pair are cast into the sea. A talisman brings them safely to a desert island, where they are fortunate enough to find their way to a miniature Eden created by the sage hermit Alfonso. Here Rezia, now christened Amanda, gives birth to a son but the couple suffer many further temptations and tribulations before their exemplary constancy reconciles the fairy monarch and gains them pardon. The adventures of Huon and Rezia are parallelled in the traditional way on a lower, comic level by those of Scherasmin and Rezia's hand-maiden Fatme. In the welter of incident Wieland does not lose sight of the graver moral theme and the poem has power to move as well as to entertain.

With *Agathon* Wieland initiated a new phase in the evolution of the German novel; with *Oberon* he virtually brought to a close the tradition of the verse romance. As the last possible variation on the themes and forms of the medieval tale it had no obvious successors but its influence may be detected in the drama and the opera—not only in Carl Maria von Weber's *Oberon,* which is based, alas, on a travesty of Wieland's poem, but also in Mozart's *Zauberflöte* and the whole genre of the Viennese "Zauberposse".

Wieland's concern with the cultivation of the individual personality is complemented by a practical interest in social and political organisation. Indeed, in his view, the quality of communal life depends on the maturity of the individuals who compose it. In one of his many essays on the French Revolution he remarks, "Soll es jemals besser um die Menschheit stehen, so muß die Reform nicht bei Regierungsformen und Constitutionen, sondern bei den einzelnen Menschen anfangen."[22] For Wieland, as a convinced monarchist, this principle applied *a fortiori* to the personality of the sovereign. The great variety of political conditions in the Germany of his day could only confirm him in his belief that the prosperity of the state and the happiness of its subjects depended almost wholly on the character of its ruler. This is the lesson of *Der goldne Spiegel oder die Könige von Scheschian* (1772), which recounts in an entertaining framework reminiscent of the *Arabian Nights* the vicissitudes of a legendary kingdom under its successive rulers. As a moderate by temperament as well as on principle Wieland picks his way between divine right and social contract, absolutism and democracy, clericalism and free thought. The work culminates in the advocacy of a constitutional monarchy on the English pattern. This "Fürstenspiegel" failed to attract the favourable attention at the court of the Emperor Joseph II that Wieland had hoped for and he was unable to play the part of the philosopher Danischmend in Vienna. However, it induced the Duchess Anna Amalia to summon him to Weimar, where his talents no doubt had more scope than they might have had under the autocratic Joseph. All the same, it is interesting to speculate what influence a mind as liberal as Wieland's might have had on Imperial policies—always supposing he did not suffer the fate of Agathon in Syracuse!

In the early stages of the French Revolution it seemed to Wieland that the ideal of *Der goldne Spiegel* was about to be realised and it was with some satisfaction that he hailed the novel as an unwitting prophecy:

> "Ich selbst ließ mir damals wenig davon träumen, daß noch vor meinem sechzigsten Jahre das, was ich für die kühnste aller meiner Dichtungen gehalten hatte, unter dem Nachfolger Ludwigs XV, wenigstens einem großen Teil nach, in Erfüllung gehen würde, und es war also sehr natürlich, daß ich bei den ersten, so viel versprechenden Anscheinungen eines so wenig gehofften Wunderwerks nichts weniger als einen gleichgültigen Zuschauer abgeben konnte."[23]

The reign of terror rapidly demolished these early hopes but Wieland continued to follow events in France and their repercussions in Germany with keen interest and no little sagacity, as is shown, for example, in a dialogue of March 1798 which predicted the rise of Napoleon—at that time in Egypt—to absolute power. So accurate was his forecast that the St. James Chronicle of January 25, 1800 accused Wieland of being party to an international conspiracy dedicated precisely to this end, his dialogue being "nothing else but a hint dropt from the pen of Weiland (sic), with which perhaps he had been inspired by the Illuminati, in order to render their plan familiar to Europe, and to try beforehand to make their hero acceptable to the French nation."

The French Revolution was in some sense the violent climax

to an international debate concerning "nature", "man", "society" and "culture". In this debate, which was nourished by growing knowledge of primitive societies and a more systematic study of anthropology, the writings of Rousseau occupied a central position. In Germany the call of "back to nature" inspired in writers of the "Sturm und Drang" that atavistic admiration of the primitive and instinctive that has been termed "Kulturpessimismus". Wieland participated in the debate through a series of essays published in 1770 under the title of *Beiträge zur geheimen Geschichte des menschlichen Verstandes und Herzens*. He takes issue with Rousseau, contradicting the theory of natural man as essentially anti-social and repudiating the myth of an arcadian Golden Age from which man had degenerated in proportion as society had grown more civilised. With his enlightened belief in the perfectibility of the human race Wieland rejects the opposition of "culture" and "nature". He sees a cultural instinct as part of man's nature :

"Wenn es die Natur ist, die im Feuer leuchtet, im Kristall sechseckig anschießt, in der Pflanze vegitiert, im Wurme sich einspinnt, in der Biene Wachs und Honig in geometrisch gebauten Zellen sammelt, im Biber mit anscheinender Vorsicht des Zukünftigen Wohnungen von etlichen Stockwerken an Seen und Flüsse baut und in diesem sowohl als in vielen anderen Tierarten mit einer so zweckmäßigen und abgezirkelten Geschicklichkeit wirkt, daß sie den Instinkt zu Kunst in ihnen zu erhöhen scheint : warum sollte es nicht auch die Natur sein, welche in Menschen nach bestimmten und gleichförmigen Gesetzen diese Entwicklung und Ausbildung seiner Fähigkeiten veranstaltet? Dergestalt, daß, sobald er unterläßt in Allem, was er unternimmt, auf ihren Fingerzeig zu merken; sobald er aus unbehutsamem Vertrauen auf seine Vernunft sich von dem Plan entfernt, den sie ihm vorgezeichnet hat,—von diesem Augenblick an Irrtum und Verderbnis die Strafe ist, welche unmittelbar auf eine solche Abweichung folgt."[24]

"Nature" for Wieland embraces human nature and it is not static but dynamic. There is in his view no primal "state of nature" from which man has fallen away through self-consciousness and reason and to which he might return, in Kleistian terms, only by some barely imaginable "circumnavigation of the globe". It is possible for communities to deviate from the line of development prescribed for them by nature, but Wieland is confident that such a community will ultimately return to its true path—"unless it is overtaken by some calamity". This view of natural development in harmony with reason conflicts to some extent with Wieland's innumerable representations in his works of arcadian and utopian states. These persist far beyond the "moralische Unschuldswelten" of his seraphic period. There is hardly a major work which does not feature some miniature Eden or island of the blest. Such visions seem to fulfil an emotional need and are possibly evidence of a fundamental, unacknowledged pessimism concerning the evolution of civilised societies. The hermit figures who appear so frequently in his novels and poems embody a similar pessimism : frustrated in their attempts to reform society they become outsiders and "Sonderlinge" on the model of Diogenes.

The satirical novel *Die Geschichte der Abderiten* may be regarded as a continuation of the *Beiträge* : it is referred to obliquely as such in the preface to the edition of 1776. The community here described is an anti-Utopia, a society which has taken a wrong turning and deviated from the path of its natural development. The work was conceived and written over a number of years and consequently has a somewhat disjointed character. The first two of its five books are compounded of legends about the Thracian city of Abdera, regarded in antiquity as a city of fools, and the frustrating personal experiences of the author as town clerk of Biberach, a city whose constitutional situation offered affinities with the smaller Greek city-states. The follies into which the Abderites are led by their over-fertile imagination, their conceit and deficient judgment are scourged by the rationalist philosopher Democritus, who speaks with the voice of Wieland. The later books of the novel, added after an interval of years, are more mellow in tone and seem to stress the "ideal" character of Abderite folly. The Abderites are no longer just fools, they are perfect fools, and even this kind of perfection has its appeal to the discriminating intellect :

> "Die Dummheit hat ihr Sublimes so gut als der Verstand, und wer darin bis zum Absurden gehen kann, hat das Erhabene in dieser Art erreicht, welches für gescheite Leute immer eine Quelle von Vergnügen ist. Die Abderiten hatten das Glück, im Besitz dieser Vollkommenheit zu sein. Ihre Umgereimtheit machte einen Fremden anfangs wohl zuweilen ungeduldig; aber sobald man sah, daß sie so ganz aus *einem* Stücke war und (eben darum) so viel Zuversicht und Gutmütigkeit in sich hatte, so versöhnte man sich gleich wieder mit ihnen und belustigte sich oft besser an ihrer Abderitheit als an andrer Leute Witz."[25]

Perhaps the finest part of *Die Abderiten* is the fourth book, *Der Prozeß um des Esels Schatten*. Round this supremely insubstantial object of dispute Wieland develops a satirical masterpiece of characterisation and motivation. He demonstrates how men's reason, seduced by their appetites and ambitions, drives them into absurdly irrational antics. In this story the ideal character of Wieland's satire emerges most clearly. It is not simply a two-edged attack on the parochial politics of the German imperial cities and on those less admirable aspects of Classical antiquity ignored by over-enthusiastic disciples of Winckelmann : it is also a universal satire on perennial human folly, "eine idealisierte Composition der Albernheiten und Narrheiten des ganzen Menschengeschlechts".[26] Abdera is everywhere and timeless.

The philosopher Democritus is defeated by the invincible complacency of the Abderites and retires to pursue his scientific studies in the seclusion of his country estate. Like the physician Hippocrates, who features in the second book, and the dramatist Euripides, who comes into the third book, he belongs to the invisible "Order of Cosmopolitans", a self-selecting company of men of all periods and cultures bound together by no formal oaths but simply by a community of ideals. They have no specific political function or aim but are dedicated to tolerance and reason. They seek to enlighten and persuade by argument and example.

It was in the spirit of cosmopolitanism that Wieland began his journal, *Der Teutsche Merkur*, in 1773. He had observed a growing anarchy in matters of taste and scholarship and no doubt sensed the irrationalism and nationalism that were beginning to make themselves felt in the "bardic" movement. The aim of *Der Teutsche Merkur*, modelled on *Le Mercure de France*, was to widen the intellectual horizons of the German nation and to liberate it from ancient ideological and theological controversies. Wieland hoped to seize the tide of Enlightenment at the flood in order to launch his progressive ideas throughout Germany and carry his fellow-countrymen into a new era :

"Wir leben in einer Zeit, wo die Aufklärung der europäischen Nationen über ihr wahres Interesse täglich zunimmt und sie immer mehr den Grundgesetzen nähert, welche die Natur der menschlichen Gattung vorgeschrieben, und an deren Beobachtung sie die öffentliche und Privatglückseligkeit unzertrennlich gebunden hat. Die Musen als treue Gehilfinnen der Philosophie sind dazu bestimmt, die Seelen, welche diese erleuchtet, zu erwärmen; die ungestümen Leidenschaften nicht anzuflammen, sondern zu besänftigen und in Harmonie mit unsern moralischen Pflichten zu stimmen, und den Wert der häuslichen Glückseligkeit und den Reiz der Privattugenden, die uns derselben fähig machen, in rührenden Gemälden vorzustellen; uns den Geist des

Friedens, der Duldung, der Wohltätigkeit und allgemeinen Geselligkeit einzuflößen; den Menschen durch die Allmacht des Gefühls einzuprägen, daß sie Brüder sind und nur durch Vereinigung und Zusammenstimmung glücklich sein können; den Fürsten—nicht zu schmeicheln—sie nicht in dem Wahne zu bestärken, daß sie alles dürfen, was sie wollen—daß die Kunst zu unterdrücken, zu würgen und zu erobern, sie zu Helden mache—daß es recht sei, wenn sie zu Befriedigung ihrer Privatleidenschaften und Launen ihre Provinzen entvölkern, glückliche Länder verwüsten und mit dem Leben der Menschen ein grausames Spiel treiben; sondern daß sie entweder wohltätige Väter und Hüter der Völker oder hassenswürdige Tyrannen sind. Dies ist, däucht mich, in den Zeiten, worin wir leben, mehr als jemals die wahre Bestimmung der Dichtkunst, und zu dieser edeln Bestimmung fordern wir uns selbst und alle Priester der Musen auf."[27]

The function of literature was, then, not simply self-expression, nor should the poet write for a small select circle. He had a social responsibility towards the public at large. Wieland was one of the first writers in Germany to state so unambiguously the ethics of a higher journalism. German writers, he believed, had a special duty not only to promote enlightenment in general but also to give the nation the sense of cultural identity which, because of its political fragmentation, it so far lacked :

"Sie sind gewissermaßen die eigentlichen Männer der Nation, denn ihr Wirkungskreis ist ganz Deutschland; sie werden überall gelesen, ihre Schriften dringen nach und nach bis in die kleinsten Städte, und durch sie fängt es bereits selbst in solchen Gegenden an zu tagen, auf welchen vor fünfundzwanzig Jahren noch die dickste Finsternis lag."[28]

For nearly forty years Wieland laboured in *Der Teutsche Merkur* to fulfil these obligations, writing assiduously on history, art, all the major literatures, seeking to inform his readers on topics as diverse as the latest discoveries in archaeology, early experiments in aeronautics and the topical events of the French Revolution. He bore with urbane dignity the slings and arrows of outrageous "Stürmer und Dränger", blandly recommending Goethe's lampoon on his *Alceste, Götter, Helden und Wieland,* as "ein Meisterstück von Persiflage und sophistischem Witz."[29] Only in private did he reveal how much it distressed him.

Wieland outlived the "Sturm und Drang", as did Goethe, and the two men became firm friends in Weimar. However, with the advent of new critical philosophies, the turmoil of the French Revolution and the Napoleonic Wars, as well as the change of taste and outlook represented by Romanticism, Wieland found himself increasingly out of sympathy with the world around him. The moralistic rigour of Kant—so abhorrent to a philosopher of the Graces—the abstruse speculations of Fichte, the chauvinism and religiosity of the Romantic school were all equally distasteful to him. His became a voice crying in the wilderness and although he may have had the ear of the older generation he failed to impress the young. He began to feel that his ideals could be achieved only in a close-knit Utopian community, of which the most elaborate and manifestly didactic account is given in the novel *Agathodämon* (1799). He withdrew more and more into his shell, seeking a mental refuge in his beloved Classics—Horace, Cicero, Lucian—and, like Democritus, a literal refuge on his estate at Oßmannstädt. In the political upheavals of his last years he saw a parallel with the age of Cicero, whose letters he was translating :

"In der Tat ist die Ähnlichkeit zwischen der Geschichte des auf einen derben Stoß zusammengefallenen deutsch-römischen Reiches (aus dessen Ruinen wir, mehr oder minder beschädigt, wieder hervorkriechen) mit dem zu Ciceros Zeit erfolgten Umsturze der weltbeherrschenden römischen Republik sehr auffallend."[30]

Through his translation of Horace's letters and satires Wieland had already attempted to set up a model of "Grazie" to counterbalance the enthusiasm of German poets for "Genie". It was inherent in his ideals, however, that they could not be propagated with the vulgar zest of his rivals. He had not the vocal power to distract his countrymen from the pursuit of ruder gods. His hope of turning the Latin poet into a native classic to match the German Shakespeare was doomed to failure. A last attempt to evoke the golden age of late Greek Classicism, the novel *Aristipp und einige seiner Zeitgenossen* (1800–1), found little response. Its picture of an urbane aristocratic culture was entirely out of keeping with the turbulent spirit of the age. Besides, Wieland's besetting sin of prolixity, of which he was well aware, had not improved with age : *Aristipp* has distinctly tedious passages.

Although it was not given to Wieland, as it was to Goethe, to crown his life's work with a masterpiece, his hey-day had been long and brilliant. It came to an end not so much because of a decline in his poetic powers but because the age which he represented was eclipsed. His contribution to the refinement of the

German literary language and poetic idiom had been incalculable. After his death, however, Wieland's fame faded rapidly. He had not excelled in those genres which offer the best guarantee of immortality : he had not the temperament for the lyric and, although he could claim to have written the first German tragedy in blank verse, *Lady Johanna Gray* (1758), he himself admitted that he had no dramatic vein. Even in the "Singspiel", of which *Alceste* and *Rosamunde* are brilliant examples, he was not fortunate enough to attract composers of the first rank. But the main reason for the decline of Wieland's reputation in his own country was a fundamental change of outlook on the part of his countrymen. Grand transcendental philosophies replaced the optimistic pragmatism of the Enlightenment. Reason was elevated into an absolute principle instead of being regarded primarily as a simple human faculty and the guide to right conduct. Cosmopolitanism, imperfectly as it had been practised even under the old régime, was now no less than a cardinal sin in an age of nation-states. Wieland was condemned as "undeutsch" and "französierend". Critics who were obsessed with the mysteries of poetic creation, with "problematic" personalities or the historical mission of the German race had no time for Wieland. They were scandalised equally by his cheerfulness and his sexual morality— although no one could assert that his personal life had been anything but blameless.

Modern readers are most unlikely to be shocked by the delicate salaciousness that features in some of Wieland's poems. His pragmatic view of man and society, which is rare among German writers, may now be more esteemed than it was in the nineteenth century. It ought perhaps to appeal more to an English taste than it has done to the Germans. However, Wieland's art and his thought are so much a part of the eighteenth century that it requires no small imaginative effort to appreciate them fully. This is "Poesie des Stils" : it represents a taste that rates elegance and polish above originality and spontaneity, urbanity above vehemence, it allows for argumentation and considers entertainment and instruction compatible and proper aims of literature. For those who are prepared to surmount the premisses and prejudices of Romanticism and enter the imaginative worlds of *Oberon,* *Agathon* or *Musarion* the rewards in entertainment—and even enlightenment—are great. Much that Wieland has to say is still surprisingly relevant. We may laugh at the Abderites who were eventually driven from their homes by the uncontrolled increase of their sacred frogs. If we substitute cars for frogs the idea does not seem quite so fantastic. No matter how complex our society may become, Wieland's constantly reiterated insistence that man is the measure of all things and reason his sovereign gift ought not to be forgotten. In times of fanatical extremism and violently radical solutions which solve nothing we might still learn much from the poet whom Goethe commemorated in his *Maskenzug:*

> Wieland hieß er! Selbst durchdrungen
> Von dem Wort, das er gegeben,
> War sein wohlgeführtes Leben
> Still, ein Kreis von Mäßigungen.
>
> Geistreich schaut' er und beweglich
> Immerfort aufs reine Ziel,
> Und bei ihm vernahm man täglich :
> Nicht zu wenig, nicht zu viel."[31]

NOTES

1. I have not yet lived a full nineteen years but I have learned full well how infinitely wicked men are.

2. Her friendship and finally my association with her, brief as it was, turned me quite suddenly into a totally different person. . . . I became steadfast, tender, noble: a friend to virtue and religion.

3. Nothing is more certain than the fact that, had fate not brought us together in 1750, I should not have become a poet.

4. I believe and confess that I am of Milton's opinion that man is made less for thinking than for feeling. On the other hand I also believe that all our thoughts should be turned into feelings and our feelings into thoughts; or that truths should proceed from the heart to the reason and from the reason to the heart. If the heart does not fully partake of all truths then such truths I value less than the comely errors of certain poets which fill the heart with sweet and propitious emotions. Man is made for happiness. But such cannot be proper to man unless it is a wise joy of which the reason partakes. True wisdom is the art to make ourselves and others well and truly happy. Hence I censure and despise the two false paths that lead us away from wisdom, that by which many—indeed most—stumble into the depths of bestiality, or float among the clouds.

5.   Despicable fools,
> To whom virtue is sufficiently slight to be sacrificed.
> To the witty *impromptu* born of the convivial glass.

6. In Zürich people took me for a spirit of a superior sort, incapable of descending to sensual joys. For my part I dwelt only in platonising waking dreams.

7. The earth is but the nursery of Heaven. Our Judge is himself the curator and the witness of our lives. And what is this life but a condition of trial and preparation in which everything is linked to another world.

8. We experience a lively pleasure just as rapidly when we witness a virtuous act as we do when we catch sight of a fair countenance. Both things are natural to our soul, except when our sensibility is constrained by some more powerful force. And these two faculties, so nearly akin to each other and inseparable from a rational creature, ultimately constitute what we call le Sens-commun, which we cannot forfeit unless we forfeit our humanity itself. . . . Now, since Nature has herself fixed so firm a bond between the Beautiful and the Good, then it is quite natural that a close connection must exist between our moral sense and good taste. The Beautiful is destined solely to make the Good the more pleasing to us.

9. But this is the great condition without the observance of which it is beyond the power of the Almighty Himself to make us happy: we must remain true to the Nature that He has given us. So that we might be happy, He created us good; if we became evil, we make our own misfortune and undo His work. He created us for Truth and Virtue. This is our Nature.

10. The entire perfection of man consists in faculties which lie as it were enfolded in the womb of the soul and require time, propitious influences and the germinating warmth of moderate affections to make them blossom in reality.

11. In such a man our Wieland discovered not a predecessor whom he might follow, nor a comrade with whom he might work, but a veritable elder twin brother in spirit whom he truly resembled without being formed in his image.

12. What has most contributed to effect this transformation, or, if you prefer, this reconstitution of my former cast of mind, from which the magic of enthusiasm had driven me, is above all the sorry tale of misfortune, distress and affliction that has pursued me since I returned to my birth-place. It was then I experienced the emptiness of all the grand words, all the radiant phantoms which hold such charms in sweet solitude or at the side of a Guyon or a Rowe for a heart as sensitive as mine or an imagination that was the more active in that it had to compensate me for all that my senses lacked.

13. . . . by which the foundations were laid to make of me at one and the same time a passably useful character to head the administration of an imperial city, an author of *Idris* and *Agathon* and (as people flatter me) a fairly agreeable companion for those who are more than just cannibals and orang-utangs.

14. In the case of Agathon we see *how* he acquires all those qualities which so commend him to us.

15. (Poetry) must rise above mere imitation of individual Nature, above the narrow ideas of particular societies, above the imperfect models of particular works of art; it must shape ideal forms from the collected features of the beautiful that is diffused throughout the whole of nature.

From these forms it must construct the basic patterns upon which it operates.

16. . . . that man—akin on the one hand to the beasts of the field and on the other to the higher beings and the Deity Himself—is equally incapable of being either a mere beast or a mere spirit; but that he lives in accordance with his nature only when he constantly strives upwards; that each successive level of wisdom and virtue has always been the true measure of public and private felicity amongst men, and that this single pragmatic truth, which no incertitude can invalidate, disperses all the sophistries of the Hippiasses and establishes upon unshakeable foundations the wisdom of Archytas.

17. For to be morally good requires only that one should seriously wish to be so.

18.   The gracious philosophy
That cheerfully enjoys what Nature and Fate vouchsafe
And gladly does without the rest.
   . . .
Speaks not constantly of virtue and, speaking
Of it, waxes heated,
But practises it without reward and from taste;
And, happy or unhappy, regards the world
As neither Elysium nor Hell.

19. As long as poetry shall remain poetry, gold gold and crystal crystal, so long will Wieland's *Oberon* be loved and admired as a masterpiece of poetic art.

20. . . . the peculiar beauty of the plan and the composition of this poem.

21.   With eager draughts his never-sated mouth
Gulps from her lips a sensuous oblivion;
His yearning grows intrepid and, alas!
Instead of Hymen, Amor crowns their union.

22. If things are ever to improve with mankind, then reform must begin not with forms of government and constitutions but with the individual.

23. I myself scarcely dreamed that before I had completed my sixtieth year I would see what I had thought to be my most daring fiction come into being, at least in large part, under the successor of Louis XV, and it was natural that I could not be an indifferent spectator of the first promising appearances of a prodigy so little expected.

24. If it is Nature that glows in fire, forms hexagonal crystals, informs the growth of the plant, spins the caterpillar's cocoon, collects wax and honey in the geometrically constructed cells of the bee, builds, as does the beaver, dwellings of several storeys by lakes and rivers with apparent thought for the future, and operates in this animal and in other species with such deliberate and precise dexterity that it seems to elevate instinct in them to the level of art; then why should it not also be Nature that contrives in man according to specific and uniform laws this development and training of his faculties? In such a manner that, immediately

he neglects to mark her admonition, immediately he departs from the plan she prescribes through relying incautiously on his reason—from that moment error and corruption is the penalty that ensues upon such a deviation.

25. Folly has its sublimity as well as good sense, and whoever can pursue it to the point of absurdity has achieved the sublime in this kind, which is always a source of delight for men of sense. The Abderites were fortunate enough to be in possession of this perfection. Their perversity, it is true, often made strangers impatient at first; but as soon as they observed that it was so much of a piece and (for that very reason) had so much self-confidence and good-nature in it, then they were reconciled and were often as entertained by their Abderitism as by the wit of others.

26. . . . an idealised compound of the stupidities and follies of all mankind.

27. We are living in an age when the enlightenment of the European nations as to their true interest increases daily; it is bringing them ever nearer to those fundamental laws which Nature has prescribed for the human race and to which public and private happiness are indissolubly bound. The Muses, as the faithful hand-maidens of philosophy, are destined to warm the souls that philosophy has enlightened; not to inflame violent passions but to soothe them and to attune them in harmony with our moral duties, to represent in affecting images the worth of domestic happiness and the attraction of the private virtues that make us capable of this happiness; to imbue us with the spirit of peace, of tolerance, of benevolence and universal fellowship; to impress upon men through the supreme power of feeling that they are brothers and can only be happy through unity and harmony; not to flatter princes nor to encourage them in the delusion that they may do everything they wish, that the art of suppression, slaughter and conquest makes heroes of them —that it is right in satisfaction of private passions and whims to depopulate their provinces, to lay waste happy lands and to play a cruel game with the lives of men; but that they are either benevolent fathers and protectors of their people or else hateful tyrants. This is, it seems to me, in the times in which we live, more than ever the true end of poetry, and we exhort to this noble end ourselves and all other priests of the Muses.

28. They are up to a point the true men of the nation, for their sphere of influence is the whole of Germany; they are read everywhere, their writings penetrate little by little into the smallest towns and through them dawn is beginning to break, even in those regions which twenty-five years ago were plunged in the deepest darkness.

29. A masterpiece of persiflage and sophistical wit.

30. Indeed the similarity between the history of the Holy Roman Empire which has collapsed under a single powerful blow (and from the ruins of which we are now crawling more or less damaged) and the overthrow of the world-wide Roman republic in Cicero's time is most striking.

31.   Wieland his name! His life acquaints
                Us with the truth his words proclaim;
                Serene he lived and free from blame,
                Tracing his circle of restraints.

                With sharpest eye and witty touch
                He kept his pristine aim in view
                And day by day he'd say anew:
                Not too little, not too much.

SELECT BIBLIOGRAPHY

Wieland's Works
Sämtliche Werke, Leipzig, Göschen, 1794–1802 (30 vols + 6 supplementary vols). This is the "Ausgabe letzter Hand", but the editions commonly quoted are the following:
  Sämtliche Werke, ed. J. G. Gruber, Leipzig, Göschen, 1824–8 (53 vols.)
  Wielands Werke, ed. H. Düntzer, Berlin, Hempel, n.d. (1879?) (40 vols.)
  A critical edition, *Gesammelte Schriften,* was planned by the Preußische Akademie der Wissenschaften to occupy 50 vols in three divisions (*Werke, Übersetzungen, Briefe*); it began to appear in 1909 under the general editorship of B. Seuffert, who was later succeeded by W. Kurrelmeyer. 17 vols of *Werke* and 4 of *Übersetzungen* have appeared so far. A first volume of a complete collection of Wieland's letters, ed. H. W. Seiffert, was published by Akademie-Verlag, Berlin, 1963, followed by a vol. of notes (1968).

  The following select editions are excellent:

Werke. Hsg. F. Martini, H. W. Seiffert, R. Döhl. Hanser Vlg., München 1965–8 (5 vols.).
Werke. Hsg. H. Böhm, Akademie Vlg., Berlin 1967 (4 vols.).
  Paperback eds of the following works are available in the Goldmann series: *Musarion und andere Verserzählungen*; *Don Sylvio von Rosalva*; *Die Abderiten; Oberon; Agathon; Menander und Glycerion/Krates und Hipparchia.*
  An annotated edition of *Der Prozeß um des Esels Schatten* (*Die Abderiten*, Book IV) by W. E. Yuill is included in the Clarendon Series of the Oxford University Press (1964).

Secondary literature
J. G. Gruber   *Wielands Leben.* Leipzig 1827–8 (vols. 50–53 of
                    Sämtliche Werke).
F. Sengle   *Christoph Martin Wieland.* Stuttgart 1949.
J. Hecker   *Wieland.* Weimar 1966.
H. Wolffheim   *Wielands Begriff der Humanität,* Hamburg 1949

E. Ermatinger	*Die Weltanschauung des jungen Wieland.* Frauenfeld 1907.
V. Michel	*C. M. Wieland. La formation et l'évolution de son esprit jusqu'en 1772. Paris n.d. (1938?)*
A. Fuchs	*Les apports français dans l'oeuvre de Wieland de 1772 à 1789.* Paris 1934.
A. Anger	*Literarisches Rokoko.* Stuttgart 1962.
C. Elson	*Wieland and Shaftesbury.* New York 1913 (reprinted 1966).
P. Michelsen	*Laurence Sterne und der deutsche Roman des 18. Jahrhunderts.* Göttingen 1962.
W. Monecke	*Wieland und Horaz.* Köln 1964.
W. W. Beyer	*The enchanted forest.* Oxford 1963 (Oberon and the English Romantics).
F. Beissner (hsg.)	*Wieland. Vier Biberacher Vortäge.* Wiesbaden 1954 (contains a "Forschungsbericht" by H. W. Seiffert).
F. Martini	*C. M. Wieland und das 18. Jahrhundert.* In: *Festschrift für Kluckhohn und Schneider.* Tübingen 1948.
J. Jacobs	*Wielands Romane.* Bern/München 1969.
R. Schindler-Hürlimann	*Wielands Menschenbild. Eine Interpretation des Agathon.* Zürich 1963.
W. Buddecke	*C. M. Wielands Entwicklungsbegriff und die Geschichte des Agathon.* Göttingen 1966.
A. Fuchs	*Geistiger Gehalt und Quellenfrage in Wielands Abderiten.* Paris 1934.
B. Seuffert	*Wielands Abderiten.* Berlin 1878.
F. Martini	*Die Geschichte der Abderiten.* In: *Der deutsche Roman,* hsg. B. v. Wiese. Düsseldorf 1963.
W. E. Yuill	*Abderitis and Abderitism.* In: *Essays in German Literature I.* Ed. F. Norman. London 1965.
E. Boa	*Wielands Musarion and the rococo verse narrative.* In: *Periods in German Literature.* Ed. J. M. Ritchie. London 1970.
E. Staiger	*Wielands Musarion.* In: *Kunst der Interpretation.* Zürich 1955 (also in *Wieland. Vier Biberacher Vorträge.* hsg. Beissner. See above).

The Anacreontic Poets
GLEIM, UZ AND GÖTZ

The Anacreontic Poets
GLEIM, UZ AND GÖTZ
by J. M. RITCHIE

I

ANACREON was an Ionian from Teos. Famous in his own time as a poet his range was wide and included songs, iambs and elegies which the Alexandrians edited in five books. When in later times these works were lost fascinating legends of his life as a poet kept his memory alive, legends which it must be said gave rise to a view of Anacreon very far removed from the truth. And yet this false Anacreon was to exercise a greater influence over the poetry of Western Europe in general and that of France and Germany in particular than could possibly have been achieved by a knowledge of the genuine works and the historical facts of his life. In addition to the legends of his life, or perhaps arising out of them a whole spate of Greek pseudo-anacreontic poems continued to be produced right down to Byzantine times.

Out of all the rich variety of metres of which Anacreon had been such a master these later imitations generally restricted themselves to metres like the catalectic iambic or the anaclastic ionic dimeter. Hence "anacreontic" poetry came to be associated with these particular verse forms. It is poetry of this kind which will be discussed here as "anacreontic", though as the term has come to be used much more widely for practically all poetry of wine, women and song some consideration will have to be given to the subject matter as well as the form.

Poetry of this kind first became a real force in European poetry with the publication in Paris in 1554 by Henri Estienne of a collection of poems reputedly by Anacreon. Henri Estienne did not at the time reveal the manuscript source he had used for these poems, however, a source did come to light later with the discovery of the Heidelberg Manuscript of the anthology of Konstantinos Kephalas (the so-called Codex Palatinus). In a tenth century manuscript version appended to this codex the "anacreontic" poems were contained.

In the year 1623 after the capture of Heidelberg this codex was taken to the Vatican library along with many other valuable manuscripts and then came back to Paris in 1797. It was finally returned to Heidelberg in 1815 but without the anacreontic appendix which by this time had been lost. The 1554 printed version by Henri Estienne was assumed to be based on this same manuscript which had in the meantime been published by Spaletti and Levesque thereby allowing for comparisons. Ever since the Fall of Constantinople manuscripts had been in circulation which seemed to contain fragments of epigrams and odes by Anacreon, but in general these various anthologies and collections contained everything from genuine works of classical Greek to pieces of much later provenance. Henri Estienne's collection was the first to gain general acceptance as presenting a true series of genuine works by the lost poet Anacreon. Occasional doubts and discrepancies were pointed out, but for the most part only the scholarship of a much later age was able to prove conclusively that these "anacreontic" poems could not be by Anacreon himself and must in fact be imitations. Hence with the so-called *Anacreontea* the reader is involved in something very much akin to the story of MacPherson's Ossian, not that there was any intentional literary fraud involved. Anacreon had existed, he had been a great poet, but his works had been lost. *The Anacreontea,* representing only later imitations of a certain very small sample of his work, was only too readily welcomed as genuine by poets and scholars alike, was widely discussed, translated into various languages and imitated. Within two years the first edition had been followed by a second, to be followed in turn by various versions offering both Greek text and Latin translations. Soon there was a veritable flood of editions in England, France, Italy and Spain introducing additional material, interpretations, references to newly discovered manuscripts, etc. Scholarship and imagination went hand in hand. As well as translations with commentary, poems in the "anacreontic" manner also began to appear, though very little attempt was made at first to observe the metrical form of anacreontic song.

Interest in the *Anacreontea* continued throughout the seventeenth and into the eighteenth century, particularly in France, and without any doubt it was French and Latin translations, imitations and commentaries which led certain German poets and critics to attempt something similar in their own language. But there is no need to despair over this as yet another example of German enslavement to outdated French fashions. There had been nothing pejorative about the seventeenth century concept of imitation of classical models and there still was nothing debasing about it at the beginning of the eighteenth century. Even the French themselves were producing mere imitations of imitations. This was, after all, not only the age of imitation but also the age of translation, and by the eighteenth century a great deal of critical thought was being given to the theory and practice of this art.[1] Here again there need be nothing shameful about such obvious lack of "originality". Indeed it has been argued that German literature is always at its best and richest when most open to foreign influences and most receptive to foreign models as in that other great age of translation the age of Romanticism.

Certainly the concern over the philological and poetic problems involved in successfully reproducing "Anacreon" (and Horace) at this time was to provoke one of the most fruitful developments of German lyric and song.

<h1 style="text-align:center">II</h1>

Until fairly recently the names Gleim, Uz and Götz tended to be passed over very quickly in most surveys of German literature in the eighteenth century. No one doubted that as men of letters they had enjoyed a considerable reputation in their own day but little attempt was made to fathom why this should have been so. To the nineteenth and twentieth century critics and historians they seemed mere imitators of imitations, translators of translations, exponents of all that was worst in the artificial, unnatural, classicistic, frenchified mode of the time. In the last few years, however, a considerable reappraisal has been taking place thanks mainly to the magnificent pioneering work of scholars like Alfred Anger and Eric Blackall. As a result of their efforts anacreontic poetry and indeed the whole of rococo literature, of which it is a part, is being seen in a wholly new, and more objective, light. The weaknesses and limitations of the so-called anacreontic poets are still plain for all to see, but there is now a greater awareness of the positive part they had to play in the "emergence of German as a literary language". Translations and imitations of classical and pseudo-classical models were, as has been seen, by no means a uniquely German phenomenon, hence what needs to be examined is *not* the extent to which German men of letters like Gleim, Uz and Götz "merely" imitated French, English or pseudo-Greek anacreontic models, but why anacreonticism should emerge in Germany when and where it did, why it was so immediately successful and what kind of needs it met and satisfied in Germany.

Friedrich von Hagedorn (1668–1722) is the man who is generally named as the initiator of the new wave of merry "anacreontic" poets. Born into a noble family with wide diplomatic connections he was naturally at home not only in the "galante Dichtung" of the previous age but also in the *poésie légère* of France and England in his own time. Indeed he could read and write English and French as well as he could German. What interests us here is the collection of *Odes and Songs* which he published in Hamburg in 1742 with music by Görner. The music is important. Just as a baroque work tended to be a kind of "Gesamtkunstwerk" combining emblem, words and music on the page to produce simultaneous visual, literary and musical effects, so too on a smaller scale the anacreontic lyric was for singing. Read in the study by literary critics the texts naturally look light-weight and contrived. What must be remembered is that, as Günther Müller has pointed out, this was the real source of the great German "Kunstlied."[2] Poems such as these were written for the Rococo Age of Song, they were deliberately contrived as amusing trifles, they were never intended to be immortal contributions to the high art of mankind :

> Den itzt an Liedern reichen Zeiten
> Empfehl ich diese Kleinigkeiten :
> Sie wollen nicht unsterblich sein.[3]

Yet in their own modest way they were to be immortal for in Hagedorn's joyful songs of love, wine, freedom and joy ("Freude, Göttin edler Herzen !") one can hear not only the faint voice of Schiller but that of Goethe who was to be an admirer and practiser of anacreontic poetry all his life. For this new note in German song Hagedorn naturally turned not only to the modern poetry of France and England but also to the ancients, Horace, whom he admired so much,[4] and also to Anacreon. The choice of Anacreon as the model was a deliberate combination of the ancient and modern :

> Ihr Dichter voller Jugend,
> Wollt ihr bei froher Muße
> Anakreontisch singen,
> So singt von milden Reben,
> Von rosenreichen Hecken,
> Vom Frühling und von Tänzen,
> Von Freundschaft und von Liebe
> Doch höhnet nicht die Gottheit,
> Auch nicht der Gottheit Diener,
> Auch nicht der Gottheit Tempel.
> Verdienet, selbst im Scherzen,
> Den Namen echter Weisen.[5]

And sing the Anacreontic poets did of tender vines and rose-bushes, of spring and dancing, friendship and love. The Gods and Goddesses worshipped now were generally Bacchus and Venus yet the aim, as Hagedorn suggested, was still wisdom and moderation : [6]—i.e. not abstract metaphysics or gloomy religion but the quest for the gay science of how best to live one's life. The Age of Rococo was an age fascinated by China and even here one detects traces of the Chinese sage who imparts practical guide lines for living.

If Hagedorn prepared the way the man who really developed this strain of light and graceful lyric was Johann Wilhelm Ludwig Gleim (1719–1803). For Hagedorn poetry had been the "playmate of his leisure hours" whose point was to "smooth the rough passage of life, assuage grief and sorrow and bring as much pleasure as possible" :

> O Dichtkunst, die das Leben lindert!
> Wie manchen Gram hast du vermindert,
> Wie manche Fröhlichkeit vermehrt!"[7]

This was the aesthetic that Gleim then pursued throughout his extremely long life. Without a doubt this man of letters was often out of touch with the truly great forces of his age being totally out of sympathy for example with the dazzling heights of speculative philosophy reached by Kant and Fichte and equally out of sympathy with the French Revolution. By the beginning of the nineteenth century which he lived to see he had experienced Storm and Stress, Romanticism, Classicism and had been under attack from all quarters. Yet equally without a doubt he had at least for a time by his propagation of the anacreontic mode in the 1740s been one of the great men of letters of his age even though he never really developed beyond anacreonticism. And throughout his long life he kept in touch with the leading literary figures of the eighteenth century in an astounding manner.

At the university in Halle 1738 he had studied under Christian Wolff the rationalist and Alexander Gottlieb Baumgarten, the man who first made aesthetics a separate philosophical discipline. Gleim pays tribute to the latter in these words :

> Lehrer, den die Gottheit lehrte,
> Lehrer, den die Weisheit liebet,
> Lehrer, der mit Licht und Leben,
> Und mit freundlichen Beweisen,
> Tugend, Witz und Warheit stiftet,
> Sieh, wie stark sind deine Lehren!"[8]

All the key concepts of the Enlightenment are contained in these few lines :—

wisdom, light, friendliness, virtue, wit, truth.

In Halle he also became friendly with two other like-minded students, Johann Peter Uz and Johann Nikolaus Götz, but they were not to be long together at the university. In the course of the various positions to be held in Berlin, Potsdam and elsewhere Gleim became acquainted with Ewald von Kleist, Ramler, Pyra and others. In 1747, he became established in Halberstadt and his contacts now included Sulzer, Bodmer, the Bremer Beiträger, Klopstock and Jacobi. Tiedge came to stay with him, then Herder. With those whom he could not meet personally he kept up an extensive correspondence and was often able to help them financially. Hence he had connections with Lavater, Bürger, Schiller and Jean Paul. Even Heinrich von Kleist was sure of a warm welcome when he visited Gleim in Halberstadt in 1801 on his way to Paris.

Friendship was no empty ideal with Gleim. Like Hagedorn he was unbelievably kind and generous. In an age plagued with literary jealousies and animosities it is pleasurable indeed to find such men of letters putting the sentiments of their poems into practice in terms of money and real help to fellow writers. Friendship is of course almost exclusively a male prerogative in the eighteenth century and the modern reader tends to be suspicious of the somewhat excessive language in which these batchelor poets conducted their lengthy correspondence with each other. (Hagedorn was however married.) The admiration for the beautiful male was doubtless one feature of Greek poetry (and anacreontic poetry in particular) which appealed to these unmarried poets. Hence in a sense it is misleading to repeat as nearly all histories of literature do that this is the poetry of wine, women and song. It is just as often the poetry of wine, *boys* and song. For example :

> *An einen Knaben*
> Anmuthsvoller Knabe,
> Welcher Mädgens gleicht,
> Dir, dir lauf ich nach;
> Und du willst nicht hören,
> Und du willst nicht wissen,
> Daß du, als ein Fuhrmann,
> Meinen stolzen Geist
> Wie am Zügel lenkst.[9]

Be that as it may Gleim was able to gather round him in

Halberstadt a group of poets and young people prepared to make poetry a merry sociable activity. Halberstadt was, however, no golden age Arcadia entirely removed from the turmoils of the world, indeed during the course of the Seven Years War (1756–63) the township was several times occupied by the French. This too is reflected in his writing.

One of the curious features of Gleim's work was that the poet of the notoriously unwarlike anacreontic poetry should also be the poet whom local patriotism for Prussia and admiration for Frederick the Great inspired to the famous *Preussische Kriegslieder*. *Mit Melodieen* (Berlin 1758) in the metre of *Chevy Chase* :

> Auf Brüder, Friedrich, unser Held,
> Der Feind von fauler Frist,
> Ruft uns nun wieder in das Feld,
> Wo Ruhm zu hohlen ist.[10]

Yet the difference between the anacreontic and the Prussian poems is not so great as might appear at first. For one of the great attractions of the anacreontic manner was naiveté and simplicity of tone.

And this Gleim maintains in his *Preussische Kriegslieder*, for he made them songs of a simple soldier. It was this tone too that he adopted for his *Zwey Lieder eines armen Arbeitsmannes* (1772).

> Die Reichen alle mögen sich
> In Gold und Seide kleiden,
> Und schmausen; Christen, sie will ich,
> Ich Armer, nicht beneiden,
> Sie mögen ohne Leibesnoth
> In Erdenfreuden leben!
> Nur, ihre Herzen rühre Gott,
> Daß sie uns Arbeit geben!"[11]

It was a common-place and much admired piece of anacreontic wisdom that one should reject wealth in favour of the simple things in life. So Hagedorn could write :

> Stumme Hüter toter Schätze
>   Sind nur reich.
> Dem, der keinen Schatz bewachet,
> Sinnreich scherzt und singt und lachet,
> Ist kein karger König gleich."[12]

Hagedorn's most famous poem along these lines was the tale of *Johann der Seifensieder* who lost the power of song as soon as he started to accumulate money. Such sentiments were fairly safe

9—GMOL-6   *   *

and harmless yet there was a vein of social criticism in Gleim's poetry which, while it should not be exaggerated, is very definitely present. And this same critical voice of the simple man directed again the excesses of the rich and the powerful is also present as an undercurrent in much anacreontic poetry.

Apart from the *Zwey Lieder eines armen Arbeitsmannes* Gleim also wrote *Lieder für das Volk* (1772) in the same simple tone. But even more interesting in this connection are his *Poems after the Minnesinger* (1773) and his *Poems after Walter von der Vogelweide* (1779) especially if one considers similarities in style and content between these and the *Lieder nach dem Anakreon* (1764):

Die Erinnerung
Erster Th.S. 113

Unter'n Linden,
Wo sie mir zur Seite saß,
Könnt ihr finden,
Blumen und gebrochnes Gras,
Vor dem Walde, Dal de Dall,
Schön sang uns die Nachtigall!

Under de linden An der heide
Da unser zvveier bette vvas Da mugent ir vinden
Schone beide Gebrochen bluomen und gras
Vor dem vvalde in einem tal
Tandaradai schone sanc dú nachtegal[13]

German critics long convinced of the artificiality of anacreontic poetry do not take kindly to suggestions of affinity between it and "Minnesang". And yet it was the great Swiss Bodmer who first pointed out the "sympathy of spirit" existing between Gleim and the "ancient" German poets, and these "Nachdichtungen" are needless to say dedicated to him. The idea of similarities between "Minnesang" and Anacreon was certainly not foreign to the German poets themselves.

Hence Götz for example, in the notes to his translation of Ode XX after drawing attention to similar lines by Heinsius, Ovid and La Motte quite naturally quotes the following lines "from the Age of the Emperor Friedrich":

Ich wolte, das der anger sprechen solte,
als der Sytich in dem glas,
Und er mir danne rehte sagen wolte,
wie gar sanfte im hure was,
do mine frowe blumen las

ab im, und ir minneclichen fuesse
ruehrten uf sin gruenes gras.[14]

The truly anacreontic collection of poems which established Gleim's literary reputation was *Versuch in scherzhaften Liedern*, published anonymously in Berlin in 1744. A second part appeared the following year. Gleim himself later pointed out in his fragmentary autobiography the part which the Halle poets Lange and Pyra played in forming his literary and aesthetic ideals. Certainly as far as the anacreontic poetry is concerned the *Freundschaftliche Lieder* by Pyra and Lange proved most important, not only because of the emotional significance of the friendship motif but also because of the sustained attack they contained on the "alleged adornment of rhyme". Their *Freundschaftliche Lieder* tended to become experiments with unrhymed metres and strophes. For the poetry of the period the battle over rhyme was almost the major issue beside which the choice of the appropriate classical model—Horace, Pindar, Anacreon—was almost secondary.[15] Pindar was seriously considered as a possibility but he only really came into his own with the Goethe of the "Sturm und Drang" period. Next to Anacreon it was the Horace of the Odes who proved most attractive as a model for Gleim, Uz and Götz.

Lange's complete translation published in 1752 showed the kind of significance that contemporaries attached to his works.[16] Unfortunately Lessing's famous critique of the translation and the resultant obliteration of Lange tends to be remembered while the importance of Horace for the age is forgotten.

The poetry of Lange and Pyra was for the most part serious, pietistic and gloomy. Gleim and his friends determined to use the new rhymeless forms for poetry that was light and bright and gay. The poem entitled *Anacreon* placed at the head of the *Versuch in scherzhaften Liedern* was programmatic enough.[17]

> *Anacreon*
> Anacreon, mein Lehrer,
> Singt nur von Wein und Liebe;
> Er salbt den Bart mit Salben,
> Und singt von Wein und Liebe;
> Er krönt sein Haupt mit Rosen,
> Und singt von Wein und Liebe;
> Er paaret sich im Garten,
> Und singt von Wein und Liebe;
> Er wird beim Trunk ein König,
> Und singt von Wein und Liebe;
> Er spielt mit seinen Göttern,

Er lacht mit seinen Freunden,
Vertreibt sich Gram und Sorgen,
Verschmäht den reichen Pöbel,
Verwirft das Lob der Helden,
Und singt von Wein und Liebe;
Soll denn sein treuer Schüler
Von Haß und Wasser singen?

After the first few lines so often misleadingly quoted in histories
of literature to show how trivial and ridiculous anacreontic poetry
can be, come the more important, programmatic lines. Gleim like
Anacreon, *plays* with his Gods, *laughs* with his friends, *dispels* care
and sorrow, *despises* the rich, *rejects* the worship of heroes and
sings of wine and love. The anti-Herrenhuter, i.e. anti-pietistic
intention is also quite outspoken on more than one occasion :

An Herrn ***
Ich trink, ich lieb, ich lache,
Indem ihr euch, ihr Helden,
Die Köpfe spaltet.
Ich trink, ich lieb, ich lache,
Indem, du müder Geitzhals,
Für Arbeit schwitzest.
Ich trink, ich lieb, ich lache,
Indem sich Herrenhuter
Zu Tode beten,
Ich trink, ich lieb, ich lache,
Ich singe frohe Lieder,
Wann Priester schimpfen.[18]

Most critics and historians have been a little too ready to
dismiss Gleim's poetry as limited in scope and repetitive in theme,
even while admitting his formal proficiency in handling the short
lines and classical metres. In fact, however, he is not nearly so
restrictive as he himself appears to claim. He does not really write
only of girls and wine. There are poems about a wide variety of
subjects—serious subjects as well as those of a more frivolous
nature. A glance through the list of titles shows this clearly enough :
"Thoughts of Death"; "Life's Obligations"; "The Atheist"; "The
Astronomist"; "The Comet"; "The Rainbow"; "Brotherhood"; "A
Dream"; "Longing"; "The Will"; "The God of War"; etc.

The difference now is the manner in which such serious themes
are treated. Sickness, old age, winter, death need not, it is argued,
give rise to sadness and gloom or meditations on the transience of
human happiness. Gleim insists on the pleasures of life and

refuses to let life-denying ministers of the church take these away. Rarely does he lose his good humour or become offensive and even poems like the *Tierchen ohne Namen* about the louse on the lady's bosom is dealt with so lightly that no reader need ever feel that "good taste" is being in any way undermined.

In general Gleim did not translate the *Anacreontea* directly. Anacreon, as he said in the first poem of the collection, was his teacher. From him he took merely a thought or a poetic conceit which he then expanded in his own way. The man who did successfully translate Anacreon was Johann Nikolaus Götz (1721–81) one of the group of students at Halle who turned to the poetry of Horace and Anacreon. If he had a claim to fame it is for his version of the *Anacreontea* (1746). As could be expected of the sociable nature of anacreontic poetry the translation into unrhymed verse was a joint effort with Johann Peter Uz. What is not always so clear is why this translation should have been so well received at the time and why it was so influential. As has been seen translations had been appearing in England and France at irregular intervals for decades ever since the appearance of Henri Estienne's edition in 1554 and even in Germany there had been sporadic attempts for nearly a hundred years. But these versions of odd poems by Weckherlin, Opitz, Moscherosch, Schirmer, Taubmann and others always failed to capture the essence of "Anacreon". As far as the content was concerned they were either too crude and vulgar or too moralising and reflective. And all sorts of other aspects were wrong—the language of the seventeenth century was too awkward, the baroque poets' mastery of metre was not great enough, their rhetorical devices were too excessive—Johann Christian Günther's versions might have been a step in the right direction but these were unfortunately lost. Hence Götz's collection of the *Anacreontea* which was not even the first attempt to present all the poems in German, this having been done by Kaspar Ernst Triller in 1698, was the first successful presentation of "Anacreon" as a delightful model for mankind. Here at last was a guide to something genuine, simple and natural. Götz who had learned from Hagedorn how to write German clearly and logically was able to cut through the jungle of irrelevances like rhyme and rhetoric and present his master in a style appropriate to him. In this he had some help from Gottsched who as early as 1733 had published some samples of anacreontic song in unrhymed verse to demonstate how it could be done in German even to the very metrical form of the original. It was his example that Götz and Uz followed.

As with most works of joint authorship it has proved impossible to determine after the event the part played by each in the work, and as so often happens in such cases the authors themselves prove the least reliable guides to the facts. And as with attempts to determine the individual French models for particular German poems in the anacreontic manner so here too, the identification of the particular translator of particular odes has proved an exercise in fruitless scholarship. What is definite is that Götz and Uz separated shortly after the translation was first published anonymously in 1746. Götz apparently left Halle suddenly without explanation and relations between himself and Uz remained strained to say the least. From then on Gleim too became involved in the continuing attempts to produce better and better versions of the odes, but in the end it was left to Götz to finalise the first complete translation making up for what were thought to be the various deficiencies of the hastily produced edition of 1747. This appeared in 1760. Gleim meanwhile resumed composition of odes in the manner of Anacreon leaving the philological labour of accurate but poetic translations of the odes to Götz, while Uz moved on to works of a more serious and philosophical vein.

The basis for the Götz-Uz translation was the edition by the French bluestocking Mme. Dacier who had herself built on the scholarly work which her father T. Le Fèvre had done on the text before her. Her first edition of the Greek original using her father's commentary had appeared in 1681. The most important feature of this edition was the inclusion by Mme. Dacier of her own translation of the original into French *prose*. A second edition followed in 1699. The third edition of 1716 had as a further addition the de Lafosse translation into French *verse*. It was this third edition which Götz and Uz used for their own translation work. The German poets' interest in the *Anacreontea*, in other words, did not represent an anachronism. They were responding to a scholarly-poetic tradition which was still very much alive in France as indeed in England where Addison's English version appeared in 1735.

The main attraction of Madame Dacier's edition for Götz and Uz was the fact that it not only gave what was as far as possible a philologically accurate text for the Greek, it also attempted to avoid obscurity caused by previous attempts at verse translation by giving a nice clear straight-forward prose version. Götz and Uz followed this example by trying to reveal in German the real Anacreon :

"as he really spoke, in keeping with his times and the people he associated with and the playful ways they were accustomed to then; we have not wilfully altered any expression in which references to customs and tales of the times were contained, we have avoided changing the thoughts, altering the Greek text, all additions, expansion of images, avoided even as far as possible increasing the number of the lines, without laying down any hard and fast rules about all this. So as translators we have at all times had to keep Anacreon uppermost."

However, they did go beyond Madame Dacier to some extent in that they rejected the idea of a prose translation which would simply convey the sense, in favour of a verse translation which would also impart something of the grace and charm of the original. In this they were following the example not of De Lafosse but of Gottsched who had shown by his model translations of one or two odes into *unrhymed* verse that the grace of the Greek verse need not be lacking in the German. Hence, if the inspiration for the Götz-Uz version was French, the direct model was German. It was Gottsched who, by his model versions of the first three anacreontic odes published first in *Beiträge zur Critischen Histoire Der Deutschen Sprache, Poesie und Beredsamkeit* (1733), set the pattern for the German "anacreontic" verse of the future. That these versions were to be poetic but *unrhymed* was as far as Gottsched was concerned beyond discussion or question. But in addition, he pointed out the unsatisfactory nature of all previous attempts to reproduce the original anacreontic metre in English, French, German or whatever and instead of the catalectic or acatalectic iambic dimeter, himself introduced a form of trochaic dimeter.[19]

What Gottsched had realised was that the metrical form was crucial to the particular charm and grace of this kind of poetry and that everything possible should be done to retain it. It was he who first insisted on keeping the same number of syllables as the original, the same number of lines and with the one change to the trochaic dimeter the same metre. In effect, as he argued in his *Versuch einer Übersetzung Anakreons in reimlose Verse,* this became a kind of test case for his whole theory of translation :

"As far as the anacreontic odes are concerned an attempt was being made to establish whether a German equivalent could be found for the Greek metre, and the conciseness and gentleness of this poet could be expressed in German. To this end the same verse forms have been adopted as Anacreon used in each ode ! So that not one single extra line has been used for any ode. If we still knew the actual melodies this poet sang in days gone by, then these German experiments could be sung to exactly the same ones. So our countrymen can have some idea of the Ancients' taste."[20]

By these model versions of the anacreontic odes Gottsched was attempting to indicate the direction that German poetry might take with the assistance of metrical forms from other languages. It was left to others, in particular Pyra and Lange, Bodmer and Breitinger, to lead the discussion of metrical forms and their future development into wider channels, whereupon the whole question of whether verse should be rhymed or unrhymed became a particular bone of contention.

As Zeman has pointed out Götz and Uz assume a position between the battle fronts which were forming over these issues.[21] On the one hand Gottsched had presented them with the concrete models they could follow, on the other hand they could not totally approve of his excessively rationalistic approach, when what they wanted was a poetry of playfulness and delicate niceties, a poetry expressive of the pleasures of this life on earth. Nevertheless, from another point of view it was to Gottsched that they owed the awareness that the "natural" simplicity of language, the "naiveté" of the anacreontic odes *could* be reproduced in German. Unfortunately, the debt to Gottsched has since been easily forgotten, for naiveté and simplicity of poetic diction was something which most contemporary writers were seeking and finding not only in the Ancients like Anacreon, Catullus and Ovid but also in the Moderns like Marot, Scarron, Voiture and La Fontaine. German critics of later generations have generally condemned anacreontic poetry as contrived and unnatural, while the poets themselves thought they were being "simple" and "natural". What the critics have consciously or unconsciously been objecting to in part is not the lack of naturalness, but the fact that Götz and Uz insist on not taking things too seriously. They always maintain a certain ironic distance. *Scherz* is the aim of the game and later readers brought up on the "sincerity" and personal involvement of the Storm and Stress generation or the "outpourings of the heart" of the Romantic generation were loath to recognise that they were here being offered a different kind of simplicity and naturalness.

Certainly contemporary readers were in no doubt about the significance of this new translation of the *Anacreontea*. The translation and the new poetic diction it employed had an impact not only on the continuing spate of poetry and song in the anacreontic manner,[22] it was still being hotly discussed many generations later. The idea that Gleim, Uz and Götz and the anacreontic poetry they propagated were but a brief and passing phase in the development of German lyric poetry is yet another of the many fictions of German histories of literature. Lessing and Goethe have already been named as two major figures who clearly owed a great deal to anacreontic poetry and Goethe in particular made no secret of his continuing love for it throughout his life. In later times Mörike needed no great urging to continue the work of perfecting German versions of Anacreon and readily took over the task of producing yet another translation of a translation.[23] His version of *Anakreon und die sogenannten Anakreontischen Lieder* appeared with his commentary as late as 1864. In his edition of *Die Gedichte Anakreons und der Sappho Oden*, a facsimilie of the 1760 edition, Herbert Zeman includes in the appendix various versions of the second ode starting with Gottsched's translation which first pointed the way in the new direction. He also includes a version by Gleim and the edition itself has of course the Götz version though he is careful to mark the variants between this and the 1747 version. Mörike using an even later translation by Degen arrived at this version :

Naturgaben
Es gab Natur die Hörner
Dem Stier, dem Roß die Hufe;
Schnellfüßigkeit dem Hasen,
Dem Löwen Rachenzähne,
Den Fischen ihre Flossen,
Den Vögeln ihre Schwingen;
Und den Verstand dem Manne.
-So bliebe nichts den Frauen?
Was gab sie diesen?—Schönheit;
Statt aller unsrer Schilde,
Statt aller unsrer Lanzen!
Ja über Stahl und Feuer
Siegt jede, wenn sie schön ist.[24]

Anacreontic poetry had clearly a lot to offer. As in so many other spheres it was the great rationalist Gottsched who had shown the way but the poets who came after him proved remarkably successful in avoiding excessive rationalism and making a strong appeal to the emotions as well as to the head. As Blackall has put it, there is indeed feeling in this poetry but it appears not as passion but as sentiment.

> "*Witz* embodies refinement, a refinement of the reason; *Herz* is naked and direct expression of the emotions. Only when it has undergone similar refinement can it coexist with *Witz*. The word used to denote this refinement of feeling is *Empfindung*."[25]

Blackall is equally right when he singles out "Witz" and "Empfindung" as the hallmarks of civilisation. It is certainly true that

historians and critics of eighteenth century literature have failed in
the past to recognise the connection between these two cultures.
The culture of feeling was neither a later reaction against, nor a
simultaneous counter-current to, the culture of reason. "Both are
inherently connected as different aspects of the movement towards
sophistication in a country which needed it."[26] Sophistication by
itself may not sound very far removed from the artificiality of
which anacreontic verse is often accused but it all depends on the
contexts in which such concepts are seen. The aim was not artificiality as such but artifice leading to art. Lightness of touch was
all and as such certainly an acceptable alternative to the weighty
"Wucht" of the baroque poets. Clarity too was a welcome innova-
tion after seventeenth century obscurities, and formal precision a
necessary counter-force in a German literary tradition which was
always threatening (as with Klopstock) to fly off into formless
effusions.

The worst crime of anacreontic poetry in the eyes of many critics
was that it was undoubtedly popular and successful. Why this
should have been so baffled later generations but perhaps it was
simply because it was *not* serious. German literature has never
had any shortage of metaphysics, but has never reacted favourably
to lightness and sparkle whenever these qualities did appear.
Popular reaction, however, showed that there was a public for such
poetry. The eighteenth century was an age of morality and there
were many who did not take kindly to such outspoken advocacy
of the joys of this earth. At the same time there were enough people
who had had enough moralising forced upon them and were only
too glad of a little harmless frivolity. For there is no doubt the
anacreontic poetry was fairly harmless. As Blackall has pointed out
it was not so much the immorality of anacreontic poetry which
constituted its appeal. It was never really immoral and even the
language it employed indicates the extreme care which was taken
to ensure that there was never any offence against the canons of
good taste and discretion. Nor was there ever any suggestion that
the middle-class reader should apply the pressing invitations to
drink and pursue boys and girls in the course of his own daily
life. Instead by the device of the anacreontic mode the reader was
transported into a Golden Age of Innocence out of time in which
such pleasures were part of the simple life and therefore not in
any way in conflict with the moral dictates of the real.

There may have been much implicit wishful thinking but there
was certainly no need for any kind of guilt feelings. The reader
could enjoy the poems and the thought of the simple pleasures
portrayed, while the ironic detachment of their tone made it clear

that they committed no-one to anything just in the same way as the author was in no way totally committed to what he was saying :

> "Never draw conclusions about a writer's morals from his writings. You will be wrong; for they write only to demonstrate their wit even if they thereby place their virtue under suspicion. They do not characterise themselves as they really are, but as the manner of the poems demands and they accept most gladly that system which allows most opportunity for being witty. The mathematical proofs of the Wolffians enhance no poem, and the philosophy of Plato is not appropriate as the theme for frolicsome songs. I favour poets who praise the Goddess."[27]

Yet anacreontic poetry was never merely a game played with pastoral motifs from a classical age. That had been a feature of the seventeenth rather than the eighteenth century. Never before in the history of German literature had a classical poet been singled out as a model in this way. This (false) Anacreon was intended as something more than an artistic game. He was felt to be a model who could influence the character, life and morals of the age. At the same time the Ancient combined with the Modern in a characteristically eighteenth century manner and the artistic and other qualities of Anacreon fused with those of the later French poets.

Hence far from being out of date or anachronistic the anacreontic poetry of the 1740's was felt to be somehow very modern. The themes and motifs had, it is true, been to some extent the common literary property of Europe since time immemorial, but they were being dealt with in a modern manner. Nor was this modern manner by any means exclusively French. Earlier critics were unfortunately too ready to dismiss German anacreontic poetry as mere imitations without asking why German poets should have waited until the 1740's before incorporating material which had been to hand for so long. More recent examinations have shown that the German anacreontics were extremely selective about what they took over especially from the French and quickly developed their own particular German themes. The incontrovertible fact remains that anacreontic poetry was enormously popular in Germany from the 1740's on. It was not only welcome, it seems to have been an *essential* stage in the development of German poetry. Certainly Günther Müller was correct in realising that the irrestible attraction of anacreontica for all the leading poets of the age was a sure sign that something very deeply rooted in the aspirations of the time was finding expression thereby.

The process of seeking out an authority whether ancient, modern or both together was not a new one, but the tempo of change from translation and imitation to assimilation was now much quicker. The process whereby the new lyrical tone developed in German was indeed so fast and so successful that it was only too easy for later critics to underestimate the value of the anacreontic phase in this process. The new note resulted in the lyrical poetry of Goethe. He (like Mörike later in the nineteenth century) was never one to disparage the anacreontic vein, unfortunately others were not so kind or so perceptive.

Anacreontic poetry was then the product of a Germany at a certain point in its artistic development. It clearly belonged in the age of Enlightenment, at the same time it was equally a product of the Rococo culture of that age. That it should have appeared where it did, when it did, namely in Halle and Halberstadt has been fairly conclusively pinned down to the influence of Pietism of which this was one of the great centres. At the same time anacreontic poetry represented to a large extent a kind of "secularisation of pietism" in the sense that despite the often apparently erotic themes the same language of feelings and the soul is used. There is no simple contrast between anacreontic and sentimental or "empfindsame" lyrics at this time, for one of the great attractions of anacreontic poetry right from the start was the sensitivity with which emotional values were explored.

NOTES

1. See: *Some problems of translation in the eighteenth century* in Edna Purdie: *Studies in German literature of the eighteenth century.* London 1965 pp. 111–131;
T. Huber: *Studien zur Theorie des Übersetzens im Zeitalter der deutschen Aufklärung 1730–70* Meisenheim am Glan 1968;
Anneliese Senger: *Deutsche Übersetzungstheorie im 18. Jahrhundert (1734–46).* Bonn 1971.
2. G. Müller: *Geschichte des deutschen Liedes vom Zeitalter des Barocks bis zur Gegenwart.* München 1925 pp. 170–3.
3.   To the times now rich in song
        I recommend these trifles
        They have no desire to be immortal
        F.von Hagedorn: *Gedichte (An die Dichtkunst)* p. 5
4. See Hagedorn op. cit:
                Die Lust, vom Wahn mich zu entfernen
                Und deinem Flaccus abzulernen,
                Wie man durch echten Witz gefällt,

Die Lust, den Alten nachzustreben,
Ist mir im Zorn von dir gegeben,
Wenn nicht mein Wunsch das Ziel erhält.
The desire to avoid what is wrong
And to learn from your Horace
How to please with genuine wit,
The desire to emulate the Ancients,
Was given to me by you in rage
If my wish does not keep the goal.

5.
You poets full of youth
If in your merry leisure
You wish to sing anacreontically
Then sing of gentle vines,
Of rose-rich hedgerows,
Of spring and of dances,
Of friendship and of love,
But do not scorn the Goddess,
Nor yet Her servants,
Nor yet Her temple.
Earn, even while playful
The name of genuine sages.

Hagedorn op. cit. *Anakreon* p. 22.

6. See Gleim's *An Doris* in J. W. L. Gleim: *Gedichte* (Reclam) p. 88.

7.
O poetry, you who make life smooth!
How much grief you have assuaged,
How much enlarged life's pleasures!

Hagedorn op. cit. *An die Dichtkunst* p. 5.

8.
Teacher, whom the Goddess taught,
Teacher, whom Wisdom loved,
Teacher, who with light and life,
And with friendly means of proof
Established virtue, wit and truth,
Behold how strong your teachings are!

An Herrn Professor A. G. Baumgarten in Frankfurth in *Versuch in Scherzhaften Liedern* Zweeter Theil, Berlin 1745 hsg. Alfred Anger p. 94.

9.
To a Boy
Charming boy,
So like a girl,
It's you I'm after;
And you don't want to hear,
You don't want to know,
That you hold the reins,
As it were,
That steer my proud spirit.

J. N. Götz: *Die Gedichte Anakreons und der Sappho Oden* Faksimiliedruck nach der Ausgabe von 1760, hsg. H. Zeman p. 178.

10.
Onwards Brothers, Frederick our hero,
The enemy of sloth and delay,

Calls us yet again to battle
Where there's fame to be won.

From *Schlachtgesang bey Eröfnung des Feldzuges 1757* in J. W. I.
Gleim *Gedichte* (Reclam) p. 74.

11. Let the rich all dress
In silk and gold
And enjoy themselves to the full.
Christian brothers, I poor wretch
Do not envy them,
They can live a life of pleasure
Free of hardship for all I care!
Only may the Lord move their hearts
To give us work!

From *Zwey Lieder eines armen Arbeitsmannes* in Gleim *Gedichte*
(Reclam) p. 103.

12. Dumb guardians of dead treasures
Are only rich.
The man who keeps watch over no treasure,
Makes intelligent fun and sings and laughs
Is far better off than any mean king.

From Hagedorn *An die Freude, Gedichte* (Reclam) p. 14.

13.   *The Memory*
    First Part p. 113
Under the Linden Tree
Where she sat by my side
You can find
Flowers and broken grass,
Beside the wood, Dal de Dall,
Beautifully sang the nightingale!

Under the lime tree. On the heath
There the two of us had our bed.
There you may find both
Broken flowers and grass
Before the wood in a valley.
Tandaradei, brightly sang the nightingale.

Gleim *Gedichte* (Reclam) p. 118.

14. I would that the meadow might speak
Like a parrot into a mirror,
And that it would tell me truly
How much it enjoyed this year
When my lady picked flowers
From it, and her lovely (dainty) feet
Touched its green grass.

Minnesinger Hsg. F. H. v. d. Hagen 4 Bände Leipzig 1828 Ed. 1 112[a]
Götz: *Die Gedichte Anakreons und der Sappho Oden* hsg. H. Zeman
p. 58.

15. Claus Schuppenhauer: *Der Kampf um den Reim in der deutschen Literatur des 18. Jahrhunderts.* Bonn 1970.

16. See Samuel Gotthold Lang: *Horatzische Oden.* Faksimiliedruck nach der Ausgabe Halle 1747. Hsg mit einem Nachwort von Frank Jolles Metzler, Stuttgart 1971.

17.
Anacreon

Anacreon, my teacher,
Sings only of wine and love;
He annoints his beard with oils,
And sings of wine and love;
He crowns his head with roses,
And sings of wine and love;
He finds his lover in the garden
And sings of wine and love;
In his cups he is a king,
And sings of wine and love;
He plays with his gods,
He laughs with his friends,
Drives away care and worry,
Despises the rich rabble,
Refuses to praise heroes,
And sings of wine and love;
Is then his faithful pupil
Expected to sing of hatred and water?

In Gleim *Gedichte* (Reclam) p. 3 and in Alfred Anger ed. *Versuch in Scherzhaften Liedern* p. 5.

18.
To Mr. XXX

I drink, I love, I laugh,
While you, you heroes,
Rack your brains.
I drink, I love, I laugh,
While you, you tired miser,
Sweat with your labours.
I drink, I love, I laugh,
While pietists
Pray themselves to death,
I drink, I love, I laugh,
I sing merry songs
When priests swear at me.

Reclam p. 32; A. Anger p. 117.

19. W. Bennett: *German Verse in Classical Metres.* The Hague 1963 p. 80: The normal form was:

$$\ddot{}\cup{}^{\prime}\cup|\ddot{}\cup{}^{\prime}\cup$$

It originated from the Anacreontic verse $\cup\cup{}^-\cup{}^-\cup{}^-\cup$, which is found among the German Anacreontic poets, Götz, Gleim and others, following the example set by Gottsched who attempted a translation of Anacreon.

Goethe made use of the form in *Magisches Netz* and *Nektartropfen;*
also in *Musageten:*

Oft in tiefen Winternächten
Rief ich an die holden Musen:
"Keine Morgenröthe leuchtet
Und es will kein Tag erscheinen,
Aber bringt zur rechten Stunde
Mir der Lampe fromm Geleuchte."

Oft in deep winter nights
I called to the gracious muses:
"No dawn brightens the sky
And day refuses to break,
But bring me at the right hour
The lamp's pure glow."

20. H. Zeman op. cit. p. 41.
21. H. Zeman op. cit. p. 42.
22. See Goedeke Vol. IV/I pp. 51–7.
"Zur Modedichtung wurde diese Art der Lyrik durch die hallischen
Freunde Gleim, Uz, Götz, denen eine zahllose Schar jüngerer Dichter
folgte ..." Goedeke then lists 58 authors of anacreontica and various
anonymous works.
23. See *Mörike Kommentar zu sämtlichen Werken* von Helga Unger.
München 1970 pp. 156–160 (Anakreon und die sogenannten anakreontischen Lieder).

24.   *Nature's Gifts*
Nature gave the steer horns,
The steed hooves,
The hare fleetness of foot,
The lion sharp teeth,
The fish their fins,
The birds their wings,
And man his reason.
—So there was nothing left for women?
What did it give them?—Beauty,
Instead of all our shields,
Instead of all our lances!
Truly, any woman can conquer
Steel and Fire when she is beautiful.

Mörikes Werke hsg. Harry Maync 3 Bände. Bibliographisches Institut,
Leipzig n.d. p. 497.
25. E. A. Blackall: *The Emergence of German as a literary language*
p. 390.
26. Blackall op. cit. p. 391.
27. From the playful introduction to *Versuch in Scherzhaften Liedern*
Zweeter Theil. Hsg. A. Anger p. 71.

SELECT BIBLIOGRAPHY

Anacreontic Poetry

Alfred Anger — *Literarisches Rokoko.* Stuttgart 1962.

Alfred Anger — *Deutsche Rokokodichtung. Ein Forschungsbericht.* In *DVj Schr.* 36 Jg., 1962, I. Tl.: S 430–479, II Tl. S. 614–648. This chapter leans most heavily on pp. 614–626 i.e., Anakreontik. Rokokolyrik.

Fr. Ausfeld — *Die deutsche anakreontische Dichtung des 18. Jhts. Ihre Beziehungen zur französischen und antiken Lyrik.* Straßburg 1907.

Eric A. Blackall — *The Emergence of German as a literary language.* C.U.P. 1959.

Paul Böckmann — *Formgeschichte der deutschen Dichtung.* Hamburg 1949.

John Lees — *The Anacreontic Poetry of Germany in the eighteenth century, its relation to French and German Poetry.* Aberdeen 1911.

Texts

Anakreontiker und preußisch-patriotische Lyriker. Hsg. Franz Muncker. Stuttgart 1893 (Deutsche Nationalliteratur Bd. 45).

J. W. L. Gleim — *Gedichte.* Hsg. Jürgen Stenzel (Reclam Universal Bibliothek Nr. 2138/39).

J. W. L. Gleim — *Versuch in Scherzhaften Liedern und Lieder* kritisch hsg. Alfred Anger. Tübingen 1964.

J. N. Götz — *Die Gedichte Anakreons und der Sappho Oden.* Faksimiledruck nach der Ausgabe von 1760. Mit einem Nachwort von Herbert Zeman. Metzler 1970.

J. C. Gottsched — *Ausgewählte Werke.* Hsg. Joachim Birke (Ausgaben Deutschen Literatur des XV. bis XVIII Jahrhunderts) Berlin 1968. Bd.1 *Gedichte und Gedichtübertragungen.*

F. V. Hagedorn — *Gedichte.* Hsg. A. Anger (Reclam Nr. 1321–3)

J. P. Uz — *Sämtliche Poetische Werke.* Hsg. August Sauer. Stuttgart 1890 (Deutsche Litteraturdenkmale des 18. und 19. Jahrhunderts, Bd. 33–8). Modern Reprint available.

Friedrich von Hagedorn

Friedrich von Hagedorn

by BRIAN KEITH-SMITH

Friedrich von Hagedorn was born on April 23, 1708 in Hamburg, which apart from his student days at Jena and two years in England was to be his home for the rest of his life. Son of a senior representative of Denmark, of a diplomat and man of letters, he was brought up in the centre of one of the most progressive social environments of the time. Encouraged to make full use of his father's library of French books and to write from early days, he was also taught by the best tutors, and until his father suddenly died in 1722 seemed to have an assured future. In 1723 he entered the Akademisches Gymnasium where he acquired a lifelong taste for several classical Latin writers. In 1726 he went to study law at Jena, but concentrated on languages and literature whenever he was not leading a riotous student life. At the end of 1727 he had to leave his studies incomplete and return to Hamburg to live apart from his mother and try to make his way as a poet and with occasional teaching posts. In 1729 he was taken on as private secretary to the Danish Envoy in London where he took full advantage of the opportunity to study the contemporary English literature and meet its authors. In two years he completely reeducated himself so that he became as he put it "half English". His hopes on return to Hamburg for a further assignment in Denmark came to nothing, and he took up posts as private tutor. In 1732 his mother died, and he went to Halle to visit his younger brother Christian Ludwig the artist and later Director General of the Saxon Art Academies and Royal art collections. A year later Friedrich obtained the post of Secretary to the "English Court" in Hamburg, headquarters of an old trading company. This brought him daily work, free accommodation, also direct access to the best social circles in Hamburg and close contact with British affairs. He married the daughter of an English tailor, said to have been neither beautiful nor rich, although he hoped her dowry would have cleared off his debts. Despite his extravagant living, enjoyment of endless picnics, boat-trips, regular club meetings and frequent banquets and dinner parties, she apparently cared devotedly for him and nursed him through attacks of gout, which eventually after weeks of pain and distress brought him to his death from dropsy in 1754.

STUDENTS of German literature find Hagedorn sandwiched traditionally with other eighteenth-century writers at the beginning of a course on the classical age "somewhere between the 'Aufklärung' and Goethe". Together with Klopstock

149

and Haller, Gleim and Brockes he is mentioned all too often as a forerunner of the classical tradition, dimly related somehow to Lessing ("the founder of modern German literature")—perhaps a distant great uncle ("father of the Anacreontics"), a gouty old reveller staunchly conservative in provincial Hamburg, a name to be dropped at the start of an examination answer on Goethe's lyrical poetry, a poet doomed to be represented by a few short pieces in the most representative anthologies.

Hagedorn's contemporaries, however, held him in great esteem. Gellert, Ebert, Giseke, J. E. Schlegel, Haller, Klopstock, Nicolai, Heinse, Zachariä and Uz all praised his poetry or his character. Lessing, aged 17, described him as "the greatest poet of our times", an opinion he never withdrew publicly. Hamann admired the way in which Hagedorn tempered natural depth of feeling and good taste into valid harmonious expression. Herder saw in his moral tales and epigrams the fruit of a great native tradition. Goethe as a young man hoped he would be honoured one day and named together with Hagedorn and other great poets, and he was still quoting Hagedorn in 1831 only a few months before his death. Yet already in 1792 Gleim was deploring the passing out of fashion of the song praising virtue and the short-lived ideals of the Anacreontic tradition in his and in Hagedorn's poetry. Bodmer too, despite the extensive correspondence and respect he shared with Hagedorn, was honest enough to comment that Hagedorn's work was gradually losing favour. Used for entertainment at ladies' parties in the 1790's, Hagedorn's poetry was to be all but forgotten by the Romantics, and hailed by the literary critics of the nineteenthy century in general as functionally important for its influence on the improvement of good taste in eighteenth century Germany. From Hermann Hettner onwards Hagedorn was seen as the forerunner of a new age of polite behaviour based on an ideal of social morality alongside and not necessarily dependent on a religious ethic. An understanding of the place of his poetry as a renewal of pre-Baroque folk poetry and of a simplicity reaching back to the Minnesänger only came at the end of the century in a short introduction to an edition by August Sauer. Hagedorn as a popular poet, as a poet steeped in literary traditions from different ages and peoples, and as one of the chief poetic explorers of the implications of "Aufklärung attitudes"—these have become recognised approaches in monographs on him. His achievements have been praised for several reasons : as a revealer of taste as a natural culture, as a creator of a new light harmonious language from which Goethe and others were to draw so much, as an incorporator of the irrational in effective closed poetic forms, as the leading adaptor of all that was best in French court poetry to German middle-class life, as the leading singer to joy after a period of depression and war, as the founder of a cult of friendship that would play such an influential part in literary and social life in the closing years of the eighteenth century, as an important pointer to the way from a religiously based cultural life to a secular one, as the only consistently natural-sounding writer in an age of playful conceit and artificiality, and as the essential transitional figure in German literature during the eighteenth century.

To understand Hagedorn as a turning-point limits our understanding of Hagedorn as a personality. Admirable though the historical approach may be to place such a writer in perspective, Alfred Anger's description of him as the first singer of the new optimistic love of life developed out of a release of enjoyment based on Shaftesbury's doctrine of "moral grace", and his explanation of his popularity due to the flatness and dryness of early "Aufklärung" poetry suggest that Hagedorn's value is at best that of a reaction against a stultifying norm in thought and literature or as a glimpse of better things to come. It is part of the literary historian's functions to look for transitional figures between the great crises or peaks in the development of thought and culture both on a national and international scale. German literature in particular seems to offer great temptations to do this. Yet it takes most students little time to realise that neither the literary historical approach nor that of the interpretation of the individual work of art is entirely satisfactory as a mode of value judgement. The action and reaction theory, and for German literature in particular the general movement versus genius theory of "literary development" can lead to a distortion of focus as soon as an individual man's work overall is under scrutiny. The former has tended to denigrate Hagedorn, the latter can lead easily to the assumption that because he can be read in so many different ways (some of which have already been listed) he might perhaps have been an erratic genius with different stages and emphases within his own character and creations. A more accurate interpretation of his personality and of his products might be achieved by an examination of the immediate influence of his background and of the apparent contradictions that appear thereby.

Hamburg during Hagedorn's life was exceptional in many ways. It had not suffered from the ravages of the Thirty Years War, and thanks mainly to its excellent inland connections had become one of the leading cities in eighteenth century Europe. With direct and complex business relations with England, Holland and Denmark, it also enjoyed an international status and outlook more important for Germany than even perhaps Bordeaux for France. For alongside its commercial activity grew a flourishing cultural life including the first German opera house from 1678, several of the first moral weeklies such as *Der Vernünfftler* (1713–4) and *Der Patriot* (1724–6) based on the English *Tatler*, *Spectator* and *Guardian* and read throughout Germany, the re-establishment of literary societies, and a vigorous if less important musical life. The English style of life, more democratic and open-minded than in many of the other German towns with their more or less benevolent despots, turned Hamburg into a haven for political refugees and a birthplace for progressive ideas. A serious-minded search for honest civic values and a personal code of conduct aimed at helping others rather than enjoying oneself was conducted by Hamburg societies whose confidence suggests the spirit of social experiment rather than rigid adherence to the past or to traditions from other lands. French manners were ridiculed for their excesses, British poise adopted for its naturalness. The aesthetic debates to come about rules and individual expression were foreshadowed by the self-confidence and willingness to learn of the Hamburg citizen. Typical of the current attitude are the two satirical letters published in 1726 by Hagedorn in *Der Patriot* which already show a keen eye for ridicule and a precocious understand of the relationship between authentic self-expression and moral education. The second letter written in an impossibly over-laden Frenchified style by a self-styled "Gentilhomme" comes to the heart of the matter in two phrases :

"Frankreich hat nicht mich, und ich nicht Frankreich gesehen . . . ja ich halte ein REVERENCE besser, als die schönste BIBLIOTHEQUE."[1]

Culture and wisdom already implied direct personal discovery for Hagedorn; inherited tradition could only have significance for him if it confirmed and effectively expressed truths gauged by his own experiences. Such an openness to life marks Hagedorn's character and informs most of his writings. It might be seen fitting, then, that an openness to what Hagedorn actually said and how he said it rather than attention to the forces against which he may be said to have reacted, would lead to an interpretation at once unpatterned by and devoid of potentially distorting comparisons.

Apart from some early occasional poems that his father had printed in a few copies as broadsheets for family friends, also some schoolboy attempts in Italian and French, Hagedorn's first significant publication was entitled *Über die menschliche Seele* for the periodical edited by the uncle of J. G. Hamann : *Die Matrone* in the 48th number. This ended on a suitably repentant note :

Weil meine Seel' ein Werk, o Gott, von deiner Hand,
So laß auch dir zum Ruhm den Willen und Verstand
Sich nicht von ihrem Zweck, und nie von dir entfernen,
Und mich bei ihrem Werth, und ihrer Eigenschaft,
O Schöpfer, immer deine Kraft
An meinen Kräften kennen lernen!
Dein Wille heil'ge meinen Willen,
Und deine Weisheit sey stets der Gedanken Licht,
So fürcht' ich Fehl' und Irrthum nicht,
So kann das Gute nur mit Wunsch und Sehnsucht stillen![2]

From another poem written at this time came the later *Schreiben an einen Freund* as an introduction to his moral poems, where an essential point is made in reference to Pope and which clearly invites a critical approach to Hagedorn not as an imitator but as a recreator :

"Aber der Character dieses vortrefflichen Poeten ist gewiß nicht in der gewöhnlichen Nachahmung zu suchen. Keiner ist reicher an eigenen, neuen Gedanken, glücklicher im Ausdruck, edler in Gesinnungen. Sogar seine Nachahmungen aus dem Horaz sind meisterhafte, freye Originale."[3]

Some of the early poems, including satires in the style of Canitz, festival poems modelled on Günther and König, the first version of *Der Wein* still overladen with ornamental features in the style of Opitz's *Lobgesang Bacchi,* and a love poem with neither feeling nor originality, were collected together in 1729 in *Versuch einiger Gedichte, oder auserlesene Proben poetischer Nebenstunden.* Hagedorn was later to regret this necessary early stage in his development as a poet and hope he would not be judged by it. Already he mentioned the need to continue all the time with improvements to first versions of poems. All unnecessary ornament and rhetoric he wished to remove, and overhasty eagerness to publish he hoped to repress. There is no sign in these of the light touch and inner warmth of his later lyrics perhaps precisely because they are too conscious imitations of the traditions of Günther and others. With a few major exceptions Hagedorn may be said to have been held back by over-attention to traditional forces, held back from the full expression of his own poetic voice.

Hagedorn's two years in England were in themselves no more than an interlude, but the tastes he developed there were to play a central part in his life and work and were to have a surprisingly

widespread influence on other German writers who were in correspondence with him. He took full advantage of reading such writers
as Pope, Prior, Gay, Addison, Steele, Thomson, Shaftesbury and
many others. After his return Hagedorn became a leading importer
of the most recent English books, and his knowledge of English
literature was respected and used by such writers as Bodmer and
Ebert.

It would be misleading to suggest that Hagedorn's debt to
England was solely a literary one; rather than attempting to list
obvious direct borrowings or to construct possibly false impressions
from the scanty evidence of his stay in London, it is customary to
compare the content and form of his pre-London writings with
those he wrote after his return, and from this to suggest that all
the new elements stem from direct English influence. What Hagedorn learnt in England was a natural development of features in
his own character and Hamburg background; put in a phrase
from Addison he learnt that "the whole man must move at once".
Personal freedom and a love of personally selected social life,
freedom to find and express oneself through consideration of and
personal application to literary models—such were the leading
emphases he developed in his life and works on his return to
Hamburg. In the introduction to his *Moralische Gedichte* he states
the case for kinship of spirit with other writers rather than slavish
imitation of their works:

"Die schönste Übereinstimmung zwischen zwei Dichtern beruhet
so wenig auf Worten, als die edelste Freundschaft. Geist und
Herz sind in den besten Alten und Neuen die lebendigen, oder
vielmehr die einzigen Quellen des glücklichen Ausdrucks gewesen.
Er leidet zum öftern unter dem Joche einer blinden Folge und
kümmerlichen Knechtschaft. Man sollte nachahmen, wie Boileau
und Lafontaine nachgeahmt haben. Jener pflegte davon zu sagen :
Cela ne s'appele pas imiter; c'est jouter contre son original."[4]

When we turn to Hagedorn's later writings it is clear that he took
this very much to heart and realised that the pithy epigrammatic
wit, the cheerful ironic tone of English moral poetry, and the love
of solitude and personal reflection away from the demands of town
society expressed in contemporary English literature corresponded
to essential parts of his own character and situation. Hagedorn's
introduction of the moral poem into German literature together with
the device of the heroic couplet, the ease with which he transposed
the brevity and antithetical style of Pope's writing in particular,
and the essentially Deistic attitudes which he expressed in a personal
and optimistic manner reveal him as a revolutionary force in Ger-

man literature. Yet he would have been the last to have wanted such a role. Hagedorn, like Pope, was no extremist but a staunch believer in the value of virtue as a harbinger of happiness, peace and good health. This Hagedorn did not see as a moral duty but as a challenge to each individual. To suggest that as a central aim in life one could make oneself into the person of one's choice, that each man could be the artist of his own life, was one of the first signs of the emancipation of the individual along secularised paths before one of the culminations of this in Goethe's writings and life. Hagedorn's visit to England was however only one of the liberating forces in his life. Another was the way of thought of his own brother whose independence in taste and aesthetic theory was later to find expression in his *Betrachtungen über Malerei* (1762). In this reason and taste are claimed to have equal importance for the appreciation of a work of art. Art for Christian Ludwig had the object of increasing joy in living, a theory put into practice by his brother in his writings. Most important for both was the belief that a study of both nature and classical art and life are necessary foundations to the creation of individual art. Where nature taught correct choice of colour, classical art brought an understanding of the importance of line.

The mastery of Hagedorn's poetic language is already evident in 1732 with his translation of Ranchin's triolet :

> Le premier jour du mois de Mai
> Fut le plus beau jour de ma vie.
> Le beau dessein que je formai
> Le premier jour du mois de Mai !
> Je vous vis & je vous aimai.
> Si ce dessein vous plut, Silvie,
> Le premier jour du mois de Mai
> Fut le plus beau jour de ma vie.

Hagedorn in a note to this quotes Ménage who called this "un Triolet si joli qu'on peut l'apeller le Roi des Triolets" and another writer who admires its simplicity, naivety and tenderness. Its charm depends on "tant de Naturel au milieu de tant de difficultés". His own version catches just those qualities, and shows a terseness, lightness and ease of syntax missing in German poetry since some of the early Minnelieder of the twelfth and thirteenth centuries :

> Der erste Tag im Monat May
> Ist mir der glücklichste von allen.
> Dich sah ich, und gestand dir frey,
> Den ersten Tag im Monat May,

Daß dir mein Herz ergeben sey.
Wenn mein Geständniß dir gefallen;
So ist der erste Tag im May
Für mich der glücklichste von allen.[5]

In Hagedorn's first book of fables published in 1738 these poems,
the first he had published for six years, announce almost a different
poet from the author of the *Versuch einiger Gedichte*. . . . There
is a marked enjoyment in telling a tale, a clear ease of presentation
and adaptation from older models in a form that was relatively
new to German. For the first time in his writings a clear moral
didactic purpose shows through. A note of Socratic irony creeps
in, and although much is unashamedly borrowed and the debt
acknowledged, the process of adaptation is raised to the level of
assimilation of the models to his own taste and manner. A fine
example of this is *Das Hühnchen und der Diamant*:

Ein verhungert Hühnchen fand
Einen feinen Diamant,
Und verscharrt' ihn in den Sand.

Mögte doch, mich zu erfreun,
Sprach es, dieser schöne Stein
Nur ein Weizenkörnchen seyn!

Unglückselger Ueberfluß,
Wo der nöthigste Genuß
Unsern Schätzen fehlen muß![6]

The indiscriminate annoyance of the hen is caught in an almost
epigrammatic form. La Fontaine's original is far more studied, a
narrative in miniature rather than a well-turned thought:

Un jour un coq détourna
Une perle, qu'il donna
Au beau premier lapidaire.
'Je la crois fine, dit-il,
Mais le moindre grain de mil
Seroit bien mieux mon affaire.'

Un ignorant hérita
D'un manuscrit, qu'il porta
Chez son voisin le libraire.
"Je crois, dit-il, qu'il est bon;
Mais le moindre ducaton
Seroit bien mieux mon affaire."

Hagedorn's hen goes hungry—concentration on the essential detail for its own sake rather than as an example or symbol for something else is one of the attractive features of his fables. The art in these often lies hidden; what is left out is often more important or persuasive than what is expressed. Yet on occasion, as in *Der Wolf und der Hund,* Hagedorn adds useful motivation missing in all the models (Phaedrus, Hugo von Trymberg and La Fontaine). One special feature of his fables results from Hagedorn's dislike of giving too much wisdom in them to the animal figures, as this would distort reality and hence detract from their likely credibility. Not all use the device of animal figures directly, indeed Breitinger in his *Critische Dichtkunst*[7] singled out for praise the adaptation of the Book of II Samuel Chapter twelve in *Das geraubte Schäfgen* by which the judgement of the Lord is turned into impartial self-condemnation. What in the Old Testament appears as just punishment to a somewhat naive David now becomes an appeal to commonsense through David's example. *Wallraff und Traugott* has almost a Goethean cadence. Sometimes Hagedorn can add to traditional fables general mottoes of his own as in *Philippus, König in Macedonien, und Aster* at the beginning, and in *Ben Haly* (one of a series with an oriental setting) at the end. Some are interspersed with personal statements that seem to crystallise Hagedorn's own beliefs and desires; thus in *Apollo, ein Hirte* the direct first person form is used and an idyll of contentment is evoked. At times, as in *Wein und Liebe,* a precarious balance is sought as a result of disappointment, usually expressed in praise of wine and in defiance of the illusion of women.

But by far the most important and successful poem in this first collection of fables is the well known *Johann, der Seifensieder.* E. K. Grotegut has pointed out how Hagedorn relied mainly on La Fontaine's *Le Savetier et le Financier* out of a whole list of traditional sources. Hagedorn has successfully lightened the whole story with "Witz" and by spending no unnecessary time on transitional details from one scene to the next. The whole poem comes alive because Hagedorn has learnt how to make use of dramatic asides by the characters which tie the scenes together and do not prejudge the issue. Each character has far more of a personal individuality because Hagedorn has different aims from La Fontaine. Where La Fontaine explains his moral purpose, Hagedorn concentrates on the narrative itself thereby allowing the moral to stand out clearly through the context. Johann is depicted with care and sympathy and is designed to have immediate appeal on a social as well as intellectual level. His schooling is that of life which has taught him to remain open to experience. Yet this innocence leads Johann to believe that happiness comes through objects external to himself. He is even led to boast and is suitably mocked for this. Johann develops in fact from being a wise man into a fool and thereby learns his way to freedom and happiness. Where La Fontaine produced a neat drawing-room story, Hagedorn creates a living character and fate, individual yet exemplary, a poem that in its precision and form is a minor masterpiece.

The first of the major moral poems : *Der Gelehrte* was written in 1740 and published first with some ten others separately in quarto format for Hagedorn's friends, only later being included in his *Sämtliche Werke*. *Der Gelehrte* is a fine ironic piece that manages to avoid caricature yet portrays in 120 lines the quiet joys of a scholar as opposed to the more strident life of the business and political world. As with so many of Hagedorn's poems it is written as a "captatio benevolentiae" to his own way of life. The companion poem to this is *Der Weise* originally written in 1729 but rewritten in 1741. It includes fulsome praise for England and the particular freedoms enjoyed there. For Hagedorn the wise man is he who unites all virtues in his heart and way of life. He faces up to reality and avoids all forms of illusion, thus he must be courageous and resilient. Nature, because it is true and does not follow false values, is his inspiration. To nature and to the great works of art he responds with his heart, for to respond merely with reason would be to restrict both his experience and his scope for development. Out of a moral precept comes the basis for an aesthetic more and more removed from the teachings of the "Aufklärung". A step is taken towards restraint of the passions, but not by the intellect, rather by a sense of proportion whose mentors are a natural law and independence of spirit. The wise man achieves balance and harmony by getting to know himself and by learning as consciously and objectively as possible the limitations and possibilities of his own spirit. The main freedom Hagedorn prized, taking the British as examples, is freedom from all superfluous needs. Through such poems as *Die Glückseligkeit* (1743), *Schreiben an einen Freund* (1747) and *Die Freundschaft* (1748) the true reflective Hagedorn expresses himself. Such lines as :

> Es stamt die Freundschaft nicht aus Noth und Eifersucht :
> Sie ist der Weisheit Kind, der reifen Kenntniß Frucht,
> Ein Werk der besten Wahl, und kann nur die verbinden,
> Die in der Seelen Reiz die grösste Schönheit finden[8]

suggest a writer who could see through and thus enjoy freedom of selectivity in his life. Only perfection and not similarity or temporary satisfaction are the ideals that Hagedorn demanded of himself and of his friends. Such perfectionism is to be seen in his repeated rewriting of poems, in his critical detachment from any partisan views (most obvious in his public stance in the Gottsched-Bodmer literary feud), in his frequent allusions to the insufficiency of translations (especially from the English), in his positive yet restrained self-confidence, and even in the unrestrained epicureanism of his later years.

However Hagedorn's moral poems are in no sense systematically planned expositions of a carefully prepared and defined ethical standpoint. The principles that they praise have to be sought out by implication, or by way of a number of digressions, or deduced by application of commonsense. Often quite banal situations are dressed up as allegories in a highly subjective manner. Nevertheless they convince because of the light-heartedness and optimism resulting from the grace and ease of the measure of the poetic lines. They have been called aptly "eine Rhapsodie edler Gedanken";[9] and it is their urbane sense of elegant and positive detachment from the sufferings of life, in brief their healthy self-critical satiric humour that justifies Hagedorn's title of "the German Horace". All longing for material prosperity and political power is shown as vain compared with the eudaemonistic culture of personal qualities, private friendships, and full enjoyment of the immediate surroundings. Nobility of character is to include such virtues as contentedness, simplicity of motive, lack of self-interest, repose, a health-giving balance between moments of solitude and social festivities, and a conscious formation of the value of living. Happiness for Hagedorn is the product of each individual's heart, not the result of chance or circumstance. This is no quietist or self-satisfied quality, but the natural style of a "gesetzter Geist".[10] For lack of knowledge is the cause of many ills :

> Stolz, Aberglaube, Zorn, Bewundrung, Geiz und Neid
> Sind alles, was sie sind, nur durch Unwissenheit.[11]

The direct achievement of a "gesetzter Geist" is the necessary stage to prepare for friendship.

It is the application of this attitude and the use of it to deliberately justify the "Dichter" that allow us to understand Hagedorn as a poet with a social purpose beyond that of entertaining himself and his chosen friends. In the two sections of *Horaz* (1751) the exemplary mission of the poet is directly referred to :

> Der ist beglückt, der seyn darf was er ist,
> Der Bahn und Ziel nach eignen Augen misst,

> Nie sklavisch folgt, oft selbst die Wege weiset,
> Ununtersucht nichts tadelt und nichts preiset,
> Und, wenn sein Witz zum Dichter ihn bestimmt,
> Natur und Zeit zu seinen Führern nimmt.[12]

And even clearer :

> Ein Dichter lehrt das menschliche Geschlecht
> Der Tugend Reiz und ihrer Thaten Recht.
> Ein Dichter stellt für Zeiten, die entstehen,
> Exempel dar, den Mustern nachzugehen,
> Erleichtert oft des Armen Last und Hohn,
> Und mäßiget des Kranken Klageton.
> Die den Homer, wie du, mit Einsicht lesen,
> Sehn, daß schon er ein Menschenfreund gewesen.[13]

Hagedorn praises Horace because in reading his works he has learnt to hate prejudice, has illuminated his wit and lightened his heart. Horace, that is, had a social, technical and personal influence on him. Hagedorn does not ask for fame, but to be enjoyed as he enjoyed Horace :

> Wann werd ich einst, in unbelauschter Ruh,
> Nicht so berühmt; nur so vergnügt, wie du?[14]

Hagedorn as "Father of the Anacreontics" is a misnomer. His three poems most obviously imitating Anacreon (*Anacreon, Chloris* and *Der Traum*) were published in 1747, a year later than the first edition of Götz's Anacreon and three years after the first appearance of Gleim's *Versuch in scherzhaften Liedern*. Herbert Zeman in his commentary on his edition of Götz's *Die Gedichte Anakreons und der Sappho Oden* (Deutsche Neudrucke 1970) sketches the fifteenth, sixteenth and seventeenth century interest in Anacreon, and refers to several German adaptations before Götz. Hagedorn's role is not found worthy of more than a passing mention. And Gleim (called by Uz the "German Anacreon") could only be interested in one of Hagedorn's odes—*Anacreon*—according to Hagedorn's letter to Gleim of May 12, 1747. Although several minor poets were to imitate Hagedorn's occasional pastoral style and hence encourage an image of a poet praising only wine women and song, Hagedorn's few poems directly in the Anacreontic style were themselves modish imitations of a well established tradition. Thus in the *Vorbericht* to his *Oden und Lieder* Hagedorn shows detailed knowledge of French and Italian writers, but also a critical detachment from the artifices of French rhyme schemes (a point of view also frequently expressed in his letters), an understanding of the limitations of much Petrarchan style ("zu pindarisch, zu voller

Figuren, zu sinnreich, auch zu lang"),[15] and a realisation thanks
to Bodmer's *Critische Briefe* that the German native traditions of
the thirteenth century and earlier might be far more useful to him
than French and Italian models. Hagedorn is quite prepared to look
not only to England, but also to Slavonic and Russian traditional
songs for his inspiration. He claims he knew and understood
Anacreon's poetry well; typically he commented on Gleim's *Versuch
in scherzhaften Liedern* in a letter to Bodmer of April 13, 1744
that they were "natürlich, feurig, schalkhaft, spielend, mit einem
Worte fast alle anakreontisch".[16] He appreciated the dangers of
excess in the Anacreontic way of life—thus the poem *An Celsus,
einen jungen anacreontischen Dichter*:

> Erheb und zeige dich dem deutschen Vaterlande!
> Doch, sollen itzt noch Kuß und Wein
> Der Inhalt deiner Töne seyn;
> So singe beyder Lob nicht zu der Sitten Schande!
> Wie dir Anacreon gefällt,
> So heisse stets der klugen Welt
> Ein Weiser, wie er hieß, in jeglichem Verstande!
> Auch folg einst einem Rath, der weder eilt noch irrt,
> Sey nicht der Grille gleich, die bis zum Tode schwirrt![17]

Hagedorn's gift to the German Anacreontic poets was not so
much a series of poems directly in the Anacreontic style but,
through a long note to *An Celsus* and through the poem *Anacreon,*
a reinterpretation of Anacreon as a philosopher of life, as a man of
wisdom. That they were to make use of his different styles and
learn from the new found flexibility of the German language to
express traditional Anacreontic themes was not his prime intention.

In one of his technically most successful and most sprightly odes:
An die Freude the true Hagedorn is seen at his best, for in it
there are both the light-hearted, almost jubilant tone of a secular
Te Deum laudamus and the serious realisation of the educative
force of joy. It is a paean to friendship and love, but the choice of
language immediately suggests the more serious lessons of the moral
poems. Nobility, not a trifling engagement with the everyday,
comes from joy. Further to this, poetry itself stems from such joy—
the poem is the naive natural outcome of contemplation of joy and
is a defiant answer to the cynics and hypocrites:

> Freude, Göttinn edler Herzen!
>   Höre mich.
> Laß die Lieder, die hier schallen,
> Dich vergrossern, dir gefallen:
> Was hier tönet, tönt durch dich.

Muntre Schwester süsser Liebe!
     Himmelskind!
Kraft der Seelen! Halbes Leben!
Ach! was kann das Glück uns geben,
Wenn man dich nicht auch gewinnt?

Stumme Hüter todter Schätze
     Sind nur reich.
Dem, der keinen Schatz bewachet,
Sinnreich scherzt und singt und lachet,
Ist kein karger König gleich.

Gieb den Kennern, die dich ehren,
     Neuen Muth,
Neuen Scherz den regen Zungen,
Neue Fertigkeit den Jungen,
Und den alten neues Blut.

Du erheiterst, holde Freude!
     Die Vernunft.
Flieh, auf ewig, die Gesichter
Aller finstern Splitterrichter
Und die ganze Heuchlerzunft![18]

Even in the traditional occasional poems written in pastoral style with all the trappings of a well-worn tradition (lovers with names such as Phyllis and Doris set in a landscape with eagles and doves hovering over the hidden rose-bedecked corners of the arbour) Hagedorn makes use of his connoisseur's experience to show up different levels of love. Naive in thought-content such poems as *Die alte und die neue Liebe* and *Die Wunder der Liebe* may be, but the proverbial tone of their platitudes somehow lifts them above much similar writing of the time. As for the wine poems, they capture some of the excitement and vivacity to be found at their best in the poems of the fourteenth century Persian writer Hafis. A few, such as *Das Heidelberger Faß*, are no more than stylised drinking songs overladen with cliché and enthusiastic sentimentalism. Wine as the sap of life, the releaser of inhibitions and visionary insights into a Leibnizian universe of harmony inhabited by Dionysiac monads in a great primitive orgy—such is the expression of Hagedorn's more self-indulgent moments. Yet, and perhaps significantly, he claimed that such visions stuck in his throat so that he had just to drink and remain silent. Hagedorn's imagery was limited in range and precise definition, as will be shown by a study of his debt to earlier writers, especially the classical ones. Most of his odes and songs are direct apostrophes and depend for their effect on their insistent rhythms and use of refrain and simple rhyme schemes rather than on carefully selected and polished imagery. Many contain a narrative third person framework giving the usually pastoral setting to a direct conversation between two or more lovers and ending with a general solution. The challenge or offer thus presented suggests that the scene might be exemplary or at least typical of the society who would read the poem. Sometimes, as for example in *Gränzen der Pflicht,* a formula is found around which to build a set of conundrums and answers about life—a form of social game in which human virtues and failings attain the dignity of individual characters. An artifical semi-dramatic situation is constructed with abstracts in order to enliven or somewhat heavily point up a moral or truth about human life. Often, as in *Der Jüngling,* an almost too romantic situation is developed, but emotions are carefully held in check, so that a conscious retention of pleasure can be practiced without loss of individual personality. Alongside the flirtatious superficial relationship Hagedorn also sang the more lasting and formative awakening effects of directly felt love. Hagedorn's depiction of love rarely surpasses an idealisation of a young girl whose beauty offers youth, freshness and light-hearted pleasure. His understanding of love, as opposed to friendship, is summed up in suitable simplicity in the lines of *An die Liebe* :

> Tochter der Natur,
> Holde Liebe!
> Uns vergnügen nur
> Deine Triebe.
> Gunst und Gegengunst
> Geben allen
> Die beglückte Kunst
> Zu gefallen.[19]

There is an ironic playfulness both delicate and yet full-blooded artfully lurking behind the apparent simplicity of what looks at first sight and taken on its own as trite and of no great consequence. Love only gives pleasure in itself, not it would seem in its consequences. Such pleasure if equally shared leads into an art of living. And—clearly under the influence of the precepts of the "Aufklärung"—love in Hagedorn's poems must be held in bounds and shared for it to be creative. Not only does art have a purpose but love too, thus in *Nutzen der Zärtlichkeit* in which, as with many other poems, infidelity is revealed as a destructive, demoralising force. For this reason perhaps he distinguished between love and friendship in the little poem *Die Freundschaft* :

> Du Mutter holder Triebe!
> O Freundschaft! dir zur Ehre,
> Dir, Freundschaft, nicht der Liebe,
> Erschallen unsre Chöre,
> Und Phyllis stimmt mit ein :
> Doch sollte das Entzücken
> Von Phyllis Ton und Blicken
> Nichts mehr als Freundschaft seyn?[20]

In all his poems, even those uttering full praise for the glories of nature, love, friendship or wine, there is a reflective element. In none of them is the poetic self so caught up by the exuberance of the moment it describes to be fully suffused in the poem. The detachment of wit, an epicurean and almost scholarly refusal to complete commitment, together with a playful refusal to accept any struggle for either a higher station in life or a more intense outlet for his emotions, all add up to make Hagedorn a restricted revolutionary. Making the most of what one has and not wanting for more was the underlying style of his more serious moments. Such independence and emphasis on individualism are perhaps the most relevant pointers to an appreciation of Hagedorn and his work.

NOTES

1. France has not seen me, and I not France . . . yes, I esteem a ceremonial bow better than the finest library. *Der Patriot* Bd. 3 p. 59.

2. Because my soul, o God, is a work of your hands, then may will and reason too never stray from the purpose of your praise, never from your ways; and by their worth and their quality, o creator, may they always bring my powers to know yours! May your will sanctify my will, and your wisdom be always the light of thought, then should I not fear fault and error, then what is good can only soothe with wish and desire. Eschenburg Bd. IV pp. 33–4.

3. But the character of this excellent poet is certainly not to be sought in customary imitation. Nobody is richer in his own original thoughts, happier in his expression, nobler in his sentiments. Even his imitations from Horace are masterly, independent originals. I. *Theil XIX.*

4. The finest agreement between two writers rests as little on words as does the noblest friendship. Mind and heart in the foremost ancients and moderns have become the lively, or rather the only sources of the happily turned expression. It suffers too often from the yoke of blind

conformity and wretched submission. One should imitate as Boileau and La Fontaine did. The former used to say: "That's not imitating, it's tilting against one's model". I. Theil p. VII.

5.   The first day in the month of May
       To me is the happiest of all.
       You I saw, and to you did call,
       The first day in the month of May,
       My heart's love and to you did play.
       Did my avowal your pleasure befall,
       Then the first day in the month of May
       To me is the happiest of all. III Theil pp. 85–6.

6. A hungry hen found a fine diamond and buried it in the sand. If only to please me, it said, this beautiful stone were but a grain of wheat! Unhappy abundance, where the most needed enjoyment must be lacking in our treasures! II Theil pp. 42–3.

7. pp. 180–2 Volume I Reprint of the 1740 edition (Deutsche Neudrucke 1966).

8. Friendship does not come from need and envy: it is the child of wisdom, the fruit of knowledge, a work of the best choice, and can only bind those together who find in soulful allurement the greatest beauty. Theil I. p. 50.

9. A rhapsody of noble thoughts. (C. H. Schmid p. 300).

10. Mature spirit.

11. Pride, prejudice, anger, admiration, avarice and envy are all what they are just through ignorance. *Schreiben an einen Freund.* Theil I. p. 32.

12. He is happy who may be what he is, who measures out his way and aims with his own eyes, who never follows like a slave, often points out ways to others, unquestioned blames nothing and praises nothing, and if his wit turns him into a poet takes nature and time as his leaders. Theil I. p. 80.

13. A poet teaches the human race the charms of virtue and the justice of their deeds. A poet offers for times now rising an example of how to follow models, often lightens the burden and mockery of the poor man, and restrains the lamentation of the sick. Those who, like you, read Homer with understanding see that he already was a friend of man. Theil I. p. 81.

14. When will I one day in a peace where I am no longer listened to become not so famous but only as much enjoyed as you? Theil I. p. 82.

15. Too like Pindar, too full of figures, too ingenious, and too long. Theil III p. V.

16. Natural, ardent, roguish, playful, in one word almost all anacreontic. Guthke p. 38.

17. Rise up and show yourself to the German fatherland! But, should kisses and wine now still be the content of your songs, then sing the praise of both but not to the shame of good manners! As Anacreon pleases you, then may you always be called a wise man of the shrewd world, as he was called, in every form of reason! And follow too a piece of

advice that neither makes you rush on nor holds you back, be not like the cricket who buzzes himself to death! Theil I pp. 100–1.

18. Joy, goddess of noble hearts, hear me. May the songs which here resound enlarge you and please you: whatever sounds here, sounds through you. Bright sister of sweet love! Heavenly child! Power of souls! Half of life! Ah, what can fortune give us, if we do not win you too? Silent protectors of dead treasures are only rich. No mean king can be compared with him who watches over no treasure, who jokes wittily and sings and laughs. Give to those who know, to those who honour you, new courage, new jest to active tongues, new skill to youth, and to the old new vitality. Gentle joy, you enlighten reason! Flee for ever the faces of all gloomy faultfinders and the whole band of hypocrites! Theil III p. 42.

19. Daughter of nature, gentle love! Only your impulses bring us pleasure. Goodwill and goodwill returned give to all the enchanted art of pleasing. Theil III p. 83.

20. You mother of gentle impulses! O friendship! In your honour, to you friendship, not to love, do our choruses ring out, and Phyllis joins in too: but should the enchantment of Phyllis' song and glances be nothing more than friendship? Theil III p. 80.

SELECT BIBLIOGRAPHY

Published works
The two main editions are:
Johann Joachim Eschenburg—*Friedrich von Hagedorn Poetische Werke. Mit einer Lebensbeschreibung und Charakteristik und mit Auszügen seines Briefwechsels begleitet. Fünf Theile.* Hamburg 1800.
Herrn Friedrichs von Hagedorn sämmtliche Poetische Werke. In dreyen Theilen. Hamburg 1757. Neuverlegt bei Herbert Lang. Bern 1968.
(This includes the first 3 volumes of Eschenburg, but not the biography, posthumous works and selected correspondence in volumes 4 and 5. Quotations are taken from this edition.)
Easily available is:
Friedrich von Hagedorn—*Gedichte* (Hsg. Alfred Anger) Reclam 1321–3.
Indispensable is:
Karl S. Guthke—Friedrich von Hagedorn und das literarische Leben seiner Zeit im Lichte unveröffentlichter Briefe an Johann Jakob Bodmer.
Jahrbuch des freien deutschen Hochstifts 1966 pp. 1–108 (Includes a 15 page introduction, 41 letters and footnotes).
The 111th number of *Der Patriot* (14.2.1726) is to be found in the third volume of the reprint (pp. 52–61) De Gruyter Vlg, Berlin 1970.

Secondary literature
A. Anger   *Nachwort* (pp. 183–201) to the Reclam edition 1968 of Hagedorn's poems.

B. R. Coffman	*The influence of English literature on Friedrich von Hagedorn. Modern Philology.* 1914 Vol. XII No. 5 November pp. 121-132; 1915 Vol. XII. No. 8. February pp. 179–196; Vol. XIII No. 2 June pp. 11–33.
M. Colleville	*Friedrich von Hagedorn.* In: *La Renaissance du Lyrisme dans la Poésie allemande au XVIIIe. Siècle.* Paris 1936 pp. 371–496.
K. Epting	*Der Stil in den lyrischen und didaktischen Gedichten Friedrich von Hagedorns. Ein Beitrag zur Stilgeschichte der Aufklärungszeit.* Stuttgart 1929. 154 pp.
E. K. Grotegut	*Friedrich von Hagedorn's "Seifensieder" and freedom. Monatshefte* 1960 LII (3) pp. 113–120.
E. K. Grotegut	*The popularity of Friedrich von Hagedorn's "Johann der Seifensieder". Neophilologus* 1960 XLIV (3) pp. 189–195.
S. List	*Friedrich von Hagedorn und die antike Literatur.* Dissertation München 1908 100 pp.
C. H. Schmid	*Friedrich von Hagedorn.* In: *Nekrolog oder Nachrichten* 1785 Bd. 1 pp. 278–321.
W. Schulze	*Die Brüder Hagedorn. Archiv für Kulturgeschichte* 1959 XLI pp 90–9.
H. Stierling	*Leben und Bildnis Friedrichs von Hagedorn.* Hamburg 1911 5 plates, 8 drawings 102 pp.
G. Stix	*Friedrich von Hagedorn. Menschenbild und Dichtungsauffassung.* Rome 1961 237 pp.
G. Witkowski	*Die Vorläufer der anakreontischen Dichtung in Deutschland und Friedrich von Hagedorn.* Leipzig 1894 43 pp.

Among other works not available for this essay are:

W. Eigenbrodt	*Hagedorn und die Erzählung in Reimversen.* Berlin 1884.
E. Briner	*Die Verskunst der Fabeln und Erzählungen Hagedorns.* Dissertation Zürich 1920.
R. Petsch	*Friedrich von Hagedorn und die deutsche Fabel.* In: *Festschrift der Hamburgischen Universität ihrem Ehrendoktor Herrn Bürgermeister Werner von Melle zum 80. Geburtstag am 18. Oktober 1933 dargebracht.* Hamburg 1934.

Georg Christoph Lichtenberg

Georg Christoph Lichtenberg

by NICHOLAS BOYLE

Georg Christoph Lichtenberg was a Sunday's child, born on July 1, 1742 in Oberramstadt near Darmstadt, where his father was pastor. As the youngest of the family he had a solitary but happy childhood, being educated at the Pädagogium in Darmstadt, to which the father (1689–1751) moved on his promotion in 1745. He was devoted to his mother (1696–1764). His constitution, probably as a result of rickets, was always frail, and he developed a pronounced hump. While still at school he showed an interest in mathematics (not at the time a normal school subject) and a passion for his hobby, astronomy. At some undetermined point in his early life he also acquired a knowledge of English. After studying mathematics and natural science at Göttingen University (1763–7) he was made Extraordinary Professor of philosophy (i.e. mainly mathematics) in 1770 and Ordinary Professor there in 1775. During this period he made two visits to England (March-May 1770 and August 1774—December 1775). On his first visit he met George III at the royal observatory in Richmond; on the second the king, for the sake of Queen Charlotte, but also for the sake of Lichtenberg's charming conversation, admitted him to the intimacy of his family circle. While in England Lichtenberg visited Oxford, Stratford (purchasing himself a shilling's worth of the Bard's chair), Birmingham and Bath, but spent most of his time in London, going to the theatres, making the acquaintance of scientists (Cook's second voyage had just come to an end), and mingling with all classes of society. After returning to Göttingen on December 31, 1775 Lichtenberg did not leave it again for more than three weeks at a time.

Lichtenberg's scientific interest had always been physical rather than mathematical. In 1777, when his collection of instruments was already worth some 1500 Thaler (in 1789 it was bought from him as the basis of the University's collection), he began to take over the lectures in physics previously given by his deceased friend J. C. P. Erxleben, and in the same year he discovered, while erecting some electrical apparatus, what are now known as the Lichtenberg figures. These are the starry shapes that appear—e.g. in dust—on a non-conductor over which an electrical discharge has taken place, and at the time they were thought to be an important discovery, offering a new hope of understanding the mysterious "electrical fluid". In the 1780's his interests extended themselves to the rapidly advancing chemistry of gases, and in his last years meteorology held out to him the false promise of a simultaneous solution of disputed points in both chemical and electrical science. In 1780 he erected the first lightning-conductor in Göttingen, much to the alarm of the inhabitants. The house of the bookseller Dieterich—in which Lichtenberg lectured as well as lived from 1776 to 1799—became notorious for the poppings and flashings and bangings that emerged from it when "the Professor" was at work. From 1777 to 1799 he edited the *Göttinger Taschenkalender*, from 1780 to 1785 the *Göttingisches Magazin*. In 1788 he was made *Hofrat* and in 1793 Fellow of the Royal Society. His lectures were always popular and his pupils included Thomas Young, Alexander von Humboldt, Franz von Baader and Ludwig Tieck.

In 1777 Lichtenberg had taken into his house a twelve-year-old flower-seller, Dorothea Stechard, with whom he lived in great happiness until her death in 1782, which desolated him. In 1783 her place was taken by Margarethe Kellner, who bore him six children. A formal marriage did not occur until 1789 when Lichtenberg fell severely ill with a nervous complaint from which he never fully recovered and which gave free rein to his hypochondria. In the 1790's he took to drink and adultery, even though this was also the period of public recognition and honour, and he died of a chest-infection on February 24, 1799.

THE name of Lichtenberg is not a familiar one to most English readers. This is strange not only because this Göttingen professor of physics was perhaps the most sympathetic and knowledgeable observer of English affairs that German literature has produced, was for the greater part of his life a subject of George III (the Electorate of Hanover being at the time in personal union with the English crown), and was a Fellow of the Royal Society and "the real link between Göttingen and the [English] court"[1] in the arrangements which led to the three youngest princes' spending a not particularly educational four years at the University there. His *Briefe aus England* provide "the only source from which it is possible to get a clear idea of Garrick's acting",[2] he wrote an exhaustive commentary on Hogarth's engravings,[3] and his death was reported, with an attention to medical detail which would have appealed to his hypochondriac temperament, in the *Gentleman's Magazine*.[4] The obituary refers to him as "one of [Germany's] most ingenious writers, who to profound knowledge in the most sublime sciences, united an inexhaustible fund of original genius"; and contemporary estimation of him as a scientist is best indicated by Alexander von Humboldt, who wrote in 1792 that a metaphysical question about the nature of chemistry could be decided only by Lichtenberg or Kant.[5] Had Lichtenberg been only this, an eighteenth century pundit, writing Letters from England as Letters are now written from America, English ignorance of him would hardly be unjustifiable. What does make that ignorance odd is the fact that Lichtenberg is no literary fossil. His admirers have included Jean Paul, Goethe and Mörike, Grillparzer and Hebbel, Kierkegaard, Schopenhauer, Nietzsche, Freud and Wittgenstein.[6] But the truth is that none of these admired him for the reasons which might appeal peculiarly to the English reader. They admired him for something, in fact, which has never appealed to any large public,[7] German speaking or not, something which played no part in establishing Lichtenberg's fame during his lifetime. When in 1904 Tolstoy, in conversation, equated Kant and Lichtenberg,[8] his reason for doing so was not Alexander von Humboldt's. His reason was, simply : Lichtenberg's aphorisms. That is, the mass of "miscellaneous ideas, digested and undigested, events that in peculiar concern me, now and again extracts and remarks noted more exactly elsewhere, or otherwise used by me"[9]—which Lichtenberg, from the age of at least twenty-two, continuously accumulated in the notebooks that he referred to as "waste-books" ("Sudelbücher").[10] The contents of these notebooks were partially published after his death and called by his literary executors "remarks" (Bemerkungen). It would appear to have been Hebbel who baptised them "aphorisms",[11] and the name was officially confirmed by Albert Leitzmann's definitive edition of the surviving waste-books (1902–8). It is this second, posthumous, Lichtenberg, the private, not the public, writer, who has secured the enthusiastic affection of a constellation of minds of international brilliance. During the nineteenth century the public Lichtenberg slowly died. The scientific writings were the first to disappear from the collected editions, then the journalism, and by 1900 editorial interest was confined to the manuscript and nothing but the manuscript— letters, waste-books and unpublished fragments. In recent years, however, there have been signs[12] of a reinstatement of the Lichtenberg who so impressed his contemporaries—the journalist, the satirist, the professor. Though this new interest can really only be archaeological it is nonetheless welcome. For Lichtenberg's two literary lives were distinct, but they were not separate. To understand his sensitivity to the demands imposed by writing for a public is a necessary precondition of understanding what he noted down for himself in private.

Lichtenberg's first published work reads like an overture to the rest of his *oeuvre*. It is a short essay of 1766, *Von dem Nutzen, den die Mathematik einem* Bel Esprit *bringen kann*,[13] in which he immediately establishes himself in the role which, with more nuances, he is to play throughout his public life—that of a

"witziger Kopf", what a more sanctimonious age calls an "intellectual". Then, as now, one joined the charmed circle by
libelling it.[14] The essay canvasses the literary potential of analo-
gies drawn from mathematics, instead of from the traditional poetic vocabulary—"asymptote", for example, or "equation" or "centre
of gravity". It is typical that Lichtenberg should disguise an
intellectual ambition—to demonstrate the human and literary
significance of scientific thought—as a public crusade—against the
pastoral fopperies of an effete Germany. It is typical too that
the ambition should be achieved only in a string of unrelated
examples, each of which could stand on its own as "an idea".[15]
Finally, it is typical that the attempt to force these various serious
little jokes into coherence should result only in a pedantic and
undirected sarcasm, "the enthusiastically exaggerated claims that
youth will always make for its own speciality."[16] In this unpromis-
ing form the main themes of Lichtenberg's literary career are
introduced.

Appropriately, Lichtenberg's name first became widely known
as that of the author of a pseudonymous work dedicated to
Oblivion. In 1769 Lavater, a young Christian pastor in Zurich,
challenged Moses Mendelssohn, the Jewish philosopher in Berlin,
12 years his senior, to confute certain arguments for Christianity
or to make his submission. Mendelssohn's measured reply declined
both, but Lavater would not let the matter rest. A sermon that
he preached on the baptism of two Jews in 1771 is the object
of Lichtenberg's satire in *Timorus,* purportedly a defence of
the two converts by one Conrad Photorin, "der Theologie und
Belles Lettres Candidat",[17] whose name is a transparent Grecisa-
tion of Lichtenberg's. But Photorin is more than a pseudonym—
he is almost a character : anxiously seeking the approval of
entrenched Protestant orthodoxy, no doubt with his eye on future
preferment, he undertakes the defence in the first person. The
result is that Lichtenberg's irony is confused by the superabundance
of targets : there is Lavater, almost lost to view save for a few
parodistic allusions to his ecstatic style, there are the Jews, whose
rascality is beyond doubt, despite the sophistries with which
Photorin tries to veil it, there is dogmatic ecclesiastical authority,
which approves of conversion but disapproves of Jews and of
Enlightenment and therefore also of Lavater, and there is
authority's catspaw, the juvenile enthusiast Photorin, himself the
most obvious object of satire in the tract. Lichtenberg has plenty
of material, but the only unity he can impose on it is his desire to
be satirical about all of it. How he is satirical does not matter—
there is no unity of purpose. When for example Photorin has to

explain away the fact that one of the Jews is a convicted thief, his argument—that the Jew has not done anything less honourable than the courtier who welshes on his debts—has only its crudity in common with the argument, used elsewhere, that the Jew desired to spend so much time in prison in order to weigh the proofs of the Christian religion. There is no common satiric object to the arguments : they are there not because they contain the pith of the whole satire (as do the arguments in Swift's *Modest Proposal*) but because they enable Lichtenberg to turn these particular points to humorous advantage, and any other argument would have served as well. Similarly, Lichtenberg cannot resist studding his sentences with detached witticisms :

> "welcher natürlich ehrliche Mann, *von den künstlichen will ich gar nicht einmal reden,* wird dazu stille sitzen können?"[18]
> "Es sind zwar von der Nase bis an die Seele, *vorausgesetzt daß sie zu Hause ist,* etwa drittehalb Pariser Zoll."[19]

—the italicised phrases are pure Lichtenberg : they break into, and break up, the comic character of Conrad Photorin; they are inserted not because they could plausibly come from Photorin, but because they happen to amuse Lichtenberg. Lichtenberg has chosen to address the public from behind a mask; but it is only *gaucherie,* or not knowing his own mind, that has caused him to do so, since half the time he feels sufficiently protected by his disguise to be comic *in propria persona.* As a result Photorin's arguments never emerge as the views, or as the caricature of the views, of any one party in the controversy. At best Photorin is the caricature of certain aspects of Lichtenberg's own personality. Lichtenberg was always old for his years : his coming up to Göttingen University was delayed by poverty; after that his progress was rapid and favoured by his superiors, and some of his notes testify to a fear that it had outstripped his ability[20]; it was his misfortune to be just a few significant years older than the literary revolutionaries of the "Sturm und Drang",[21] whom he never tires of charging with immaturity and undergraduate —or even sixth-form—sentimentality,[22] that is, with errors from which he had only recently escaped himself.[23] Lichtenberg's anxiety to preserve pseudonymity (he at first denied his authorship even to his friend, landlord and publisher Dieterich) is evidently not a simple matter. Photorin's grating precocity is something of a self-castigation on Lichtenberg's part, just as Photorin's assumption of the task of defending both true faith and his academic and ecclesiastical elders and betters is a parody of a secret but serious and lasting ambition of Lichtenberg's : the ambition of writing the great German satire. Because that ambition races ahead of the author's interest in the literary means by which it is to be attained, because Lichtenberg wants the satire to be at every moment and in every sentence achieved, *Timorus* is one of the jokes that fall flat because they have tried too hard.

> "Oft wenn mir Zeit und Genie zuraunte: jetzt, Photorin, jetzt schlage zu, werde der Retter deines Vaterlands, du kannsts, so habe ich gepfiffen oder an den Fensterscheiben getrommelt."[24]

Lichtenberg was never to make himself known as Germany's satirical Messiah. It is one of his most appealing characteristics that, besides cherishing this ambition—along with many others—, he also, on occasion, recognised its absurdity : and anyway inclination and opportunity coincided too rarely for him to be capable of bringing forth a major, homogeneous, work.[25] From 1774 to 1776 he planned a polemic against the "Sturm und Drang" (again under the pseudonym of Conrad Photorin), from about 1785 to 1793 a satirical novel—neither plan succeeded in imposing any order on his heaps of fragmentary notes, which remained unpublished during his lifetime. Nonetheless, in the decade which followed the appearance of *Timorus,* Lichtenberg established a reputation as a writer to be feared with a series of lesser satirical and polemical campaigns. In 1776, just returned from England and fired by his admiration for the letters of Junius (in full flight during his first visit to the country in 1770), as well as by his affection for Dieterich, he wrote two pamphlets against Tobias Göbhard, a publisher in Bamberg, who had pirated a legal text-book on Dieterich's list and had then attempted to justify himself on the ground that Dietrich's prices were extortionate.[26] Lichtenberg is merciless in his exposure of the feeble subterfuges by which the piracy is defended—their own contradictions show up Göbhard's dishonest intent—and there is none of the moral equivocation that there is in *Timorus*. But the occasion is in itself too insignificant to give rise to important satire, and the plain-speaking comes close to vituperation. Lichtenberg is still trying too hard. Much the same is true of his contributions to a lengthier and more distressing controversy, that with the poet, scholar and boor J. H. Voß, in 1781 and 1782.[27] However, though the subject of dispute may seem even more trivial—Voß's plan for a reformed spelling of names transliterated from the Greek—its import is in fact rather wider. Lichtenberg criticises first the philological inadequacies of the proposal itself, showing how questionable are Voß's basic assumptions, then the overweening pedantry that would displace living, established, international usage in favour of such a dubious schematism, and finally— and only after the greatest personal provocation—he criticises the moral distortions caused by this intellectual obsession : Voß had been grossly and publicly rude to his teacher and benefactor, the great classicist Heyne, and there is, Lichtenberg concludes,

"kein verächtlicheres Geschöpf unter der Sonne [. . .], als einen Menschen, der über der Lumperei von einem Laut eines Buchstabens bei einem ausgestorbenen Volk, Undank verübt : das heißt ein Verbrechen, das ein rechtschaffener Mann nicht um den ersten Thron der Welt begehen würde."[28]

Voß's moral transgression—allowing personal obligations to be overturned by intellectual convictions—is put in parallel with the philological transgression of allowing something as ephemeral and idiosyncratic as pronunciation to overturn something as public as an agreed orthography. Both errors proceed from the same loud-mouthed egotism (for which Lichtenberg finds further evidence in Voß's literary taste). But once again Lichtenberg was a prisoner of circumstance, constrained by the occasion : of course, he was not himself inflating a triviality but protesting at its inflation by others, but nonetheless all he did in fact was to add to the clamour. Again, it may be true that the academic and speculative preoccupations of intelligent Germany at the time did unfit it to produce the great social, satirical and "menschenbeobachterisch"[29] literary culture of contemporary England, but to satirise *those* preoccupations was merely to play the pedants' own game. Even when the satire was a refusal to play it :

"Ich werde [Hrn. Voß] nie *ernstlich* antworten, ich wollte lieber —o, ich weiß nicht, was ich lieber thun wollte—o ich wollte fast lieber Hr. *Jäsus* schreiben."[30]

Yet even if the quarrel with Voß shows that Lichtenberg did not possess the imagination to escape from the vicious circle of arid academic controversy, it does reveal his true strength. His ability to see the widest intellectual issues in the microcosm of a single dispute, his conviction that intellectual and personal integrity are inseparable, and his constant reference to the principles of public life and public debate in "des lieben Gottes Unterhauß [wo] er selbst uns Sitz und Stimme aufgetragen hat" (J26)[31] —these are doughty virtues even when practised with an excess of moral effort reminiscent of the excessive formal effort shown in *Timorus*. But when the effortfulness falls away, when his interest is concentrated solely on the subject in hand, and no

longer on the ambitions that he is satisfying, in fact, when he is
fired by passion for the simple truth, then Lichtenberg's polemical
writing is at its best. It is noteworthy that this best is brought out
in him by issues that have a scientific turn. From 1780 to 1783 he
sought, in a series of articles, to assuage the public anxiety aroused
by the amateur astronomy of one Superintendent Ziehen.[32] This
good churchman had concluded from his observations of the stars
that the earth was about to split in half. Lichtenberg is intolerant
of the "sceptical indolence" that would allow that Ziehen might
be right since "all our knowledge is vanity" anyway. Ziehen can
be convicted of specific ignorances, inaccuracies and confusions. But
Lichtenberg insists that he must be put down with the right wea-
pons, and actually argues on his victim's behalf when the counter-
arguments are inadequate or fallacious. His main polemical instrument, in fact, is his power of kindly, picturesque and—even in
anger—devastatingly rational exposition. And Lichtenberg's concern that the prestigious name of Science should not be misused to
impress and impose upon a vulnerable readership is the animating
principle of his satirical masterpiece, *Über Physiognomik*.[33] More
than anything else he wrote, this essay established him as a
popular educator and guardian of the public intellect. Lichtenberg
here once more crossed swords with Lavater, who in 1772 had
written the relatively brief and abstract *Von der Physiognomik*
and in 1775 had begun the publication of a series of profusely
illustrated quarto volumes of *Physiognomische Fragmente*. Of
course the craze for physiognomy Lavater unleashed—for the
analysis of character on the evidence of facial features alone—
was to a large extent a society fad. It coincided with the easy
production and reproduction of individual silhouettes, is suited
the temper of a decade that had opened with the publication
of Sterne's *Sentimental Journey,* and it provided that opportunity
for slight sociable indecency which other ages have found in
phrenology or table-turning or the interpretation of dreams or
blots or doodles. But, like all society fads, it had more serious
pretensions, and it touched on some of the deeper anxieties of
the day. It promised to extend into the study of human behaviour the exactitude if not of Newtonian physics, at any
rate of Linnean botany. It would categorise, and predict, and
attach everything supposedly mental to a material counterpart.
Those left unimpressed by Lavater's wordy paeans to the
Creator (who had so perfectly harmonised body and spirit)
could not rid themselves of the fear that the observations might
all the same be right. And without the ecstasy Lavater's universe
was a godless piece of clockwork. Lavater therefore gave Lichten-

berg what neither Göbhard nor Voß was able to give him : the opportunity for quite untrivial satire. Lichtenberg took the opportunity (perhaps without recognising it for what it was).[34] Lavater's metaphysical justification of physiognomy—that in the clockwork universe, where everything is affected by everything else, everything is therefore reflected by everything else as well—is cogently ridiculed :

> "An dieser absoluten Lesbarkeit von Allem in Allem zweifelt niemand [. . .] Besonderes Tröstliches folgt hieraus für Physiognomik, ohne nähere Bestimmung, nichts, da eben dieses Lesen [. . .] die Quelle unserer Irrthümer, und in manchen Dingen unserer gänzlichen Unwissenheit ist. [. . .] Bezieht sich denn Alles im Gesicht auf Kopf und Herz? Warum deutet ihr nicht den Monat der Geburt, kalten Winter, faule Windeln, leichtfertige Wärterinnen, feuchte Schlafkammern, Krankheiten der Kindheit aus den Nasen?"[35]

The appeal to metaphysics is worthless when physiognomy cannot even approximate to the model of a science afforded by ordinary physics. The conclusions of physiognomy are not subject to experimentation, calculation or generalisation, for every new face is an exception, demanding the invention of a new rule. Lavater's *Fragments* have neither the immediacy of life, nor the simplicity of science, they are

> "Ein weitläuftiges Werk, und zwar eines, welchem Weitläuftigkeit wesentlich ist [. . .] die Physiognomik wird in ihrem eigenen Fett ersticken."[36]

Physiognomy was supposed to teach people to know one another better so that they would love one another more. Lichtenberg shows that this claim to knowledge is fraudulent since Lavater admits that he offers knowledge merely of disposition (Anlage), of potential not of actual character.

> "Was der Mensch könnte geworden sein, will ich nicht wissen. Was hätte nicht jeder werden können? Sondern ich will wissen, was er ist. [. . .] Um aller Welt willen, was ist für uns *in praxi* eine verdorbene gute Anlage? nichts weiter als eine gerade Linie, die man krumm gebogen hat; eine krumme."[37]

Lavater complained with some justice that trying to answer Lichtenberg was "like endeavouring to hold an eel by the tail."[38] It is true that in one sense Lichtenberg was evasive. His essay put together many different arguments, mainly extracted from his notebooks, and the different standpoints from which these different criticisms were made were not always compatible. He found it difficult to justify his own suggested study of "pathogno-mics"—the study of the expressions of the human face, rather than of its anatomy—without being guilty of the very fallacies for which he had criticised Lavater. But all in all, Lavater's com-plaint simply means that Lichtenberg had run rings round him. There is no need to say more here of the literary quality of *Über Physiognomik*, as an excellent discussion of the work is already accessible in English.[39]

Über Physiognomik was first published in the autumn of 1777, in the *Göttinger Taschenkalender* for the year 1778. By February of 1778 all 8000 copies had been sold[40] and a second, revised, edition of the essay was published separately. Professor Mautner has suggested that the reason for this considerable success is to be found not only in the topicality of the controversy and the intrinsic brilliance of Lichtenberg's contribution to it, but also in Lichtenberg's own growing reputation.[41] He was becoming known as a satirist and a populariser of enlightenment, and also as an expert on English affairs. He explicitly relates his English experiences to his physiognomical interests in the foreword to the second edition of *Über Physiognomik* :

> "Im Jahr 1770 sowohl als in 1774 und 1775 stellte ich in England mit großem Eifer physiognomische Beobachtungen an, die oft so gefährlich waren als die über die Gewitterelektricität [. . .] Ich habe dort Männer gesehen und gesprochen, berühmte und berüchtigte durch einander, die mit unter die merkwürdigsten der neuern Zeit gehören [. . .] Allein was war am Ende das Resultat aller meiner Bemühungen? Nichts als ein wenig nähere Bekanntschaft mit dem Menschen und mir, und dann ein Mißtrauen gegen alle Physiognomik [. . .]"[42]

In the same month as this foreword the third and last of Lich-tenberg's *Briefe aus England* was published in the *Deutsches Museum*, the first two having been published in the same journal in 1776.[43] Their subject, theatrical life in contemporary London, was bound to arouse the greatest interest. Germany never looked to England more than in the 1770's—in this decade the German translation of English novels reached its eighteenth-century peak.[44] Nationally, England had long been laying an evident claim to primacy in Europe. And in these years between the Wilkes riots and the outbreak of the American War, London, a unique, teeming, commercial metropolis was possessed of a public life and a public consciousness that no other city in the world could match. A part, if politically an insignificant part, of that public life took place in the theatre, and the prestige and independence of the London stage could not but impress a Germany still struggling to establish, amidst a superfluity of court-theatres, a single repertory theatre for plays in the national language. Moreover, London had Garrick. London acting, on the whole, did not seem to Lichtenberg to set a standard beyond the reach of the products of the German theatrical "Treibhäuschen".[45] But Garrick was unique, his reputation was European. His skill alone was enough to attract Lichtenberg to life in England. Garrick's art seemed to him to be a studied reflection of the hectic and colourful London world which appealed to him so much for being so unlike the provincial placidity of Göttingen. In London, the alert observer could learn every law, and every eccentricity, of human behaviour, and that, Lichtenberg felt, was just what Garrick had done. Variety, appetite, energy, self-esteem, this was what Lichtenberg prized in the Englishmen of his day, and Garrick's skill was, he believed, to have shown the same force and adaptability in exactly observing their habits and in recreating them on the stage. Garrick's stagecraft provided the real answer to the physiognomists : an art of human observation was possible, but it was to be found in the detail and precision of his acting technique, not in the verbal effusions of Lavater.

"Der Mensch lag seinem beobachtenden Geiste offen, von dem ausgebildeten und ausgekünstelten in den Sälen von S. James's an, bis zu den wilden in den Garküchen von S. Giles's. Er besuchte die Schule, in welche Shakespeare ging, wo er ebenfalls, wie jener, nicht auf Offenbarungen paßte, sondern studirte, (denn in England thut das Genie nicht Alles, wie in Deutschland), London meine ich, wo ein Mann mit solchem Talent zur Beobachtung seinen Erfahrungssätzen in einem Jahre leicht eine Richtigkeit geben kann, wozu kaum in einem Städtchen, wo Alles einerlei hofft und fürchtet, einerlei bewundert und einerlei erzählt, und wo sich Alles reimt, ein ganzes Leben hinreichend wäre [. . .] ich wundere mich, daß London nicht mehrere bildet, ich meine nicht mehrere Garricke oder Hogarthe oder Fieldinge, sondern Leute die zwar etwas Anderes wären, aber so würden, wie jene. Kenntniß der Welt gibt dem Schriftsteller in jeder Classe Überlegenheit."[46]

Lichtenberg is in love with the milieu that produced Garrick. But also he admires the man because this peculiar talent seems to confirm his own most cherished beliefs about the nature of art. Art, in Lichtenberg's view, is the concentrated arrangement of significant detail. Knowledge of the detail is acquired by observation, observation of the hurly-burly of an active world. But the detail is *significant* detail—it is not collected and presented because it is interesting for its own sake, but because it corroborates a story, because it points to a general fact about human nature, or reinforces a particular theme in the particular work. It is a fact of the greatest importance that Lichtenberg is in love with the England and the art of Fielding (though he quite misunderstands them), but has little or nothing to say of the England or the art of Richardson. In England he sees politics but not class, opulence but not money, unbuttoned sensuality but not privy prurience. In art, detail is for Lichtenberg what makes the imagined world more rich and substantial, it is not, as it is for Richardson, itself a way of imagining the world anew. Lichtenberg retained a lifelong admiration for a particular constellation of English minds : Garrick, Hogarth, Fielding and—in his own peculiar understanding of him—Shakespeare. All these artists (so Lichtenberg thought) combined a wealth of reference to the particularities of English life—which it always gave him great personal pleasure to elucidate—with a deliberateness in their presentation of the details of human behaviour which stood up to the closest critical scrutiny. A man could achieve what these men achieved only by assiduity in observation and calculated *désinvolture* in performance—an aesthetic which neatly combines those qualities in which Lichtenberg was obviously strongest, observation and calculation, with those in which he felt himself most deficient, assiduity and ease— :

> "Er muß reich genug sein an Bemergkungen, eine hinzuwerfen, auch wo er nicht gewiß ist, ob sie gleich gefunden werden wird, und Goldstücke hinzugeben mit einer Miene, aus der sich gar nichts auf den Gehalt schließen läßt : und nicht wie unsere [i.e. German] Prächtigen, rothe Heller mit einer Majestät zurückschmeißen, daß, wer bloß die Miene sieht, denken sollte, es wären Goldstücke."[47]

These words come from what can only be called the *reductio ad absurdum* of Lichtenberg's notion of art : *Vorschlag zu einem Orbis Pictus für deutsche dramatische Schriftsteller* . . ., published in 1780, and its *Fortsetzung* of 1785.[48] "Ich habe einen guten Vorrath von Bemerkungen liegen,"[49] says Lichtenberg, finding German authors not "sufficiently rich in observations" to bear comparison with their English contemporaries, and so he offers them a helping hand. These extracts from his own observations of certain social types will, he hopes, enable Germans to write better plays and novels in future. It is true that the same sharp eye that watched the corners of Garrick's mouth or the creases in his coat is at work here, as for example in these lines from the section "*Die Bedienten* "a) männliche B) Für den Schauspieler" :

"Er liest gern Federn vom Hute, und hascht Fliegen wie ein Sterbender, dreht den Hut vor dem Nabel wie eine Windmühle. Dieses muß sparsam gebraucht werden. [. . .]
Macht sich, wenn er bei Geringern ist, mit ausgespreizten Beinen kleiner, als er ist, und spricht wichtig. Dieses thun zuweilen sogar die Kurzen, wenn sie bei Langen stehen. [. . .]"[50]

Individually the observations are harmless and amusing enough. But as soon as Lichtenberg attempts to put them together into a methodical, discursive, presentation of the servant class, to provide a work of reference for the German novelist, the tone becomes disagreeably utilitarian and patronising. The reason is that Lichtenberg cannot take his system, and his supposed purpose, as thoroughly light-heartedly as he would like to. Unlike the ventures of Rabelais and Sterne in the same genre, Lichtenberg's humorous classifications are not parodies of classification itself. There is always the reservation that perhaps there is something in the system after all. He cannot wholly emancipate himself from the belief that perhaps a *bel esprit* might really be able to draw some profit from mathematics.

Orbis pictus shows clearly how Lichtenberg conceives of art. And it also shows that art so conceived is not very far from being tabulation, an exhaustive handlist of things noticed. That at any rate is what Lichtenberg made of the task of explicating the work of one of those favourite artists of his, a task which in one form or another occupied him during the last 15 years of his life. *G. C. Lichtenbergs ausführliche Erklärung der Hogarthischen Kupferstiche . . .*[51] appeared in five bulky, more or less annual, fascicles from 1794 onwards, but was preceded and, until 1796, accompanied by another series of briefer commentaries published in the *Göttinger Taschenkalender* (from 1784). The new work was a prestige publication, with reproductions by Riepenhausen of 32 engravings, and (to the displeasure of Goethe, who was at the time embarking on his classicising venture with Schiller) it was received with great enthusiasm.[52] Though practically all of Lichtenberg's factual knowledge about the engravings and their allusions was derived from existing commentaries in English, he was nonetheless right to claim that his work was unprecedented in its attempt to reproduce in words the "tone", the "mood" or "whimsicality", of the original.[53] Hogarth's pictures seemed to him to be most interesting for the mass of independent though ironical details with which they were charged. Reproducing the tone, therefore, meant giving himself the freedom to pass from feature to feature making only the connections that he chose to make, rather than those that the point of the picture demanded :

> "Mir aber ist es verstattet, die Vergleichung zu machen, bloß als Wendung, die zu der darauf folgenden Bemerkung führt."[54]

The humorous atmosphere is consequently established more when Lichtenberg digresses than when Hogarth is elucidated. This is how Lichtenberg explains the fact that in the sixth plate of the *Marriage à la Mode* series a meal is being taken at 11.05 a.m.

> "Elf Uhr des Morgens ist allerdings spät für den Mann, der schon um vier beim Rentenbuch wacht. Am *westlichen* Ende der Stadt speist man zu Mittage, wenn es hier in *Osten* schon fünf Uhr ist. Dieses gibt also der Stadt *London* eine sittliche Ausdehnung in *Länge* von sechs Stunden in Zeit oder 90 Graden im Bogen. Sollte sie noch ferner zunehmen, wozu man die beste Hoffnung hat, und der König von Spanien sich je wieder einmal rühmen, daß die Sonne in seinen Staaten nie unterginge, so könnte ihm jeder *Cockney* getrost antworten : seine *Vaterstadt* allein sei schon so groß, daß die Sonne, sie stehe auch, wo sie wolle, immer irgendeine Familie beim Mittagessen antreffe."[55]

The example is extreme but it does show Lichtenberg finding every detail of Hogarth's significant, that is, interpretable, and it also shows that the digression, even if its conclusion seems a wholly independent piece of fantasy, is in fact dependent on its original occasion, that is, on a feature of Hogarth's picture : it is not possible to say at what point in the development the initial suggestion—that the time of day has an economic and social meaning—finally fades away. This digressive method ensures that, sentence by sentence, whatever the commentary has to say is somehow *related* to the picture. It does not ensure that, taken as a whole, the commentary says anything very pertinent *about* the picture.[56] In 1799 Goethe published a "Novelle", *Der Sammler und die Seinigen*,[57] which concludes with a—rather Schillerian—classification of various kinds of onesidedness in art. Here the character-painter (Charakteristiker) is reproached with "pure rationality" (bloße Verstandesoperation) which is inadequate to art, while the miniaturist, paradoxically but shrewdly, is said to find his greatest difficulty in achieving unity. In terms of Goethe's scheme, Lichtenberg is a *"Pünktler* und *Punktierer,"*[58] capable only of scattered, local effects. Goethe, of course, gives pride of place to an organic, many-sided perfection—but then his eyes are turned towards Greece, "das heilige Grab der schönen Künste", as Lichtenberg has it in *Orbis pictus*.[59] The two artists, the classicist and the miniaturist, the two imaginary worlds, the Greek and the English (for that too is a figment), are so far apart that the pious hope of the *Frankfurter Gelehrte Anzeigen* in 1780, reasonable though it was at the time, and much though it testifies to Lichtenberg's reputation, can now seem only grotesque :

"Es sollten Lichtenberg, Goethe und Herder sich vereinigen, uns einen Shakespear zu geben, wo man es ganz vergässe, eine Übersetzung zu lesen."[60]

Lichtenberg's devotion to England was a kind of personal metaphor for his devotion to a set of artistic values which was bound to alienate him from the main schools of contemporary German literature and which was all of a piece with his incapacity for thinking connectedly on a large scale. It is ironical that he should have regarded the copies of the *Ausführliche Erklärung* that he presented to Kant and Goethe as counterparts for their gifts, respectively, of the *Kritik der reinen Vernunft* and *Wilhelm Meisters Lehrjahre*.[61]

Ironical, but not at all incomprehensible. Herbert Schöffler[62] poignantly reminds us how the ailing and prematurely aging Lichtenberg of the 1790's must have fingered the 1500 printed pages of his commentary and felt that, in comparison with the infertile tangle of near-misses of which his literary *oeuvre* had so far consisted, here at last was real achievement. It contrasted particularly with the hackwork by which he earned his daily bread— and, one might add, his household fame. From 1777 until his death he lived rent-free in Dieterich's capacious home in exchange for his work in editing—and to a great extent writing—the *Göttinger Taschenkalender*. The gilt-edged 16mo volume, illustrated with the engravings on which Lichtenberg first practised his commentator's art, appeared annually every autumn in readiness for the festive season at the turn of the year. From 1776 it was also published in French. Lichtenberg had to provide the Bilderklärung at the end of the book and a long essay by way of introduction, as well as a miscellany of smaller pieces, to fill the space between the two. *Faits divers* culled from foreign periodicals, hints on household management, little squibs (mostly damp), popularisations of scientific or medical advance, the contents of this middle section add up to a dismal harvest. There are exceptions of course, which are still worth reading. Connoisseurs of ephemera will enjoy the gracefulness of *Geschichte der Lichtputze* (1785), *Von der Äolus-Harfe* (1792), *Warum hat Deutschland noch kein großes öffent-*

liches Seebad? (1793),[63] though the factual material in them is rather exiguous. Lichtenberg shows genius in the art of making something out of nothing only when his scientific and his imaginative self are both equally engaged and are together fired by some philosophical or satirical purpose: *Ein Traum* (1794),[64] for example, the sum of a lifetime's reflection about the limits of scientific knowledge; *Rede der Ziffer 8* (1799),[65] which combines a satirical glance at the events of the end of the eighteenth century with a precise discussion of the year in which the new century can be said to begin; and the piece which must rank highest among all Lichtenberg's essays, *Amintors Morgenandacht* (1791),[66] an intimation of the wisdom that comes with knowledge and experience and with the experience of the search for knowledge, a wisdom which for that very reason cannot be put into words, but by which alone the upright man can live.

The search for knowledge was Lichtenberg's profession. His literary activity was a luxury, if a usual one, his editorship of the *Taschenkalender* was a chore. Science, on the other hand, was his first love and so the cause of his most painful disappointment. Despite his interest in Kant, Lichtenberg was first and foremost an experimentalist. Partly because whether he was peering from an upper window down on to a London street, staring into the darker corners of a Hogarth print, or searching the night-sky for the latest astronomical novelty, he was a self-confessed addictive observer. Partly because, untroubled by any Goethean inhibitions about torturing the phenomena, he delighted in instruments, both in themselves, and because they extended the range of observation. Kästner looked down his nose at his colleague's "Experimentalphysik", but it was Lichtenberg, a deft and witty impresario, whose lecture-room was full. And partly Lichtenberg was an experimentalist because that was his cast of mind. From the early days when he admired Wieland, to the last days, when he doubted Kant, Lichtenberg, often coarsely, took the side of the senses against all pretentiousness, whether aesthetic, moral, or philosophical. In the two great scientific controversies of his lifetime—over the nature of electricity and the nature of fire—what roused his anger was the sight of fools rushing in with theories where angels feared to tread with facts :

> "was ich im Collegio beständig sage, das ist, *untersucht* und nie *entschieden*, wo man über das Zeugnis der Sinne hinausgeht. Ich glaube, ohne dieses große Principium its kein wahrer Fortgang in der Physik zu hoffen."[67]

Yet, though he planned to expunge the word "theory" from the science text-book that he did not live to write,[68] Lichtenberg could not with justice have said of himself *hypotheses non fingo*. For he *did* make hypotheses, but with this peculiarity : they were the hypotheses of a sceptic, designed to show that there were alternatives to the hypotheses of others. They were not intended as explanations in their own right but as pointers to unasked questions. Even the phlogiston theory, of which he was one of the last defenders, was dear to Lichtenberg not because he thought it correct (for he thought that of no theory) but because he was used to it and so felt that it did not get in the way of his observation of the facts. When in 1789 the successful electrolysis of water by Paets van Troostwyk and Deimann was hailed as final confirmation of the new chemistry of Lavoisier, Lichtenberg objected that no one had asked the questions : what was the chemical composition of electricity itself? and what role was electricity supposed to have played in the experiment?

> "Wenn man die elektrische Materie aus Sauerstoff und Wasserstoff mit Wärmestoff bestehen ließe, [. . .] und den Erklärungen das Gepräge von Thatsachen aurdrückte, so ließe sich mit ein wenig Witz und Schreibart ein Gebäude einer elektrischen Chemie errichten, das dem antiphlogistischen an äußerm Scheine wenig nachgeben würde.[65]

Not that Lichtenberg, who certainly possessed "wit and style", had the intention, or indeed the ability, to construct such an electrical chemistry. Like the "pathognomics" he had outlined as a contrast to Lavater's physiognomy, it was a polemical device whose purpose was to draw attention away from invisible transcendental mechanisms and back to the observable surface of things. To this extent Goethe was right to say that Lichtenberg's was not a constructive nature.[70] An especial sadness attaches therefore to Lichtenberg's unfulfilled longing to make, in what anyone could see to be a time of notable scientific advance, some great discovery. It is not simply hindsight that justifies us in saying that he was not capable of it. There is one natural phenomenon that bears Lichtenberg's name (apart from the lunar crater christened in his memory) : the Lichtenberg figures were an *accidental* discovery. No doubt Lichtenberg might accidentally have discovered something else more important than these proved to be. But what of the great moment that passed him by when in June 1783 Montgolfier's fire-balloon (quickly followed by gas-balloons) inaugurated, as it seemed, a new era? Months before, Lichtenberg had been playing in his laboratory with soap-bubbles filled with hydrogen.

"Montgolfiers Erfindung war in meiner Hand"[71] he wrote after the event. And in later life he alternated between blaming himself for not making the discovery, and attributing all great discoveries to chance anyway. His most substantial scientific achievement lay in his editorial work[72] and above all in his lecturing, in the enthusiasm and the clarity of his exposition, virtues which attracted students from all over Europe, and which can be seen in his longer popularising essays, *Über das Weltgebäude* (1779),[73] for example, or *Dreht sich der Mond um seine Achse?* (1796)[74] or the posthumously published *Schreiben an Herrn Werner in Gießen, die Newtonische Theorie vom Licht betreffend*.[75] What is striking about these essays is their robust confidence, not that they are right, but that they are following the correct method—a lecturer cannot be a sceptic, and Lichtenberg's manner here is firm and patient, for once an embodiment of his own stated principles :

> "man soll immer bei Untersuchung der Wahrheit so verfahren, daß selbst erleuchtetere Zeiten dereinst, wo nicht unseren Glauben selbst, doch unser Verfahren dabei zum Muster nehmen können."[76]

In *Amintors Morgenandacht* this rather dusty-sounding "procedure" is revealed as the spirit of religious devotion in which a whole life of more and less serious investigation has been led :

> "es sei nichts weniger als jene physico-theologische Betrachtung von Sonnen, deren uns deutlich sichtbares Heer nach einer Art von Zählung auf 75 Millionen geschätzt würde. Er nannte diese Art von Betrachtungen bloße Musik der Sphären, die anfangs den Geist, wie mit einem Sturm von Entzücken, fast zur Betäubung hinreiße, deren er aber endlich gewohnt werde; allein das was davon immer bleibe, unstreitig das Beste, fände sich überall und vorzüglich in dem mit in die Reihe gehörigen Geist, der dieser Betrachtungen fähig sei. Es sei vielmehr eine zu anhaltendem Studio der Natur sich unvermerkt gesellende Freude über *eigenes Dasein,* verbunden mit nicht *ängstlicher* sondern *froher Neugierde* (wenn dieses das rechte Wort ist), [. . .] zu erfahren, mit diesen Sinnen oder mit analogen, oder Verhältnissen anderer Art, die sich von jeder Art des Daseins hoffen lassen, *was nun dieses Alles sei und werden wolle.*[77]

Yet neither Lichtenberg's public failure, literary or scientific, nor his despair over it, nor even perhaps his recovered serenity, would be of interest to us if we did not have access to something else, to a back-room of his mind (to quote Montaigne) where he shuts the door on the noisy disorder outside and draws up the reckoning alone—or, rather, alone with us. For it is difficult to determine how private the "Sudelbücher" really are.

"Es ist fast nicht möglich Etwas Gutes zu schreiben ohne daß man sich dabey Jemanden oder auch eine gewisse Auswahl von Menschen denckt die man anredet [. . .]" (L614)[78]

They are certainly more private than Lichtenberg's letters, for example. These, naturally, are addressed to a wide range of different audiences—other members of the international scientific community (such as Volta and Herschel) are at one extreme, his own wife and Dieterich are at the other. But all along this spectrum the letters tend towards the strained facetiousness that is characteristic of the published rather than the unpublished works. This conclusion is confirmed by what Lichtenberg wrote in the 1790's: while the letters proclaim nothing but outrage at the French Revolution, the "Sudelbücher" are sympathetic even towards its excesses.[79] (At that time the potential audience for any letter always included the censor.) On the other hand, the "Sudelbücher" do not represent an inmost fastness, they are not a confessional. During the last decade of his life Lichtenberg also kept a diary, and this reveals a world horrifyingly different from anything the waste-books or the letters contain. It is a record of neurotic illness and adulterous domestic misery, of pain, depression, and terror of pregnancy, with special symbols for the beginnings and ends of quarrels and each erotic act carefully noted and assessed.[80] The diary proves that the waste-books do not owe their unique attraction simply to the fact of being private documents: the diary was the most private thing that Lichtenberg wrote, but the waste-books were the most personal. When he was gathering up the day's crop of ideas, Lichtenberg was already in communion with a public, with posterity. This is shown by the care he took of the volumes themselves and by the fact that he did not conceal their existence: the family knew of them, as did Dieterich,[81] and Lichtenberg even hinted at their existence in public.[82] It is quite clear, too, that they are not working note-books[83] but were in some sense complete in themselves. However it is also true that (particularly in F) there is much material that was actually used later in published works, and that many of the entries in the books at all periods take the form of ideas, or even paragraphs, for larger projects, or just of words and turns of phrase that one day might come in useful. The result is a considerable ambiguity of literary intention. Lichtenberg writes:

"Wenn ich dieses Buch nicht geschrieben hätte, so würde heute über 1000 Jahre Abends zwischen 6 und 7 zE. in mancher Stadt in Deutschland von gantzen andern Dingen gesprochen worden seyn, als würcklich gesprochen werden wird." (D54)[84]

and by "this book" he probably means something (indefinite) that he never did write, though as it happens the remark is likely to prove a good deal more true of the "Sudelbücher" than it ever would have been of the work he was planning. Through this suspension of literary purpose, through the recognition, which is implicit in the act of writing the idea down, that he does not know what to do with it, Lichtenberg, half-intentionally, creates his aphorisms.

"Wie viele Ideen schweben nicht zerstreut in meinem Kopf, wovon manches Paar, wenn sie zusammen kämen, die größte Entdeckung bewirken könnte [...] Wenn wir beym Nachdenken uns den natürlichen Fügungen der Verstandesformen und der Vernunft überlassen, so *kleben* die Begriffe oft zu sehr an andern, daß sie sich nicht mit denen vereinigen können, denen sie eigentlich zugehören. Wenn es doch da etwas gäbe, wie in der Chemie Auflösung, wo die einzelnen Theile leicht suspendirt schwimmen und daher jedem Zuge folgen können."[85]

We have to be grateful that the two predestined ideas never came together in Lichtenberg's head—for if they had he would not have needed to transcribe the rest of its contents, and we should be without the waste-books. These are precisely such a "solution" as he refers to : each thought in them keeps all its options open.

Unless there is purpose there cannot be suspension of purpose and Lichtenberg's aphorisms were possible only at the cost of a lifetime's frustrated ambitions. The sheer plenitude of the aphorisms tells us how powerful that ambition was. But one cannot but be glad that the price was paid. The ambition and its frustration are two distinct factors, both of which are necessary for the production of the aphorism : in the first place Lichtenberg notes some detail down—a word, a question, a joke, a quotation—not just because he has come across it but because he sees in it some sort of significance, some sort of entelechy, because he thinks he can do something with it; and then he finds himself unable to do violence to that entelechy by incorporating it in one of the false contexts, the false continuities, the false personae that he had to build in the works he published. And so this thought, along with all the other thoughts, is left to lie, innocent, untouched and tantalising as ever. Indolence and integrity are here indistinguishable. It is with relief that we exchange the satirical messiah for "p.m."[86] Yet far from being lost the satirical intention has now taken on a more valuable form :

> "Während man über geheime Sünden öffentlich schreibt, habe ich mir vorgenommen, über öffentliche Sünden heimlich zu schreiben."[87]

Emancipated from his responsibility for public enlightenment, Lichtenberg avoids the German dilemma and is non-ideological without being unpolitical :

> "Sie fühlen den Druck der Regierung so wenig als den Druck der Lufft. (J1217)[88]
> Das Traurigste, was die französische Revolution für uns bewirkt hat, ist unstreitig das, daß man jede vernünftige und von Gott und Rechtswegen zu verlangende Forderung, als einen Keim von Empörung ansehen wird."[89]

He sees that the intellectual and literary ferment (in which his public self took part) compensates for political tutelage :

> "Polen wird getheilt, der Orden der Jesuiten aufgehoben, Hollstein an Dänemarck abgetretten. Davon reden 10 bis 15 politische Zeitungen wie es sich gehört mit unterthänigst devotester Trockenheit. Aber nun hört einmal. Bahrdt travestirt das neue Testament. Da wird in allen gelehrten und ungelehrten Zeitungen gedonnert, gezischt, geklatscht, gepfiffen und getreten, Gläser entzwey geschlagen, Bleystiffte stumpf notirt [. . .]" (D253)[90]

And he notes the artificiality of the resulting literary revival (he after all had surrendered literature rather than accept this artificiality) :

> "Der Deutsche ist nie mehr Nachahmer als wenn er absolut Original seyn will, weil es andere Nationen auch sind, den Original Schrifftstellern andrer Nationen fällt es nie ein Original seyn zu wollen" (D364)[91]

But one should not give the impression that satire in the aphorisms is a matter of sour grapes. The aphorisms are not a private revenge on an uncongenial world. The concern for Germany's future in the published satires, that at least is not a pose, and after 1775, despite regrets, Lichtenberg's eyes are not always fixed on the other side of the Channel. The wider world has given him clarity of vision, but he does not seriously think he could belong to it :

> "Ein Mädchen, 150 Bücher, ein paar Freunde und ein Prospect

von etwa einer deutschen Meile im Durchmesser, war die Welt
für ihn.[92]
Was würde es geben, wenn man einmal in London die 10
Gebote während als es 12 schlüge aufhübe". (F299)[93]

Indeed the observer can see quite enough without even looking out
of his window :

"Wenn ich bisweilen viel Caffee getruncken hatte und daher
über alles erschrack, so konte ich ganz gnau mercken, daß ich
eher erschrack ehe ich den Krach hörte, wir hören also gleichsam
noch mit andern Werckzeugen, als mit den Ohren. (A49).
Um eine fremde Sprache recht gut sprechen zu lernen, und
würcklich in Gesellschafft zu sprechen mit dem eigentlichen
Accent des Volks, muß man nich allein Gedächtniß und Ohr
haben, sondern auch in gewissem Grad ein kleiner Geck seyn."
(E173)[94]

At this provincial Calvary the martyrdom is quiet, but not for that
less terrible :

"Die Balcken von Häusern anzusehen, die Zeugen waren von
Hofnungen, die nun nach 25 Jahren nicht erfüllt sind. O Gott
O Gott. [. . .] (L444)
Pusillanimitaet ist das rechte Wort für meine Kranckheit, aber
[wie] benimmt man sich die? Diese zu überwinden würde
Ehrensäulen verdienen, aber wer sezt dem Menschen Ehrensäulen,
der sich aus einem alten Weibe zum Manne macht?" (J320)[95]

The modest consolation, however, is not ignored :

"Wenn jemand alle glücklichen Einfälle seines Lebens dicht
zusammen sammelte, so würde ein gutes Werk daraus werden.
Jedermann ist wenigstens des Jahres Einmal ein Genie. Die
eigentlich so genannten Genies haben nur die guten Einfälle
dichter. Man sieht also wie viel darauf ankommt, Alles auf-
zuschreiben."[96]

Yes, the consolation is accepted, but its price is not concealed :

"Ich habe den Weg zur Wissenschafft gemacht wie Hunde die
mit ihren Herren spatzieren gehen, hundert mal dasselbe vorwärts
und rückwärts, und als ich ankam war ich müde." (J470)[97]

There is of course much in the waste-books that does not refer
directly to the circumstances of Lichtenberg's life. They are not,
it will be remembered, diaries, not even spiritual diaries. There
are the common forms of maxim and witticism that most obviously
link him to other aphorists :

"Wahrhafftes unaffectirtes Mistrauen gegen menschliche Kräffte in allen Stücken ist das sicherste Zeichen von Geistesstärcke." (F323)[98]
"Wenn die Menschen sagen, sie wollen nichts geschenkt haben, so ist es gemeiniglich ein Zeichen, daß sie etwas geschenkt haben wollen."[99]

There are the little fantasies of the common life that he made so peculiarly his own :

"Da liegen nun die Kartoffeln, und schlafen ihrer Auferstehung entgegen."[100]
"Der Esel kommt mir vor wie ein Pferd ins Holländische übersetzt."[101]

Then there are forms that are clearly related to his scientific activity, though they have been extended to cover life as a whole : rules of procedure, for example :

"Immer sich zu fragen : sollte hier nicht ein Betrug Statt finden? und welches ist der natürlichste, in den der Mensch unvermerkt fallen, oder den er am leichtesten erfinden kann?"[102]
"Man muß nicht zu viel in Büchern *blättern* über Wissenschaften, die man noch zu erlernen hat. Es schlägt oft nieder. Immer nur das Gegenwärtige weggearbeitet!"[103]

or the tabulation :

"Die Bewegungs Gründe, woraus man etwas thut, könten so wie die 32 Winde geordnet werden, und die Nahmen auf ähnliche Art formirt werden. Brod Brod Ruhm oder Ruhm Ruhm Brod, Furcht, Lust." (D367)[104]

But if, *per impossibile,* there is a *characteristic* form among the aphorisms (and there are about 6000 of them), it is the hypothesis. Though this is really a whole genus of forms running from bizarre suggestion to metaphysical fancy :

"*Särge von Korbwerk* könnten wohlfeil und doch schön gemacht werden; man könnte sie schwarz und weiß anstreichen. Sie hätten den Vortheil, daß sie leicht verfaulten."[105]
"Wenn der Mensch, nachdem er 100 Jahre alt geworden, wieder umgewendet werden könnte, wie eine Sanduhr, und so wieder jünger würde, immer mit der gewöhnlichen Gefahr, zu sterben; wie würde es da in der Welt aussehen?"[106]
"Es wäre ein Thier möglich dessen Gehirn die See wäre, und dem der Nordwind blau und der Südwind roth hieße."(F33)[107]

The hypothesis, as a form of the aphorism, derives from doubt, from the disabling doubt, or from the doubt that expressed disablement, that accompanied Lichtenberg's infertile scientific struggles. It is—like the satirical observations and notes from the literary context—failure transmuted into gold,

> "Selbst unsere häufigen Irrthümer haben den Nutzen, daß sie uns am Ende gewöhnen zu glauben, alles könne anders seyn, als wir es uns vorstellen." (J919)[108]

Lichtenberg's aphoristic hypotheses are simply statements of ways in which things could be different. Because they are only statements of possibility it is wrong to treat them as anticipations of modern developments (psychoanalysis, for example, or linguistic philosophy) just as it is wrong to reconstruct literary works from the fragments of novels and satires that also occur among the aphorisms. Between the covers of the waste-books, the hypotheses are "in suspension". Because he is fascinated by the existence of so many possibilities, Lichtenberg can seem to be a nihilist like so many aphorists before and after him. But his doubt is not even Cartesian, it is not *systematic* doubt:

> "Zweifle an Allem wenigstens Einmal, und wäre es auch der Satz: zweimal 2 ist 4."[109]

"At least once"—doubt that is applied thus piecemeal is an instrument for writing aphorisms, not for constructing a philosophy.

> "Solte nicht manches von dem was Herr Kant lehrt, zumal in Rücksicht auf das Sittengesetz Folge des Alters seyn, wo Leidenschafft und Neigungen ihre Krafft verloren haben, und Vernunfft allein übrig bleibt?" (L733)[110]

This is not [111] an irresponsible jibe at Kant's expense by one who could not live up to the demands of his philosophy, but a hypothesis as earnest—and as playful—as any other that Lichtenberg propounded—it is the possibility of another "way of looking at"[112] the Kantian philosophy. Why should one not doubt Kant, "at least once"? Why should philosophy always have the last word? Why not natural history? Why should there not be a natural history of philosophers?

> "Was denkbar ist, ist auch möglich."[113]

Indeed if, again *per impossibile,* there is a characteristic subject-matter to the aphorisms it is this: thought is a fact. It is what consoled Amintor: thought itself is a phenomenon that belongs, "mit in die Reihe", to the universal order. It is a part of nature, something to rejoice in.

"Dieses ist dem Menschen so natürlich als das Dencken, oder das werfen mit Schneebällen." (C155)[114]

True, for the deformed Lichtenberg the recognition that thought also is a part of the human condition comes by way of harsh personal experience:

"Die gesundesten und schönsten, regelmäßigst gebauten Leute sind die, die sich Alles gefallen lassen. Sobald einer ein Gebrechen hat, so hat er seine eigne Meinung."[115]

But the principle is general and applies to all kinds of thought:

"Solte nicht der Mensch seine Ideen von Gott eben so *zweckmäßig* weben können, wie die Spinne ihr Netz zum Fliegenfang? oder mit andern Worten: solte es nicht Wesen geben, die uns wegen unsrer Ideen von Gott und Unsterblichkeit eben so bewunderten wie wir die Spinne und den Seidenwurm?" (L736)[116]

Lichtenberg's most famous expression of the idea puts it in metaphysical terms:

"*Es denkt,* sollte man sagen, so wie man sagt: *es blitzt.* Zu sagen *cogito,* ist schon zu viel, so bald man es durch *Ich denke* übersetzt. Das Ich anzunehmen, zu postuliren, ist praktisches Bedürfniß."[117]

It also has a moral form, which is all the more impressive for being one of the last aphorisms that Lichtenberg wrote, a kind of summing-up in fact:

"Ich glaube der Mensch ist am Ende ein so freyes Wesen, daß ihm das Recht *zu seyn* was er glaubt zu seyn nicht streitig gemacht werden kan." (L745)[118]

Lichtenberg thought much, and to no purpose, and for that very reason his thought was pure. His aphorisms retain a childish integrity which no other aphorist possesses: there is *no* limitation, no intellectual reservation or corruption, in every fragment he gives his whole life up for a thought. And he pays the price—all else he does is waste, time gone for ever, entropy gained, at the end he is "weary". He has held nothing back, and so, crazy though the claim may seem, there is something Shakespearean about the "Sudelbücher". Certainly it ill behoves the critic to reproach with moral immaturity the man who wrote

"O wie oft habe ich der Nacht gebeichtet, in der Hoffnung, daß sie mich absolviren würde, und sie hat mich nicht absolvirt!"[119]

Lichtenberg is a natural among intellectuals: he lives unself-consciously with selfconsciousness, speculation and doubt—and everything else. He knows that his is the human condition, but he also knows that to discover one is human is not to make a remarkable discovery. (As Montaigne or Pascal or Nietzsche thought it was.) What is always worth doing, always worthy of remark, is finding out about, showing off found bits of, that condition, and knowing those bits for what they are. Moreover, as his generous appreciation of his intellectual heroes, but also of colleagues and friends, shows, Lichtenberg is not insensitive to human greatness: he knows about that too, and while he admires the greatness what interests him is the humanity. Perhaps he knows about it because in part he possesses it.

"Es macht allemal einen sonderbaren Eindruck auf mich, wenn ich einen großen Gelehrten oder sonst einen wichtigen und gesezten Mann sehe, dabey zu dencken, daß doch einmal eine Zeit war, da er den Maykäfern ein Liedchen sang um sie zum auffliegen zu ermuntern." (L163)[120]

NOTES

Abbreviations

PhM   Vols. 6–9 of the *Vermischte Schriften* 1800–6, which contain the *Physikalische und Mathematische Schriften*.

VS   *Vermischte Schriften* 1844–7.

Grenzmann *Gesammelte Werke* ed. Wilhelm Grenzmann 1949.

Br. ed.   Vol. IV (Briefe) of *Schriften und Briefe* ed. Wolfgang

Promies   Promies 1967.

References to the aphorisms follow the numbering of Leitzmann's edition. This consists of a letter (A to L), which Lichtenberg assigned to the MS volume in question, and a number, assigned by Leitzmann to the individual aphorism. MS volumes, G, H (1779–89), and most of K (1793–6) are lost. For further details of all these editions see Bibliography.

    1. S. Frensdorff *Die englischen Prinzen in Göttingen* in: *Zeitschrift des historischen Vereins für Niedersachsen* 1905 p. 435.

    2. W. A. Darlington in: *Daily Telegraph* October 22, 1958. Quoted in: J. P. Stern *Lichtenberg* (see Bibliography) p. 338.

    3. Of which two separate translations have been made in the last five years. See Bibliography.

    4. Vol. 69 (1799) pp. 347, 434.

    5. A. Leitzmann (ed.) *Aus Lichtenbergs Nachlaß* Weimar 1899 p. 180.

    6. To make any show of completeness, the list would also need to mention: Hofmannsthal, Karl Kraus, Robert Musil, Kurt Tucholsky, André Breton, Thomas Mann and W. H. Auden.

7. In a piquant essay, *Die Frauen und Lichtenberg,* Herbert Schöffler suggests this is because it has never appealed to women: *Lichtenberg. Studien zu seinem Wesen und Geist* (ed. Götz von Selle) Göttingen 1956 pp. 31–43.

8. "I am reading Kant and Lichtenberg [. . .] I am fascinated by the clearness and grace of their style, and in particular by Lichtenberg's keen wit [. . .] I do not understand how the Germans of today can so neglect this author [. . .]" Hugo Ganz *The Downfall of Russia* London 1904 p. 300. German original: *Vor der Katastrophe* Frankfurt 1904 p. 296.

9. Title of notebook J (translated).

10. E46: Shopkeepers have their Waste book ("Sudelbuch", "Klitterbuch" in German, I believe) in which they enter day by day everything they sell or buy, all higgledy-piggledy [. . .] This deserves to be imitated by the learned [. . .] a book in which I enter everything as I see it or as my thoughts come to me [. . .].

11. P. Requadt *Lichtenberg* (see Bibliography) p. 16.

12. Notably the selection of essays in Grenzmann's edition (1949), and in the edition—still being published—of W. Promies (1967–), as well as the considerable amount of space devoted to these ephemera in F. H. Mautner's standard study *Lichtenberg. Geschichte seines Geistes* (see Bibliography).

13. On the profit to be drawn from mathematics by a *bel esprit* VS III 53–62. It appeared in the *Hannoversches Magazin.*

14. p. 55. Lichtenberg is more circumspect in dealing with individual personalities. His teacher and academic patron, the vain, malicious, tyrannical and regrettably long-lived A. G. Kästner, receives three flattering mentions in the first three pages.

15. "mein Gedanke" p. 59.

16. O. Deneke *Lichtenbergs Leben* (see Bibliography) p. 63.

17. Student of theology and *belles lettres.*

18. VS III 85 How can a man's natural honesty, not to mention the artificial varieties take that sitting down?

19. VS III 116 To be sure, it is perhaps two and a half inches, Paris measure, from the nose to the soul, always provided the latter is at home. . . .

20. D90 (1773), E174 (1775).

21. Though he would have thought himself to be the same age as Herder (cp. F1207) he was in fact two years older.

22. e.g. C49 (1772), D526 (1774).

23. See for example B78 (1769), B333 (1770), both from letters to Ljungberg, B344 (the motif of castration is not uncommon at this time).

24. See Leitzmann's note to D647 (ca. May 1775) (*Aphorismen* Bd. I Tl.2 p. 328). Time and Genius have often whispered in my ear: Now, Photorin, strike now, and save the country, you can do it, and I have hummed a tune, or drummed upon the window-pane. Stern p. 72.

25. Cp. letter to Nicolai of September 2, 1776 (*Br.* ed. Promies pp. 273–4).

26. *Epistel an Tobias Göbhard* . . . VS III 137–162, *Friedrich Eckard an den Verfasser der Bemerkungen* . . . ibid. 163–180. The reference of Lichtenberg's pseudonym is again personal: Friedrich was the name of one of his brothers, Eckard his mother's maiden name.

27. *Über die Pronunciation der Schöpse* . . . VS IV 243–265, *Über Hrn. Vossens Vertheidigung gegen mich* . . . ibid. 266–332, cp. also ibid. 235. An exhaustive documentation of the controversy will be found in *Ein Jahrhundert deutscher Literaturkritik* Ed. Oskar Fambach Bd. III (1750–1795), Berlin, 1959, pp. 215–309.

28. VS IV 332 no more contemptible creature under the sun than a man who, for the rubbishy sake of the sound of some letter of an extinct people, is guilty of ingratitude: a crime, that is, which an upright man would not commit for all the world.

29. psychological.

30. VS IV 265 I will never give Mr. Voss a *serious* answer, I would rather—oh, I do not know what I would rather do—oh, I would almost rather write "Lord Jasus". (Voß had defended himself against Heyne's humorous suggestion that consistency demanded he should adopt this spelling of "Jesus".)

31. the good Lord's Lower Chamber, in which he himself has entrusted us with a seat and a vote.

32. *Über die Weissagungen des* [. . .] *Herrn Ziehen* . . . (1780) VS V 3–13, *Noch ein Wort über Herrn Ziehens Weissagungen* (1782) VS V 14–27, *Antwort auf das vorstehende Sendschreiben* (1783) VS V 87–110, *Bemerkungen über ein Paar Stellen* . . . (1783) VS V 28–32. The first of these pieces was twice printed and twice pirated (VS V 27).

33. VS IV 3–72. Lichtenberg himself published only one further contribution to the controversy, a notice *An die Leser des Deutschen Museums* (VS IV 103–106). The *Fragment von Schwänzen* (1783), VS IV 109–119, appeared without his permission.

34. cp. letter to Nicolai, February 15, 1778 (*Br*. ed. Promies p. 314) "auf einem Gartenhause flüchtig zusammengeschrieben." But the abundance of notes in F on physiognomical topics shows that Lichtenberg was deeply involved in the issue.

35. VS IV 21–22, 24 That, in an absolute sense, everything can be read in everything else, is doubted by nobody. [. . .] This yields no particular consolation for physiognomy unless we are more specific, since this very "reading" [. . .] is itself also the source of our errors and, in many matters, of our total ignorance. [. . .] Is *everything* in the face to be referred only to head or heart? Why do you not see the date of birth, the cold of the winter, the dirty napkins, the careless nursemaids, the damp bedchambers, the childhood illnesses, in the shape of the nose?

36. VS IV 41 A long-winded work, indeed a work that is of its very nature long-winded [. . .] Physiognomy will die choked by its own fat.

37. VS IV 30–31, 27 I do not want to know what the man could have become. What could not anybody have become? No, I want to know what he is [. . .] In heaven's name what does it mean in practice,

a good disposition that has been perverted? It means no more than a straight line that has been curved—a curve, in fact.

38. Quoted from *Physiognomy* [. . .] *A complete epitome of the original work of J. C. Lavater* London 1866 p. 169. Cp. letter to Schernhagen, February 10, 1778 (*Br.* ed. Promies p. 312).

39. Alan Marshall *Lichtenberg's Satirical Writings* in: *Essays in German Language, Culture and Society* [presented to Roy Pascal] London 1969 pp. 46–58. The bibliographical information on p. 54 is incorrect.

40. See e.g. letter to Schernhagen, February 15, 1778 (*Br.* ed. Promies p. 313).

41. F. H. Mautner *Lichtenberg* p. 188.

42. VS IV 14–15. In England in the year 1770, as well as in 1774 and 1775, I industriously took physiognomical observations that often proved as dangerous as observations of atmospheric electricity [. . .] There I saw and spoke to men, famous and infamous alike, who are among the most remarkable of the modern age [. . .] Yet what in the end was the result of all my exertions? Nothing, save a slightly closer acquaintance with mankind and myself, and then a distrust of all physiognomy [. . .].

43. All three letters are reprinted in VS III 197–268.

44. M.B. and L.M. Price *The Publication of English Literature in Germany in the eighteenth century* Berkeley 1934 p. 14.

45. VS III 219 Hot-houses.

46. VS III 212 All men were an open book to his observant spirit, from the civilised and sophisticated in the salons of St. James' to the savages in the eating-houses of St. Giles'. He went to the school that Shakespeare attended, and there like Shakespeare he did not wait for revelations to come to him, but applied himself to study (for in England not everything is done by genius as it is in Germany), I mean London, where a man with such a talent for observation can in a year give his empirical principles an accuracy for which a whole lifetime would hardly suffice in some small town, where all hopes and fears are the same, all marvels are the same, all stories are the same, and everything rhymes with everything else [. . .] I am surprised that London does not produce more, I do not mean more Garricks or Hogarths or Fieldings, but people who are something different but have come to it in the same way as they. Knowledge of the world gives superiority to writers of any category.

47. VS IV 193 He must be sufficiently rich in observations to toss one down even when he cannot be certain that it will be picked up straight away, and to give out gold sovereigns with an expression that says nothing about their value—and not like our swells hurl back brass farthings with such hauteur that just to see the expression you would think they must be gold sovereigns.

48. *Proposal for an Orbis Pictus for German dramatic writers . . . and its Continuation . . .* VS IV 186–227.

49. VS IV 197 I have a good supply of observations in store.

50. VS IV 205 *Servants.* a) male B) For the Actor: He likes to pick fluff off his hat and catch flies like a dying man, and to spin his hat in front of his navel like a windmill. This is to be used sparingly [. . .] When he is with his inferiors he straddles his legs so as to look smaller, and makes his talk impressive. Short ones even do this sometimes when facing tall ones.

51. *Complete Commentary on the Engravings of Hogarth.* This is at present most accessible in Wilhelm Grenzmann's edition of Lichtenberg's works, vol. II pp. 669–1181. (N.B. on p. 681 for "1784" read "1794") For English translations, see Bibliography.

52. 600 copies of the first fascicle were sold in three months (Schöffler *Lichtenberg* p. 85). It was such a success that Dieterich, the publisher, could not let the project drop when Lichtenberg died, but completed it partly by reprinting material from the *Taschenkalender* and partly by engaging hacks to fill out the lacunae that remained. Goethe's comments (in the *Tag-und Jahres-Hefte*) will be found in the Weimar edition vol. 35 pp. 55–7.

53. *Vorrede* Grenzmann II 672–3.

54. *Vorrede* Grenzmann II 677 I however am at liberty to make the comparison, simply as a figure that leads into the next following remark.

55. *Die Heirat nach der Mode. Sechstes Blatt* Grenzmann II 783 For eleven of the morning is late to the man who at four was already awake over his account-books. In the *West* End the midday meal is taken at a time when here in the East it is already five o'clock. This gives London town a longitudinal social extension of 6 hours of time or 90 degrees of arc. Should it continue to grow, of which there is every reason to be confident, and should the king of Spain ever again boast that the sun never sets in his domains, any Cockney could cheerfully reply that his home town alone is so large that wherever the sun chooses to stand it will find a family eating their midday meal.

56. See Ronald Paulson (*Journal of English and Germanic Philology* vol. 66 (1967) p. 597): "Lichtenberg retells Hogarth's stories in his own idiom, and makes them his own. Hogarth is partially transformed in the process: such a retelling, to catch Hogarth, would have to be in the idiom of Fielding; Lichtenberg is a whimsically pedantic German, an English approximation being a cross between Sterne and the Carlyle of *Sartor Resartus.*"

57. Weimar edition vol. 47 pp. 119–207.

58. ibid. p. 202 dotter and stippler. No names are named.

59. VS IV 197 the holy sepulchre of the fine arts.

60. Quoted by H. Uhde-Bernays in: *Der Mannheimer Shakespeare* in *Litterarhistorische Forschungen* XXV (Berlin 1902) p. 71 "Lichtenberg, Goethe and Herder should join forces and give us a version of Shakespeare where you could completely forget you were reading a translation."

61. See Mautner *Lichtenberg* p. 424.

62. Schöffler *Lichtenberg* p. 83.

63. *History of candle-snuffers* VS V 316–8; *The Aeolian harp* VS VI 3–10; *Why is the German public still without a large resort for marine bathing?* VS VI 11–23.

64. *A dream* VS VI 50–5.

65. *Speech by the figure 8* VS VI 174–194.

66. *Amintor's morning devotion* VS V 334–9.

67. Letter to F. F. Wolff December 30, 1784 (*Br.* ed. Promies pp. 598–9) which is what I am always saying in my lectures, namely, *investigation,* never *conclusions,* when you go beyond the evidence of the senses. I believe that without this great principle we cannot hope for any real progress in physics.

68. PhM IX 134.

69. *Vorrede* to Erxleben *Anfangsgründe der Naturlehre* (6. Aufl. 1794) p. XXVIII quoted from J. C. Fischer *Geschichte der Physik* . . . Göttingen 1801–8 vol. 8 p. 117. If one assumed that the electrical substance consisted of oxygen and hydrogen with caloric [Lavoisier's terminology] and impressed on these explanations the character of facts, then with a little wit and literary style the edifice of an electrical chemistry could be constructed which in outward appearance would yield little to the antiphlogistical system.

70. To Riemer. Quoted Stern *Lichtenberg* p. 128

71. PhM IX 140 Montgolfier's invention lay in my hand.

72. *Tobiae Mayeri opera inedita I* (1775) and several re-editions of J. C. P. Erxleben's compendium *Anfangsgründe der Naturlehre.*

73. *On the fabric of the universe* PhM VI 172–210.

74. *Does the moon turn upon its axis?* PhM VII 107–154.

75. *Letter to Mr. Werner in Giessen, touching the Newtonian theory of light* probably written in 1788 or 1789 (see Mautner *Lichtenberg* p. 316) PhM IX 361–432.

76. MS quoted by Paul Hahn: *Georg Christoph Lichtenberg und die exakten Wissenschaften* Göttingen 1927 p. 63. In investigating the truth we should always proceed in such a way that even more illuminated times will be able to take as a model if not our beliefs, then at any rate our procedure in arriving at them.

77. VS V 337. It was anything but that physico-theological contemplation of suns, of which the army clearly visible to us is estimated by a certain kind of calculation at 75 millions. Such reflections he called mere music of the spheres, that at first transport the nigh swooning spirit, as in a whirlwind of ecstasy, but to which the spirit finally becomes accustomed; and what was permanent in them— indisputably the better part—could be found everywhere and supremely in the very spirit, itself a link in the great chain, which was capable of these reflections. No, his was rather the rejoicing at *his own existence* that imperceptibly attached itself to an untiring study of Nature, together with curiosity (if that is the right word), a desire not *anxious* but *joyful* to discover, with our own senses, or with analogous ones, or through relations of some other kind which one can expect from every mode of being, *just what all this is about and what it is up to.*

78. It is almost impossible to write something good without imagining somebody or even a certain selection of people whom one is addressing.

79. Mautner *Lichtenberg* pp. 457–470.

80. F. H. Mautner *Lichtenbergs ungedruckte Tagebücher* ... *Euphorion* 3. Folge, LI (1957) pp. 23–41.

81. See letter to Dieterich July 8, 1773 (*Br.* ed Promies p. 145) and Leitzmann's comments *Aphorismen* Bd. I Tl. 2 p. 261.

82. VS VI 195–200.

83. See the description of these given by Leitzmann *Aus Lichtenbergs Nachlaß* p. XV. In the "Sudelbücher" Lichtenberg did *not* cross out entries once they had been used elsewhere.

84. If I had not written this book, then in many a town in Germany a thousand years from today, between 6 and 7 in the evening, say, quite different things would be talked about than actually will be talked about.

85. PhM IX 137–8. How many ideas float scattered around my head, and many a pair of them, if they came together, might produce the greatest of discoveries. When we are thinking and entrusting ourselves to the natural dispositions of the reason and of the categories of understanding, the ideas often *adhere* to each other too much so that they cannot join up with those they really belong to. If only we had something like solution in chemistry, where the several parts float in weightless suspension, and so can respond to every attraction.

86. p.m. = pellucidus mons = Lichtenberg. In the aphorisms this is a frequent substitute for the first person.

87. VS II 74 While people are writing publicly about private sins, I have resolved to write secretly about public sins.

88. They no more feel the pressure of the government than they feel the pressure of the atmosphere.

89. VS I 240 The saddest effect the French Revolution has had for us is indisputably this: that every reasonable demand, that God and common justice approve, will be regarded as a seed of sedition.

90. Poland partitioned, the Jesuit order suppressed, Holstein ceded to Denmark. 10 to 15 political journals will mention that in befitting terms of most humble and obedient desiccation. But now just listen. Bahrdt parodies the New Testament. Then in all learned and unlearned journals what a thundering, hissing, clapping, whistling, and stamping, what a breaking of glasses, wearing away of pencils on margins . . .

91. The German is never more an imitator than in his absolute determination to be an original because other nations are it too. It never occurs to the original writers of other nations to want to be originals.

92. VS II 151 A girl, 150 books, a few friends and a view of about five miles in diameter, that was the world for him.

93. What would happen if one were to suspend the Ten Commandments in London one day while it struck twelve?

94. When as I sometimes do I had drunk a lot of coffee and anything made me start, I noticed quite clearly that I started before I heard the sound, so we hear as it were with other instruments besides

the ears. In order to learn to speak a foreign language really well and actually to speak in company with the genuine accent of the people, one needs not only to have memory and a good ear but also to be in some degree a nasty little fop.

95. To see the beams of houses, the witnesses of hopes which now after 25 years have not been fulfilled. O God, O God. Pusillanimity is the proper word for my sickness, but how does one rid oneself of that? To overcome that would be a deed worthy of a monument, but who sets up monuments to a fellow for turning himself from an old woman into a man?

96. VS II 168 If someone were to collect close together all the felicitous ideas he has had in his lifetime, a good book would be the result. Everyone is a genius at least *once* a year. To the geniuses properly so called the ideas just come closer on one another's heels. So one sees how important it is to write everything down.

97. I have travelled the path to knowledge like dogs that go out walking with their masters, the same stretch back and forth a hundred times, and when I got there I was weary.

98. Genuine unaffected distrust of human capacity in everything is the surest indication of a powerful mind.

99. VS I 169 When people say that they do not want something for nothing, this is normally a sign that they want something for nothing.

100. VS II 87 And there lie the potatoes, sleeping on towards their resurrection.

101. VS II 108 The donkey looks to me like a horse translated into Dutch.

102. VS II 134 Always ask myself: could there not be some deception here? and which would be the most natural for a man to fall into without noticing it, or the easiest for him to invent?

103. VS II 129 One should not *browse* too much in books on subjects one has still to learn about it. It often causes depression. Just always get the present job dispatched!

104. The motives that lead one to do something could be arranged like the 32 points of the compass, and their names formed after the same fashion. Bread Bread Fame or Fame Fame Bread, Fear, Lust.

105. VS II 139 Coffins of basketwork could be produced cheaply but prettily; they could be painted black and white. They would have the advantage of rotting easily.

106. VS II 193 If a man, after reaching the age of 100, could be turned over again like an hour-glass, and so get younger again, always with the usual danger of dying, what would things look like then?

107. An animal could be possible whose brain was the sea, and which called the north wind blue and the south wind red.

108. Even our frequent errors have this much use, that in the end they accustom us to thinking that everything could be different from how we imagine it.

109. VS II 136 Doubt *everything* at least *once,* even the proposition: twice 2 is 4. (The nature of this doubt is further elucidated in J915.)

110. Could not much of Mr. Kant's doctrine, particularly in respect of the moral law, be a consequence of old age, when passion and the affections have lost their force and only reason remains? See also what Lichtenberg says about Leibniz, F345.

111. As Requadt has it, *Lichtenberg* p. 99.

112. "Vorstellungsart" PhM IX 134.

113. What is thinkable is possible too, L. Wittgenstein *Tractatus Logico-Philosophicus* trans. D. F. Pears and B. F. McGuinness, London 1966 § 3.02.

114. This is as natural to man as thinking, or snowballing.

115. VS I 191 The healthiest and handsomest, the most regularly formed people are those who fall in with everything. As soon as someone has a defect, he has an opinion of his own.

116. Could it not be that man weaves his ideas of God to as much *purpose* as the spider weaving its web for catching flies? Or in other words: could not beings exist that would admire us for our ideas of God and immortality as much as we admire the spider and the silkworm?

117. VS I 99. We should say, "It thinks", just as we say, "It thunders". Even to say *cogito* is too much if we translate it with "*I* think". To assume the "I", to postulate it, is a practical need. (Trans. Stern *Lichtenberg* p. 270, slightly adapted.)

118. I believe man is ultimately so free a thing that his right *to be* what he believes himself to be cannot be disputed.

119. VS I 32 Oh how often have I made my confession to the night, in the hope that she would absolve me, and she has not absolved me! See also Stern *Lichtenberg* pp. 215–216.

120. It always makes a strange impression on me, when I see a great scholar or some other important and serious man, to think that there was once a time when he sang a little song to a ladybird to encourage her to fly away.

SELECT BIBLIOGRAPHY

(a) Lichtenberg's works
There is no complete edition, nor any likelihood of one this century. The works have to be pieced together from the following.
Vermischte Schriften [. . .] *aus den hinterlassenen Papieren gesammelt und herausgegeben* von Ludwig Christian Lichtenberg und Friedrich Kries. 9 vols. Göttingen 1800–6. (Volumes 6–9 contain the *Physikalische und Mathematische Schriften,* unreprinted since.)
Vermischte Schriften. Neue vermehrte, von dessen Söhnen veranstaltete Original-Ausgabe. 8 vols. Göttingen 1844–7. (Volumes I and II contain many aphorisms from waste-books that have not survived.)
Gesammelte Werke ed. Wilhelm Grenzmann. 2 vols. + Ergänzungsband. Frankfurt a.M. 1949. Vol. II includes the *Ausführliche Erklärung.*

Schriften und Briefe ed. Wolfgang Promies. 4 vols. München 1967—(only vols. I (*Sudelbücher*) and IV (*Briefe*) have so far appeared. The volume of letters brings together much material discovered since the Leitzmann-Schüddekopf edition, but is not complete.)

Aphorismen ed. Albert Leitzmann. 5 parts in 3 vols. Berlin and Leipzig 1902–8. (Deutsche Literaturdenkmale Nos. 123, 131, 136, 140, 141.) (The standard edition of the surviving waste-books.)

Briefe ed. Albert Leitzmann and Carl Schüddekopf. 3 vols. Leipzig 1901–4.

Gedankenbücher ed. Franz H. Mautner. Heidelberg 1967. (The only selection that can be wholeheartedly recommended.)

(b) Translations into English.

"Thoughts from Professor Lichtenberg". *Pocket Magazine of Classic and Polite Literature*. Arliss's series. Vol. 1 pp. 215–216. London 1818.

"The Phenomena of diseased Imagination". *London Magazine* vol. 1 No. 3 pp. 250–4 (March 1820).

"German descriptions of Hogarth's works". *London Magazine* vol. 2 No. 9 pp. 277–284, vol. 2 No. 10 pp. 388–402 (September, October 1820).

The Reflections of Lichtenberg trans. N. Alliston. London 1908.

Lichtenberg's Visits to England as described in his Letters and Diaries trans. and annotated by Margaret L. Mare and W. H. Quarrell. Oxford 1938.

The Lichtenberg Reader trans. F. H. Mautner and H. Hatfield. Boston 1959.

Lichtenberg's Commentaries on Hogarth's Engravings trans. G. and I. Herdan. London 1966.

Lichtenberg: Aphorisms and Letters trans. F. H. Mautner and H. Hatfield. London 1969. (An abridged edition of *The Lichtenberg Reader*.)

Hogarth on High Life. The marriage à la Mode Series from Georg Christoph Lichtenberg's Commentaries trans. and ed. Arthur S. Wensinger with W.B. Coley. Wesleyan University Press 1970.

A Dream trans. Meyer Schapiro *New York Review of Books* vol XV No. 3 p. 15 (August 13, 1970).

Translations will also be found in J. P. Stern's *Lichtenberg* (see below) pp. 277–327 (aphorisms and *Amintor's Morning Devotion*); *Physiognomy* London 1866 (see fn. 38 above) (Lavater's extracts from *Über Physiognomik*); and in such collections as *The Faber Book of Aphorisms* ed. W. H. Auden and L. Kronenberger. London 1964.

(c) Studies of Lichtenberg

In German:

O. Deneke	*Lichtenbergs Leben I* (*1742–75*) München 1944 (no more published).
Paul Requadt	*Lichtenberg* 2nd ed. Stuttgart 1964.
W. Promies	*Georg Christoph Lichtenberg in Selbstzeugnissen und Bilddokumenten* (Rowohlts Monographien 90) Hamburg 1964.

F. H. Mautner   *Lichtenberg. Geschichte seines Geistes* Berlin 1968.

Rudolf Jung   *Lichtenberg-Bibliographie* Heidelberg (Lothar Stiehm Verlag). In preparation.

In English:

J. P. Stern   *Lichtenberg. A Doctrine of Scattered Occasions.* Bloomington 1959. London 1963. (Indispensable.)

Carl Brinitzer   *A Reasonable Rebel* trans. Bernard Smith London 1960.

Eric G. Forbes   *Tobias Mayer: Opera Inedita.* London 1971.

Jakob Michael Reinhold Lenz

Jakob Michael Reinhold Lenz

by ALLAN BLUNDEN

Jakob Michael Reinhold Lenz was born in 1751 in a village in Livonia. He entered Königsberg University in 1768; but, unable to settle to his theological studies, he went to Strasbourg in 1771 as travelling-companion to the von Kleist brothers, who planned to enter French military service. There Lenz met Goethe, and devoted his energies to the Salzmann literary circle. The Strasbourg years were his most fruitful period of work, and it was here that he wrote *Der Hofmeister* (1774), *Der neue Menoza* (1774), *Das Tagebuch* (1774–5), *Die Soldaten* (1775), and *Der Engländer* (1775–6). Early in 1776 he moved to Weimar, but spent much of the summer in the country, at Berka. Here he wrote *Der Waldbruder*. In December the Duke expelled him from the court for some unspecified social blunder. Disillusioned and unbalanced in mind, Lenz drifted aimlessly in Switzerland and southern Germany until 1779, when his brother fetched him home to Riga. He failed to obtain a teaching post there, tried unsuccessfully to join the army in St. Petersburg, and went to Moscow in 1781, where he lived obscurely, dependent on the charity of friends. He was found dead in the street in May 1792.

"Diese Schrift ward zwei Jahre vor Erscheinung der Deutschen Art und Kunst und des Götz von Berlichingen in einer Gesellschaft guter Freunde vorgelesen. Da noch manches für die heutige Belliteratur drin sein möchte, das jene beiden Schriften nicht ganz überflüssig gemacht, so teilen wir sie—wenn nicht anders als das erste ungehemmte Räsonnement eines unparteiischen Dilettanten—unsern Lesern rhapsodienweis mit."[1]

WITH this urbane apologia Lenz introduces his *Anmerkungen übers Theater* (published in 1774). It is the most famous of his critical essays, for literary history has accepted the claim which the author puts forward under the cover of diffidence—that his essay is of the same revolutionary importance as *Von deutscher Art und Kunst* and *Götz von Berlichingen*. Certainly it belongs to a recognisable family of writings, which also includes Gerstenberg's *Briefe über Merkwürdigkeiten der Literatur* and H. L. Wagner's *Neuer Versuch über die Schauspielkunst* (translated from the French of Mercier). Like these, Lenz' essay presents the "naturalist" dramaturgy of the "Sturm und Drang", contemptuous of all rules: he attacks the

French theatre as artificial and poor, and rejects the unities of time and place as totally irrelevant. All that matters is the unity of action, which is conveniently undefinable : "Der Dichter und das Publikum müssen die eine Einheit fühlen aber nicht klassifizieren".[2] He is here combining the petulant cry of Gerstenberg—"Weg mit der Klassifikation des Drama !"[3]—with the Goethean sense of richness residing in the very word "Gefühl" :[4] we think at once of Faust's "Gefühl ist alles",[5] and "Wenn ihrs nicht fühlt, ihr werdets nicht erjagen".[6]

Lenz contemplates with rapture the achievement of Shakespeare, and like all the "Stürmer und Dränger" he infers from the greatness of the plays that Shakespeare himself was a man of Promethean personality : "Mensch, in jedem Verhältnis gleich bewandert, gleich stark, schlug er ein Theater fürs ganze menschliche Geschlecht auf. . . ."[7] Such an inference is, of course, the corollary to their own ambition; aspiring to Shakespeare's achievement, they naturally attributed to him their own feelings of titanic creative potential. We observe that the "Stürmer und Dränger" had a special level of rhetoric reserved for mention of Shakespeare : the *nec plus ultra* of this may be read in Gerstenberg's *Briefe über Merkwürdigkeiten der Literatur,* where he defines the material of Shakespeare's drama as "Der Mensch ! die Welt ! Alles !"[8] That, as Mr. Harry Secombe once remarked to a fellow Goon, seems to exhaust *that* particular line of argument.

Lenz' language is indeed rhapsodic where he speaks of Shakespeare. To be more precise, the language of the *Anmerkungen* is irritatingly careless in places. Yet Lenz' style here is not typical of his writing, which in most of his essays and letters is quite unremarkable in its sobriety. The exuberant and chaotic style of the *Anmerkungen* derives, rather, from the subject-matter and the mood with which such discussion was associated. Any rebellion of youth against the past, once it has become intellectually self-aware and articulate, will adopt and jealously guard a language (that is to say, a jargon) of its own : in our own time, pop-culture and the Underground have both evolved a discourse which is frequently incomprehensible to the outsider, and where it is comprehensible it often appears to be gratuitous. When we consider the origins and diffusion of such an alternative discourse—*langage* as opposed to *langue*—the relative degrees of creative originality and unintelligent imitation are difficult to apportion. For both are responsible for the evolution of such a language. It begins either as a new way of expressing the world experienced by the speaker, or as a means of repudiating the experience and the sensibility of an older generation as outmoded, dishonest, or whatever. And it hopes to justify the viability of its new vision by establishing itself as a social bond between adherents of the new way of life. The frequently opaque critical prose of Hamann, Gerstenberg, Herder, Lavater, and the young Goethe functions more as a social bond than as the adequate or convincing expression of a creative originality; their letters to each other often affect the same "inspired" tone. Doubtless they regarded such a style as "nervicht" (Lenz)[9] or "körnigt" (Wagner-Mercier),[10] succumbing here to the same virility syndrome which informed their thinking about Shakespeare : and obviously there was a desire to *épater le bourgeois* behind it all. Lichtenberg, with his customary perceptiveness, has the wry observation : "Ob das Elend in Deutschland zugenommen hat, weiß ich nicht, die Interjektions Zeichen haben gewiß zugenommen. Wo man sonst bloß ! sezte (sic), da steht jetzt ! ! !"[11]

Lenz' originality is most apparent in his three main dramas, *Der Hofmeister* (1774), *Der neue Menoza* (1774), and *Die Soldaten* (1775). They do not fit into any conventional literary categories. In the nineteenth century, when critical values were largely derived from Weimar classicism, it was usual to regard the plays, more or less disparagingly, as typical "Sturm und Drang" efforts, "unartistic" and "excessive" (though the criteria of sufficiency were not made apparent). Recently, Karl Guthke has argued that Lenz' dramas (excluding *Der neue Menoza*) are the first real tragi-comedies in German literature.[12] Lenz himself referred to *Der Hofmeister* ("Eine Komödie") as "mein Trauerspiel"[13] in letters, while *Die Soldaten* was a "Komödie"[14] before it was finally published as a "Schauspiel".[15] In a letter to Gotter of May, 1775 Lenz writes :

> "Mein Theater ist . . . unter freyem Himmel vor der ganzen deutschen Nation, in der mir die untern Stände mit den obern gleich gelten die *pedites* wie die *equites* ehrenwürdig sind. Findt sich niemand in meinen Stücken wieder so bedaure ich Oel und Mühe—ob sie übrigens spielbar sind bekümmert mich nicht. . . ."[16]

It is clear from this, as well as from the *Anmerkungen* and the plays themselves, that he was more interested in characters than in dramatic construction, and more concerned to offer a compendious abundance of content than to achieve an aesthetic economy of form. Neither comedy nor tragedy was his conscious aim, and the result was a depiction of "life"—he habitually refers to his plays as "Gemälde".[17]

Lenz' best plays are quite properly regarded as social dramas. The three plays mentioned all have a love-story as a central element in the plot : but the development and frustration of passion, and the life of the family unit which is its immediate setting, are seen against a broad contemporary background. Whereas in a French classical tragedy the passion is intense precisely because it is divorced from any wider social context, existing as a thing absolute and universal, in Lenz' dramas the social context is explored so thoroughly and depicted in such a many-sided way that the "passion" seems petty or squalid in its struggling dependence on circumstance. Lenz' dramatic technique of presenting a large number of scenes, which are often extraordinarily short (the briefest, in *Die Soldaten,* contains six spoken words), creates a sense of epic breadth which effectively intimates the presence of a society beyond the domestic milieu. Successive scenes often take place in different towns, and sometimes in different years as well. Hence the action we see is consistently rooted in a scale of time and place which applies in real life, but not in the conventional theatre. What the situations in Lenz' dramas point to is not an abstract scheme of values, as in Goethe's *Iphigenie,* or even in *Götz von Berlichingen,* but the unordered substance and complexity of social existence. Lenz' mode of dramatic writing is more akin to the cinema than to conventional eighteenth-century theatre : the camera (they say) cannot lie, but most poets, as Plato observed, generally do, and it is some measure of Lenz' veracity that his plays contain no heroes or heroines, no clear moral message, and no facile hope that people might be "improved" by experience.

Der Hofmeister was published anonymously in 1774, the year of the *Anmerkungen.* It is a dark forest of a play—some would say a jungle—and we can see why some contemporary reviewers attributed it at first to the author of *Götz.* Läuffer, the tutor of the title, secures a post in the house of Major von Berg, where he is charged with the education of the Major's two children. Gustchen, the daughter, is the childhood sweetheart of her cousin, Fritz von berg, whose father is a "Geheimer Rat" (Privy Councillor). When Fritz goes away to university in Halle, Läuffer seduces Gustchen; it seems to be more the inevitable consequence of boredom and confinement than an act of real passion. When Gustchen becomes sure that she is pregnant, Läuffer absconds and takes refuge with Wenzeslaus, a village schoolmaster. Gustchen runs away too, but not with her lover. Distraught with fury and grief, the Major pursues them. Meanwhile Fritz has his own adventures in Halle, trying to help his student friend Pätus, who gets into financial difficulties and compromises the daughter of his music teacher, Herr Rehaar. Läuffer, who remains with Wenzeslaus, finally castrates himself (it is not clear why). Gustchen, who has been living with a peasant woman, is discovered by her father as she is about to drown herself, and is subsequently reunited with Fritz, who agrees to marry her despite her illegitimate child. Pätus is reunited with his father, whose harshness has been the cause of his chaotic financial circumstances, and he agrees to marry Jungfer Rehaar. To complete this extraordinary happy ending, Läuffer plans to marry Lise, a simple country girl who asks for nothing beyond companionship. It will be clear from this summary that there is no single clearly delineated plot. The different areas of the action are developed in apparent isolation; the links between them derive solely from the circumstance that a character in one plot knows, or is related to, a character in another plot. The expanded dimensions of time and place serve precisely to accommodate such "lifelike" diffuseness, and to render it fully probable—and hence dramatically acceptable—within the context of the play's own world.

What is remarkable in *Der Hofmeister*, as in *Die Soldaten*, is simply the astonishing variety of social encounters which Lenz renders. His concern is to explore character and relationships through dialogue; the corollary to this is that he achieves an illumination of certain problems of communication through characteristic uses of language in these situations. This, indeed, is what distinguishes Lenz' work from the bulk of "Sturm und Drang" drama, and by this means he conveys such a wide range of social observations that what we have is not one-sided polemic but complex and rich analysis. Where other writers impart a simplistic social concern through plot and action and a more or less contrived rhetoric, Lenz is able to characterise people by their speech-habits, which in their turn suggest the social determinants of individual personality.

It is true that people are characterised by speech-habits in Baroque comedy. Gryphius' *Horribilicribrifax* (1663) contains memorable examples of the *miles gloriosus* and the pedantic scholar. But this is sheer spectacle, a gallery of caricatured types, who are funny precisely because we do not conceive them to be of the real world we know. Nor was the technique refined during the century that followed Gryphius' death in 1679—if indeed it was used at all to any important degree. Characters in Lessing's dramas, for instance, all share the same level of discourse; all are equally and similarly eloquent. What distinguishes them from each other are differences in opinions, desires, and moral standards, but these things are not significantly reflected by modulations in linguistic expression. Lenz, however, suggests that there is a relationship between what a man is and what a man says. This is not just a matter of a "local colour" type of realism : Stammler is correct, but uninteresting, when he tells us that "der Major flucht wie ein Soldat".[18] At its crudest level "characteristic" speech does merely serve to "place" a character by superficial association with the reader's experience. Because a dramatic personage talks "like a soldier"—in other words, answers any single one of our (not very exacting) expectations of a soldier's language—we are satisfied that he *is* a soldier, and there the function of characteristic speech ends. What Lenz shows us is not only that a man talks like a soldier because he is one, but also that he is a soldier because he talks like one. To put it less paradoxically, the individual is moulded and limited by the pattern of life, and the pattern of speech associated with it, which he inherits or adopts.

Lenz' concern for language in its social function was unique for his time. Herder, of course, was interested in the origins of language, its historical and ethnic significance, and its expressiveness considered in terms of the individual. All the "Stürmer und Dränger", and Lenz himself, shared these interests to a greater or lesser extent. But Lenz was alone in relating language to society, and only he had a creative concern for the way speech-habits condition our psychology and even our morals. In an essay which he wrote for the Strasbourg literary circle, entitled *Über die Bearbeitung der deutschen Sprache im Elsass, Breisgau und den benachbarten Gegenden* (1775), he writes of language in general:

> "Soll ich Ihnen zu bedenken geben, wie viel nicht allein in den Wissenschaften, wie viel selbst im Handel und Wandel, und allen andern Begegnissen des menschlichen Lebens, die Liebe und die Freundschaft selbst nicht ausgenommen, auf die Sprache ankomme, auf die Art andern seine Gedanken und Wünsche auszudrücken? Die Natur hat schon die Tiere gelehrt, sich durch gewisse Laute und Schreie mit einander zu verbinden; das hülfloseste unter allen Tieren, der Mensch, hat dieses innigen Bandes aller Gesellschaft und Menschenliebe am meisten vonnöten. Treffen wir mit andern in Ansehung unserer gemeinschaftlichen Sprache keine Verabredung, so vereinzeln wir uns selbst auf die allergrausamste Weise."[19]

It purports to be a politico-geographical analysis, but he finds himself relating his argument to domestic and personal situations, love and friendship and family life. To call man "the most helpless of all beasts" is a paradox, and a particularly strange remark for a writer of the late eighteenth century: it is intelligible only in the light of Lenz' view of language as a crucial factor in human affairs. Language, for him, does not simply express—it shapes and influences as well. Fulfilment and happiness, Lenz says, are achieved only through communication and sharing, so that language becomes the key to the good life.

Lenz sees that language does not, in practice, offer us an infinite range of expressive possibilities, which is the assumption behind all those "Sturm und Drang" eulogies of Shakespeare's diction and the poetry of primitive peoples. In his view very nearly the opposite is true : instead of an unlimited number of permutations, each approximating to an "individual" style of speech, and each rendering the nuances of a unique experience, there is a comparatively limited range of rhetorics, each evolved within a social group and becoming a part of that group's identity. The group might be a class or a profession (these being the most obvious social groupings) or it could be a literary coterie—"Stürmer und Dränger", therefore, just as much as "Aufklärer". Communication is effected in terms of a particular and identifiable rhetoric, so that in social intercourse, in our speaking and our writing, we can be neither infinitely clear nor infinitely original. Lenz shows how people's personalities can become circumscribed by the speech-conventions they adopt, which leads to a refusal or an inability to achieve any understanding with people from a different social background.

In the light of this we can now look in detail at some of the characters in Lenz' dramas, returning first of all to *Der Hofmeister*. Wenzeslaus is the first of a series of Lenzian figures who are of a scholarly or philosophical cast of mind. He is a solitary bachelor, locked in a comfortable routine of work and domesticity : "Und da werd ich dick und fett bei und lebe vergnügt und denke noch ans Sterben nicht."[20] Some critics have seen him as the epitome of the Rousseauistic simple life. Rozanov, Lenz' biographer, calls him "ein liebenswürdiger Brummbär",[21] and it is clear from the way he describes the Läuffer-Wenzeslaus relationship that he sees it as an antithesis between corrupt Civilisation and unspoilt Nature : "Ein betresster, wenig Kenntnisse besitzender, verwöhnter Hofmeister wird hier einem sich wirklich Abmühenden, einem einfachen, ehrlichen, strebsamen Dorfschulmeister gegenübergestellt."[22] It is true that Wenzeslaus' absorption in his work and in the daily round of chores seems at first to be indicative of a laudable self-possession and an enviable strength of character. Läuffer bursts into the schoolroom and asks for protection; he is being pursued by Graf Wermuth and some armed servants (the Graf, a fop and a braggart, has had his own designs on Gustchen). Seemingly unperturbed by Läuffer's agitation, Wenzeslaus chats away about the exercises he is marking, about the life of a private tutor, about the health hazards it involves; when the Graf arrives some minutes later Wenzeslaus ejects him with frosty politeness—and then picks up the thread of his rambling monologue in mid-sentence.

But a closer reading of the play cannot support Rozanov's view. Wenzeslaus' loquacity may imply for some that he is "lovable", but almost invariably he talks about himself and his own interests. We learn nothing at all about his pupils, for the simple reason that Wenzeslaus takes no personal interest in them. His reaction to Läuffer's castration is grotesquely indicative of his insensitivity. For he registers only momentary astonishment—"Wa—Kastrier—"[23]—and then congratulates Läuffer on doing a fine heroic thing, calling him "ein zweiter Origenes".[24] He slips with relish into a sermonic mode, full of all the homiletic clichés; Läuffer is an "auserwähltes Rüstzeug", "eine Leuchte der Kirche", "ein Stern erster Größe".[25] The wretched tutor points out that his motives have nothing to do with self-martyrdom, that the act was the consequence of empty and aimless despair, but Wenzeslaus ignores him and resumes his rhapsodic sermon with a piece of tribal history culled from Josephus. (The same bizarre association of ideas occurs, interestingly enough, in the almost contemporary *Die Räuber* : Spiegelberg says "Lies den Josephus, ich bitte dich drum!" to which Karl Moor replies "Pfui! pfui über das schlappe Kastraten-Jahrhundert...."[26]) One suspects that Wenzeslaus' joy is due to his own sexual frustrations, which are apparent whenever the topic of love is mentioned. If *he* cannot enjoy the pleasures of marriage, for whatever reasons, then he is glad that Läuffer, young and lusty as he is, is now irrevocably condemned to chastity. Hence his anger when Läuffer proposes to wed Lise shortly after this episode.

Wenzeslaus is frustrated because his experience is limited in the extreme, and his experience is limited because he is self-centred. That commendable self-possession now appears as the grotesque *inability* to enter into a human relationship, to adapt his responses to the feelings of the people he is with; he talks *at* people, not to or with them. For his language and his habits of mind have become conditioned by the rhetoric of scholarship or the pulpit, and book-learning has become a substitute for real experience of people and their problems. Hence all the classical tags, the references to the authority of the ancients—"Habt Ihr den Valerius Maximus gelesen?"[27]—and his predilection for wise sayings. When Läuffer asks him why he should not marry Lise, Wenzeslaus' reply is a splendid example of how he has no answers of his own, but can only reproduce the generalised wisdom of the past : "Ei was—*Connubium sine prole, est quasi dies sine sole....* Seid fruchtbar und mehret euch, steht in Gottes Wort. Wo Eh ist, müssen auch Kinder sein."[28]

Equally empty, because full of *idées reçues,* is the language of Major von Berg and his wife. They represent another social type which reappears throughout Lenz' work, namely the arrogant aristocrat. The Majorin is a stupid snob, while her husband is a rather dim old soldier whose speech derives clearly enough from the military milieu which Lenz portrays so vividly in *Die Soldaten.* His language characterises him not as an individual but as one of a class—for indeed a mindless acceptance of the ways of his class is the essence and extent of his personality. There is a delightful scene when he interrupts a lesson which Läuffer is giving to his son Leopold (who never once speaks). The Major now behaves as if they were on the parade-ground, with the bizarre implication that culture and military discipline are synonymous : "Wie steht's, kann er seinen *Cornelio*? Lippel! ich bitt dich um tausend Gottes willen, den Kopf grad. Den Kopf in die Höhe, Junge!"[29] At one point he gives himself away and has to correct himself : "—und wenn die Kanaille nicht behalten will, Herr Läuffer, so schlagen Sie ihm das Buch an den Kopf, daß er's Aufstehen vergißt, oder wollt ich sagen, so dürfen Sie mir's nur klagen."[30] It is a nice moment : the boorish aristocrat apologises to the obsequious bourgeois tutor whom he acknowledges, with a mixture of fear and contempt, as a more accomplished scholar than himself.

He wants Leopold to be a soldier, predictably enough : "ein Kerl, wie ich gewesen bin."[31] The word "Kerl", which is frequent in "Sturm und Drang" writings, implies a hearty, back-slapping kind of admiration for animal spirits—in the *Anmerkungen* Lenz says that we respond to tragic heroes with the feeling "Das sind Kerls!"[32] Similarly the Drum Major in Büchner's *Woyzeck* (1836) boasts : "Der Prinz sagt immer : Mensch, Er ist ein Kerl!"[33] But the *Anmerkungen,* which represent Lenz' overt commitment to the "Sturm und Drang", are an exception in his work, as was suggested earlier : it is clear that he could not take seriously the exclamatory vulgarity and desperate pathos which informs much contemporary writing. We associate such a crude and hyperbolic style with *Götz von Berlichingen,* "Kraftkerle", "Machtweiber", and all that; but Lenz places this vocabulary in the mouth of a man who is anything but a rebel or a titan, a man who is loyal to King and country : "Potz hundert! wenn er Major wird und ein braver Kerl wie ich und dem König so redlich dient als ich!"[34] This is barrack-room royalism, not revolutionary ardour : both in their nationalism and in their rhetoric the "Stürmer und Dränger" owed more to the past than they cared to realise. The students in

Der Hofmeister also speak a kind of "Kraftsprache", not because they are "Originalgenies", but because students talk like that. The inference is plain : what is implied by violent and extravagant language, for Lenz, is not genius and creative energy, but a social milieu.

This kind of speech reaches its grotesque extreme with Donna Diana, the "Spanish countess" in Lenz' second major play, *Der neue Menoza* (1774). The plot is slight : an enlightened ruler, Prince Tandi, who has been brought up in "Cumba" (wherever that may be—it hardly matters), visits Europe to observe civilisation at work, but he reacts to European society in the manner of Rousseau and is disgusted by its artificiality and effeteness. He falls in love with Wilhelmine, his host's daughter, and they eventually find happiness. Wilhelmine is pursued temporarily by Graf Camäleon, who is pursued in turn by Donna Diana, his jealous former mistress. In his *Rezension des neuen Menoza* (1775) Lenz defends his play against the criticism that his characters are exaggerated by maintaining that a certain degree of exaggeration is *necessary* for an effective dramatic characterisation. So he willingly concedes that Donna Diana is a caricature, defending himself somewhat unconvincingly—indeed inconsistently—with the argument that truth is stranger than fiction.

Although a countess, she is emphatically no lady. She calls Babet, her nurse and confidante, "verdammte Hexe"[35] and "Kot von Weib",[36] indulges in extravagant threats—"ich bohr dir das Herz durch !"[37]—and hits her like a petulant child : indeed her behaviour springs from the childish frustration she feels when her will is not immediately executed. Donna Diana has the energy of a man—albeit a madman—within the body of a woman, and her life is poisoned by the humiliating knowledge that she is of the weaker sex : ". . . . ich halt mich nichts besser als meinen Hund, so lang ich ein Weib bin. Laß uns Hosen anziehn und die Männer bei ihren Haaren im Blute herumschleppen. . . . Ein Weib muß nicht sanftmütig sein, oder sie ist eine Hure, die über die Trommel gespannt werden mag."[38] (Klinger has this image in the first scene of *Sturm und Drang* (1776).)

Like Kleist's *Penthesilea*, Donna Diana reacts with perverse ferocity against the sexual submission of the woman, and like Penthesilea she aspires to the opposite extreme, to a rôle of sadistic and characteristically male dominance. She affects the language of a "Kraftmensch" because she feels this to be the language of men at their most manly. She associates it with energy, mastery, achievement. In fact the dynamism of the language is a *substitute* for the energies and the fulfilment that it seems to body forth, and the verbal experience becomes a substitute for real experience : or rather for Donna Diana it is an alternative kind of real experience. As she says later : ". . . es ist mir Wonne, wenn ich davon reden kann."[39] The jargon of the "Genie" betrays frustration, not achievement; she cannot "drag men by the hair through their own blood", but she talks as though she had the energy to do so. The archetypal "Machtweib", this parody of "Sturm und Drang" Prometheanism, is burning herself out not with deeds but with words.

None of Lenz' plays is so rich in telling caricatures as *Der neue Menoza*. The aptly-named Zierau[40] introduces himself to the enlightened Prince Tandi as "Ein Baccalaureus aus Wittenberg",[41] and proudly adds : ". . . doch hab ich schon über drei Jahr in Leipzig den Musen und Grazien geopfert."[42] (Leipzig, it should be remembered, was so fashionable that Goethe was obliged to alter his style of dress when he went there in 1765 : and it was in Leipzig that Läuffer had spent his time frequenting coffee-houses and dances.) This rococo preciosity, this fondness for an allusive and esoteric language which is nothing but a string of fashionable clichés, immediately irritates Tandi, and there ensues a delightful exchange, whose flavour is best rendered by an extended quotation :

Prinz: Was führt Sie zu mir?
Zierau: Neugier und Hochachtung zugleich. Ich habe die edle Absicht vernommen, aus welcher Sie Ihre Reise angetreten, die Sitten der aufgeklärtesten Nationen Europens kennen zu lernen und in Ihren väterlichen Boden zu verpflanzen.
Prinz: Das ist meine Absicht nicht. Ja, wenn die Sitten gut sind—setzen Sie sich—
Zierau (setzt sich): Verzeihen Sie! Die Verbesserung aller Künste, aller Disziplinen und Stände ist seit einigen tausend Jahren die vereinigte Bemühung unserer besten Köpfe gewesen, es scheint, wir sind dem Zeitpunkte nah, da wir von diesen herkulischen Bestrebungen endlich einmal die Früchte einsammeln, und es wäre zu wünschen, die entferntesten Nationen der Welt kämen, an unsrer Ernte Teil zu nehmen.
Prinz: So?
Zierau: Besonders da itzt in Deutschland das Licht der schönen Wissenschaften aufgegangen, das den gründlichen und tiefsinnigen Wissenschaften, in denen unsere Vorfahren Entdeckungen gemacht, die Fackel vorhält und uns gleichsam jetzt erst mit unsern Reichtümern bekannt macht, daß wir die herrlichen Minen und Gänge bewundern, die jene aufgehauen, und ihr hervorgegrabenes Gold vermünzen.
Prinz: So?[43]

Zierau's speeches are rich parodies of the self-important, shallow optimism of the popularised "Aufklärung", with all the resounding clichés that in the twentieth century we would associate with political propaganda or advertising. Metaphors drawn from agriculture are incongruously mixed with metaphors of light, while the gloom of "die herrlichen Minen und Gänge" presumably counterbalances all that light, of which Herder once wrote: ". . . in unserm Jahrhundert ist leider so viel Licht!"[44] By his use of the first person plural Zierau implies that he is participating in this European movement, contributing to "progress", but in effect his enthusiasm is in inverse proportion to his understanding; only a man without an idea in his head will subscribe so totally and consistently to the rhetoric of other men, taking it to be his own. As Kierkegaard once observed, with his gift for witty paradox : language is used by many people to hide the fact that they have no thoughts.[45] We find precisely this type of facile cliché, grotesque in the context of the world in which it is uttered, in Büchner's *Dantons Tod* (1835), when the "first gentleman" says : "Ich versichre Sie, eine außerordentliche Entdeckung! Alle technische Künste bekommen dadurch eine andere Physiognomie. Die Menschheit eilt mit Riesenschritten ihrer hohen Bestimmung entgegen."[46] In the age of the Pathé News it all sounds horribly familiar.

Die Soldaten (1775) is probably the best and certainly the most influential of all Lenz' works. *Minna von Barnhelm* (1767) stimulated literally hundreds of "Soldatenstücke", all of them sustaining the magnificent myth that the army still contained the flower of the nation's chivalry. In these plays, most of which were dreadful, army officers were portrayed as honourable gentlemen; they were liable, certainly, to get themselves and others into trouble, but with impeccable magnanimity they always did the decent thing in the end. Lenz' play suggests that this popular image of the army does not correspond to the facts. He shows that relations between the civilian population and the army are extremely ugly, particularly in times of peace, for then the officers become idle and bored. Consequently they exploit their position as a privileged caste to "lie, whore and steal" at the expense of the civilians. Without a doubt, Lenz' play has more in common with Brecht's *Mutter Courage* than with Lessing's benign drama of reconciliation.

Die Soldaten examines a particular case of this abuse. Mariane Wesener, daughter of a bourgeois dealer in fancy goods, is betrothed to Stolzius, a young draper. But Desportes, an army officer, begins to flirt with her : her father is alarmed, then flattered, and his equivocal attitude encourages Mariane to accept Desportes' attentions. She is seduced by him, having broken off her engagement to Stolzius. Desportes then absconds to avoid paying his huge debts, and entrusts his colleague Mary with the task of placating Mariane. Stolzius takes service with Mary, as part of his plan to revenge himself on Desportes, and when his chance comes he poisons both Desportes and himself. Mariane has meanwhile been taken into the house of Gräfin de la Roche, who hopes to protect her from evil influences and reform her. But Mariane runs away from the Gräfin's house; Wesener sets out in pursuit, and finds her on the road when she accosts him as a prostitute, not realising who he is. Thus they meet, and thus we leave them.

The four officers who compose the central clique—Desportes, Mary, Haudy, and Rammler—are portrayed as brutal and cynical, worthy ancestors to the enormity of Büchner's Drum Major. When they are together they speak the language of Donna Diana, hearty, hyperbolic, and vulgar, and in this way Lenz presents the paradox of army comradeship : beneath the fellowship of a common life and language lies a fierce individualism, an uncompromising and arrogant self-assertiveness. The force of their speech is to affirm the speaker's ego, to mirror that ego to himself, and thus to convince him and his hearers, by the vigour of his diction and the extravagance of his threats, that he is not a man to be trifled with—"Das sind Kerls !" The traditional military ethic of personal honour is here debased to the level of crude egotism. In different company the officers' speech changes in tone, but the strategy is similar—to get the better of the other person. When Desportes is wooing Mariane he adopts a courtly and gallant level of discourse, which the bourgeoisie regards as "cultivated"; Mariane's father speaks a clumsy and exaggerated form of the same jargon, full of Gallicisms and coy diminutives: ". . . mein Marianel wird Sie ennuyiert haben . . ."[47] (Rehaar, the music teacher in *Der Hofmeister*, adopts a similarly wheedling and obsequious tone with his student clients.)

In an important essay of 1958 Walter Höllerer has shown how Mariane's style of speech is progressively contaminated by Desportes, who replaces her father as the model of "proper" language.[48] His gallant flattery succeeds in seducing her : but what is *then* significant is her intuitive understanding of what such language is designed to do. It functions not as self-expression, but as a tool with which to manipulate or hurt other people, and it is part of Mariane's moral decline that she learns how to wield that tool. In the scene where she commits herself to Desportes, both by her compliancy of manner and by writing a letter to Stolzius to break off their engagement, she addresses Jungfer Zipfersaat, an evidently unsophisticated but faithful friend, with sarcastic and malicious elegance. She mimics Desportes, not naively, but in a deliberate attempt to confuse and embarrass the other woman :

> *Mariane (hier und da launigt herumknicksend)* : Jungfer Zipfersaat hier hab ich die Ehre dir einen Baron zu präsentieren der sterblich verliebt in dich ist. Hier Herr Baron ist die Jungfer von der wir soviel gesprochen haben und in die Sie sich neulich in der Komödie so sterblich verschameriert haben.[49]

When Mariane starts to talk like Desportes we know that her sexual surrender is imminent, because his very use of language is determined by his moral degeneracy. Indeed, in two productions of *Die Soldaten* this scene has ended with the consummation of Mariane's seduction just offstage.

The same connection between language and morals is seen in the behaviour of Gräfin de la Roche's son, who takes up with Mariane later in the play. He comes home late one night and complains about the servant's absence—"wo ist denn der Bediente, die verfluchten Leute, . . .?"[50]—threatening to "break every bone in his body". This is precisely the language of the officers, of Donna Diana, and of Major von Berg, characters who seduce, assault, and tyrannise respectively. Clearly the young nobleman has picked it up from Mariane in her corruption, and although he responds at once to his mother's admonition, we can see how readily he has absorbed the speech-habits, and consequently the habits of mind, of a brutalised milieu.

One of the officers, called Pirzel, is a character in the same tradition as Wenzeslaus and Zierau. He is an eccentric, living on the periphery of the main clique, and his life, unlike theirs, does not revolve round drinking and womanising. He is characterised in the words of chaplain Eisenhardt—"Der philosophiert mich zu Tode"[51]—in the same way that Wenzeslaus is summed up in Läuffer's bitter observation : "Der wird mich noch zu Tode meistern."[52] Eisenhardt remarks that all the officers seem to be fawning on Stolzius, to which Pirzel replies : "Woher kommt's, Herr Pfarrer? Daß die Leute nicht denken."[53] He repeats this formula on two further occasions, elevating specific human problems to a pseudo-philosophical level where there are no useful answers, but only trite generalisations. His language is so rationalised, so entangled in its own narrow logic, that he ends up saying absolutely nothing at all :

Pirzel: . . . Es ist ein vollkommenstes Wesen. Dieses vollkommenste Wesen kann ich entweder beleidigen oder nicht beleidigen.

Einer aus der Gesellschaft (kehrt sich um): Nun fängt er schon wieder an?

Pirzel (sehr eifrig): Kann ich es beleidigen *(kehrt sich ganz gegen die Gesellschaft)* so würde es aufhören das Vollkommenste zu sein.

Ein anderer aus der Gesellschaft: Ja, ja Pirzel, du hast recht, du hast ganz recht.

Pirzel (kehrt sich geschwind zum Feldprediger): Kann ich es nicht beleidigen—*(Faßt ihn an die Hand und bleibt stockstill in tiefen Gedanken.)*[54]

His colleagues do not listen to him—but then his words are hardly directed at any listeners, being more a kind of thinking out loud. He communicates nothing but his own obsessions: it is a one-way traffic, the monologue of a self-centred intellectual. We are reminded of Prince Tandi's words: " . . . wer auf der Studierstube ein System zimmert, ohne es der Welt anzupassen, der lebt entweder seinem System all Augenblick schnurstracks zuwider, oder er lebt gar nicht."[55]

The final scene of *Die Soldaten* is notorious. The Gräfin and Colonel von Spannheim discuss the problem of the ruin which dissolute army officers bring upon bourgeois families, and it is suggested that units of "official" prostitutes should be recruited to satisfy the needs of the men. Now elsewhere (in his essay *Über die Soldatenehen* (1776)) Lenz submits that the answer to this problem is to remove the customary prohibition on army marriages. He was aware of the discrepancy between the two proposals, for he told Zimmermann that the essay would give the play "ein größeres Gewicht und einen ganz andern Ausschlag."[56] So clearly he was satisfied that each solution was valid in its own context. The idea of a corps of prostitutes *is* absurd in moral terms. But if one accepts the premise that soldiers should not marry, the suggestion becomes perfectly logical and acceptable. What is absurd, therefore, is the premise itself, and by extension the whole conception of an alternative military society, which terrorises the civilian population it is supposed to be protecting. The vision of *Über die Soldatenehen* is of a citizen army, where every man is a valiant warrior who fights not for money but for home and fatherland: as such it is the dream of a Homeric Golden Age, and ultimately of a world without war. Conversely, the plan for "eine Pflanzschule von Soldatenweibern"[57] is only a *reductio ad absurdum* of the situation that existed. Strangely, many critics have not realised that Lenz' intention was ironic : Rozanov, outraged by what he takes to be a serious suggestion, calls this scene "eine überflüssiger antikünstlerischer Ballast."[58]

It will be clear from what has been said that Lenz' critique of the aristocracy does not rest on the popular "Sturm und Drang" assumption that the lower and middle classes are the repositories of all virtues. The middle-class Läuffer is a weak, ambivalent character, and the behaviour of Mariane and her father is more disturbing than that of the officers, who at least are consistent in their cynicism. Lenz is deeply preoccupied with social division, but the problem he presents is not simply that the privileged upper classes oppress and abuse the deprived but virtuous lower classes. Gräfin de la Roche points out that Mariane's great mistake was to try and get above her station in life, which might seem like a betrayal of the play's apparently anti-aristocratic purpose : for to deny in these terms the possibility of social advancement is also to deny implicitly the desirability of a radical reorganisation of society. But for Lenz the evil lay not so much in the existence of a class structure *per se* as in the abuse of one class by another. The maltreating of the lower classes by the aristocracy has already been indicated clearly enough, and the misery of Mariane, the agony and suicide of Stolzius, are a direct consequence of the pleasure-loving and selfishness of Desportes and his friends. Such a critique is a commonplace of the "Sturm und Drang". But in a letter to Sophie von La Roche of July 1775, where he speaks about *Die Soldaten*, Lenz has a remark which suggests that there was a need to enlighten as well as to admonish : "Überhaupt wird meine Bemühung dahin gehen, die Stände darzustellen, wie sie sind : nicht, wie sie Personen aus einer höheren Sphäre sich vorstellen."[59] In an age when we pay lip-service, at least, to the desirability of social equality, it requires a considerable effort of the imagination to appreciate that the upper classes of that time probably did not regard their treatment of their social inferiors as untoward exploitation, but simply as the natural way of the world. This may have required a slightly elastic conscience, but it certainly does not presuppose wilful, Machiavellian malice. Auerbach's critique of *Kabale und Liebe* (1784) is concerned with precisely this point;[60] Schiller implies that the black picture of evil tyranny which he paints is true of German principalities in general, which is not the case. Like many a "Sturm und Drang" play, *Kabale und Liebe* preaches to the already converted. In suggesting that the upper classes needed to be educated in the realities of the social system Lenz was by no means exculpating them for oppressing the lower classes. He was simply offering a more complex and therefore more accurate critique than Schiller's.

Mariane's case illustrates the delusions which the bourgeoisie harboured about their social superiors. With certain exceptions, such as the Geheimer Rat von Berg and Gräfin de la Roche, Lenz portrays the aristocracy as stupid, selfish, and vulgar. Yet the upper classes were regarded not as oppressors, but as a refined and elegant élite, and to emulate them was the very height of middle-class aspiration. Times, it may be observed again, do not change. In his short story *Der Landprediger* (1777) Lenz talks of "(der falsche Firnis). . . . den die Imagination der geringern Stände gemeinhin sich um die höheren lügt, und der dem Gefühl ihres eignen Glücks so gefährlich ist."[61] Now this is the obverse of the same problem; the bourgeoisie do not *know* what the upper classes are like, and vice versa. Hence the curious paradox that elegant and precious speech is the language which is used *between* the bourgeoisie and the aristocracy, by Wesener, Desportes, Rehaar, and Zierau, but it is not the language which the aristocrats use among themselves. It fulfils a merely ritual function, as the acknowledgement of social difference. And the trouble is that both parties appear to enjoy the game of maintaining the façade, which only deadens their awareness of the basic alienation of one class from another.

For Lenz the problems of human relationships are not capable of being solved by social reform. Class structures aggravate these problems by sanctioning and affirming the differences between individuals, but they provide the occasion rather than the cause : therefore the answer cannot lie in programmatic legislation. In the two "social" plays the recognisably social problem is dealt with in one scene of intensive discussion; in the argument between the Geheimer Rat and Läuffer's father in *Der Hofmeister*, and in the final scene of *Die Soldaten*. Rozanov is taking a regrettably narrow view (though it is one that many have shared) when he writes, categorically : "Diese Stücke, die ein bestimmtes Thema behandeln und diese oder jene These verteidigen, sind tendenziös, polemisch und suchen zu überzeugen."[62] The stuff of both plays is a rendering of social reality which is far more complex, and far more interesting, than the mere illustration of a social evil and its proposed reform. The sources of social abuse, Lenz tells us, lie more deeply, in aspects of human behaviour whose manifestations are not confined to the particular context of class relations —selfishness, pretentiousness, ambition, and, not least, imagination. We are explicitly told that the inhabitants of Prince Tandi's

Cumba, whom we must suppose to be as happy and innocent as
the people of Voltaire's Eldorado, are not troubled by imagination.
Herr von Biederling, the Prince's host, tells Graf Camäleon
what the Prince has said :

"... dabei haben sie nicht nötig den Phantaseien nachzuhängen,
denn die Phantasei, sehen Sie, das ist so ein Ding . . . warten
Sie, wie hat er mir doch gesagt? . . . in Gesellschaft ist es
ganz vortrefflich, aber zu Hause taugt's ganz und gar nicht, es
ist wie so ein glänzender Nebel, ein Firnis, den wir über alle
Dinge streichen, die uns in Weg kommen, und wodurch wir sie
reizend und angenehm machen."[63]

When Gräfin de la Roche pauses to reflect on the implications
of her philanthropic zeal, she realises that imagination and the
self-deception it engenders may be necessary for happiness in
society as it is—and perhaps also in society as it ever humanly
could be :

"Ich weiß nicht ob ich dem Mädchen ihren Roman fast mit
gutem Gewissen nehmen darf. Was behält das Leben für Reiz
übrig, wenn unsere Imagination nicht welchen hineinträgt;
Essen, Trinken, Beschäftigungen ohne Aussicht, ohne sich selbst
gebildetem Vergnügen sind nur ein gefristeter Tod."[64]

It is what we might call the moth view of human behaviour.
Moths are irresistably drawn to the flame which often kills them :
but without the light which the flame sheds, there would be no
fun in being a moth.

In another letter to Sophie von la Roche (also written in July
1775) Lenz reflects how good it would be to work for a better
understanding between individuals, but he sees that it is something
which cannot be achieved by public measures. The problem, he
feels, is more fundamental : how do we know what a person is
really like, when personality—and communication—are so contingent upon fashion, convention, and other social structures?

"Ich sage immer : die größte Unvollkommenheit auf unsrer
Welt ist, daß Liebe und Liebe sich so oft verfehlt, und nach
unsrer physischen, moralischen und politischen Einrichtung,
sich fast immer verfehlen muß. Dahin sollten alle vereinigte
Kräfte streben, die Hindernisse wegzuriegeln; aber leider ist's
unmöglich. Wer nur eines jeden Menschen Gesichtspunkt finden
könnte; seinen moralischen Thermometer; sein Eigenes; sein
Nachgemachtes; sein Herz. Wer den Augenblick haschen könnte,
wo sich seine Seele mit der andern zu vereinigen strebt."[65]

What we are reminded of when we read these words is not the work of another "Stürmer und Dränger", but the spiritual crisis of Kleist.

Nearly all of Lenz' later plays and most of his significant imaginative prose works were written to explore the author's personal problems, and they reflect the difficulties he found in his own relationships. They also illustrate precisely those dangers of the imagination which Lenz shows to be partly responsible for the failed relationships of his dramatic characters. *Das Tagebuch* (1774–5) is the account of Lenz' involvement with Cleophe Fibich, the Strasbourg jeweller's daughter who was betrothed to the elder Baron von Kleist. (There are traces of this background in the setting of *Die Soldaten*; indeed in a letter to Herder of March 1776 Lenz implies that the correspondances are so obvious that the play will serve to deter von Kleist from behaving towards Cleophe as Desportes behaves towards Mariane. Naturally the play had no such effect, and von Kleist did jilt Cleophe.) The Diary begins at the point when "Scipio" (the elder brother) has gone away to obtain his father's permission to marry. "Der Schwager", his younger brother, has arrived at the same time, and the intrigue commences : Lenz thinks that the latter has conceived a passion for "Araminta" (Cleophe), and he himself falls in love with her as well. In the introduction, addressed to Goethe, Lenz is convinced that he was only trying to deter "der Schwager", and that he was thereby safeguarding Scipio's interests; the younger brother appears as the only villain of the piece. But the text itself is a document of Lenz' tortured passion, an account of his attempts to persuade himself that he alone is the one whom Araminta loves. So we have an astonishing day by day record of Lenz' visits to her house, and of his every encounter with Araminta and "der Schwager"; every glance, every word is noted and anxiously scrutinised for evidence of her love for him, and every sign of favour that the other man receives embitters their "rivalry" to fantastic degrees.

A particularly tense moment comes during an outing in the country, when all three of them are travelling together in one of the carriages : "Wir machten Knüttelverse, ich : 'ich wünschte diesen Bennenkarg, dir zum Hochzeitsbett mir zum Sarg.' Der Schwager sah sich um, sie schien böse und machte geschwind folgenden : 'ich sitz' auf einem Bennenkarren und hab' neben mir einen Narren.' "[66] This kind of language-game recurs throughout the Diary : through an oblique and allusive use of language Lenz tries to elicit a response which shows that the allusion has been understood and accepted. If the reply also communicates through an oblique reference, so much the better. He appeals to a shared understanding about the indirect use of language because he takes such an understanding to indicate a spiritual affinity, and a complicity, which together betoken love. He is mistaken, of course : for although Araminta's reply shows that she has comprehended the erotic suggestion in Lenz' couplet (the images of marriage-bed and coffin evoke sexual intercourse and death, and thence "death" in the transferred rococo sense of "orgasm"), this proves nothing about her feelings. It is simply a comment on her understanding and wit—and, incidentally, on her tact. On another occasion, both Lenz and "der Schwager" cut pens for Araminta, so that she can write a letter. She tests the pens, and writes "bester Freund" with von Kleist's pen, "Mein Herz" with the one that Lenz has trimmed : ". . . ich verlor alle Sinnen. Der Schwager wie der Teufel merkte es, die Angst gab mir Gegenwart genug, dem einen andern Verstand anzudrehen."[67] It seems likely enough that both forms of address relate to the letter she is about to write, which is no doubt intended for her fiancé; but Lenz at once jumps to the conclusion that these casual scratchings are a deliberate ploy to reveal Araminta's "true" feelings for "der Schwager" and himself.

Araminta/Cleophe was simply a flirt, as Lenz himself came to realise later : we find an account of his disillusionment in his *Moralische Bekehrung eines Poeten*, written in the early summer of 1775. Yet even the sobriety of hindsight here is possible only because one idol has been replaced by another, namely Goethe's sister Cornelia, wife of Lenz' good friend Schlosser. Admittedly his feelings for her were more sentimental than the eminently sensual passion he conceived for Cleophe. *Das Tagebuch* contains a few self-critical remarks; but the intention of the work is to render the workings of fantasy, not to rationalise them. A whole world of pain and joy is constructed and hungrily enjoyed on the basis of Araminta's chance remarks or glances, and what disappoints Lenz ultimately, perhaps, is not so much her failure to love him as her failure to grasp the power of his imagination and the depths of feeling which she has so casually evoked. He seeks a response not because he loves Araminta, but in order to give substance to his fantasy : through being realised it will also be justified.

Der Waldbruder (1776), which Schiller described as "pathological", is a thinly disguised picture of Lenz' passion for Henriette von Waldner, a lady whom he knew only through reading some of her correspondance (which, incidentally, was not even addressed to him !). Several of his later plays, including *Der Engländer*

(1775–6) and *Die Freunde machen den Philosophen* (1776), are based on this affair; the hero, who represents Lenz—in the latter play he is even called Reinhold—falls in love with a woman who is beyond his reach. One play ends with the hero's suicide, the other with a fairy-tale happy ending, but the latter is as disastrous as the former in terms of failing to relate fantasy to reality. *Der Waldbruder* is in letter form, which is one of the reasons why Lenz called it "(ein) Pendant zum Werther"[68], and it consists partly of letters written by Herz, the "hermit" of the title, and partly of letters written to him, or about him, by his friends and acquaintances. Herz leaves the town to live as a hermit in the forest—reflecting Lenz' move from Weimar to Berka —and is only persuaded to return when the "Countess Stella" (Henriette) learns of his plight and his obsession and promises an interview. When they meet, Herz seeks for indications that his "love" is requited. Naturally enough he finds them : "Ich bekam nur Seitenblicke von ihr, und sie sah meine Augen immer auf den Boden geheftet und doch begegneten unsere Blicke einander und sprachen ins Innerste unsers Herzens was keine menschliche Sprache wird ausdrücken können."[69] There is no further plot, and no conclusion; Herz remains deluded—for of course Stella does not love him, and indeed she is already engaged. He oscillates between extremes of hope and despair, while his friends contrive a plot to entice him to America as a soldier. Herz' closest friend is Rothe, in whom we are to recognise Goethe : he is portrayed as a cynical hedonist in a society which Lenz clearly regards as the epitome of corrupt and inane frivolity. The celebrated "mystery" of Lenz' expulsion from Weimar a few months later really does not seem all that mysterious ! But Rothe's assessment of Herz is an accurate one, and to Plettenberg, Stella's fiancé, he writes : "Er lebt und webt in lauter Phantasien und kann nichts, auch manchmal nicht die unerheblichste Kleinigkeit aus der wirklichen Welt an ihren rechten Ort legen."[70]

That this was equally true of Lenz himself is quite clear. When he heard that Henriette Waldner was about to marry Baron von Oberkirch he wrote a spate of letters to his friends, urging them to try and dissuade her from what he regarded as an unworthy match. He even drafted a letter to her himself, although he had not met her and had no personal acquaintance with Oberkirch. Critics have been impatient of this aspect of Lenz' character, and frequently they have been all too ready to adopt a tone of moral condemnation. Since the imagination, with its attractions and its dangers, was an important element in Lenz' way of understanding and portraying the world, this critical prejudice has not helped to form a balanced and intelligent view of his achievement. The later plays and the prose are written off as "subjective" indulgences, the somewhat embarrassing outpourings of a mind already unbalanced.

What has generally not been realised is the extent to which Lenz understood the power of his own imagination, and was capable of sufficient detachment to *render* the state of mind to which he so often fell victim. *Der Waldbruder*, by its very structure, involves a critique of Herz—and thus an acute self-analysis. Although rococo society is effectively satirised, there is no corresponding apologia for Herz' behaviour. Nor is such an apologia implicit in the satire itself. The letters written about him, especially those from the pen of "Honesta", whose name indicates her impartiality, contain convincing analyses of his psychology and conduct; the unsparing irony of the work proves that Lenz was fully aware of how hopeless his infatuation was. Just as Donna Diana was a parody of the "Machtweib", so Herz (the name is significant) is a parody of the "Gefühlsmensch", that tortured soul whom we know from Goethe's Werther and Jacobi's Woldemar, and from many a figure of European Romanticism. Rothe, whose acuteness we have noted, puts it very nicely : " . . . ich klage Dir meine kleinen Empfindungen auf der Querpfeife, wie Du Deine auf dem Waldhorn."[71]

Through such self-irony Lenz doubtless achieved a kind of confessional catharsis, a coming to terms with his unhappiness and guilt through recreating them as a third-person experience. As he wrote in the *Moralische Bekehrung* : " . . . ich fühle der einzige Rat sein Los in der Welt zu tragen ist daß man sich ganz aus sich heraussetzt, sich für einen fremden und andern Menschen als sich ansieht. So kann ich mich bisweilen lieben . . ."[72] In *Zerbin*, a short story he wrote in 1775, Lenz had written many aspects of his own character into a narrative which was based on an actual Strasbourg scandal. Zerbin is introduced as "ein junger Berliner, mit einer kühnen, glühenden Einbildungskraft",[73] and we are told that he has "ein reizbares, für die Vorzüge der Schönheit äußerst empfindliches Herz."[74] He explores various kinds of relationship with women, including an infatuation with Renatchen, a flirt in the manner of Cleophe/Araminta. Renatchen wants to attract the attentions of Graf Altheim, to whom Zerbin acts as "Führer und Mentor",[75] so she deliberately flirts with Zerbin in order to bring herself to Altheim's notice. When he is finally disillusioned, Zerbin despairs of finding true love. But he falls in love, suddenly and spontaneously, with Marie, the girl who attends him in his lodgings. She is a gentle, innocent

"Naturkind" in the sentimentalised "Sturm und Drang" tradition
—"lesen mochte sie nicht, aber desto lieber tanzen"[76]—and
she becomes a devoted and loving mistress. Yet Zerbin abandons
her, because he is not prepared to contemplate a *mésalliance*.
Their child is born, Marie is executed for concealing her pregnancy,
and Zerbin commits suicide.

The hero is viewed ironically throughout, and the flippant
tone of the early pages—"er stand wie Saul unter den Propheten,
sobald er in eine Gesellschaft von Damen trat"[77]—gives way
to a more severe manner of writing as Zerbin ceases to be just
silly and becomes involved in guilt. There is one scene in particular
which is an uncanny parallel to a scene in *Das Tagebuch* (where
the protagonist in question is, of course, Lenz himself). He describes
a card game in which the players are Zerbin, Renatchen, Altheim,
and Hohendorf, an officer to whom Zerbin teaches military
architecture (a subject in which Lenz himself was deeply
interested) :

"Jede Karte hatte in des armen Liebessiechen Ideen eine
Bedeutung, deren geheimer mystischer Sinn nur ihm und
seinem Abgott anschaulich war, und sie dachte gerade bei
jeder Karte nichts. Er spielte erbärmlich und machte sie eine
Partie nach der andern verlieren, und wenn sie im Ernst böse
auf ihn ward, hielt er das für die feinste Einkleidung ihrer
unendlichen Leidenschaft für ihn, die kein anderes Mittel wüßte,
sich ihm, ohne von den andern bemerkt zu werden, verständlich
zu machen."[78]

In *Das Tagebuch* we find the following account :

" . . . in der Verwirrung abwechselnder Empfindungen . . .
vergaß ich einmal—ihr die Karten zu geben, die ganze Gesellschaft lachte und sie schien erstaunend böse über diese
Vernachlässigung. Aber ihr Blick sagte mir welch Vergnügen
es ihr gemacht hätte. Ich war wie albern für Freude als wir
fortgingen . . ."[79]

So the situation which he describes in ironic terms in *Zerbin* is
precisely the one which he relates so naively and openly in the
Diary. And if we should think that self-irony of this kind is an
easy way out, a comfortable way of coming to terms with one's
own folly by merely laughing it off, we need only turn to
the passages in the *Moralische Bekehrung eines Poeten* where
Lenz has a dispassionate and penetrating analysis of the fantasy
world of *Das Tagebuch:*

"Ich erinnere mich der Zeit noch wohl da ich Tiefen des Genies in meiner geliebten C. zu entdecken glaubte—wie wohl war mir dabei—alle meine Kräfte arbeiteten, wie Shakespear sagt, meiner Narrheit das Ansehen der Vernunft zu geben, und zu jeder ihrer unbedeutendsten Handlungen einen Schlüssel aufzusuchen . . . die Schönheiten die Vollkommenheiten die ich ihrem Geist und Herzen lieh, haben bloß in meiner Imagination gesteckt, ich sah allen Zauber um Armiden verschwinden und ein gemeines und weh daß ich's sagen muß, häßliches Porträt stand da wo mein betörter Kopf vor einem Augenblick Ideale gesehen hatte."[80]

It seems there is nothing we can say about Lenz' fantasy which he has not already said himself. Through the unsparing self-revelations of *Das Tagebuch* we see how Lenz' experience led him to the same conclusion which Gräfin de la Roche reached about Mariane—that life, unredeemed by imagination, consists of "eating, drinking, occupations that lead nowhere". Yet in the acute ironies of *Der Waldbruder* and *Zerbin,* and in the cool self-critique of the *Moralische Bekehrung,* Lenz shows that the escape from ennui which fantasy offers is not satisfactory because it cannot be translated into real experience, real involvement. "Und am Ende war nichts drin, sondern alles hatten *wir* hineingetragen."[81] What then are we to make of this astonishing ambivalence, this co-existence of two modes of feeling and writing which, on the face of it, are mutually exclusive and self-contradictory? Lenz himself provides an answer in a narrative aside in *Zerbin:*

> "Daß des Menschen Herz ein trotzig und verzagtes Ding sei, ist ein Gemeinspruch, der auch den Allereinfältigsten auf den Lippen schwebet, den aber, wenn er sich an uns selbst wahr macht, kein menschlicher Scharfsinn, wär' es auch des größtmöglichen universellsten Genies, daß ich so sagen mag, auf der Tat ertappen und ihm mit gehörig zubereiteter Brust begegnen kann."[82]

The implications of this most casual and undramatic observation are extremely important; for, in noting that there is no necessary link between "common knowledge" and individual actions, Lenz is implicitly rejecting the old Socratic paradox. Lenz admired Socrates, although like Nietzsche he saw that the Socratic sensibility meant the end of a certain primitive and instinctual power in Greek culture; but the optimistic belief that knowledge is virtue simply did not measure up to his own experience. Yet precisely this belief was central to the "Aufklärung"—as its very name suggests. The didactic dramatists of the eighteenth century took it for granted that there was a necessary cause-effect relationship between knowing and doing, and they felt no need to apologise for writing "improving" literature. But for Lenz this link was not self-evident. His work as a whole, from the irony of the "solutions" in his social dramas to his own repeated and conscious failures, in the prose works, to "learn from experience", questions the very existence of such a link. Literature, he tells us, does not work like that, and nor does life.

If our lives cannot be governed entirely, or even satisfactorily, by reason and knowledge, then perhaps we are wrong to suppose that they should. This at least is the implication of Lenz' enigmatic remark in his *Moralische Bekehrung*: "Das aber muß ich mir gestehen daß meine Imagination mir schlimme Streiche gespielt hat, meine Vernunft aber vielleicht noch schlimmere."[83] Reason alone, he is saying, is not enough to make a man happy, to keep a man on the right path. The imagination, the irrational, must be allowed their part. Or, as John Henry Newman put it: "Reason is God's gift; but so are the passions. Reason is as guilty as passion." What has for so long been seen as a private aberration in Lenz, the inability to control imagination by reason, is in fact a statement of the common experience. It is an extreme statement, no doubt: but the difference is one of degree, not of kind. The patronising tone of so much Lenz criticism tells us more about the repressions of the critics than it does about Lenz: they try to isolate Lenz from the common experience, which merely tells us the more cogently that he is part of it. For our moralising is never so eloquent as when we are attacking our own faults in others.

In its utopian zeal the "Sturm und Drang" has more in common with the "Aufklärung" than with Lenz. For Lenz shows us what *is*. Instead of reiterating moral imperatives, telling us what ought to be, he renders the paradox of human behaviour without attempting to resolve it. And truly it is insoluble: to know that something is irrational, foolish, or just unsatisfactory, and *yet* to do it, is more true to human experience since the Fall than any rational theories of behaviour, especially where that knowledge, and the "Gemeinsprüche" which articulate it, relate by definition to the general and not to the particular. Truth will always be more paradoxical than polemic: and moths, if we may recall Mariane Wesener, will continue to be singed by candles. This, and not talk of Shakespeare and the three unities and Nature and genius, was the vital revolution in sensibility which made possible a new kind of literature, a literature which was the opposite in every way of the classical mode of Weimar.

The chief representatives of that new, anti-classical writing are far better known than Lenz himself. Kleist's doubts about the reliability of language as a means of communication are an extension of Lenz' awareness that language has its limits, that communication is a kind of ritual or game whose success is determined by the interplay of complex social and psychological factors. Büchner's debt to Lenz is immense, as many critics have noted. He derived parts of his critical theory from the *Anmerkungen*; he wrote the short story *Lenz,* an imaginative reliving of Lenz' spiritual predicament rather than a description; and above all his dramatic technique, his macabre view of human behaviour, especially in *Woyzeck,* owe much to the dramas of Lenz. In the twentieth century Wedekind's plays have a patent affinity with those of Lenz, both in their form and in their concern with the problem of sexuality and society. It is an eloquent testimony to that affinity that Wedekind should have contemplated editing a new edition of Lenz' works. Brecht's adaptation of *Der Hofmeister* for the modern stage is well known. More recently, the late B. A. Zimmermann's opera *Die Soldaten,* based on Lenz' text, has been acclaimed as the most important opera since Berg's *Wozzeck*—an interestingly appropriate comparison.

There are a number of reasons why Lenz' work should enjoy fresh popularity in the twentieth century, though they are not the same reasons which explain his transient fame in the 1770's, when he was once called Goethe's "twin". His loose dramatic structures, his sometimes violent theatricals, his techniques of irony and caricature (of which Brecht's theory of alienation is a development), and his pessimism—all these have been welcome to a theatre which has not been able or willing to sustain the heterocosmic "well-made play". Above all, perhaps, it is the sexuality of Lenz' plays which has made them readily accessible to the twentieth-century sensibility, the sexuality which also gave birth to the fantasies which he indulged and portrayed. In the post-Freudian age, where psychology covers a multitude of sins, these plays that show men and women deadened by boredom and frustration, seeking release in sexual adventure, impelled by their animal desires, their social pretentions, and motivated always by that "Selbstliebe" (self-love) which Rothe believed to be essential for survival in society—such plays reflect the imaginative life, not of a schizophrenic or a psychopath, nor even of a poet, but of the age we live in.

NOTES

1. This paper was read out to a group of good friends, two years before the publication of *Von deutscher Art und Kunst* and *Götz von Berlichingen*. Since there may be many things in it which are still relevant to present-day writing, and which have not been rendered entirely superfluous by those two works, we are laying it before our readers in all its rhapsodic extravagance, if only as the first unrestrained reflections of an impartial dilettante. (Goverts I, p. 329).

2. The writer and the public must feel the single unity—but not classify it. (ibid., pp. 344–5).

3. Away with all this classification of the drama!

4. Feeling.

5. Feeling is all.

6. If you do not *feel* it, you'll not achieve it.

7. A man, equally at home and equally strong in every situation, he set up a theatre for the whole of mankind. (Goverts I, p. 362).

8. Man! The world! Everything!

9. Sinewy.

10. Gritty.

11. Whether there has been an increase of misery in Germany, I cannot tell, but there has certainly been an increase in exclamation marks. Where people used to write ! one now sees !!!

12. See Bibliography.

13. My tragedy.

14. Comedy.

15. Drama.

16. My theatre exists under the open skies and before the whole German nation, in which the lower classes count for just as much with me as the upper classes; the *pedites* and the *equites* are equally deserving of honour. If anybody cannot find himself in my plays, then I consider that I have wasted my lamp-oil and my time. Whether or not they can be performed does not bother me. (*Briefe I*, p. 105).

17. Paintings, portraits.

18. The Major curses like a soldier. (See Bibliography)

19. Must I remind you how much depends on language, on the way we express our thoughts and desires to others, not only in the sciences but even in general day to day transactions, and in every other contingency in human life, not excluding love and friendship themselves? Nature has taught the beasts to communicate with each other through certain sounds and cries; man, the most helpless of all beasts, has the greatest need for this close bond of all society and love between men. If we do not reach an understanding with others in respect of our common language, we isolate ourselves in the most gruesome way imaginable. (Goverts I, p. 456).

20. And so I grow fat and plump, live happily, and don't need to think about dying yet awhile. (III, 4).

21. A lovable old grumbler. (Rozanov, p. 202).

22. A beribboned, ignorant, spoilt tutor is contrasted here with a man who really works himself hard, a simple, honest, industrious village schoolmaster. (ibid, p. 203).

23. Wha—castra— (V, 3).

24. A second Origen. (ibid.).

25. Chosen instrument; a light of the Church; a star of the first magnitude. (ibid.).

26. You really must read old Josephus!—Damn! Damn this snivelling age of eunuchs . . . (I, 2).

27. Have you read your Valerius Maximus? (V, 10).

28. But come now—a marriage without children is like a day without sunshine. . . . Be fruitful and multiply, it says in the Bible. Where there's a marriage there are children. (ibid.).

29. How's it going? Does he know his Cornelio, eh? Leo! By God and all the saints, keep your head *straight*! Look *up,* boy! (I, 4).

30. —and if the rascal won't remember things, Herr Läuffer, just clout him round the head with the book so that he won't be able to stand up in a hurry—er—no—what I meant was—er—you come along and report him to me. (ibid.).

31. A chip off the old block. (I, 2).

32. Now *those* are men for you! (Goverts I, p. 359).

33. The Prince always says to me: By heavens, you're a man and no mistake!

34. But damn it all! As long as he becomes a Major and a good chap like me, and serves the King as faithfully as I have! (I, 2).

35. Damned witch. (II, 3).

36. Filthy bitch. (III, 4).

37. I'll stab you through the heart. (II, 3).

38. . . . as long as I'm a woman I count myself no better than my dog. Why don't we put trousers on and drag men by the hair through their own blood . . . A woman has no business being meek and mild— if she is, then she's a whore, and her carcase is fit for nothing better than a drumskin. (ibid.).

39. . . . it's such ecstasy to talk of it. (III, 4).

40. His name recalls the adjective "zierlich", meaning "dainty", "decorative", "elegant".

41. A Bachelor of Wittenberg. (I, 7).

42. . . . but in Leipzig I have sacrificed three years and more in the service of the Muses and Graces. (ibid.).

43. *Prince:* What brings you to me?
Zierau: A combination of curiosity and respect. I have been apprised of the noble intent with which you embarked upon your travels, which was, to seek knowledge of the customs of Europe's most enlightened nations, and to transplant them to your native soil.
Prince: That is not my intent. Now, *if* the customs are worthy—do sit down—
Zierau (sits down): By your leave! The progressive improvement of all

arts, disciplines, and conditions of men has been the common endeavour of our most outstanding minds for some thousand years now, and it seems that we are approaching the time when we shall at last reap the fruits of these Herculean exertions. It is to be hoped that the most far-flung nations of the earth will come to share in our harvest.

Prince: Really?

Zierau: And particularly since the light of the Fine Arts has now dawned in Germany, to illumine the way forward for those painstaking and profound sciences in which our forefathers made discoveries, and, as it were, to make us aware for the first time of our priceless riches, so that we marvel at those splendid mines and passages which those who went before us have hewn out, and can turn into good coin the gold which they brought forth.

Prince: Really? (ibid.)

44. . . . in this century of ours there is, alas, so much light!

45. Quoted by Otto Jespersen (*Mankind, Nation and Individual,* London 1946).

46. A most remarkable discovery, I assure you! It will change the face of all the technical arts. Mankind is hastening with massive strides towards his lofty destiny.

47. . . . my little Mariane will have bored you . . . (I, 3).

48. See Bibliography.

49. *Mariane (doing a facetious little curtsey every now and again):* Miss Zipfersaat it is my honour to present to you a Baron who is mortally enamoured of you. Herr Baron here is the maiden of whom we have talked so much and with whom you fell so mortally in love the other day at the theatre. (II, 3).

50. And where's the servant? These bloody people . . . (III, 8).

51. He'll philosophise me to death. (III, 4).

52. He'll schoolmaster me to death before he's finished. (III, 4).

53. And what, reverend Sir, is the reason for that? Why, people don't *think,* that's the reason. (II, 2).

54. *Pirzel:* . . . There exists an utterly perfect Being. I am free either to insult this utterly perfect Being, or not to insult Him.

One of the assembled company (turning round): He's not starting on *that* again, is he?

Pirzel (very excitedly): If I am free to insult Him *(turns right round to face the others)* then He would cease to be utterly perfect.

Another of the assembled company: Yes, Pirzel, yes, you're right, you're absolutely right.

Pirzel (turning suddenly to the chaplain): If I am free *not* to insult Him—*(takes hold of the chaplain's hand and stands quite still, deep in thought.)* (ibid.)

55. . . . a man who sits in his study and constructs a system without relating it to the real world is either living a life that goes flat against his own system the whole time, or he's not living at all. (II, 6).

56. Rather more weight and a completely different effect. (*Briefe I,* p. 183).

57. A nursery of soldiers' molls. (V, 5).

58. Superfluous ballast which offends against the laws of art. (Rozanov, p. 309).

59. Indeed my whole aim will be to portray the classes as they really are, and not as people of a higher social standing imagine them to be. (*Briefe I*, p. 115).

60. *Mimesis*, chapter 17.

61. (the false gloss) . . . with which the imagination of the lower classes generally overlays the upper classes, and which threatens to prevent them from appreciating and enjoying any happiness of their own. (Blei V, p. 154).

62. These plays, which deal with a specific topic and put forward this or that point of view, are tendentious, polemical, and seek to persuade. (Rozanov, p. 194).

63. . . . . and they don't need to chase after fantasies, because fantasy, you know, is a funny old thing . . . just a minute, how did he put it? . . . in society it's quite splendid, but at home it's no earthly use at all. It's like some glowing mist, a shiny gloss which we paint over all the things we encounter, so as to make them attractive and pleasant. (III, 1).

64. I don't know whether I can deprive the girl of her little romance in all good conscience. What has life got to offer, if our imagination does not invest it with some kind of attraction? Eating, drinking, occupations that lead nowhere, all these are just a postponement of death unless we contrive pleasures for ourselves. (IV, 3).

65. I've always said that the greatest imperfection in our world is the fact that two loving hearts so often fail to meet, and indeed are pretty well bound *not* to meet, given the physical, moral, and political climate of our time. All our available resources ought to be directed towards removing the obstacles; but unfortunately it is not possible. If only we could find every single person's point of view; his moral thermometer; his individuality; his assumed characteristics; his heart. If only we could catch the moment when his soul is struggling to unite with another. (*Briefe I*, p. 113).

66. We were making up doggerel verse. I said: "I wish this carriage of ours could be, a marriage-bed for you, a coffin for me." The brother-in-law looked round, she seemed annoyed, and quickly capped it thus: "As upon this carriage I sit, here at my side there sits a twit." (Goverts I, p. 222).

67. . . . I felt dizzy. The brother-in-law noticed, the sly devil, but fear gave me enough presence of mind to pretend that it all meant something different. (ibid., p. 215).

68. A pendant to *Werther*. (*Briefe I*, p. 200).

69. All I got from her were sidelong glances, and she saw my eyes fixed upon the ground the whole time. Yet our glances met, and spoke to our inmost hearts, uttering things that no human language can express. (Goverts I, p. 298).

70. He lives and moves in nothing but fantasies, and he can't put

anything from the real world in its proper place, sometimes not even the most insignificant trifle. (ibid., p. 317).

71. . . . I sing you my little feelings on the fife, as you sing me yours on the French horn. (ibid., p. 288).

72. . . . I feel that the only way to bear one's fate in the world is to put oneself right outside oneself, to see oneself as a different person, a stranger. If I do this I can love myself from time to time. (ibid., p. 280)

73. A young man of Berlin, with a bold, fiery imagination. (Blei V, p. 79).

74. A susceptible heart, highly sensitive to the attractions of beauty. (ibid., p. 82).

75. Guide and mentor. (ibid., p. 81).

76. She wasn't one for reading, but she was passionately fond of dancing. (ibid., p. 93).

77. He stood there like Saul among the prophets if ever he came into a room full of ladies. (ibid., p. 86).

78. In the poor love-sick fellow's eyes every card had a meaning whose secret significance was accessible only to him and his idol—but to her not one of the cards meant a single thing. He played abominably, and caused her to lose game after game; if she really got annoyed with him he supposed this to be a highly subtle disguise for her boundless passion for him, which could find no other way of communicating with him without attracting the attention of the others. (Blei V, p. 87).

79. . . . in the confusion of my ever-changing feelings . . . I once forgot to give her the cards. Everybody laughed, while she seemed remarkably annoyed by this lapse. But the look in her eyes told me what pleasure it had given her. I was almost crazy with joy when we left. (Goverts I, p. 220).

80. I can still recall clearly the time when I thought I discerned depths of genius in my beloved C. How happy it made me! All my faculties conspired to lend wisdom's warrant to my folly, as Shakespeare puts it, and to seek a key to her every little action, however insignificant. . . . the beauties, the perfection which I attributed to her mind and heart, existed solely in my imagination; the magical fascination surrounding this Armida melted away before my eyes, and there before me was a common and, sad to say, an ugly portrait, in which a moment earlier my infatuated head had seen ideals. (Goverts I, pp. 255–6).

81. And in the end there was nothing there—it was we who had read everything into it. (ibid., p. 259).

82. That the human heart is an obstinate and timorous thing is a commonplace that comes readily to the lips of the most simple-minded among us; but when it turns out to be true for *us,* no human perspicacity, not even that of the greatest, most universal genius, can catch the heart in the act, so to speak, and meet the danger with a bosom adequately steeled. (Blei V, p. 89).

83. I must admit that my imagination has played me some bad tricks: but my reason has perhaps played me some worse ones. (Goverts I, p. 255).

SELECT BIBLIOGRAPHY

J. M. R. Lenz   *Gesammelte Schriften,* vols. I-V. Hsg. Franz Blei.
                     München—Leipzig 1909–13.
J. M. R. Lenz   *Werke und Schriften,* vols. I-II. Hsg. Titel und
                     Haug. Goverts Verlag, Stuttgart 1966.
J. M. R. Lenz   *Gesammelte Werke,* vol. I. Hsg. Daunicht. München
                     1967.
J. M. R. Lenz   *Der neue Menoza.* Hsg. Walter Hinck. Berlin 1965.
J. M. R. Lenz   *Über die Soldatenehen.* Hsg. Karl Freye. Leipzig
                     1914.
Briefe von und an J. M. R. Lenz, vols I-II. Hsg. Freye und Stammler.
                     Leipzig 1918.

Freidrich Beissner   *Studien zur Sprache des Sturms und Drangs* in
                     Germanisch-romanische Monatsschrift 22 (1934).
Elisabeth Genton   *J. M. R. Lenz et la scène allemande.* Paris 1966.
Karl Guthke   *Lenzens "Hofmeister" und "Soldaten". Ein neuer
                     Formtypus in der Geschichte des deutschen Dramas*
                     in *Wirkendes Wort* 9 (1959).
Walter Höllerer   *J. M. R. Lenz: Die Soldaten* in *Das deutsche Drama
                     vom Barock bis zur Gegenwart,* vol. I. Hsg. Benno
                     von Wiese. Düsseldorf 1958.
Heinz Kindermann   *J. M. R. Lenz und die deutsche Romantik.* Berlin
                     1925.
Werner Kliess   *Lenz in Sturm und Drang. (Friedrichs Dramatiker
                     des Welttheaters).* Hannover 1966.
Volker Klotz   *Geschlossene und offene Form im Drama.* München
                     1960.
M. N. Rozanov   *J. M. R. Lenz. Sein Leben und seine Werke.* Trans-
                     lated C. von Gütschow. Leipzig 1909.
Erich Schmidt   *Lenz und Klinger. Zwei Dichter der Geniezeit.*
                     Berlin 1878.
Max Spalter   *Brecht's Tradition.* Baltimore 1967.
Wolfgang Stammler   *"Der Hofmeister" von J. M. R. Lenz.* Halle 1908.

An exhaustive bibliography may be found in Elisabeth Genton's book.

Friedrich Maximilian Klinger

Friedrich Maximilian Klinger

by H. M. WAIDSON

Friedrich Maximilian Klinger was born in Frankfurt am Main on February 17, 1752. With his two sisters, he was brought up in straitened circumstances by his mother after the father's death in 1760. Klinger became a student of Law at Gießen University in April 1774. While a student he wrote his first dramas, and after the summer of 1776 he had a period as playwright to Abel Seyler's theatre company. In 1778 he took part in the War of the Bavarian Succession as a lieutenant in Austrian service, and was recommended for Russian service in 1780. One of his early duties here was to accompany the Grand-duke Paul on a journey through Austria, Switzerland, Italy and France. He held a number of offices as an educational administrator, including that of Curator at the University of Dorpat. He married in Russia, and although he kept in touch with German friends, including Goethe, he did not revisit Germany after he had settled in Russia. He died in St. Petersburg on February 25, 1831, having retired from most of his administrative activities by 1817.

ALTHOUGH he came to regard his main contributions to literature as lying in the sequence of novels that he wrote in the 1790's, it was as a playwright that Klinger first became known in Germany. The play originating from his early years in Germany which he regarded with most affection in his later life was *Die Zwillinge* ("The Twins", 1775). He included this drama alone of his writings of the 1770's in the collected edition of his works. It was this, his third play, which made the author's name known to the theatre-going public. Written as an entry for the drama competition promoted by Sophie Charlotte Ackermann and her son Friedrich Ludwig Schröder, *Die Zwillinge* was shaped to conform to their requirements of an original play that should be practicable for performance on the stage without involving excessive costs. With its cast of seven and its indoor settings in a country house, this play depends primarily on characterisation and atmosphere for its impact, and dispenses with those features of Shakespearean drama which were influential on Goethe's *Götz von Berlichingen* and also on Klinger's first play *Otto* (1774), itself modelled also on *Götz* in part. *Die Zwillinge* is straightforward in its action, the obsessive hatred of Guelfo for his twin-brother Ferdinando moving directly from the first scene to the later catastrophe where hatred finds its outlet in murder. The time-sequence is compact, as in a classicist play. Schröder's award of the prize to Klinger launched *Die Zwillinge* as a literary and theatrical success, though not without arousing controversy, since some thought that the prize should have gone to Leisewitz' *Julius von Tarent*. The violent impulsiveness of Guelfo has been unable to find satisfactory expression because since his boyhood he has been aware that his twin-brother, the gentler and cleverer Ferdinando, has been excessively favoured by their father. Guelfo's sombreness of mood is underlined through his friendship with the melancholy Grimaldi who mourns for the death of Guelfo's sister. The mother Amalie and Kamilla, Ferdinando's fiancée whom Guelfo also loves, are anxious for family reconciliation. It is Guelfo and his father who are incalculable and passionate; the father is unable to understand that his actions should be seen as unjust by Guelfo, while the latter cannot explain his viewpoint to his father with any clarity. A weakness in the action is that the critical scene where the father strikes the son is recounted subsequently and not presented directly. If the language is at times exaggerated, the play evokes a consistent tragic mood, supported by some premonitions of uncanny nature. *Die Zwillinge* made a considerable impression upon K. P. Moritz, and, in the nineteenth century, on Otto Ludwig.

Die Zwillinge is one of five completed dramas which Klinger wrote between 1774 and May 1776, the period when he was a student at Gießen. It was during the summer of 1776, the months when Klinger, with Lenz, was living in Weimar and hoping that his friendship with Goethe would stand him in good stead at the court there, that he wrote *Sturm und Drang,* the play whose title was to give the name to the literary movement with which the early work of Goethe and Schiller, as well as that of Klinger and others of their contemporaries, is associated. It may be regarded as its author's last contribution to this early phase of his writing. Klinger's original title was *Der Wirrwarr* ("Confusion"), and the title "Storm and Stress" emanated from a suggestion made to the author in September 1776 by a contemporary with whom he had brief acquaintance at that time, Christoph Kaufmann. The first performance of the play was given by Seyler's company in Leipzig on April 1, 1777. Two days later the author referred to this in a letter :

"Am Dienstage führten sie hier Sturm und Drang von mir auf, und eröfneten damit die Bühne. Es ist meine Lieblings Arbeit—

und da saßen sie nun, konnten nicht fassen und begreifen, und doch schüttelte sie das Ding mächtig zusammen."[1]

The work is full of fantasy and whimsy, extravagance and exaggeration. The setting is an inn somewhere in America during the War of Independence. However, Klinger makes little of the topical material, concentrating as he does on the theme of a feud between two families. The central figure is Wild, the restless wanderer who is "eternally chasing after phantoms" though "full of strength and health", and who is not averse to seeking a termination to his troubled emotions in death :

"Ich habe gelitten in der Welt, habe gelitten und meine Sinnen sind etwas wirr geworden. Ungestüm bemeistert sich oft meiner."[2]

He has impulsively crossed from Europe to America, "where everything is new, everything significant", dragging his two friends La Feu and Blasius with him. La Feu would like to transform reality into something magic and imagined, while Blasius describes himself as overcome by inner strife and melancholy. After Wild has met Caroline, whom he has not seen for ten years, and they have re-affirmed their devotion to each other, there is the further problem of the strife between the families. Caroline's father, Lord Berkley, has long been embittered by the harm which he believes has been done to him by Lord Bushy, Wild's father, while the aggressiveness of Berkley's son Harry has sought to wreak havoc both on Bushy and Wild. Finally a reconciliation becomes possible, though one with undertones of disharmony and sadness. The main weakness of *Sturm und Drang* lies in the haphazard plot-construction; the atmosphere of eccentric moodiness generated by a number of the characters is not without originality and charm.

With *Der Derwisch* ("The Dervish", 1780) Klinger moved away from the heroic melancholy of *Die Zwillinge* and *Sturm und Drang* and designed a comedy in the Rococo manner; the remoteness of a timeless Orient is further emphasised by the liberal use of fantasy, including transposed heads and princesses transformed into pocket-watches. Klinger succeeds here in presenting a mood of light comedy with elements of the farcical; at the same time, however, he includes elements of social criticism that recur in others of his works. In the scenes at the Sultan's court appears satire at the expense of a régime in which the head of the state neglects his duties of government for the sake of ephemeral pleasures. The Dervish is the one man who can be independent of the Sultan's whims, and who can embody the aspiration towards a life of poverty that is close to nature and virtue. The third act contains a scene in which the Dervish speaks plainly and with didactic intent to the Sultan; it is a dialogue that has parallels to the central scene between Saladin and Nathan in Lessing's *Nathan der Weise*, or that between Philip and Posa in Schiller's *Don Carlos*. The Dervish, who likes to laugh and be carefree, has the gift of being able to bring back the dead to life, and has been initiated into the secrets of an Order of wise men in Egypt:

> "Dort wohnt Weisheit, Klugheit, Wissenschaft. Da wird das Innre der Natur entwickelt, so weit der schwache Mensch nur dringen kann . . . Ich forschte in den Dunkelheiten der Natur, ließ mich von meinen Brüdern leiten, und fand tief im Mark der innern, geheimen Schöpfung, das Licht, womit ich Todte an die Sonne rufen kann."[3]

Finally, however, the Dervish takes advantage of an opportunity to go to the Ganges, together with his beloved Fatime and her mother, to a happier environment in which he is "closer to the origin of my being, and to the creation of my ideas".[4] This comedy has a neatness and charm which are missing in Klinger's sprawling erotic first novel *Orpheus* (1778–80).

With Klinger's entry into Russian state service the "Bohemian" phase of his life was over. He evidently adapted well to the demands of the new environment and found considerable satisfaction in the performance of his administrative duties. There now followed over two decades during which his imaginative writing continued, as a spare-time occupation, with great productive vigour. In the twelve dramas of the 1780's, whether treating historical themes, or a contemporary setting, or a classical background, Klinger showed a sober, even austere approach in his handling of characterisation and style. He sums up his changed attitude in the "Vorrede zum Theater 1785",[5] where he puts himself at a distance from his earlier plays, though retaining affection for "these explosions of youthful spirit and discontent", and proclaims ideals of "simplicity, order and truth"; German drama, he says, should not be closely bound to French or English novels, and should be distinctive through vitality and action. Another factor which emerges in the course of the 1780's is the author's growing interest in the delineation of problems of ideas and ethical situations in his plays, thus anticipating subsequent developments in the novel-sequence.

The two *Medea* dramas may be cited as characteristic and successful examples of Klinger's later manner as a playwright. The dominating figure of the heroine in *Medea in Korinth* (1786) arouses fear and mistrust in the alien Greek environment, not only in the calculating minds of Jason and King Kreon but also in the irrational resentments of the people. Although she has laid aside her supernatural powers, she still retains an insight into the motives of others and some capacity to foresee future events. However, these are separating factors, as are her different cultural background, her sense of being apart from others through the guilt of her earlier acts of violence, and in general her sombre, fierce temperament. To Kreon Medea's power appears as "the image of death", and he sees her as treating the existence of ordinary human beings as if it were "an insubstantial dream". Jason resents the feeling of inferiority and dependence that his relationship with her has brought, and hopes to find in Kreusa a more malleable companion as well as the means to succeeding her father as king of Corinth. The third Act, with its confrontations between Medea, Kreusa and Jason, gives Medea the opportunity to plead for her point of view in forceful poetic prose. In the family drama Medea has a role reminiscent of that of Guelfo in *Die Zwillinge*; she has reason to feel that she has been ill treated, and is driven to an act of desperation that brings about catastrophe. The allegorical figure of Fate introduces the action and, together with the Eumenides, draws it to a close which emphasises the puniness of the scheming of Kreon and Jason. In a letter of April 10, 1790 Klinger referred to *Medea in Korinth* as his "favourite play", and on December 4, he announced the completion of its sequel, *Medea auf dem Kaukasos,* referring to this latter as being "certainly the best that I have ever written".[6] In solitude in the Caucasus Medea looks back to her past with longing and remorse, but a visit from three members of an indigenous tribe gives her an opportunity to renew human contacts with a possibility of doing good work of a socially useful nature. The Medea of the Corinth period was absorbed by self-consuming passions, but now the plight of a tribe that is subject to superstitious belief in a destructive deity who requires human sacrifices arouses in her a reforming zeal that is to further human progress through moral idealism. The figure of Fate forewarns us of the likely consequences of Medea's impetuosity :

"Töricht wird sie sich den Menschen abermals vertrauen . . .
Rasch wird sie vollziehen wollen, was in Jahrtausenden kaum
reift."[7]

If the young couple Saphar and Roxane appreciate her helpfulness, the other members of the tribe are unable to rise above the narrow and inhumane traditions of their Druids. Medea can only save Roxane from death by summoning for a last time her own supernatural powers of destruction, in spite of her avowed intention to conserve, and not to destroy. But when she tells the truth about herself, she encounters not the understanding that Goethe's Iphigenie finds from King Thoas, but the ruthless hostility of the Druids that causes her to take her own life rather than to be their sacrificial victim. In Corinth Medea had in desperation killed her two sons; in the Caucasus she meets death herself, but not before earning the gratitude of Saphar and Roxane whom she has protected and taught as if they were her own children. The affirmation of the humane ideal, but in terms of some scepticism and caution, points the way to the novels of the 1790's.

The preface to Klinger's sequence of novels, which speaks of a plan of ten quite different works, is important in presenting a summary of the author's aims in this largest structural unit that he devised. In the first place Klinger speaks of his primary aspiration as being to give in these volumes his views on the whole "moral existence" of man, a picture that shall include reflections on society, government and religion. He realises that the individual novels may not fit in one with another to comprise an obvious monolithic structure, for in experimenting with various approaches, he may well have presented situations in one novel that appear to negate what a previous volume has constructed. Apparent discrepancies in the conclusions to be inferred from the various works will be due to the author's empirical rather than *a priori*, normative attitude to his material. Klinger sums up something of his views of the meaning of the universe, thus preparing the reader with a preliminary author's comment. The stage where man plays his part is wonderful, strange and terrible. On it he may easily feel lost, since the "spirit of humanity", that allegorical figure representing man's nobler aspirations who appears on various occasions in the course of the novel sequence, receives no reassurance in answer to his questions concerning the purpose of life. Yet the miracle of the universe is all the more impressive because in this darkness each must seek his own independent solution. But the author gives some account of the qualities he would generally see as of guidance to man. He contrasts virtue ("Tugend") as the only true vision in which the divinity reveals itself to us, with illusion ("Wahn"), the idol that men have set up for themselves. Truth and courage are the qualities needed by man if he is to envisage the world in its great contrasts of ideal and base. Such factors will reveal man in his nobility and his folly, and will also lead him to appreciate that happiness is to be acquired in a life of natural simplicity and idyllic self-restraint. A good man in his striving is led towards that happiness intended for him by nature, while the wise man resigns himself to leaving the complexity of the universe as an unsolved mystery. Man lives in an environment of fear, uncertainty and doubt, but he has "intimations of a higher, spiritual world", being the miraculous son of a higher, incomprehensible creation :

"Und auch nur so beweist er, daß ihn ein wirkender, schaffender Geist beseelt, daß er dieses selbst ist, und frei, würdig seines Urhebers—die Gewalt der physischen Notwendigkeit allein anerkennend."[8]

The "Humanität" of Klinger's outlook as revealed in the later plays and the novels is akin to that of Goethe, Herder and Schiller; it is closely sympathetic to some of the moods of Weimar Classicism, particularly in its affinities with the Enlightenment in general. But already in the preface to the novels there is evidence of a sombre mood of resignation that is particularly characteristic of Klinger's imagination.

The opening novel, *Fausts Leben, Thaten und Höllenfahrt* ("Faust's Life, Deeds and Descent into Hell"), is in some ways the most challenging and uncompromising work in the sequence. It is full of incident and broad in its scope, alternating discussion of its general issues with a wealth of action, perhaps over-sensational in the presentation of some of its episodes, often succinct and concentrated. Faust is the inventor of printing, but is frustrated that none of the leading citizens in his town expresses any interest in his work. He would like to surprise the world and gain its recognition for the achievement of his intellect, as well as to rise from the poverty in which he and his family find themselves. He is indignant that his role in life is always that of the "vessel", the "tool", and would like to see some fulfilment of his urge towards the expression of the freedom and strength he feels within himself. The conjuration of Leviathan, the emissary of hell, leads to the dialogue, at the close of the first book, which gives further evidence of Faust's aspirations and leads to the cementing of the pact. It is not for the sake of wealth and pleasure alone that Faust has entered upon this undertaking, but in order to discover the cause of evil and injustice in the world and the purposes of creation :

"Ich will des Menschen Bestimmung erfahren, die Ursach des moralischen Uebels in der Welt. Ich will wissen, warum der

Gerechte leidet und der Lasterhafte glücklich ist. . . . Du sollst mir den Grund der Dinge, die geheimen Springfedern der Erscheinungen der physischen und moralischen Welt eröffnen. Faßlich sollst du mir den machen, der alles geordnet hat, und wenn der flammende Blitz, der diesen Augenblick durch jene schwarze Wolke reißt, mein Haupt sengte und mich leblos in diesen Zirkel der Verdammniß hinstreckte."[9]

Leviathan makes it clear that he as a devil no longer has insight into exalted mysteries, but a pact is agreed upon; as they travel through the world, Faust will aim to demonstrate to his companion that there is moral value in mankind, while Leviathan offers to show a disillusioned picture of man in his nakedness. It is part of the paradox of the situation that Faust, while seeking examples of unselfish simplicity in the people he encounters, will be susceptible to a wide range of sensual, material pleasures which Leviathan makes available to him.

Faust's adventures lead him from the narrower world of Mainz, through visits to other parts of Germany, and then to countries which offer even more repulsive examples of depravity— France under Louis XI, England under Richard III, and as culmination of these travels, Rome at the time of Pope Alexander VI. The return from Italy to Germany shows Faust's despair and the collapse of his mood combining defiant vitalism with occasional interventions in the hope of righting instances of wrong. In expressing his weariness of life and his readiness to go to hell, Faust allows Leviathan to have won the wager. The novel closes with a satirical scene in hell, which has an earlier counterpart in the episode in the first book immediately prior to Leviathan's appearance before Faust. The world that Leviathan has shown to Faust, and to the reader, is one calculated to lead to despair, not merely to what Klinger describes as "atheism of reason" but in addition to an "atheism of feeling". However, the author is at pains to indicate that Faust has followed the wrong path, though these directives may at times not be wholly convincing as part of the narrative structure. In particular, there is the extended retrospection where Leviathan re-interprets Faust's experiences for him, explaining that he has shown him not a full vision of man, but a deliberately partial picture, not the courts of good and just rulers, but only those of the wicked, and that he has deflected his attention from those cottages of simple people where the ideals of modesty and resignation were to be found. Within his own family Faust's father warns him of the temptations of wealth, remaining for him an example of the rightness of persisting within "bürgerliche Ordnung".[10] If the world of spirits with which Faust has contact remains in the reader's memory primarily as a vision of hell, decked out in satirical terms, it should be recalled that the Spirit of Humanity, supported by Faust's family, intervenes to warn Faust against conjuring up evil spirits, offering him in lieu of his more ambitious expectations "Demuth, Unterwerfung im Leiden, Genügsamkeit und hohes Gefühl deines Selbsts; sanften Tod und Licht nach diesem Leben".[11] After his flight from Rome, while on the way back to Germany, Faust experiences a dream-vision in which the Spirit of Humanity plays a prominent part. On a large, flourishing island surrounded by a stormy sea this figure is busy guiding work on the construction of the temple of humanity, though he and his human supporters are impeded by various allegorical figures of destructive intention; it is through his qualities of constancy and sublimity that the Spirit of Humanity can encourage strength, patience and endurance among those who are working for him. The three great rocks on which the temple is built are recognisable as symbols of patience, hope and faith. Faust is thus portrayed for the reader in the context of his actions and thoughts in his earthly environment, and also as he appears in his relationship to hell and Leviathan and to the Spirit of Humanity; but the forces of evil have a specific, dramatically concrete role to play here, as in any *Faust* story, while the voice of goodness is only heard occasionally and has little effective influence on the central character's actions. There is no major scene in Klinger's work equivalent to Goethe's "Prologue in Heaven" which so triumphantly establishes the framework of divine harmony and purpose before introducing Mephistopheles. However, Klinger's *Faust* is a novel with an authorial narrator, and although authorial intervention is by no means obtrusive, the device does allow for comment from a vantagepoint that must be broader than that of Faust, Leviathan or other figures in the story. Authorial comment does in fact support the attitude of Faust's father and of the Spirit of Humanity. Near the opening of the fifth book, for instance, it is pointed out that Faust's loss of faith in the goodness of divine purpose as a result of what befalls him during his travels may be seen more as a reflection on Faust's own personal shortcomings than as attributable to the nature of his experiences:

". . . der Edle sieht die Laster und Verirrungen der Menschen bloß als Dissonanzen an, welche dazu dienen, die Harmonie seiner Brust in ein helleres Licht zu setzen und ihm sein eigenes Glück fühlbar zu machen."[12]

Klinger's *Faust* is least convincing in its retailing of subsidiary episodes illustrating the evil in the world, but the framework of the hero's quest for self-fulfilment and knowledge and of his relationship with Leviathan is presented with robust vigour and sharp outlines. One misses the finer nuances of poetic sensibility in the delineation of personal relations, but there are moments, such as his acceptance of the pact, with the words "ich springe über die Gränzen der Menschheit",[13] when Klinger's Faust is by no means without his own form of grandeur.

Geschichte eines Deutschen der neuesten Zeit ("Story of a German of the Most Recent Time") clearly indicates by its title the author's aim of presenting a novel that is to be concerned with specifically German issues in a contemporary setting. Most of the action is set in an unnamed German state, partly at the court, and partly on the estate of the hero, Ernst von Falkenburg. In internal politics the main issues are the methods by which agricultural resources should be developed, and the relationship of the land-owning aristocracy to their country workers. The Prince is a benevolent figure, fully prepared to support Ernst's reforming measures, which, however, meet with the opposition of the aristocracy, the chief spokesman of the latter being Ernst's uncle, the President. World events make their impact on this small and outwardly untroubled state; Hadem, Ernst's first tutor, spends a considerable period in America, while the French Revolution and subsequent French advances on to German territory produce strong reactions in the German community. Klinger succeeds well in his blending of topical, social-political factors with the main lines of his plot, so that the narrative moves effectively towards its climax.

As well as being a "Zeitroman", this work is a novel centring upon the inner development of an individual and tracing his educational progress at various stages. Although Ernst has a friendly and respectful relationship with his father, the latter plays little part in his son's education, having entrusted the boy to Hadem, whom he knows to be a sympathetic tutor. From first to last it is his tutor Hadem who inspires Ernst. He soon notices Ernst's quiet inwardness and "high moral strength", and directs his sympathies towards Ernst who can be relied upon to live in the spirit of the "quiet virtues" and not to subordinate means to ends, but his "solemnity" and "quiet melancholy" are seen by Hadem as indications of his vulnerability. In a letter to Ernst from America he writes :

"Besonders, Geliebter, hüten Sie sich vor den Folgen des Mißlingens guter Absichten auf Ihr Herz ! Dieses ist der gefährlichste

Felsen, der unter den Fluthen des Lebens verborgen liegt; nicht selten scheitert der Edle an ihm."(14)

If Faust succumbs to despair, one of the reasons for this is that a few actions of his that were intended as good deeds could be shown to him by Leviathan to be disastrous in their outcome. In the case of Ernst, there is no question of his ever being accessible to the multifarious actions which lead to Faust's damnation; he is consistently noble in the motivation of his undertakings, and the fault is seen as lying in the insufficient resistance which he offers to the blows of misfortune and misunderstanding. However, Ernst has to contend with a succession of losses and disasters which quite understandably would account for his despair : the infidelity of his wife, the deaths of his son and his father, the threat of execution in revolutionary Paris where he vainly hoped to meet Hadem, and the increasing personal hostility which he encounters in his own country. The political situation arouses extremes of feeling, whereas Ernst wishes to maintain a position of balanced moderation; but his ill-starred visit to Paris introduces him to an atmosphere of "anarchy threatening everything with disintegration" that adds to his disillusionment. Hadem's influence on Ernst has to contend with that of the President who unsuccessfully tries to persuade the boy that his own form of sceptical realism is more appropriate than Hadem's moral idealism. The first major crisis of Ernst's life occurs when his uncle through intrigue compels Hadem to leave. Ernst's future development is thereby threatened, although at the age of seventeen and with Hadem's gift of the writings of Rousseau, he will be able to resist the very different teaching of his new tutor, a protégé of the President. Ernst's years at the university and on his travels are quickly passed over. He returns to seek political-administrative employment with his Prince and soon gains his favour. His formal education is now complete, but the narrator intends to follow his hero's life for some distance further, in order to point out the danger of discouragement to the man of good will. Already in Ernst's early days with Hadem, his tutor had been anxious lest the boy's enthusiasm for virtue might be turned to "chimerical over-excitement", and when he is compelled to leave, Hadem prays that Ernst may retain "the holiness of his heart", as it is at this time. At the opening of Book Three, the narrator anticipates the growing sombreness of the story and warns the reader that he will have to tell :

". . . was Dummheit, Bosheit und Neid thaten, einen Geist zu erschüttern, der gegen alle Schläge des Schicksals durch ein

Gefühl gestählt ist, das zwar nicht vernichtet, aber doch
verdüstert werden kann—nun wird mein Geschäft bei jedem
vorwärts gethanen Schritte trauriger und schmerzlicher."[15]

On his return from France Ernst withdraws to his estates, where
even his own country workers regard him with suspicion and hostility. Having lost faith in his ideal, he is full of self-reproach
because of this. Even when Hadem arrives, it is some time before
Ernst can be persuaded, by a self-denying action of the older man,
to renew his belief in moral idealism.

Subsidiary action is provided in the figure of Ferdinand, the
son of a friend of Ernst's father, who is brought up with him.
From early on in the novel Ferdinand is described as having the
more volatile and fierce imagination and the less reliable moral
sense. After Hadem's departure Ferdinand is prepared to accept
the approach of the new tutor who sponsors a more worldly concept
of "honour" rather than Hadem's faith in "virtue". Ferdinand
spends some years in France and is compelled by the Revolution
to return home; his royalist sympathies make him willing to regard
his old friend with some suspicion. The main purpose of Ferdinand's presence in the novel is to act as a foil to Ernst; his love-
affair with Ernst's wife Amalie, together with his unintentional
responsibility for the fall leading to the illness and death of Ernst's
child, are further pointers to the contrast between the two men and
to the way in which Ernst's goodness is requited with ingratitude.
Geschichte eines Deutschen moves over an extended period of time,
and includes some static, descriptive passages as well as scenes in
dialogue form. The gradual quickening of the pace, especially after
the reactions to the French Revolution may come in, and the series
of personal blows that then befall the hero, are effectively devised.
The presentation of Ernst's development may be regarded as over-
dependent on didactic emphases, but the author keeps close to
his key mood with consistency. With an elevated, occasionally
rhapsodic style Klinger follows through the fortunes of his idealistic
hero, refusing in this novel to countenance the sceptical approach
that he can reveal on other occasions. As Ernst says to Amalie, the
role of the imaginative writer is to demonstrate man's links with
the eternity of the ideal world :

"Sie [die Dichter] erwecken durch ihre schaffende Kraft, durch
die hohe Darstellung ihres innern Sinnes den schlafenden Funken
in unsrer Brust, und beweisen uns durch seine Entzündung unsre
Abstammung aus jenem Lande und unsre Wiederkehr dahin.
Ohne sie würde sich der Mensch nie über das Irdische erhoben
haben."[16]

The Poet in *Der Weltmann und der Dichter* (1798) stands close to Ernst in his outlook and in his conception of the role of the art. This novel Klinger described as a "pendant" to the *Geschichte eines Deutschen,* and indeed the two, taken together, may be seen as presenting a complementary unit. It is *Der Weltmann und der Dichter* which modifies some of the more abrupt and passionately proclaimed aspects of *Geschichte eines Deutschen* and by its more reconciliatory spirit conveys a mood of broader understanding and an atmosphere containing some touches of late-summer warmth. The conciseness of its presentation and the unsensational nature of its plot are further factors which make for the sense of balance which characterises this work. It is in dialogue form throughout, consisting of nine conversations between the Man of the World and the Poet who visits him at his office. The contrast between the two men gives ample dramatic sharpness, especially in the initial conversations where the Poet emerges as suspicious and indignant of the way of life he believes to be that of his school contemporary of many years earlier, while the Man of the World is easy and relaxed, countering traces of acidity with touches of condescension. When the Poet takes pride in his closeness to nature and appreciation of moral ideals, his interlocutor doubts whether one such as he would be suited to any but a subordinate administrative position. The Poet has come to plead for justice on behalf of the young man who has married the eldest of three orphaned children whom the older man has been struggling to support in his quiet country abode; but he goes away feeling discouraged. It seems as if the courtly administrator and the imaginative writer have nothing in common in middle life. In their personal styles too they are well apart, the Poet with his emotional fervour and the Man of the World with his scepticism and dry wit. The sequence of the dialogues shows the Poet being gradually drawn to a closer understanding of the other man, for it is the latter who, paradoxically, does most of the talking and feels the more pressing inward compulsion to confide his feelings and experiences to the Poet. It is the Poet who emerges as the self-contained character, while the Man of the World, at this particular point in his life, is the one in need of the other's sympathy.

The initial differences of the two men, after becoming narrowed over the conversations of several months, or a year or so perhaps, become resolved when the Man of the World reveals himself as not dissimilar from the Poet in the well-meaning quality of his intentions towards others. The Man of the World, however, has been moulded by, and has adapted himself to, the demands of practical politics and administration at a German court. Although it is a relatively small and unsophisticated community in comparison with the governing bodies of larger nation-states, as he points out to the Poet, it has been of a character that has taught him over the years to exercise caution, discretion and compromise. He has assumed that the means are to be justified by the ends. Coming from an unprivileged family background, he has needed dogged persistence and calculation from his schooldays onwards in order to make his way in the world. His account of his progress reflects frankly his long-standing desires to further his own career; as time goes on and he meets with success, he is more in a position to look at wider issues and to take into account the interests of others, even when they are not bound up with his own. To make one's way at court, he says to the Poet, costs quite as much effort as composing an epic poem. The main point, he insists, is that each individual should endeavour to be what he himself is and what he has set before himself as his purpose. Then will emerge a true tolerance and understanding which will transcend the limitations of narrow self-absorption. The Man of the World has found his way through mazes of intrigue, and is thankful to be where he is, without wishing to have much substantial influence upon the country and Prince whom he serves; here again his cautious realism prevents him following the path of Schiller's Marquis von Posa, or exposing himself to the risks run by Ernst von Falkenburg. The greatest "folly" of his adult life, as the Man of the World sees it, was to fall in love with an attractive young woman from a wealthy and influential family. At the time of his betrothal and the first years of his marriage he hoped to combine domestic contentment with a useful adjunct to his career-prospects through the alliance with an important family. The latter expectation was realised, but the discovery of his wife's infidelity shattered his illusory hope of stable family life. The later revelation that his favourite Sophie is not his own daughter, and that therefore it will be impossible for her to marry the man whom she loves, is a blow which comes upon the Man of the World shortly before the close of the novel. His attitude of undemonstrative resignation and forbearance over this personal distress arouses the admiration of the Poet, who has repeatedly expressed misgivings about the Man of the World's various moves in his administrative career which had been central features of the Man of the World's earlier confidences.

Thus it is the Man of the World who has most to say and the Poet who listens and makes his comments. The life of the man of letters is to be found in his books, the Poet tells his friend when the latter asks him to recount his life-story. The Poet maintains that he needs to keep away from worldly affairs and to live close to nature and the moral ideal; the Man of the World counters that this urge to withdraw from public life would seem to confirm his own pessimism about human nature, and that a poet should have to wake from his dreams occasionally. Both figures may be taken as representing facets of Klinger's own personality. Certainly the Poet's summary of his inner development may well reflect the author's personal feeling :

> "Ich könnte Ihnen weitläufig darthun, wie sich erst die wirkliche Welt, bloß durch den dichterischen Schleier, meinem Geiste darstellte—wie die Dichterwelt bald darauf durch die wirkliche erschüttert ward, und dann doch den Sieg behielt, weil der erwachte, selbständige, moralische Sinn Licht durch die Finsterniß verbreitete, die des Dichters Geist ganz zu verdunkeln drohte. Dieses alles könnt ich Ihnen Schritt für Schritt, Grad nach Grad aufzählen—könnte Ihnen darthun, wie des Dichters kleine, schwache Schwingen immer mehr an Ausdehnung und Kraft gewannen—wie der Genius auf dieß und jenes hinwies —dieß und jenes eingab—zu welchem Zweck, in welcher Stimmung, in welcher Hoffnung—aber dieses alles liest sich noch besser in dem, was er eingegeben hat.[17]

Klinger's plan to present a cycle of ten novels was not carried out in entirety. Seven major novels were completed, which illustrate in complementary, though not repetitive manner the principal themes which the author summed up in the preface to the novels. After *Faust* there followed in *Geschichte Raphaels de Aquillas* ("Story of Raphael de Aquillas", 1793) the narrative of a man whose belief in moral idealism has to contend with many disasters and suffering. His acceptance of determinism leads him to an attitude of resignation, but with occasional angry revolts against outrageous situations. The setting is the early seventeenth century, largely in Spain. *Geschichte Giafars des Barmeciden* ("Story of Giafar the Barmecide", 1792, 1794) resembles *Faust* in its introduction of Leviathan as diabolical tempter, though Giafar remains faithful in his adherence to his moral principles. In an oriental setting Giafar rises to activity in government, where, however, he is a victim of the whims of the Caliph. The dream-sequence in the second section anticipates Grillparzer's *Der Traum ein Leben* ("Life as a Dream"). *Reisen vor der Sündfluth* ("Travels before the Flood", 1795) depicts the bewilderment of Mahal, the simple man, as he discovers the follies of society at the time when Noah is anticipating the Flood. Mahal's search for knowledge and meaning finds very little in the way of positive answer; this work is critical and satirical. In *Der Faust der Morgenländer* ("The Faust of the Orient", 1797) the hero Abdallah remains throughout convinced of the rightness of moral action. Temptation in his case takes the form of the availability to him of superior knowledge and insight which deprive him of emotional spontaneity, for (contrary to the experience of *Giafar*) not reason but the heart is to be motive-force of unselfish deeds. *Geschichte eines Deutschen* and *Der Weltmann und der Dichter* then follow and round off the sequence of the principal novels. However, Klinger added three more works. *Sahir, Eva's Erstgeborner im Paradiese* ("Sahir, Eve's Firstborn in Paradise", 1798), with its oriental background, satire and fantasy, has a place by the side of the other novels of the 1790's, but is a revision of an earlier work, *Geschichte vom Goldnen Hahn* ("Story of the Golden Cock", 1785). The "fragment", as Klinger subtitled it, *Das zu frühe Erwachen des Genius der Menschheit* ("The Premature Awakening of the Spirit of Humanity", 1803), is the last fictional contribution to the cycle; here Klinger again expresses his reactions to the French Revolution, taking up a motif from *Geschichte eines Deutschen*.

Klinger's own selection of his Works concludes with the substantial collection of aphorisms, *Betrachtungen und Gedanken über verschiedene Gegenstände der Welt und der Literatur* ("Reflections and Thoughts Concerning Various Subjects in the World and in Literature", 1803–5). After devoting himself in the first place to dramatic writing, and then, above all in the 1790's, to the novel, he now finds a third genre to which he can turn with considerable pleasure. It is his final literary contribution, placing before his readers a personal summing-up of his observations as man of letters and as administrator in Russian official service. Voltaire and Rousseau have been guides in much of his thought, with Kant occupying some of his attention, though to a lesser degree. Goethe and Schiller he appreciates, if with occasional reservations. The new Romantic movement in Germany he regards without sympathy. Ethical purpose remains the first characteristic of a literary work that will appeal to Klinger. A number of the aphorisms confirm the sceptical point of view of the Man of the World, or even the more scathing assessment of man's place and potentialities presented by Leviathan. The incompatibility of virtue with court life is again emphasised. However, the place of moral idealism in the scheme of things recurs insistently, and Klinger examines not only the place of morality in earthly life but also on occasions asserts a faith in the soul and its immortality.

With the aphorisms Klinger rounds off his work as a creative writer. It is a substantial whole, an individual's reactions to personal experiences and to the stimulus of the ideas in particular of the eighteenth century. Apart from the author's early work produced while he was in Germany, his writings composed in Russia take their place as a worthy and unique contribution to European Enlightenment and to German Classicism.

TRANSLATIONS AND NOTES

1. On Tuesday they performed my "Storm and Stress" here and opened the theatre season with it. It is my favourite work—and there they sat now, could not grasp and understand, and yet the thing shook them up mightily. (M. Rieger, *Klinger in der Sturm und Drangperiode*, p. 407)

2. I have suffered in the world, I have suffered and my senses have become somewhat confused. Often I am overcome by impetuosity. (*Dramatische Jugendwerke,* ed. Hans Berendt and Kurt Wolff, vol. 2, p. 296)

3. Wisdom, sense and knowledge live there. The inner being of nature is developed there, as far as weak man can penetrate. . . . I searched in the dark region of nature, let myself be guided by my brothers, and deep in the marrow of inward, secret creation I found the light with which I can recall the dead to the light of the sun. (*Dramatische Jugendwerke*, ed. Hans Berendt and Kurt Wolff, vol. 3, pp. 271–2)

4. Ibid., p. 269.

5. Reprinted in *Dramatische Jugendwerke,* ed. Hans Berendt and Kurt Wolff, vol. 3, pp. 349–52.

6. M. Rieger, *Briefbuch zu Friedrich Maximilian Klinger, Sein Leben und Werke II*, pp. 15 and 18.

7. Once more she will foolishly entrust herself to human beings. . . . She will attempt to complete with rapidity that which scarcely ripens in thousands of years. (F. M. Klinger, *Sämmtliche Werke*, Stuttgart and Tübingen 1842 [= S.W.], vol. 2, p. 228)

8. And also it is only in this way that he proves that he is inspired by an active, creative spirit, that he is this himself, and free, worthy of his Creator—acknowledging only the force of physical necessity. (S.W., vol. 3, p. VIII).

9. I wish to learn what is man's destiny, the cause of moral evil in the world. I wish to know why the just man suffers and the wicked man is happy. . . . You are to reveal to me the ground of things, the secret springs of the phenomena of the physical and moral world. You are to make comprehensible to me Him Who has ordered all, even if the flaming lightning which tears this moment through that black cloud should scorch my head and leave me stretched out lifeless in this circle of damnation. (S.W., vol. 3, pp. 50–1)

10. Civic, middle-class order.

11. Humility, submissiveness in suffering, contentedness and high feeling of yourself; a gentle death, and light after this life. (S.W., vol. 3, p. 14)

12. . . . The man of noble spirit sees the vices and errors of men merely as dissonances which serve to display the harmony of his heart in a brighter light and to make him more aware of his own happiness. (S.W., vol. 3, p. 234)

13. I leap over the limits of humanity. (S.W., vol. 3, p. 59)

14. In particular, dear fellow, be on guard against the consequences of the failure of good intentions upon your heart. This is the most dangerous rock that lies concealed beneath the torrents of life; it is not rarely that the man of noble disposition is shipwrecked on it. (S.W., vol. 8, pp. 197)

15. . . . how stupidity, malice and envy unnerved a mind which has been steeled against all blows of fate by a feeling that, it is true, cannot be destroyed, but can none the less be darkened—now with each step forward my task becomes sadder and more painful. (S.W., vol. 8, pp. 122–3)

16. They [the poets] arouse the sleeping spark in our breast through their creative power and through the elevated delineation of their inner mind, and prove to us by the illumination of this spark our descent from that land and our return to it. Without them man would never have raised himself above the earthly level. (S.W., vol. 8, p. 209)

17. I could describe to you at length how firstly the real world revealed itself to my mind, only through the veil of poetry—how the world of poetry was soon afterwards convulsed by the real world, and then nevertheless overcame, because the awakened, independent moral sense spread light through the darkness that threatened to obscure the poet's mind entirely. I could recount all this to you step by step, degree by degree—I could describe to you how the poet's small, weak wings increasingly gained in extent and power—how the inspiring spirit pointed to this and that—stimulated this and that—for what purpose, in what mood, with what hope—but all this it is even better to read in the writing that this spirit has inspired. (S.W., vol. 9, pp. 198–9)

SELECT BIBLIOGRAPHY

F. M. Klinger   *Dramatische Jugendwerke*, 3 vols., ed. Hans Berendt and Kurt Wolff, Leipzig 1912-13.

F. M. Klinger   *Sämmtliche Werke*, 12 vols., Stuttgart and Tübingen 1842.

F. M. Klinger   *Werke*, 2 vols., ed. Hans Jürgen Geerdts, Weimar 1958.

August Sauer (ed.)   *Die Sturm- und Drangperiode. Kürschners Deutsche Nationalliteratur,* vol. 79. Berlin and Stuttgart 1883.

Spreckelmeyer (ed.) *Klingers Romane, Deutsche Literatur in Entwicklungsreihen, Reihe Irrationalismus,* vol. 14. *Leipzig* 1941.

H. H. Borcherdt *Klingers Romanzyklus,* in *Der Roman der Goethezeit.* Urach 1949.

H. J. Geerdts *Friedrich Maximilian Klingers "Faust"-Roman in seiner historisch-ästhetischen Problematik. Weimarer Beiträge,* vol. 6 1960.

Hanna Hellmann *Goethe in Klingers Werken. Germanisch-romanische Monatsschrift,* vol. 11 1923.

Christoph Hering *Klingers Romane—Das Baugesetz der Dekade. Modern Language Notes,* vol. 79 1964.

Christoph Hering *Friedrich Maximilian Klinger. Der Weltmann als Dichter.* Berlin 1966.

Ansgar Hillach *Klingers "Sturm und Drang" im Lichte eines frühen unveröffentlichten Briefes. Jahrbuch des Freien Deutschen Hochstifts* 1968.

Hartmut Kaiser *Zur Struktur von Klingers "Faust". Jahrbuch des Freien Deutschen Hochstifts* 1970.

Johannes Nabholz *The Covenant with Hell in Klinger's "Faust". Monatshefte,* vol. 50 1958.

Malcolm Pasley *Nietzsche and Klinger. The Discontinuous Tradition. Studies in Honour of Ernst Ludwig Stahl.* Oxford 1971.

M. Rieger *Friedrich Maximilian Klinger. Sein Leben und Werke.* 1. Teil, *Klinger in der Sturm- und Drangperiode.* Darmstadt 1880. 2. Teil, *Klinger in seiner Reife.* Darmstadt 1896. Zugabe zum 2. Teil, *Briefbuch.* Darmstadt 1896.

F. E. Sandbach *Klinger's Medea Dramas and the German Fate Tragedy. German Studies presented to H. G. Fiedler.* Oxford 1938.

Olga Smoljan *Friedrich Maximilian Klinger. Leben und Werke.* Weimar 1962.

J. P. Snapper *The Solitary Player in Klinger's Early Dramas. Germanic Review,* vol. 45 1970.

Ewald Volhard *F. M. Klingers philosophische Romane. Der Einzelne und die Gesellschaft.* Halle 1930.

H. M. Waidson *F. M. Klingers Stellung zur Geistesgeschichte seiner Zeit.* Dresden 1939.

H. M. Waidson *Goethe and Klinger: Some Aspects of a Personal and Literary Relationship. Publications of the English Goethe Society,* vol. 23 1954.

Hans M. Wolff *Fatalism in Klinger's "Zwillinge". Germanic Review,* vol. 15 1940.

Heinrich Zempel *Erlebnisgehalt und ideelle Zeitverbundenheit in F. M. Klingers Medeadramen.* Halle 1929.

Johann Joachim Winckelmann

Johann Joachim Winckelmann

by DAVID TURNER

Johann Joachim Winckelmann was born on December 9, 1717, the son of a master cobbler in the small Prussian town of Stendal. Despite his humble origins he enjoyed a quite sound education, first at schools in his native town, then in Berlin and Salzwedel, earning his keep during the latter years by assisting the headmaster, giving private lessons or acting as tutor to the sons of local families. The following years, 1738–43, were fairly typical for a young man of Winckelmann's circumstances who wanted to further his education: two years as a theology student at Halle and a further year studying mathematical medicine in Jena, alternating with periods as a private tutor in Osterburg and Hadmersleben. From 1743 to 1748 he was engaged as deputy headmaster at the *Lateinschule* in Seehausen, unhappy years in which his own studies were pursued largely during the night hours. In 1748 he obtained the post of librarian to Count Heinrich von Bünau at Nöthnitz near Dresden, where his duties included assisting his master in the documentation of a *Reichshistorie* and in cataloguing the vast library. Winckelmann remained in these surroundings, which provided ample opportunity for reading over a wide range of subjects and regular visits to the art treasures of the Saxon capital, for some five years, after which he moved to Dresden itself and took art lessons from the painter, Adam Friedrich Oeser. Meanwhile in 1754, after several years of negotiation, he became an official convert to the Roman faith, a necessary preparation for the cherished aim of going to Italy. And in November 1755, while still drawing an allowance from the Dresden Court, he arrived in Rome, which was to become his almost permanent home until his death. Indeed his stay in Rome was interrupted only by a succession of journeys to Naples between 1758 and 1767, undertaken for the purpose of examining the results of the recent excavations at Pompeii, Herculaneum, and other nearby sites, and by a stay in Florence during the winter of 1758 to 1759, cataloguing the great collection of gems that had belonged to the late Baron von Stosch. The years in Rome began in the close company of artists, notably Anton Raphael Mengs, but became increasingly marked by intercourse with influential and cultured figures within the Roman church, most important of whom was Cardinal Albani, a collector of many art treasures, whose librarian and companion Winckelmann became in 1759. Such contacts were valuable not only socially, but also provided access to libraries, museums and private collections, which served to consolidate his knowledge of the ancient world and so formed the further basis of his published works, most of which appeared while he was in Italy. These years were also marked by increasing recognition, such that Winckelmann was made a member of several academies and learned societies (including the Royal Society of Antiquity in London), was granted the post of Papal Antiquary (1763), and, particularly in later years, became a much sought-after cicerone to distinguished aristocratic visitors to Rome. In 1765 Winckelmann had been offered the post of librarian to Frederick the Great, but he had been unable to agree on suitable terms with the King. It was not until April 1768 therefore that he was able to set off on a journey to his homeland, a journey he was never to complete. He turned back at Regensburg and made his way via Vienna, where he was received by Maria Theresa, to Trieste. There he became the victim of a robbery and incompetent—but ultimately effective—murder.

I

EVEN through the measured prose of *Dichtung und Wahrheit*, written more than forty years after the event, it is impossible to miss the great sense of excitement felt among the young men of Goethe's acquaintance in Leipzig as they waited in the spring of 1768 for the arrival of the celebrated Winckelmann, returning to his home country after an absence of many years, impossible too to miss the subsequent sense of deep shock when the news of the great man's death came through. They had been deprived of the chance to meet a man who had earlier been a pupil of their own teacher, Adam Friedrich Oeser, but had become one of the most important figures in the cultural life of Europe. Here as elsewhere, whenever Goethe writes of Winckelmann, even with reference to his works, it is the man, or his influence on other men, that comes to the fore. This is formulated most drastically in the conversation with Eckermann on 16, February 1827:

"Man lernt nichts, wenn man ihn liest, aber wird etwas." (You learn nothing when you read him, but you become something). And in subsequent generations Winckelmann has continued to exercise a great fascination as a personality. Not that we would see him today in the same light as Goethe, who, understandably, tended to interpret his fellow-countryman as an embodiment of his own (Goethe's) classical ideal. To him Winckelmann represented, for example, something of the antique wholeness of being, in which all the faculties are developed in full harmony.[1] And yet the description he gives might more aptly be applied to his own nature. Winckelmann, by contrast, emerges as a much more singleminded, not to say exclusive character. This expresses itself not only in the perseverance with which he overcame the limitations of his background, the way in which he sought to quench his thirst for knowledge by reading even during the hours of the night or by making long excerpts from a wide range of authors, but also in the singularity of purpose with which, once he had sensed his true calling in the realm of art, he pursued this calling with unerring zeal. Further, although one cannot deny him musical awareness or —as Goethe unfairly did—poetic appreciation,[2] one is struck above all by his concentration on the visual arts and, within that sphere, on the art of sculpture and again, within that sphere, on the sculpture of Ancient Greece. Almost from the time of his move to Dresden in 1754 it is as though his eyes had found their true focus, so that everything else became relative to this.

It could also be argued that Winckelmann's homosexual tendencies detract from the picture of wholeness. Certainly it seems clear that he never enjoyed full and satisfactory relationships with women. But it is all too easy to sensationalise this aspect and isolate it from its full context within Winckelmann's life, which involves, besides an overriding interest in beauty, the cult of friendship, the need for a scholarly exchange of ideas—which in the eighteenth century almost of necessity precluded women[3]— and a strong pedagogical impulse. All these strands come together in the warmly "sentimental" dedication of one of Winckelmann's finest short works, the *Abhandlung von der Fähigkeit der Empfindung des Schönen in der Kunst* (1763). The dedicatee is the young nobleman, Friedrich Reinhold von Berg :

". . . Der Inhalt ist von Ihnen selbst hergenommen. Unser Umgang ist kurz, und zu kurz für Sie und für mich gewesen; aber die Übereinstimmung der Geister meldete sich bei mir, da ich Sie das erstemal erblickte. Ihre Bildung ließ mich auf das, was ich wünschte, schließen, und ich fand in einem schönen Körper eine zur Tugend geschaffene Seele, die mit der Empfindung des Schönen begabt ist. Es war mir daher der Abschied von Ihnen einer der schmerzlichsten meines Lebens, und unser gemeinschaftlicher Freund ist Zeuge davon, auch nach Ihrer Abreise : denn Ihre Entfernung, unter einem entlegenen Himmel, läßt mir keine Hoffnung übrig, Sie wieder zu sehen. Es sei dieser Aufsatz ein Denkmal unserer Freundschaft, die bei mir rein ist von allen ersinnlichen Absichten, und Ihnen beständig unterhalten und geweiht bleibt."[4]

In case we should need reminding of it, an earlier reference to Pindar and the young nobleman Agesidamus—as well as parallel references in the correspondence to the friendship of Theseus

and Pirithous, Achilles and Patroclus[5]—leave us in no doubt
that such relationships are to be seen as the continuation of a
time-honoured classical tradition.

Goethe also regarded Winckelmann as a true pagan in the
manner of the ancient world,[6] an interpretation which immediately
raises the whole thorny question of the "conversion". The will
Winckelmann made shortly before his death is all that one
could expect of a good Catholic : he commended his soul to
Almighty God, the blessed Virgin and all the saints; begged
the forgiveness of his sins; asked that his body be given church
burial. He is further said to have died in exemplary fashion,
having received the last rites and forgiven his murderer.[7] Faced
with the evidence of earlier years, however, one may be forgiven
for wondering whether this was not a deathbed conversion. In
the late Elector of Saxony, Augustus the Strong, there was
already a precedent for expedient conversion; membership of
the Catholic Church opened up for Winckelmann possibilities
of employment suitable to his talents and interests, contact with
men of influence in the cultural life of Italy and, above all,
access to outstanding art treasures; and, as Walter Pater suggested,
he also saw something grand and even pagan in the Roman
faith as distinct from Protestantism.[8] Moreover, the hesitations
that preceded the step, the sense of embarrassment that accompanied it, and even the mockery of the ritual, the ceremony and the
clergy that followed it[9] all point to a lack of conviction. If
Winckelmann was not entirely without religion, then it was art
and beauty as much as anything else that were his gods; the
language of mysticism he sometimes used was concerned characteristically with the contemplation of the beautiful rather than
the godhead.[10]

And yet having said all that, one cannot altogether ignore
or discount splinters of his Protestant upbringing that continue
to affect his way of life even in Italy : the strange habit, for
example, of singing favourite Lutheran chorales while preparing
breakfast,[11] or his recommendation to a friend in need that he
should seek a second support in religion—the first, inevitably, is
friendship—a remark that is reinforced by a quotation from a
favourite hymn by Paul Gerhardt.[12] In the end there remains
an element of contradiction in Winckelmann's paganism.

Such contradiction, however, seems to characterise the man
altogether. Although he prized personal independence highly,
he was continually dependent on the favour of others, so that the
image of the self-made man, conquering the narrow limits of his
origins by sheer talent and perseverance, must be modified to the

extent, that, as with most self-made men, the conquest involved
some exploitation of people as well as situations, to say nothing
of the grovelling to which Winckelmann sometimes had to submit
himself. Similarly, in his writings there emerges a love of political
freedom, sometimes even a republicanism. But this is at least
partly to be explained on aesthetic grounds, since for him autocratic rule made the highest expression of art impossible. Furthermore, his democratic tendencies did not prevent him from arguing,
with Plato, that art is not for the rabble, but for a sensitive élite
(N.E., p. 160)[13]; and since he also regarded leisure as an important prerequisite to a proper appreciation of aesthetic beauty,[14]
this inevitably meant that it was to be an almost exclusively
aristocratic élite. Finally, there is the crowning contradiction that
this man, for whom the art and civilisation of ancient Greece
represented unsurpassable peaks, never set foot in the country
itself. On a number of occasions, right up to the year of his
death, the opportunity presented itself, but there were always
reasons, real or invented,[15] to prevent him from making the
journey. On the other hand, one must be careful not to exaggerate
the significance of this omission; in view of the extent to which
the Ancient Romans had plundered Greek art treasures, the number
of works that were coming to light at the time, and the excavations
proceeding at Herculaneum and Pompeii, it is quite understandable
that Italy, and especially Rome and Naples, should still appear
the ideal place in which to study the works of classical antiquity.

II

Winckelmann first approached the ancient world as a philologist,
by way of its literary monuments. And this was a foundation which
later stood him in good stead when it came to the discussion of
works of art. Although he had some knowledge of reproductions,
it was not until after he had gone to Nöthnitz and had access
to the galleries in Dresden and more particularly when he moved
to the Saxon capital itself in 1754 and saw something of the
collection of antiquities that his eyes were opened to the world
of the visual arts and, as he put it in a letter to Berendis, his whole
heart was devoted to the knowledge of painting and antiquities.[16]
1754 was an auspicious year, too, since it saw the arrival at the
"Gemäldegalerie" of its most prized work, Raphael's *Sistine
Madonna*, which was to remain for Winckelmann a standard
for the recreation of the antique spirit in the modern world.
It was probably from his art-teacher, Oeser, that Winckelmann

derived the decisive view of the exemplary nature of Greek art—
though Oeser made no real distinction between Greek and Roman.
Once embraced, however, Winckelmann's belief in the supremacy
of Greek art never faltered; indeed it became an axiomatic principle, the compass-point by which all his other ideas were oriented.
It is for this reason that his *magnum opus*, the *Geschichte der
Kunst des Altertums* (1764), whose title might lead one to expect a
comprehensive history of ancient art, is in fact a biassed affair, with
an extended section on art among the Greeks, but decidedly
sketchy accounts of Egyptian, Phoenician, Persian, Etruscan and
Roman achievements. It is for this reason too that Winckelmann
sometimes falls into inconsistency. At the beginning of his *Geschichte
der Kunst,* for example, he argues that art developed independently and in similar ways among the various nations and, more
particularly, that Greek art, although of a later date than that of
many other countries of the Middle East, arose quite separately,
did not derive from other cultures (G.K.A. pp. 4–6). When it
comes to a discussion of the Roman style, however, the principle
is abandoned, and he is at pains to show that the Roman
artists of the older period imitated the Etruscans, while those of
later times were probably disciples of the Greeks (G.K.A. p. 291).
Still more complex is the question of imitation, the central concern
of Winckelmann's first important published work, *Gedanken über
die Nachahmung der griechischen Werke in der Malerei und Bildhauerkunst* (1755), written while he was in Dresden and very much
under the influence of Oeser and his anti-Baroque position. It is
here that those resounding and oft-quoted words occur :

"Der einzige Weg für uns, groß, ja, wenn es möglich ist,
unnachahmlich zu werden, ist die Nachahmung der Griechen."
(N. p. 3)[17]

Leaving aside the question whether imitation is not a denial of the
principle that each nation develops its own style of art, one must
still consider a further apparent inconsistency in Winckelmann's
attitude to the subject. For when he later comes to discuss the
period of decline in Greek art in his *Geschichte der Kunst* one
factor he singles out as contributing to the decline is none other
than imitation, which, he here declares, restricts the mind,
encourages a lack of individual competence, and eventually leads
to a certain fussiness (G.K.A. p. 235). It is to be noted, however,
that the imitation Winckelmann advocates is no mindless aping, but
the fruit of intimate and discerning acquaintance. The passage
quoted above continues :

". . . und was jemand vom Homer gesagt, daß derjenige ihn bewundern lernet, der ihn wohl verstehen gelernet, gilt auch von den Kunstwerken der Alten, sonderlich der Griechen. Man muß mit ihnen, wie mit seinem F[r]eunde bekannt geworden seyn, um den Laocoon eben so unnachahmlich als den Homer zu finden." (N. p. 3)[18]

Nor does Winckelmann see such imitation as a substitute for native talent; it is more of a guide in matters of taste which, if followed, might conceivably have raised outstandingly gifted artists like Holbein and Dürer above the masters of Greek art (G.K.A. p. 29).

However axiomatic, the superiority of Greek art was for Winckelmann no mere accident of history; it was rather the result of traceable causes, political, cultural, social, even climatic. Although the question of direct influence is difficult to establish, it seems clear that he did not invent this idea. In a general way his deterministic approach to historical processes may well derive from Montesquieu, from whom he made excerpts while at Nöthnitz,[19] although in its detail it has much in common with the teachings of Christian Ludwig von Hagedorn, an approximate contemporary and subsequent friend, who regarded painting as dependent on a particular nation's artistic ability as well as on the prevailing social conditions.[20] It is this kind of thinking that provides the framework for Winckelmann's discussions in *Über die Nachahmung* (particularly the *Erläuterungen*) and the *Geschichte der Kunst* of the ideal conditions that prevailed in Ancient Greece. Even the climate was temperate, which was especially advantageous for art, since it prevented the excesses of the imagination that sometimes afflicted Egyptian art (G.K.A. p. 25) and, more positively, promoted bodily perfection (G.K.A. p. 129). Moreover, since bodily beauty was greatly prized among the Greeks and both male and female beauty contests were held, since also gymnastic exercises were often practised in the nude, the artists had ample opportunity to study this beauty (N. pp. 4–8). The greater political freedom of the Greeks further encouraged the highest form of art, not only in the practical sense that by contrast with autocratic rule, it did not restrict immortalisation in art to one individual (G.K.A. p. 78), but also in the wider sense that the human mind too could develop more freely, while at the same time avoiding the twin modern dangers of book-learning and dreamy philosophising (G.K.A. pp. 132–3). Although a measure of prosperity through trade could be advantageous (G.K.A. p. 83)—a point which, like the question of freedom, will later play a role in Schiller's presentation of the development of culture in his poem *Der Spaziergang* (1795)—

Winckelmann was nevertheless aware that what he called "ein gewisser heutiger bürgerlicher Wohlstand" (N. p. 7) could have an inhibiting effect on the cultural freedom of a nation. Finally, the flourishing of art among the Greeks was encouraged by the high esteem in which artists were widely held and by the wise and sure taste of those who judged their works.

Exemplary as Greek art was for Winckelmann, it was still subject to historical laws of change. Indeed, it is on account of this view that he has been seen as the founder of all art history.[21] Yet here too the basic ideas were not new or original. Montesquieu's picture of historical development, of "grandeur" and "décadence", may have formed a basis once more, although even within the sphere of art history the notion of periodicity was already established. The tradition was so old in fact that Goethe in his essay on Winckelmann was able to make the point by quoting a source from the first century A.D.[22] More important is that Winckelmann became an influential mediator of the idea and was able to formulate intelligible and meaningful criteria for distinguishing the different periods in Greek art, many of which still stand today. Admittedly there are some variations in Winckelmann's statement of the divisions concerned. At one point, when speaking theoretically, he implies two stages: "das Heftige, das Flüchtige", and "das Gesetz[t]e, das Gründliche" (N. p. 24); elsewhere there appear to be three: "das Notwendige", "die Schönheit", "das Überflüssige" (G.K.A. p. 3); yet when it comes to a detailed account of the development of Greek art, four stages are enumerated. The older style, more reliably observable, so Winckelmann argues, on old coins, was characterised by expressive figures, but a stiff, forced posture and a lack of grace (G.K.A. pp. 218–221). The elevated style, represented among others by Phidias and Myron, emerged with a time of greater enlightenment and freedom in Greece and was characterised by beauty, simplicity, nobility and grandeur; the artists of this period based their works on the truth of nature rather than a system of rules, and this brought about a reduction in rigidity and angularity (G.K.A. pp. 224–227). These latter features were eliminated only in the "beautiful style", that of Praxiteles, Lysippus and Apelles, which, though it retained the excellencies of the earlier period, witnessed the arrival of truly undulating forms and an element of even sensuous grace. Here there was no multiplicity of expression to destroy the fundamental harmony and grandeur, no violence to disturb the basic calm (G.K.A. pp. 227–233). There then followed the period of decline, in which, as indicated earlier, imitation as a substitute for real competence, coupled with eclectic habits, produced some beauty of detail without creating an aesthetic whole. Even here, however, Winckelmann is careful to point out that this decline of Greek art was a relative matter; not everything was lost; right to the end mediocre works were still made according to the principles of the great masters (G.K.A. pp. 235–245).

Significantly Winckelmann perceives similar stages in the art both of other ancient civilisations and of more modern times. This latter point is again not original, but was probably imbibed from his reading of seventeenth-century Italian sources on art and derived ultimately from Giorgio Vasari, the sixteenth-century sculptor and founder of modern art history.[23] One is nevertheless struck by the sovereign confidence with which Winckelmann states the case, however much one may wish to carp at details of the judgement :

> "Der Stil war trocken und steif bis auf Michael Angelo und Raphael; auf diesen beyden Männern bestehet die Höhe der Kunst in ihrer Wiederherstellung; nach einem Zwischenraume, in welchem der üble Geschmack regierte, kam der Stil der Nachahmer; dieses waren die Caracci und ihre Schule, mit deren Folge . . ." (G.K.A. p. 248)[24]

In the above summary of Winckelmann's comments on the periods of art, especially within Greek civilisation, an outline pattern of his aesthetic principles will already have begun to emerge. (And it is worth remembering here that the *Geschichte der Kunst* is intended to be a "Lehrgebäude" as well as a history.) It is this pattern which must now be explored more fully, since it forms the basis of his belief in the superiority of Greek art. Not that one can take it as a picture of the real Greece; it is an ideal— and of course exercised all the power of an ideal over the literature of German Classicism. Essentially it is an ideal of beauty, in which a number of inter-related elements come together to form a whole, but at many points, explicitly or implicitly, it spills over into the realm of human behaviour and activity. In sum, it has a moral as well as an aesthetic quality to it.

A fundamental principle for Winckelmann, which will already have become apparent, is that the whole is more important than individual details, overall design more important than decoration. This also involves, however, two other principles. The first is that art should strive not simply to please, but to please *constantly,* for which reason some of the Dutch painters fall short of the ideal, concentrating too much on eye-catching naturalistic detail and too little on the total composition (N.E. pp. 130–1). The second is that essence is more important than appearance, a principle which is violated in architecture, for example, once the ornamentation ceases to serve and enhance the overall plan (B. pp. 50–1).

This leads quite naturally to another central aspect of Winckelmann's ideal : simplicity ("Einfalt"). It is a word that recurs so many times in his writings that it needs no special emphasis here. What needs to be remembered is that it is not an absolute principle, in the sense that it does not altogether exclude its opposite. In the *Anmerkungen über die Baukunst der Alten* (1762), for example, variety of ornament is seen as a perfectly desirable contribution to total beauty as long as it is not excessive, as it sometimes is with Michelangelo. It should—to recall an earlier principle —bear the same relation to the basic simplicity as twigs to a branch (B. pp. 67–8).

One hesitates to use the word balance in this connection, since simplicity and variety are not given equal weight. And yet it is a characteristic feature of Winckelmann's ideal that it embraces pairs of opposites, which are held in a kind of balance, and altogether avoids extremes or exaggerations, as well as abrupt transitions from one to the other. In a relatively minor way this is to be observed in the bodily constitution of the human figure, which, ideally, is neither too fleshy, a fault for which Rubens in particular is criticised (N. p. 16), nor too lean. The female bosom is never, as Winckelmann puts it , "überflüssig begabet", the abdomen without protruding belly (G.K.A. p. 183).

Much more fundamental, however, is the relationship between nature and the ideal, which in its turn is closely related to the interplay of matter and spirit. Briefly put, perfect beauty for Winckelmann resides in the idealisation of nature. Before looking at details of this, however, it is advisable to deal first with two possible confusions or misconceptions. Winckelmann always made a distinction between nature and naturalism; the latter he regarded throughout his writing as a clearly inferior style of art, which encouraged the portrayal of ugliness, viciousness. On the other hand, nature in the sense of naturalness was a virtue he thoroughly approved of in the realm of human behaviour as well as art. Thus beauty at its most perfect, he argues, avoids what is forced and violent[25]; and it is consequently a mark of Roman painting in decline that it went against nature, probability, and common sense (G.K.A. p. 388). Elsewhere, moreover, the context in which his remarks are made is such as to remind one not only of Rousseau, but also the more boisterous battle-cries of the "Sturm und Drang". Compare, for example, the language with which he describes the merits of Lysippus during the golden age of Greek art; Lysippus followed the way of perfection that is valid at all times :

". . . dieser Weg ist, selbst die Quelle zu suchen, und zu dem Ursprunge zurück zu kehren, um die Wahrheit rein und unvermischt zu finden. Die Quelle und der Ursprung in der Kunst ist die Natur selbst, die, wie in allen Dingen, also auch hier, unter Regeln, Sätzen und Vorschriften sich verlieren, und unkenntlich werden kann" (G.K.A., p. 344)[26]

The opposite of this course is pedantry, rigid adherence to a set of rules, the attempt to appear learned or abstruse, a trap into which Arpino, Bernini and Borromini fell in the seventeenth century. And it is, retrospectively, an illuminating comment on what imitation of the Greeks did *not* mean for Winckelmann that he should attack these artists for having thereby abandoned both nature and antiquity (G.K.A. pp. 359–360). Naturalness for him expressed itself further in the customs of the Greeks, their openness and joy, their lack of strict and therefore restricting laws, even their habit of unconcerned nakedness or—if they wore clothes— the looseness and lightness of their garments (N. pp. 7–8).

To say that naturalism is rejected and naturalness affirmed still does not give the full picture of Winckelmann's comments on nature : the ideal goes beyond nature, refines nature, ennobles nature, even when this nature is of such an exemplary kind as that of the Greek body. As Werner Kohlschmidt points out, Winckelmann's idealism is here nourished by Platonism,[27] a fact which he implicitly admits in one of his most concise statements of this principle near the beginning of *Über die Nachahmung:*

"Die Kenner und Nachahmer der griechischen Werke finden in ihren Meisterstücken nicht allein die schönste Natur, sondern noch mehr als Natur, das ist, gewisse idealische Schönheiten, die, wie uns ein alter Ausleger des Plato lehret, von Bildern bloß im Verstande entworfen, gemacht sind." (N. p. 4)[28]

The practice of the ancient artists was thus to gather together various elements of beauty from different sources—here eclecticism is not regarded as a fault!—and so form an ideal beauty. Taking up his arboricultural image again, he likens this activity to the grafting of finely cultivated slips on to a tree trunk. It is a practice that will find a clear echo later in German Classicism, for example, in Goethe's little essay, *Einfache Nachahmung der Natur, Manier, Stil* (1789) or Schiller's criticism of Bürger's poems (also 1789), with its reference to idealisation and gathering together of disparate rays to form a perfect whole.[29] But Winckelmann goes on to extend the significance of such idealisation in two important ways : first by showing it to be a part of that inborn

desire of all rational people to rise above matter to the realm of
ideas, so that, although the Greek artists were working for the
senses rather than the mind, they nevertheless strove to conquer
or inspirit matter (G.K.A. p. 157), then by implying that the idealisation in artistic beauty forges a gradual link between man at his
noblest and the divine world. He has been discussing the representation of certain male divinities, notably Hercules, and goes on :

> "Mit solchen Begriffen wurde die Natur vom Sinnlichen bis
> zum Unerschaffenen erhoben, und die Hand der Künstler
> brachte Geschöpfe hervor, die von der Menschlichen Nothdurft
> gereinigt waren; Figuren, welche die Menschheit in einer höheren
> Würdigkeit vorstellen, die Hüllen und Einkleidungen bloß den-
> kender Geister und himmlischer Kräfte zu seyn scheinen.
> So wie nun die Alten stuffenweis von der Menschlichen Schönheit
> bis an die Göttliche hinauf gestiegen waren, so blieb diese Staffel
> der Schönheit. In ihren Helden, das ist, in Menschen, denen
> das Alterthum die höchste Würdigkeit unserer Natur gab,
> näherten sie sich bis an die Gränzen der Gottheit, ohne dieselben
> zu überschreiten, und den sehr feinen Unterschied zu vermis-
> chen." (G.K.A. pp. 162–3)[30]

Here we have the idealised view of humanity such as will later be
represented, with differences of course, in Goethe's Iphigenie or
the poem *Das Göttliche* and, more closely, in the first version of
Schiller's *Die Götter Griechenlands* and the later poem *Das Ideal
und das Leben,* which, having at one point spoken of the artist
seeking to overcome matter, ends with a picture of Hercules, once
more, shedding his humanity and being accepted, transfigured,
on Mount Olympus. Indeed this concept of the narrowed gap
between the gods and men is something which Goethe saw as having had a great impact on the later eighteenth century
altogether.[31]

Although the emphasis seems to lie with the idealisation rather
than with nature itself, it is in fact a harmony of the two which
Winckelmann is upholding, a harmony that Walter Pater re-
affirms in his essay on Winckelmann when he speaks of the ideal
art of the Greeks, by contrast with the overcharged symbolism of
medieval art, as one in which thought does not outstrip or lie
beyond the proper range of its sensible embodiment.[32] But thought
there is. And its equivalent in Winckelmann's vocabulary,
"Verstand", plays an important role in his pronouncements on art.
It is closely related to his recommendation of allegory—admittedly
a fluctuating concept in his writing, but one which involves the
representation of the non-sensuous, of an idea (cf. N. p. 40, N.E.

p. 132, and elsewhere)—and is ultimately part of his attempt to combat the triviality of Rococo decorativeness (N. p. 42) and establish a fundamental seriousness in art.

But seriousness is not the same as gloom; and in order to redress the balance it must be stressed that Winckelmann's ideal of Greek art and civilisation is one which also implies joy, confidence, an openness to life, by contrast with his picture of Christian humility, which has an emphasis on self-denial that violates human nature (V.A. p. 185). Even more revealing, and of consequence for German Classicism as a whole, are his comments on the Greek attitude to death. Death was not depicted, he asserts; there were no altars to death (N.E. pp. 137–8); unlike the Etruscans, the Greeks represented cheerful scenes from life on their funeral urns (G.K.A. p. 84). This is the same rejection of Northern morbidity and gloom that Goethe later fixes on in Italy when he sees ancient tombs in the Maffeianum of Verona[33] and which is epitomised in the figure of the torch-bearing youth who appears in Lessing's *Wie die Alten den Tod gebildet?* (1769), Herder's essay of the same name (1774), and Schiller's poem *Die Götter Griechenlands* (1788).

The point in Winckelmann's ideal where aesthetic and moral considerations come closest together is probably in the crucial question of "Stille", a concept which can connote rest, calm, quiet, immobility, composure, permanence, and a number of other things, according to the context, and which is to be seen as part of the reaction against the florid movement and tensions of prevailing Baroque taste and possibly also, from the psychological point of view, as an expression of Winckelmann's personal longing for peace and calm.[34] It is a quality that Raphael, among the Renaissance artists, recaptured in his *Sistine Madonna,* but that Winckelmann sought most persistently—and most debatably—to bring out in the Laocoon group of Agesander :

"Das allgemeine vorzügliche Kennzeichen der griechischen Meisterstücke ist endlich eine edle Einfalt, und eine stille Größe, so wohl in der Stellung als im Ausdruck. So wie die Tiefe des Meers allezeit ruhig bleibt, die Oberfläche mag noch so wüten, eben so zeiget der Ausdruck in den Figuren der Griechen bey allen Leidenschaften eine große und gesetzte Seele.

Diese Seele schildert sich in dem Gesichte des Laocoons, und nicht in dem Gesichte allein, bey dem heftigsten Leiden. Der Schmerz . . . äußert sich dennoch mit keiner Wuth in dem Gesichte und in der ganzen Stellung. Er erhebet kein schreckliches Geschrey, wie Virgil von seinem Laocoon singet : Die

Oeffnung des Mundes gestattet es nicht; es ist vielmehr ein
ängstliches und beklemmtes Seufzen, wie es Sadolet beschreibet.
Der Schmerz des Körpers und die Größe der Seele sind durch
den ganzen Bau der Figur mit gleicher Stärke ausgetheilet, und
gleichsam abgewogen." (N. pp. 21–2)[35]

This is not the place to discuss whether the description is a true or
full account of the Greek character, nor to pursue the aesthetic
arguments of Lessing, who took this piece as his starting point in
Laokoon oder über die Grenzen der Malerei und Poesie (1767–9).
Suffice it to say that this representation of "Greek serenity
triumphing over the tragedy of life"—to quote Professor Butler[36]
—was to be accepted by the great figures of German Classicism :
Goethe, Schiller, and Herder. More important in the present context are, first, the nature of that serenity, which expresses itself
not only morally, in the spirit of Laocoon, but also aesthetically,
in the artistic form (the "Stellung") and, second, the reappearance
of the idea of balance ("mit gleicher Stärke", "abgewogen"), here
used principally of the physical suffering and the spiritual force
pitted against it.[37] To convey this idea of the interplay of opposing forces Winckelmann has recourse to his favourite image, that
of the sea, calm below despite its agitated surface. And the fluid
nature of this element should act as sufficient warning not to interpret the stillness of Winckelmann's ideal as rigidity or immobility.
In fact it combines stillness and movement—as it does unity and
variety. And it is no accident that when later, in the *Geschichte
der Kunst*, Winckelmann describes the beauty of youthful
figures, which resides not in rigid shapes such as circles, but in
half-irregular shapes such as ellipses, in the combination of forms
flowing into each other, he comes back to the imagery of the sea
again. The only real difference this time is that he places the
emphasis the other way round : the beauty of such forms is :

"wie die Einheit der Fläche des Meers, welche in einiger Weite
eben und stille, wie ein Spiegel erscheinet, ob es gleich allezeit in
Bewegung ist und Wogen wälzet." (G.K.A. pp. 152–3)[38]

Another of Winckelmann's aesthetic ideals, already implicit in
what has gone before is the preference for gentle transitions,
whether it be in the movement from dark to light in painting,[39]
the gentle sweep in the outline of vessels found at Herculaneum
(S.H. p. 62) or even the smooth curve of the Greek profile (G.K.A.
p. 177). And one is tempted to think that it is no accident that
the adjectives that most readily spring to mind in this context,

"undulating" and "merging", both ultimately have their origin in the sea.

For some time now we have been concerned with the nature of the ideal artistic creation. Winckelmann has also something important to say, however, about the nature of aesthetic appreciation, although it is interesting to note that some of the same concepts recur here too. Just as the senses and the spirit combine in the creation of a work of art, so also, in contemplating it, the ideal beholder employs not only his senses, which in isolation lead to lasciviousness, but also his mind ("Verstand"), through which understanding and lasting pleasure come (G.K.A. pp. 143 and 147). He is, moreover, in a state of physical and mental calm, so that his enjoyment is like the gentle dew, not a sudden shower (the essence of the passage in an image from the world of nature again!)[40] This is a frankly platonic idea—the source is probably the *Phaedrus*—and looks forward to later expositions of aesthetic freedom in parts of Karl Philipp Moritz's essay *Über die bildende Nachahmung des Schönen* (1788), Kant's *Kritik der Urteilskraft* (1790) as well as in Schiller's *Das Ideal und das Leben* and, more fully, in the *Briefe über die ästhetische Erziehung des Menschen* (1795). Consider, for example, the following passage from the *Abhandlung von der Fähigkeit der Empfindung des Schönen* in which Winckelmann sums up his view on the feeling to be cultivated for beauty :

> "Der Vorwurf dieses Gefühls ist nicht, was Trieb, Freundschaft und Gefälligkeit aufweisen, sondern was der innere feinere Sinn, welche von allen Absichten geläutert sein soll, um des Schönen willen selbst, empfindet."[41]

This is a test of aesthetic appreciation which Nero failed miserably : he had an appetite for the arts—Winckelmann uses the word "Begierde"—but no taste (G.K.A. p. 390).

There is a revealing passage in Winckelmann's correspondence on the subject of style; his aim is to be brief, but at the same time to be more expansive in dealing with original thoughts and descriptions in the elevated manner; above all he wishes his style to be worthy of its subject.[42] Whether he achieved his aim is open to question. There are certainly many elevated and "worthy" passages; on the other hand, the brevity he achieves sometimes leads to confusion. What is undoubtedly true, however, is that Winckelmann has no single manner of writing. Apart from the generally accepted change in his style from the relative clumsiness of the earlier pieces (Goethe found the language of *Über die*

Nachahmung baroque!)[43] to the more measured quality of the
works written in Italy, his method of writing can be said to
operate between opposing poles : scholarship and enthusiasm,
argument and assertion, fact and poetry, and often in such a way
that these contradictory elements occur in alternating blocks.
Winckelmann had an impressive command of ancient literary
sources, as well as of philology, and was able to muster his
knowledge, when the need arose and it served his purpose, in a
scientific way. A good example of this is the way in which he used
his philological, historical and archaeological knowledge in discussing the sites of Herculaneum, Pompeii and Stabia towards the
beginning of his *Sendschreiben von den herculanischen Entdeckungen* (1762) (S.H. pp. 5–15, and 44). And yet Winckelmann at
times shows what amounts to a suspicion of scholarship, particularly if it is regarded as a substitute for first-hand acquaintance.
Hence the simple advice he gives to his reader at the end of his
Abhandlung von der Fähigkeit der Empfindung des Schönen :

"Geh hin und *sieh* !"[44]

Furthermore, it is a cause for pride that the judgements made in his
Geschichte der Kunst are based on personal familiarity with the
works concerned. It is this that leads to those glowing descriptions
of individual works that punctuate *Über die Nachahmung* and the
Geschichte der Kunst in particular, though the resultant enthusiasm
is at times allowed to obscure the facts or to lead him into
inconsistency.

Similarly, while there are passages in which Winckelmann gives
a quite reasoned argument in support of his case, one is more
often struck by the power of his unsupported assertions, which
frequently in fact contain the core of his teaching—the supremacy
of Greek art or, in more modern times, of Raphael, for example.
Elsewhere, when evidence is lacking, he will sometimes proceed
by the deductive method with disconcerting innocence. On many
occasions he has to fall back on rather weak formulations like :
"must have been", etc. (e.g. S.H. p. 30, G.K.A. pp. 69, 73, 322,
421).

Perhaps the most striking aspect of the contrast in Winckelmann's literary method, however, is the way in which he sometimes submerges his personality entirely behind the object in
hand, yet at other times allows the whole warmth of his personality to irradiate it. The resultant difference—simply put—is
that between factual documentation and poetic description. Of the
former kind are the *catalogue raisonné* he made of the late Baron
von Stosch's intaglios (1760), his detailed account of the temples

at Paestum, with notes on the materials used, the method of building, types of architecture, and much more besides (B. Chap. I), and also parts of the *Geschichte der Kunst* such as the section dealing with the materials used in sculpture or the method of painting (G.K.A. pp. 249 and 263). The latter is represented above all by those numerous descriptions, one might almost say "recreations" of individual works of outstanding beauty that appear at intervals throughout *Über die Nachahmung* and the *Geschichte der Kunst* in particular. The fact that many were conceived, and some indeed published, separately—albeit not in an identical form—merely underlines the impression the reader gains on encountering them in their wider setting : that they are in fact poems in prose.[45] All of which, however, does not negate the fact that they are at the same time based on keen observation. One can do no better here than simply quote one such passage, that on the famous Belvedere torso from the *Geschichte der Kunst*, drawing attention to the elevated tone, the imagery, the imaginative penetration of the object represented—and, incidentally, to the summary it contains of so many of the aesthetic ideals discussed above :

"Auf das äußerste gemishandelt und verstümmelt, und ohne Kopf, Arme und Beine, wie diese Statue ist, zeiget sie sich noch itzo denen, welche in die Geheimnisse der Kunst hinein zu schauen vermögend sind, in einem Glanze von ihrer ehemaligen Schönheit. Dieser Künstler hat ein hohes Ideal eines über die Natur erhabenen Körpers, und eine Natur männlich vollkommener Jahre, wenn dieselbe bis auf den Grad Göttlicher Genügsamkeit erhöhet wäre, in diesem Hercules gebildet, welcher hier erscheint, wie er sich von den Schlacken der Menscheit mit Feuer gereiniget, und die Unsterblichkeit und den Sitz unter den Göttern erlanget hat. Denn er ist ohne Bedürfniß menschlicher Nahrung, und ohne ferneren Gebrauch der Krätte vorgestellet. Es sind keine Ardern sichtbar, und der Unterlieb ist nur gemacht zu genießen, nicht zu nehmen, und völlig ohne erfüllt zu seyn. Er hat, wie die Stellung des übrigen Restes urtheilen läßt, mit gestütztem und aufwerts gerichtetem Haupte gesessen, welches mit einer frohen Ueberdenkung seiner vollbrachten großen Thaten wird beschäftiget gewesen seyn; wie selbst der Rücken, welcher gleichsam in hohen Betrachtungen gekrümmet ist, anzudeuten scheint. Die mächtig erhabene Brust bildet uns diejenige, auf welche der Riese Geryon erdrücket worden, und in der Länge und Stärke der Schenkel finden wir den unermüdeten Held, welcher den Hirsch

mit ehernen Füßen verfolgete und erreichte, und durch unzählige
Länder bis an die Gränzen der Welt gezogen ist. Der Künstler
bewundere in den Umrissen dieses Körpers die immerwährende
Ausfließung einer Form in die andere, und die schwebenden
Züge, die nach Art der Wellen sich heben und senken, und in
einander verschlungen werden : er wird finden, daß sich niemand
im Nachzeichnen der Richtigkeit versichern kann, indem der
Schwung, dessen Richtung man nachzugehen glaubt, sich
unvermerkt ablenket, und durch einen anderen Gang, welchen
er nimmt, das Auge und die Hand irre machet. Die Gebeine
scheinen mit einer fettlichen Haut überzogen, die Muskeln
sind feist ohne Ueberfluß, und eine so abgewogene Fleischigkeit
findet sich in keinem anderen Bilde : ja man könnte sagen,
daß dieser Hercules einer höhern Zeit der Kunst näher kommt,
als selbst der Apollo." (G.K.A. pp. 368–70)[46]

As will already perhaps have become apparent, it is at least
partly because of such enthusiasms and fixed ideals that Winckelmann sometimes contradicted himself, made factual errors (many of
which he acknowledged and later sought to correct),[47] showed
lapses of taste, presented a limited or distorted view of his subject.
Most notable is his description of the Laocoon group, seen first
in a copy in Dresden. Of the many works Winckelmann singles
out for particular and favourable attention he could scarcely have
chosen one less appropriate for a demonstration of "edle Einfalt
und stille Größe". Even if it is not actually "naturalistic"[48] or
the work of a Greek Bernini[49] (both equivalent to terms of
abuse in Winckelmann's vocabulary), it nevertheless displays, as
a recent writer on Greek art has put it, "expressive modelling
and anguish of features",[50] possessing nobility and grandeur,
but hardly simplicity and calm. Apart from the general limitation
consequent upon his relative lack of interest even in painting
and architecture and his concentration on sculpture, there is
altogether a lack of appreciation of art that involves conflict or
evil, a weakness which Pater pointed out a century ago.[51] But
it stems of course from the nature of his ideal, which, although
it cast a spell over the German mind for years to come, represented
a serious distortion of Greek civilisation, omitting or suppressing
the darker and more barbaric aspects associated, for example, with
the Bacchic rites. And it is characteristic of Winckelmann's whole
approach that, in discussing the athletic customs of the ancient
Greeks, he writes of their wrestling with approval, but makes
no mention of the pancratian contests, which often involved
such niceties as gouging each other's eyes out and sometimes

ended in death.[52] Even as one reads some of Winckelmann's aesthetic pronouncements, one suspects a potential danger if the ideals are allowed one-sided prominence : the danger that proportion might become symmetry, stillness rigidity, smoothness insipidity. And it is a suspicion that other judgements by Winckelmann, particularly his fulsome praise of his painter-friend, Mengs, as the greatest artist and greatest teacher of his time, as the creator of a work even greater than anything done by Raphael himself,[53] do nothing to dispel. Before condemning Winckelmann roundly on this account, however, it is proper to recall that the work just alluded to, a fresco ceiling entitled *Parnassus* executed for Cardinal Albani's new villa and in all conscience a cold, lifeless, statuesque work, was then widely held to be one of the wonders of the world.[54] Apart from the distortion of vision that personal friendship with Mengs may well have brought—the *Geschichte der Kunst* contains after all, besides its official dedication, a consecration to "der Kunst, und der Zeit, und besonders meinem Freunde, Herrn Anton Raphael Mengs" (G.K.A. p. xxvi)—Winckelmann's unmerited encomium is probably best regarded as an expression of a common aim : the attack on prevailing Baroque taste in art.

III

Had Winckelmann been allowed to complete his full biblical span of threescore years and ten, his life would have belonged almost equally to the two halves of the eighteenth century. In spite of the abrupt and violent curtailment, however, both his life and works incorporate many of the varied and important cross-currents of the entire century in an almost exemplary way. And seen from this point of view he is again not without his contradictions.

Although in the forefront of the attack on Baroque art, he could still find words of praise for the new Villa Albani, completed in 1763 and built in the Baroque manner.[55] It has also been suggested that there is an element of Baroque stoicism in Winckelmann's ideal, embodied above all in his interpretation of the Laocoon group and the suppressed scream that Lessing had cause to re-interpret in his *Laokoon*.[56] Winckelmann in fact goes so far as to relate the sculpture explicitly to the Stoics in his *Geschichte der Kunst* (G.K.A. p. 171). Such stoicism, though a relic of the Baroque age, persisted quite widely into the eighteenth century; it is to be found, for example, in works

such as Gottsched's play, *Sterbender Cato* (1732), and Jacques
Louis David's painting, *Serment des Horaces* (1784). But as the
very titles of these works remind us, it is a philosophy customarily
if erroneously, associated with the Romans rather than the Greeks!
Again, although Winckelmann criticised the Baroque manner of
allegorising in painting, when it became too ingenious and required
explanatory inscriptions, his own prescriptions for allegorical
subjects also involve such abstraction as to be very little different
from their Baroque counterparts.[57]

The democratic strand in Winckelmann's thinking, nurtured by
his hatred of Prussian authoritarianism, and the almost Rousseauistic longing for nature implicit in his picture of Greek civilisation,
its political and moral "freedom", are sufficient to permit comparisons with the eighteenth-century developments of Enlightenment and even "Sturm und Drang". Yet here too the picture is not
entirely consistent. The dominance of reason ("Vernunft") over
imagination in the English character is seen as a distinct disadvan-
tage in artistic creation (G.K.A. p. 28), and Professor Schultz has
further demonstrated a link backwards to Shaftesbury and forwards
to Herder in the idea that artistic creation is itself like the original
act of creation, that is, it possesses a divine element.[58] On the
other hand, the force of originality is inevitably diminished when
one remembers his advocating imitation of the Greeks, or his
prescriptions for allegorical subjects.

It has even been suggested that Winckelmann was something
of a Romantic.[59] Of course there is a romantic element in his
longing for a long-lost Golden Age and in his "concentration
on an inner reality, on the vision seen by the imagination,
intuition".[60] But this is no more than one finds, for instance,
in the backward-looking gaze of Goethe's Torquato Tasso or the
lament of Schiller's *Die Götter Griechenlands*. What is more in
keeping with the specifically German Romantic movement, is
the experience of art and beauty as religion, an experience which
will find its most enthusiastic expression in Wackenroder's novel,
Herzensergießungen eines kunstliebenden Klosterbruders, published
by Tieck in 1797. Ultimately, however, this must remain a fairly
isolated point of contact with German Romanticism. Winckelmann
could never have followed the Romantics when they expressed
a preference for Christian art over antique art. And in describing
Greek civilisation as one where the mind could develop freely
while avoiding the modern dangers not only of book learning
but also of dreamy speculation (G.K.A. pp. 132–3), was he not
by implication condemning one of the tendencies that was later
to characterise a part of German Romanticism?

In seeking to assess Winckelmann's achievement and influence it is wise to make a distinction between the world of the visual arts and that of literature. In the former realm exaggerated claims have been made on his behalf, for example, that he was the founder of art history as well as archaeology. Such boldly stated claims ignore the contributions of men like Vasari with his famous *Vite* and the Comte de Caylus with his *Recueils d'antiquité*, to name but two of the most important; they also do scant justice to the influence Winckelmann derived from his painter-friends, Oeser in Dresden and Mengs in Rome. Nevertheless, making due allowance for the many influences on his thinking, it is fair to say that, even in the way in which he used insights from many sources and welded them together, he set new and high standards for the disciplines of archaeology and art history and at the same time helped to rescue ancient art from the province of pure scholarship and antiquarianism to an area where it could become of living interest as a source of pleasure in its own right. Within these disciplines too he showed an admirable desire to distinguish true from false as well as establishing valuable criteria for determining the period of particular works, even if this did not prevent him from making mistakes himself. And by advocating "imitation" of the Ancients, he joined Mengs, David, and Canova in establishing neo-classic art in Europe.

For the student of German literature and thought in the eighteenth-century, however, Winckelmann is important for different reasons; his influence is probably also more far-reaching. It might at first sight seem strange that a man who wrote almost exclusively about the visual arts should have greater consequence for the field of literature. And yet there is a kind of justice to this, since Winckelmann first approached the ancient world through its literature, not only its philosophers and chroniclers, but also its poets and playwrights. He was in fact one link in the chain of men who in the eighteenth century were gradually able to rescue the works of Greek art and literature from the neglect into which they had fallen, either because they offended religious scruples or, in the case of literature, because they were exploited solely for the purposes of grammatical instruction.[61] And it was a chain which led eventually to that fruitful and living encounter with the ancient world which we associate with the names of Lessing, Herder, Goethe, Schiller, Hölderin and others. It need hardly be said that Winckelmann's influence was particularly stimulating in the moulding of German Classicism. It is not possible to trace his influence in detail in such a short account, although some idea of its extent will already have emerged from earlier references. Of course the influence was not the same in each individual case, nor was it of a constant intensity; it was not always direct and sometimes intermingled with other influences such as Rousseau or Kant. Nevertheless, if it is true that German Classicism took the ancient Greeks as an embodiment of humanity at its greatest, most natural, most harmonious, most noble, most free, a humanity given permanence in works of art, it is also true that it was very largely through Winckelmann's eyes that the German classical writers saw them; and if it was a myth that governed their thinking and set their standards, it was a myth largely of Winckelmann's making. One has only to observe how often they refer to him or actually quote him to realise his significance for them; or, remembering the exposition of his writings given above, to enumerate some of the central ideals of German Classicism—balance or harmony; idealisation of nature, spiritualisation of matter; distillation of the essential and permanent rather than fleeting naturalism; calm and moderation as aesthetic and moral principles; the overcoming of stark tragedy—to realise how much of a living force his ideas were even years after his death.

In conclusion, still remembering that death, let us move forwards in time some hundred-and-fifty years, westwards in space some sixty miles along the Adriatic coast and, mentally, from the realm of fact to fiction; in short, from a death in Trieste to *Death in Venice*. For there are some curious similarities between the fates of Winckelmann and Gustav von Aschenbach. Both are steeped in Greek thought, both have homosexual tendencies which they regard as part of the Greek tradition, both are seekers after beauty, which they see in platonic terms, and both meet their end after an abortive attempt to return from the scene of their fascination. If this seems a far-fetched or too speculative comparison, it is worth remembering that in the long letter to Carl Maria Weber in which Thomas Mann gives a detailed exposition of his aim in writing *Der Tod in Venedig*—a work which began with the idea of the ageing Goethe's love for a young *girl*—Winckelmann is mentioned, together with Michelangelo, Frederick the Great, Platen and Stefan George, in connection with what is referred to as the "homo-erotic" interest.[62] And in fact there is a logic to all that. For what Thomas Mann is depicting in this work is nothing less than the collapse of the German classical tradition. The ideal of control and moderation, and the ideal of aesthetic contemplation advocated by Winckelmann and Schiller in particular, are here mocked and routed. Dionysus, denied for so long, now takes his revenge. And yet even the words used to describe this defeat would be unthinkable without Winckelmann :

"Die Meisterhaltung unseres Stiles ist Lüge und Narrentum, unser Ruhm und Ehrenstand eine Posse, das Vertrauen der Menge zu uns höchst lächerlich, Volks- und Jugenderziehung durch die Kunst ein gewagtes, zu verbietendes Unternehmen. Denn wie sollte wohl der zum Erzieher taugen, dem eine unverbesserliche und natürliche Richtung zum Abgrunde eingeboren ist? Wir möchten ihn wohl verleugnen und Würde gewinnen, aber wie wir uns wenden mögen, er zieht uns an. So sagen wir etwa der auflösenden Erkenntnis ab, denn die Erkenntnis, Phaidros, hat keine Würde und Strenge; sie ist wissend, verstehend, verzeihend, ohne Haltung und Form; sie hat Sympathie mit dem Abgrund, sie *ist* der Abgrund. Diese also verwerfen wir mit Entschlossenheit, und fortan gilt unser Trachten einzig der Schönheit, das will sagen der Einfachheit, Größe und neuen Strenge, der zweiten Unbefangenheit und der Form. Aber Form und Unbefangenheit, Phaidros, führen zum Rausch und zur Begierde, führen den Edlen vielleicht zu grauenhaftem Gefühlsfrevel, den seine eigene schöne Strenge als infam verwirft, führen zum Abgrund, zum Abgrund auch sie."[63]

NOTES

1. Goethe: *Winckelmann und sein Jahrhundert,* "Hamburger Ausgabe" Vol. XII pp. 98f.

2. Ibid., p. 120.

3. Cf. Carl Justi: *Winckelmann und seine Zeitgenossen,* hsg. Walther Rehm, Köln 1956 Vol. I p. 156.

4. The content derives from yourself. Our acquaintance has been short, too short for you and for me; but I was aware of the spiritual concord between us the first time I saw you. Your culture gave me cause to suppose what I desired, and I discovered in a beautiful body a spirit made for virtue and endowed with a feeling for beauty. For this reason the parting from you was one of the most painful of my life, and our common friend is a witness of that, even after your departure; for your absence, under distant skies, leaves me no hope of seeing you again. May this essay be a memorial to our friendship, which, for my part, is free of every conceivable design and remains constantly alive and devoted to you. *Kleine Schriften und Briefe,* ed. Wilhelm Senff, Weimar 1960 p. 152.

5. See the letter to Berg on June 9, 1762, in *Briefe* Hsg. Walther Rehm Berlin 1954 Vol. III p. 232.

6. *Winckelmann und sein Jahrhundert* p. 100.

7. See Horst Rüdiger: *Winckelmanns Persönlichkeit* in *Johann Joachim Winckelmann: 1768–1968*. Bad Godesberg 1968 p. 40.

8. Walter Pater: *Winckelmann* in *The Renaissance*: *Studies in Art and Poetry* (library edition) London. 1914 p. 187

9. See especially the letters to Berendis on July 12, 1754 and March 10, 1755 *Briefe* Vol. I pp. 143–7 and p. 168.

10. See Rüdiger pp. 27–8.

11. See *Briefe* Vol. IV p. 249 and elsewhere.

12. Letter to Stosch on January 28, 1764 *Briefe* Vol. III p. 11.

13. Page references given in the text are taken from Johann Joachim Winckelmann, *Kunsttheoretische Schriften*, Baden-Baden/Strasbourg, 1962– . The works contained in these volumes are facsimile reproductions of eighteenth century editions. The following abbreviations are used:

   N = *Gedanken über die Nachahmung der griechischen Werke in der Malerey und Bildhauerkunst* in Vol. I.

   N.S. = *Sendschreiben über die Gedanken von der Nachahmung der griechischen Werke in der Malerey und Bildhauerkunst* in Vol. I.

   N.E. = *Erläuterung der Gedanken von der Nachahmung der griechischen Werke, in der Malerey und Bildhauerkunst; und Beantwortung des Sendschreibens über diese Gedanken* in Vol I.

   B. = *Anmerkungen über die Baukunst der Alten* Vol. II.

   S.H. = *Sendschreiben von den herculanischen Entdeckungen* in Vol. III.

   V.A. = *Versuch einer Allegorie besonders für die Kunst* Vol. IV.

   G.K.A. = *Geschichte der Kunst der Alterthums* Vol. V.

14. *Abhandlung von der Fähigkeit der Empfindung des Schönen in der Kunst* in *Kleine Schriften und Briefe* p. 162.

15. On November 15, 1765 in a letter to Francke Winckelmann admitted that he had not seriously considered such a journey since 1759. *Briefe* Vol. III p. 137.

16. Letter of January 6, 1753. *Briefe* Vol. I p. 119.

17. The only way for us to become great, or even, if possible, inimitable, is to imitate the Greeks.

18. . . . and what someone once said of Homer, that he who has come to understand him comes also to admire him, applies also to the works of art of the Ancients, especially the Greeks. One needs to have become acquainted with them like a friend, before one can find the Laocoon as inimitable as Homer.

19. See Justi Vol. I p. 244.

20. See Wolfgang Leppmann: *Winckelmann* London 1971 p. 110.

21. See Richard Benz: *Die Zeit der deutschen Klassik*. Stuttgart 1953 p. 126.

22. *Winckelmann und sein Jahrhundert*, p. 111.

23. See Herbert von Einem in the notes to the "Hamburger Ausgabe" of Goethe's works Vol. XII p. 601.

24. The style was dry and stiff before Michelangelo and Raphael; it

is on the shoulders of these two men that the culmination of art in its renaissance rests; after an interval dominated by poor taste came the style of the imitators, these were the Caraccis and their school, with its retinue.

25. *Abhandlung von der Fähigkeit* . . . p. 176.

26. . . . this way is to seek the source oneself, and return to the fountain-head, to find the truth pure and unadulterated. The source and fountain-head in art is nature itself, which, here as in everything, can become lost and unrecognisable behind rules, precepts and regulations.

27. See Werner Kohlschmidt: *Winckelmann und der Barock* in: *Form und Innerlichkeit* Bern 1955 p. 18.

28. Those who know and imitate Greek works find in their master-pieces not only nature at its fairest, but more than nature, that is certain elements of an ideal beauy, which, as an ancient commentator on Plato teaches us, are derived from images conceived purely in the mind.

29. *Schillers Werke, Nationalausgabe* Vol XXII p. 253.

30. With such concepts nature was raised from the level of the sensuous to that of the uncreated, and the hand of the artist produced creations that were purged of every human necessity, figures representing humanity in a greater dignity, figures which seem to be the husks and forms of merely thinking beings and divine powers.

Just as the Ancients had gradually advanced from the level of human beauty to that of divine beauty, so this stage of beauty remained. In their heroes, that is, in men to whom antiquity gave the highest dignity of our nature, they came close to the limits of divinity, without crossing those limits and confusing the very fine distinction.

31. *Winckelmann und sein Jahrhundert* p. 103. See Henry Hatfield: *Schiller, Winckelmann, and the myth of Greece* in *Schiller 1759–1959: Commemorative American Studies* ed. John R. Frey. Urbana 1959 p. 34.

32. Pater pp. 204–6.

33. *Italienische Reise* "Hamburger Ausgabe" Vol. XI p. 42.

34. See Franz Schultz: *Klassik und Romantik der Deutschen* Stuttgart 1952 Vol. I p. 79.

35. The primary characteristic of Greek masterpieces in general is finally a noble simplicity and quiet grandeur, both in the posture and the expression. Just as the depths of the ocean remain forever calm, however agitated the surface may be, so also the expression in the Greek figures displays a great and steady spirit in spite of all the passions.

This spirit is expressed in the face of Laocoon (and not only the face) in spite of the most vehement passions. The pain . . . is nevertheless conveyed without anger in the face and the entire posture. He utters no terrifying scream, as Virgil sings of his Laocoon: the opening of the mouth does not permit this; it is rather a distressed and anguished sigh, such as Sadolet describes. The bodily pain and the spiritual grandeur are distributed with equal intensity throughout the entire structure of the figure and are, as it were, balanced against each other.

36. E. M. Butler: *The Tyranny of Greece over Germany* Cambridge 1935 p. 81.

37. See how elsewhere moral and artistic restraint are seen together (G.K.A., pp. 111–12).

38. ... like the unity of the surface of the ocean, which appears for some distance to be flat and still like a mirror, although it is forever in motion, rolling waves.

39. *Abhandlung von der Fähigkeit* . . . p. 174.

40. Ibid. p. 161.

41. Ibid. p. 157.

The object of this feeling is not what is displayed by instinct, friendship and favour, but what the inner, more delicate organ of perceptions, which should be purged of all design, feels on account of the beautiful *per se*.

42. See Schultz Vol. I p. 85.

43. *Winckelmann und sein Jahrhundert* p. 107.

44. Go and *see! Abhandlung von der Fähigkeit* ... p. 176.

45. See Goethe: *Winckelmann und sein Jahrhundert* p. 120.

46. Although mishandled and mutilated to an extreme degree, without head, arms and legs, this statue still shows itself, to those able to penetrate the mysteries of art, in all the splendour of its former beauty. In this Hercules the artist has created a high ideal of a body elevated above nature and a nature representing the years of manly perfection, if that nature were elevated to the level of divine contentedness—in this Hercules, who here appears as he purified himself with fire from the dross of humanity and attained immortality and a seat among the gods. For as presented here he is without need of human nourishment and has ceased to use his energies. No veins are visible, and the abdomen is made only to enjoy, not to consume, and is full without being filled. As the position of the torso that remains indicates, he has been sitting with his head supported and directed upwards, occupied no doubt with the happy contemplation of the great deeds he has performed—as even the back, bent so to speak in lofty reflections, seems to suggest. The powerfully elevated chest gives us a picture of that on which the giant Geryon was crushed to death, and in the length and strength of the thighs we see the tireless hero, who pursued the stag on feet of brass and caught it, and who wandered through countless lands to the ends of the earth. In the contours of this body let the artist admire the continuous merging of one shape into another and the floating lines which rise and fall like waves and become interlaced; he will find that no one can recapture its rightness in copying it, since the curve one thinks one is following changes direction imperceptibly and confounds the eye and the hand by the different course it takes. The bones seem to be covered with a thickish skin, the muscles are big without excess, and a fleshiness of such proportion is to be found in no other work; indeed one might almost say that this Hercules comes closer to a higher period of art than even the Apollo.

47. See Herder: *Denkmal Johann Winckelmann* in J. Winckelmann

Geschichte der Kunst des Altertums Vienna 1934 pp. 435–6 and Goethe: *Winckelmann und sein Jahrhundert* p. 121.

48. See Butler p. 47.

49. See Benz, p. 121.

50. John Boardman: *Greek Art* London 1964 p. 215.

51. Pater p. 223.

52. For a detailed description of the *pankration* see Ludwig Drees: *Olympia: Gods, Artists and Athletes* London 1968 pp. 83–4.

53. See G.K.A. pp. 170, 184; *Abhandlung von der Fähigkeit . . .* p. 172; see also Benz p. 130.

54. See Benz pp. 129–30.

55. Ibid p. 129.

56. See Kohlschmidt pp. 25–6.

57. Ibid pp. 29–30.

58. See Schultz Vol. I pp. 76–7.

59. See especially Henry Hatfield: *Winckelmann: The Romantic Element* in: *Germanic Review* XXVII (1953) pp 282–9.

60. Ibid p. 283.

61. See Humphry Trevelyan: *Goethe and the Greeks* Cambridge 1941 pp. 1–14.

62. Letter dated July 4, 1920 in *Briefe 1889–1936*. Hsg. Erika Mann Frankfurt/Main 1961 pp. 176–180.

63. Thomas Mann *Erzählungen. Stockholmer Gesamtausgabe* p. 522. The masterly tone of our style is deception and folly, our fame and position of honour a farce, the confidence that the public at large has in us ridiculous in the extreme, the education of the people and of youth by means of art a risky undertaking that ought to be prohibited. For what conceivable good as a teacher is the man who has an inborn, incorrigible and natural tendency towards the abyss? We would very much like to deny it and attain some sort of dignity, but, wriggle as we may, it draws us on. Thus we renounce the cognition that dissolves everything, for cognition, Phaedrus, has no dignity and no discipline; it is knowing, understanding, forgiving, without control and form; it is in sympathy with the abyss; it *is* the abyss. And so we reject this resolutely; from now on our sole object is beauty, that is to say, simplicity, grandeur and new discipline, a new detachment and form. But form and detachment, Phaedrus, lead to intoxication and desire, lead the noble man perhaps to hideous emotional outrages, which his own aesthetic discipline rejects as infamous, lead to the abyss, yes, they too lead to the abyss.

SELECT BIBLIOGRAPHY

J. J. Winckelmann *Kunsttheoretische Schriften* (facsimile reproduction of eighteenth century editions). Baden-Baden–Strasbourg 1962–. To date nine volumes have appeared.

J. J. Winckelmann   *Kleine Schriften und Briefe.* Hsg. Wilhelm Senff. Weimar 1960.
J. J. Winckelmann   *Geschichte der Kunst des Altertums.* Hsg. Wilhelm Senff. Weimar 1964.
J. J. Winckelmann   *Briefe, Kritisch-Historische Gesamtausgabe.* 4 Vols. Hsg. Walter Rehm. Berlin 1952–7.
Richard Benz   *Die Zeit der deutschen Klassik.* Stuttgart 1953.
R. Biedrzynski   *Begierde des Schauens* in *Johann Joachim Winckelmann: 1768–1968.* Bad Godesberg 1968 pp. 41–9.
E. M. Butler   *The Tyranny of Greece over Germany.* Cambridge 1935
Ludwig Curtius   *Johann Joachim Winckelmann: 1717–68* in *Johann Joachim Winckelmann: 1768–1968.* Bad Godesberg 1968 pp. 5–19.
J. W. von Goethe   *Winckelmann und sein Jahrhundert* in the "Hamburger Ausgabe" Vol. XII pp. 96–129.
Henry Hatfield   *Winckelmann: The Romantic Element* in *Germanic Review* XXVII (1953) pp. 282–9.
Henry Hatfield   *Schiller, Winckelmann, and the Myth of Greece* in *Schiller 1759–1959: Commemorative American Studies.* Ed. John R. Frey. Urbana 1959 pp. 12–35.
J. G. von Herder   *Denkmahl J. Winckelmanns* in *Werke.* Hsg. Suphan. Berlin 1892 Vol. VIII pp. 437–483.
Carl Justi   *Winckelmann und seine Zeitgenossen.* Hsg. Walther Rehm. Köln 1956
W. Kohlschmidt   *Winckelmann und der Barock* in *Form und Innerlichkeit.* Bern 1955 pp. 11–32.
W. Leppmann   *Winckelmann.* London 1971.
Walter Pater   *Winckelmann* in *The Renaissance: Studies in Art and Poetry* (library edition). London 1914 pp. 177–232.
Walther Rehm   *Griechentum und Goethezeit.* Leipzig 1936.
Horst Rüdiger   *Winckelmanns Persönlichkeit* in *Johann Joachim Winckelmann: 1768–1968.* Bad Godesberg 1968 pp. 20–40.
Franz Schultz   *Winckelmann und seine Wirkung* in *Klassik und Romantik der Deutschen.* Stuttgart 1959 Vol. I pp. 68–158.
H. Trevelyan   *Goethe and the Greeks.* Cambridge 1941.
B. Vallentin   *Winckelmann.* Berlin 1931.

Johann Heinrich Pestalozzi

Johann Heinrich Pestalozzi

by M. R. HEAFFORD

Johann Heinrich Pestalozzi was born in Zurich in 1746, and was educated in the city itself. After working some months from 1767–8 under J. R. Tschiffeli, an experimental farmer at Kirchberg near Bern, Pestalozzi bought a property near the village of Birr (Aarau) in 1769. In the same year he married Anna Schulthess, the daughter of an influential Zurich family.

He soon encountered financial difficulties with his farming. Therefore, in 1774, he began to take in some poor children, in the hope that he could give them an elementary education while they, by spinning, weaving, and helping on the farm, would contribute to the financial welfare of the farm. Despite his hopes, he failed to overcome his financial problems and, in 1779, the children had to be sent away.

There ensued a long, frustrating period which Pestalozzi devoted to writing and which was only finally broken in 1798 when the Swiss government requested him to set up a home in Stans for children orphaned or homeless as a result of a Swiss insurrection against French troops. Pestalozzi's stay in Stans, though it restored his confidence in his own abilities, had lasted only a few months when the building in which the children were housed was required as a military hospital. After a short rest, Pestalozzi was allowed to develop his educational ideas in the town of Burgdorf. A few months later, in October 1800, he opened his own institute in Burgdorf castle. From this moment on, Pestalozzi's reputation grew rapidly and, with it, the size of his enterprise.

When, in turn, the Burgdorf castle was taken over for administrative purposes, Pestalozzi moved to Münchenbuchsee closer to Bern. Here, for a few months, he attempted to collaborate with P.E. von Fellenberg who ran an educational establishment in the nearby Hofwyl. It soon emerged, however, that the ideas and personalities of the two men were incompatible, and their association ended when, in 1805, Pestalozzi moved on to the castle at Yverdon in French Switzerland.

Here the institute continued to grow, and with this growth Pestalozzi began to hope that the ideas he was developing would be applied to a national system of education. In fact for several years the Prussian government did send teachers to be trained at Yverdon, but the general political unrest in Europe contributed to their final departure, as it did to the instability of Pestalozzi's organisation generally. As far as Switzerland was concerned, Pestalozzi's hopes received a serious set-back with the appearance of an official report made by a commission under Father Grégoire Girard in 1810. While the report did not openly condemn the institute, its detailed analysis of the institute's work qualified every aspect of the actual achievements. Thus although Pestalozzi's message was carried all over Europe by individuals, it never received widespread support at governmental level.

A large number of teachers came to study Pestalozzi's methods at Yverdon and, as a result, the administration became increasingly top-heavy; and this, along with Pestalozzi's generosity in maintaining some pupils free or at a reduced fee, created difficulties both in finances and in human relationships. Pestalozzi came to depend more and more on his assistants, and, in particular, on Joseph Schmid and Johannes Niederer. The characters of these two men were very different and they proved unable to cooperate. Schmid left the institute in 1810, angrily and with much publicity. His eventual return in 1815 gave rise to unhappiness in many of the assistants, and the dissatisfaction reached its peak with the departure of Niederer in 1817. Niederer proceeded to attack Pestalozzi openly, bringing the whole enterprise into disrepute. The attacks culminated in the expulsion of Schmid from Canton of Vaud in 1824 and the final dissolution of the institute in 1825. Pestalozzi retired to the Neuhof, his house near Birr, and died in Brugg, nearby, in 1827, at the age of 81.

THOSE familiar with Gottfried Keller's "Novelle", *Der Landvogt von Greifensee*, will remember the charm and humour with which he depicts 18th century Zurich, especially in the episodes concerning Figura Leu. Keller's description is also historically accurate in that it pinpoints the essential characteristic of Zurich society in the middle of the 18th century— a town in which enormous social changes were taking place behind the institutional rigidity of the Church and State.

The traditional Swiss concepts of freedom and democracy had long been forgotten in a town which was governed autocratically by a "Grosse Rat" consisting of 212 citizens drawn from a comparatively small number of patrician families. All the citizens of the town were privileged in that they had the sole right to carry on trading, to fill all ecclesiastical posts, to become officers in the army, and to fill the senior administrative posts. These privileges applied not only to the town itself, but also to the whole of the surrounding countryside. Thus some 9,000 town citizens effectively controlled the 200,000 country inhabitants. Adherence to a strict social and moral code was demanded of everyone. The *"Sittenmandat"* of 1744,[1] for example, demonstrates the degree of control which the rulers imposed. Observance of the Lord's Day was the first demand :

"Man soll sich die Heiligung des Tags des Herren eiferig angelegen seyn lassen durch fleissige Besuchung der Predigten Göttlichen Worts, und der Catechisationen."[2]

Permission was required to leave the town on Sunday, and all forms of social gathering before and during Church services were prohibited. Dress too aroused the disapproval of the "Gnädige Herren" who saw the "übermachte Kleider-Hoffart" leading to the "grosser Verderbnuss und unwiderbringlichen Schaden Unserer Burgerschafft".[3] They went on to prohibit everything they found offensive from décolleté dresses to curly hair and jewellery—and in case they had forgotten anything they ended up with a blanket prohibition :

"So ist auch Unser ernstlicher Will, dass alle Neuerungen, sie seyen hierinn verbotten oder nicht, zumahlen nicht alles ausgesetzet werden kan, gänzlich . . . verbotten seyn sollen."[4]

Further regulations prohibited all forms of rowdy behaviour after dark, dancing during wedding celebrations, the consumption of game, dainties, sweets, and foreign wine at official guild dinners, all gambling and betting, travelling by coach or sedan chair without good reason, and the distribution of subversive literature. The *Mandat* concluded thus :

"Damit man aber diesen heimlsamlichen Satz- und Ordnungen mehr, als bissher geschehen, Folg leiste, und also die Züchtigung des sonst erzörnten Gottes von Unserem liebwerthen Vatterland durch wahre Bussfertigkeit abgehalten werden möge, so wünschen Wir hierzu männiglichem den Geist der Gehorsamme, welchen Gott der Herr einem jeden aus den Reichthumen seiner Güte mittheilen wolle."[5]

In the decades that followed, little changed and it is small wonder that we find Goethe mocking the rigidly structured Swiss society in the 1770's :

"Frei wären die Schweizer? Frei diese wohlhabenden Bürger in den verschlossenen Städten? Frei diese armen Teufel an ihren Klippen und Felsen? Was man dem Menschen nicht alles weismachen kann! Besonders wenn man so ein altes Märchen in Spiritus aufbewahrt. Sie machten sich einmal von einem Tyrannen los und konnten sich in einem Augenblick frei denken; nun erschuf ihnen die liebe Sonne aus dem Aas des Unterdrückers einen Schwarm von kleinen Tyrannen durch eine sonderbare Wiedergeburt; nun erzählen sie das alte Märchen immer fort, man hört bis zum Überdruss : sie hätten sich einmal frei gemacht und wären frei geblieben; und nun sitzen sie hinter ihren Mauern, eingefangen von ihren Gewohnheiten und Gesetzen, ihren Fraubasereien und Philistereien . . ."[6]

And yet behind the outward appearance of order and discipline, in Zurich at least, great changes were taking place. The ideas of Descartes, by casting doubt on all inherited systems of belief, forced the individual to think anew for himself. In Zurich his ideas, and those of other Enlightenment thinkers, began to take root. Religious belief in particular was affected, in that there was a move away from dogma towards a more individualised morality. This was the first step in a process of secularisation which was to have great consequences in the world of letters and ideas.

That these various influences managed to take a hold in Zurich was due to two important factors. On the one hand the town had a small, but highly literate, population. In 1747 Sulzer wrote to Bodmer comparing it favourably with that of Berlin : "Es sind in Zürich gewiss zehen lesende und denkende Köpfe gegen einen in diesen Gegenden",[7] and around 1752 Ewald von Kleist remarked : "Während man in dem grossen Berlin kaum drei bis vier Leute von Genie und Geschmack antreffe, finde man in dem kleinen Zürich mehr als zwanzig bis dreissig derselben."[8] On the other hand, there were one or two of these "reading and thinking" people who deliberately set out to pass on the new ideas and to stimulate discussion on their relevance to the Swiss situation. Chief amongst these were Bodmer and Breitinger who argued the merits of English literature in the famous dispute with Gottsched. Bodmer, in particular, was an ardent proselytiser and maintained a keen interest in the "staatsbürgerliche Erziehung der Jugend".[9] It was he who founded the "Historisch-politische Gesellschaft zur Gerwe" in 1762, renamed the "Helvetisch-vaterländische Gesellschaft" in 1765. The society met once a week and discussed some historical or political theme, and on more than one occasion aroused the anger of the authorities by more active forms of interference in political matters.

It was thus into a world that was on the one hand open to European intellectual influences, on the other governed by a puritanical and conservative oligarchy that Pestalozzi was born in 1746, and he was very much the product of this dichotomous world. As the son of a citizen, he was privileged to receive the best education Zurich could provide, ending up at the Collegium Carolinum where Bodmer and Breitinger were among the professors. It was here and at the "Historisch-politische Gesellschaft zur Gerwe" which he joined in 1764 that Pestalozzi found himself together with a group of young men who shared many of his own radical views on the need for instituting political reform, for eradicating administrative corruption, for improving the lot of the poor in the country areas, and for upholding moral standards.

And yet Pestalozzi differed from many of those in his immediate circle in that his interest in the poor was more than academic. His father, who had died when Pestalozzi was only six, had left his family in straitened circumstances. As a result Pestalozzi had often gone to stay with his grandfather who was pastor in the village of Höngg just outside Zurich. His grandfather maintained an active interest in the poor of his parish both by visiting them regularly and by insisting on basic standards being maintained in the village school. In Höngg Pestalozzi was both introduced to the needs of the poor and recognised the virtues of a simple country life already threatened, in his view, by corrupting town influences :

> "So ging jetzt die wachsende Abschwächung und das wachsende Verderben des Landvolks vielseitig von der Stadt aus. Auch war es unter den Pfarrern der damaligen Zeit allgemeine Klage : 'Omne malum ex urbe'."[10]

The parallel with Rousseau's view that "Les villes sont le gouffre de l'espèce humaine"[11] is obvious. And when in 1762 *Emile* and the *Contrat Social* were published, both made an enormous impact on the young and impressionable Pestalozzi. Even though later Pestalozzi accused Rousseau of having roused many impracticable fantasies in him, he fully recognised the immediate relevance of Rousseau's ideas : Rousseau, he wrote, appeared

> "wie eine höhere Natur als Wendepunkt der alten und neuen Welt in der Pädagogik. Von der allgewaltigen Natur allgewaltig ergriffen, die Entfernung seiner Zeitgenossen vom sinnlich-kräftigen ebensowohl als vom geistigen Leben wie kein anderer fühlend, sprengte er mit herkulischer Kraft die Fesseln des Geistes und gab das Kind sich selbst, gab die Erziehung dem Kinde und der menschlichen Natur zurück."[12]

However Pestalozzi may have adapted and complemented Rousseau's ideas, his debt to him remains incontrovertible.

Another book which undoubtedly had a profound influence on Pestalozzi was a work by J. C. Hirzel, a Zurich doctor, with the unprepossessing title of *Die Wirtschaft eines philosophischen Bauers*.[13] The book described the agricultural venture of Jakob Guyer (nicknamed Kleinjogg), who had established a model farm near Zurich, the success of which was based on the use of marl as a fertiliser. Interest in farming was widespread at the time, not only because of the moral superiority considered to exist in the simple country way of life, but also because it provided a practical outlet for scientific and semi-scientific experimentation. Many country pastors, in particular, took it up as a hobby and endeavoured to increase milk yield, to introduce new machinery, or to improve crops by rotation or fertilisation.[14] Pestalozzi, too, showed interest and became friendly both with Guyer and later with Tschiffeli.

Pestalozzi's first two published works reveal him very much as the product of his environment. His *Wünsche*[15] were published in 1766 in the weekly paper of the "Helvetisch-Vaterländische Gesellschaft" entitled the *Ephemeriden* and began thus :

"Ein junger Mensch, der in seinem Vaterland eine so kleine Figur macht, wie ich, darf nicht tadeln, nicht verbessern wollen; denn das ist ausser seiner Sphäre. Das sagt man mir fast alle Tage; aber wünschen darf ich doch?"[16]

Pestalozzi proceeded to draw attention to various manifestations of declining moral standards in language reminiscent at times of the *Sittenmandat*. His political and social comments, however, would have received little sympathetic response from the authorities. Amongst others he included a wish

"dass doch jemand einige Bogen voll einfältiger, guter Grundsätze der Erziehung, die auch für den gemeinsten Bürger oder Bauern verständlich und brauchbar wären, drucken liess."[17]

Although this specific reference to education can be regarded as a premonition of things to come, the work as a whole expresses the sentiments of Pestalozzi's circle as well as his own. The same could be said of his work entitled *Agis* which also appeared in 1766. Beginning with a translation of the third Olynthian speech of Demosthenes as a form of introduction, it continued with a summary, based on Plutarch, of Agis' attempts to revitalise a declining Sparta. Despite a note at the beginning assuring the reader that it was "gewiss keine Satyre auf unsere Umstände,[18] clearly parallels could be drawn between the Athens of Demosthenes, the Sparta of Agis, and the Zurich of Pestalozzi.

In one respect Pestalozzi stood apart from his young friends, namely in the seriousness with which he pursued his aims. His advocacy of political change and moral regeneration was not indulged in as an academic exercise or as the petulant expression of the younger generation's disapproval of parental conservatism. He acted as he did because he felt he had a calling to help his country. And once he had espoused a cause, nothing could divorce him from it.

It was Pestalozzi's character which made him stand apart. He described himself and his situation thus :

"Ich stand freilich in der Welt wie ein Mensch, der aus einem fremden Weltteile in den unsrigen verschlagen worden ist; aber je mehr ich mich so verschlagen fühlte, je mehr verstärkte sich in mir die Vorliebe für meine Zwecke und das Eigen meines Ganges. Aber je lebhafter mein Streben nach meinen Zwecken war, je mehr verstärkten sich auch die Folgen des Mangels der Fertigkeiten, die ich dazu bedurfte und nicht hatte."[19]

The very honesty of this self-portrayal tells us much about Pestalozzi. In addition it alludes to the dilemma with which he was continually confronted throughout his life : he was a man dedicated to action, to putting his ideas into practice, and yet to do this required both attention to practical minutiae and ability to organise efficiently the people around him, neither of which abilities he possessed sufficiently—he was, as he himself admitted, too kind-hearted and too uncritical.

Thus we find the young Pestalozzi, on the threshhold of his career, filled with ideals and seeking a practical outlet for them. Later in life he accused the multiple influences of his youth of having established aims without indicating how they were to be achieved :

"Unabhängigkeit, Selbständigkeit, Wohltätigkeit, Aufopferungskraft und Vaterlandsliebe war das Losungswort unserer öffentlichen Bildung. Aber das Mittel, zu allem diesen zu gelangen, das uns vorzüglich angepriesen wurde, die geistige Auszeichnung, war ohne genugsame und solide Ausbildung der praktischen Krafte, die zu allem diesem wesentlich hinführen, gelassen."[20]

Even Rousseau's work he saw later as "ein vorzügliches Belebungsmittel der Verirrungen".[21] Filled with an overwhelming desire to help his native land and more especially the poor in country districts, Pestalozzi finally decided to imitate Guyer and Tschiffeli by taking up agriculture. In a letter to Hirzel, Pestalozzi wrote :

"Sie wüssen, mein Herr, dass ich es zu der einigen Beschefftigung meines Lebens gemacht habe, dem Landbau obzuligen; mögen Sie glauben, dass sittliche Absichten und Liebe zu Vatterland nicht ganz davon getrent sind."[22]

It was indeed a decision which might appear to have abstracted him from precisely those social aims he was pursuing. In fact, by improving agricultural methods, he hoped he would automatically help the poor who lived off the land. And when, in 1774, he decided to take in poor children and give them an education suited to their needs, he was even more overtly beginning to achieve his ambition.

Pestalozzi felt that he was entering into the unknown. And he was doing so before he had produced a single work of educational theory. He was motivated by a desire to help the poor and a realisation that previous and existing attempts by others had proved inadequate. This desire to help was primarily born of his humanity and not of his politics. Certainly he felt that the poor child did not exist

"bloss um ein Rad zu treiben, dessen Gang einen stolzen Bürger empor hebt".[23]

But at the same time he realised the dangers of trying to alter society too fast, and therefore he insisted that the poor child's education should prepare him for a life of poverty :

"Der Arme muss zur Armuth auferzogen werden."[24]

Most benevolent institutions, he felt, left a child ill-equipped for the life he would have to lead afterwards, and all too often after leaving school he would continue to be a burden on other benevolent institutions. To achieve success an educator must have a

"tiefe genaue Kenntniss der eigentlichen Bedürfnisse, Hemmungen und Lagen der Armuth, Kenntniss des Details der wahrscheinlichen Lag ihrer künftigen Tage."[25]

Having gained an insight into a poor man's life, he could adapt his education to the domestic and industrial conditions of his own locality and the individual could be suited, according to his abilities, to his future station in life.

Putting these ideas into practice, Pestalozzi decided that an industrial training adapted to the needs of local industry should form the basis of the curriculum. The boys would supplement this with some agricultural work, the girls with some domestic work. It was essential that there should be variety in their work because monotony would stunt interest in the child and prevent the adult from adapting himself to changes of technique in the industrial field. Instruction in reading, writing, and arithmetic was to be given alongside the vocational training. Pestalozzi denied that the deleterious influence of industrial work on physical health was inevitable. Variety of activity, regularity of habits, and additional physical exercises and games would produce fit and healthy children.

Pestalozzi recognised from the first that ultimate success could only be achieved if the character of the children was also formed. Thus he proposed to give them religious instruction and to encourage everything which would lead to the "Entwicklung und Bildung ihrer Herzen".[26] Formal instruction was not so important as establishing the correct relationship between teacher and taught and thus Pestalozzi maintained that :

"Der Unternehmer soll Vater seines Hauses seyn können".[27]

The heart and "eine sanfte menschliche Hand"[28] were required if the pupils were to acquire those qualities which Pestalozzi considered essential even in a poor man : peace of mind, steadiness, thrift, above all humanity.

These ideas of Pestalozzi on the education of the poor were fashioned empirically and they are derived from his short writings of 1775 to 1779 describing his activities with poor children at the Neuhof. In practice, Pestalozzi encountered some problems which he had not foreseen. By far the greatest of these was how to win the confidence of the children and their parents. Pestalozzi quickly learnt that the middle classes were separated from the poor not only by a financial barrier, but by a psychological one also. Some of the children resented the discipline, stole, and ran away. The parents who had often let them go their own way at home, sympathised with them for having to submit to a stringent routine, and when they found their offspring well clothed and capable of earning a living, they actively encouraged them to return home. Pestalozzi recognised too that he had overestimated the children's ability to produce an article of quality, and therefore the running expenses of such an enterprise were greater than he had imagined. Indeed he himself was forced to make public appeals for financial support and was finally compelled to send the children away when this support and his own funds dwindled. But despite the failure, Pestalozzi was certain that the difficulties to which he had succumbed were ones of organisation and not of substance. With greater financial backing, more technical knowledge, active support from the authorities, and more binding agreements with parents, he believed his scheme could be made to work. In any case he felt that he had proved his point by making most of the children at least happier, healthier, and better equipped to confront the life that lay ahead of them than would otherwise have been the case.

The desire to extend education for the poor remained Pestalozzi's prime ambition throughout his life. For the moment, however, the closure of his establishment at the Neuhof put an end to all his attempts to involve himself practically in the furtherance of education, and reluctantly Pestalozzi turned to writing. Twenty years were to pass before he was given another opportunity to involve himself in the world of action. Writing was for him a means of survival, not an end in itself :

"Ich bin nicht zum Schriftsteller gebildet . . . Und für alles, was mich nicht als Bedürfnis der Menschheit intressirt, bin ich unbekümret und einer der unwüssendesten Menschen. Daher muss alles, was ich als Schriftsteller sagen kan, eine äusserst mangelhafte Seite haben."[29]

Certainly Pestalozzi was not a systematic writer—he wrote from the heart, building up his ideas around those topics about which he felt deeply, adapting the ideas, assimilating new ones, but never producing a comprehensive, definitive work. Yet his initial period of writing played a fundamental part in Pestalozzi's life. It enabled him to organise the multiple influences of his youth and to place his practical experiences at the Neuhof into a wider theoretical context.

The work which he called the preface to all he would write appeared in 1780, and was entitled *Die Abendstunde eines Einsiedlers.*[30] Man, he wrote, can only learn about himself "im Innersten seiner Natur",[31] and wisdom lay in understanding oneself and the people and situations directly surrounding one. Thus the development of the individual had to follow nature, avoiding both "Einseitigkeit" and the "zerstreute Gewirr des Vielwissens";[32] it had to be approached through "Realgegenstände",[33] and must not follow the "künstliche Bahn der Schule".[34] The task of education was to develop the humanity in man first of all, only then consider training adapted to his class and profession—and it could only succeed in doing this if it took place in a natural context, that is in a society which was a family of families. The "Vaterhaus" became the "Grundlage aller reinen Naturbildung der Menschheit",[35] and, in a wider context, "Vatersinn bildet Regenten—Brudersinn Bürger".[36] Caring for the whole world was God, the Father of all men.

A society moving towards Pestalozzi's ideal was described in his successful novel *Lienhard und Gertrud* (1781). The action took place in a small Swiss village where many of the poor inhabitants were being exploited by the bailiff, Hummel. His tyranny was eventually ended when Gertrud, the wife of a poor mason and mother of seven children, begged the new squire, Arner, to intervene. Showing great concern for the welfare of the poor, Arner removed Hummel from office. In the novel the family is seen as the central, stable element in society, and the joys to be experienced within the family are praised :

"Die häuslichen Freuden des Menschen sind die schönsten der Erde. Und die Freude der Eltern über ihre Kinder, ist die heiligste Freude der Menschheit."[37]

And it is significant that it is Gertrud, a wife and mother, who takes the initiative in ending Hummel's reign. She receives immediate sympathy from Arner who appreciates that his social position involves responsibility towards his people. When Arner complains to the pastor that the laws of the land are inadequate to deal with the corruption to be found in the country, the pastor is quick to reply :

"Keine Gesetzgebung kann das, Gnädiger Herr! aber das Vaterherz eines Herrn,"[38]

thus emphasising Arner's rôle of father to his people. However it would be wrong to see the novel simply as a conflict between Arner and Hummel. Hummel himself justified his behaviour by claiming that he was acting like many others :

"Aber wo ich mich umsehe, vom Fürsten an bis zum Nacht-wächter, von der ersten Landeskammer bis zur letzten Dorf-gemeinde, sucht Alles seinen Vortheil, und drückt jedes gegen das, das ihm im Weg steht."[39]

That Hummel was able to exploit the poor indicated that they too were weak, having allowed themselves to be corrupted by promises of material gain. Gertrud points out, therefore, that more than material rewards are needed to save the poor :

"Wenn es nichts als Arbeit und Verdienst brauchte, die Armen glücklich zu machen; so würde bald geholfen seyn. Aber das ist nicht so; bey Reichen und bey Armen muss das Herz in Ordnung seyn, wenn sie glücklich seyn sollen."[40]

The necessity for inner purification introduced the question of education, the principles of which were put forward by the pastor at the end of the book :

"Ordnung, nahe Gegenstände und die sanfte Entwicklung der Menschlichkeitstriebe müssen die Grundlage des Volksunterrichts seyn, weil sie unzweifelbar die Grundlagen der wahren mensch-lichen Wahrheit sind."[41]

It was the further implications of the novel beyond a simple localised clash between good and evil which Pestalozzi felt his readers overlooked and which caused him to add three further parts to his novel (appearing in 1783, 1785, and 1787), the main object of which was to develop his ideas on popular education.

The realisation of Pestalozzi's educational and social plans as put forward in *Die Abendstunde eines Einsiedlers* and *Lienhard und Gertrud* depended on an aristocracy which was benevolent, altruistic, and enterprising. Over this period, Pestalozzi was corresponding with influential politicians in the hope of interesting them in popular education, but as the years passed and no one made concrete proposals, he became increasingly disillusioned. The French Revolution came and it was too late. In 1792 Pestalozzi wrote to Fellenberg :

"Indessen wird 'Lienhard und Gertrud' ein ewiges Denkmal seyn, dass ich meine Krefte erschöpft, den reinen Aristokratisme zu retten; aber meine Bemühung fand nichts als Undank zum Lohn."[42]

The French Revolution itself gave Pestalozzi hopes that France might pioneer his ideas. But the violent form the aftermath of the Revolution took, alienated Pestalozzi, and, apart from being elected an honorary French citizen by the National Assembly in 1792, he was never approached by the new régime. Over this period he had to reconcile himself to the unlikelihood of his being allowed to establish a system of popular education from above, and, as a result, began to consider the alternative of attracting attention to his cause by establishing an exemplary institution which could then be taken as a model for nationwide application. In a letter of 1792, Pestalozzi admitted that the ideas of *Lienhard und Gertrud* should be tried out in isolation first :

"Selbige könen im Anfang nicht die Sach des Gesezgebers und Landesfürsten syn. Sie müssen unumgenglich durch das Privatintresse einzelner Mentschen gegründet [werden], und erst, nachdem sie im Staat als eine genzlicher Privatsach ihre Einzelwürkung entscheidend gethan, erst dann kan der Staat die Ausbreitung ihrer erheiterten und erwiesenen Grundsäzen als seine Sach ansehen."[43]

Pestalozzi's change of attitude meant that in the years to come he devoted himself much more narrowly to the field of education. But it should not be forgotten that Pestalozzi's educational ideas developed out of his philosophical, political, and social views and he continued to see education as fulfilling certain philosophical, political, and social aims.

In 1797 appeared Pestalozzi's most ambitious philosophical work, *Meine Nachforschungen über den Gang der Natur in der Entwicklung des Menschengeschlechts*.[44] In it he returned to the fundamental questions he had asked himself in *Die Abendstunde eines Einsiedlers*, but now gave revised, more comprehensive answers. Once again he turned inward to search for these answers :

"Ich kan . . . nichts suchen, als die Wahrheit, die in mir selbst liegt."[45]

And having found it, he hoped that it would be universally applicable :

"Ich bin überzeugt, meine Wahrheit ist Volkswahrheit und mein Irrthum ist Volksirrthum."[46]

He went on to distinguish three aspects of man—in a natural state, in a social state, and in a moral state. The relationship between the three states was extremely complex and most of the book was concerned with elucidating it. Basically the three states occurred progressively, but were not mutually exclusive. Natural man, an innocent creature of instinct, only existed at the moment of birth. Thereafter he was immediately subject to social needs which began to adapt and restrict his animal instincts. Thus Pestalozzi rejected the notion that the "noble savage" ever existed or that it was desirable or possible to return to a natural state :

"Also ist es nicht wahr, das der Urmensch friedlich lebte auf Erden . . . Es ist im Gegenteil wahr, das Menschengeschlecht theilte die Erde, ehe es sich auf ihr vereinigte."[47]

But the social influences on natural man did not eliminate his egocentricity or his instinctive desire for self-preservation :

"Der gesellschaftliche Zustand ist in seinem Wesen eine Fortsezzung des Kriegs aller gegen alle, der im Verderben des Naturstandes anfängt, und im gesellschaftlichen nur die Form ändert, aber um deswillen nicht mit weniger Leidenschaft geführt wird."[48]

Only by attaining to the moral state could man hope to rise above the needs and restrictions imposed by the social state, and, by so doing, ennoble himself. Only in the moral state could he prefer to suffer injustice rather than to perpetrate it. The power to raise himself to this third state lay within man himself—by application of his will he could achieve it. The essential points therefore, about the *Nachforschungen* were its adaptation of the Rousseauistic concept of nature to fit into a comprehensive view of social man, and its acknowledgement of man's capacity to approach an ideal gradually by application of his own innate will.

The period devoted by Pestalozzi solely to writing ended with the request of the Swiss government to go to Stans in 1798. From this moment until 1825 Pestalozzi was totally involved in one educational enterprise after another, and, although he continued to write, his writings were for the most part closely linked to his practical work—placing it on a sound theoretical basis, explaining it, advertising it. It was the moment Pestalozzi had been waiting for and yet, if anything, it came too late. He was already over fifty, an old man who felt he was approaching the end of his days. But without the enforced period of writing which had compelled him to organise his thoughts on basic topics in a systematic way, he might well not have had the idea which was to dominate his life until his death in 1827. To grasp the nature of this idea, it is necessary to remember that until now Pestalozzi had talked of the "künstliche Bahn der Schule".[49] For him schools had become abstracted from real life, places plunged "in das tausendfache Gewirre von Wortlehren und Meinungen".[50] Subject to the rigours of rote learning, empty repetition, and stern discipline, all joy seemed to have departed out of their pupils who became no more than "ABC-Puppen".[51] Pestalozzi, having been led to dismiss all traditional forms of education, had initially valued only education closely linked to practical aims. However, finding himself in Stans and Burgdorf in a more traditional teaching situation, he now came to the conclusion which was for him so momentous : that schools were not "per se" artificial, only their *methods* were, and that all experience, even traditional school subjects, could be taught in an *ideal way*. It was from this point onwards that Pestalozzi began to talk about his "Method", an idea which was henceforth central in all his major writings, in *Wie Gertrud ihre Kinder lehrt* (1801), in *Über die Idee der Elementarbildung* (the published version of his Lenzburg speech of 1809), and in *Schwanengesang* (1825).[52]

The "Method" was not a new teaching theory but a new way of fitting all educational experience into a coherent pattern. Thus many of the component parts of the pattern were not original, nor did Pestalozzi claim originality for them.[53] Two of the pillars of the new "Method" can be traced to Pestalozzi's younger days. The first, undoubtedly inspired by Rousseau, was that education should be child-centred. The child should not be regarded as a potential adult who had to be crammed with that knowledge necessary for adult life. On the contrary, the child was an individual whose potentialities had to be developed :

"Es gibt überall kein Positives in der Erziehung und dem Unterrichte als eben das Kind als Individuum und die Individuell in ihm vorhandene Kraft."[54]

The second idea fundamental to Pestalozzi's system derived from his early criticism of schools as places concerned with words, not objects, with theories, not practice. For Pestalozzi now maintained that, if teaching matter was to be comprehended, it had to fall within the experience of the child at his particular stage of development. A child could not be taught by being presented with abstract theories, but had to be led by his experience of the natural world around him to formulate them for himself. The teacher's task, therefore, was no longer to form the child, but to guide him.

The necessity to take into account the child's capacity to understand and the limitations of his comprehension demanded a knowledge of child psychology. It also required all experience to be presented to the child in a logical natural progression corresponding to the child's individual development. Pestalozzi divided education into its intellectual, physical, and moral aspects, and set out to discover, by continual subdivision and simplification, the basic elements of these, and then endeavoured gradually to piece the elements together again into "psychologisch geordnete Reihenfolgen".[55] In the initial stages, it was essential for a child's awareness of the external world to be involved in the learning process. In intellectual education a child moved from sense impressions, to language, and finally to thought :

"Alle drei Kräfte, die Anschauungskraft, die Sprachkraft und die Denkkraft, sind als der Inbegriff aller Mittel der Ausbildung der Geisteskraft anzuerkennen."[56]

Moral education had its roots in the relationship of a child with his mother, and in turn a child's love of his mother could be explained in terms of her satisfying his needs. Physical capacities, too, developed naturally from observation and imitation to independent actions. Thus the first task of the "Method" was the analysis of all experience followed by its organisation into a *natural* sequence in harmony with the child's *natural* growth.

Pestalozzi accused contemporary education of having become fragmented, and therefore, despite the fact that much of his own work depended on analysis, he always insisted that education be seen as a total process. The unity of education lay in man himself; hitherto people had spent too much time thinking about what they knew or what they possessed, not about what they were. The starting point of education lay therefore in the "innern Würde der Menschennatur".[57] As all education strove to form a whole individual, all aspects of it were necessarily linked, with moral education playing the most important part :

"Wir sehen alle einzelnen Theile des Unterrichts in Vergleichung
mit dem Ganzen des Charakters eines Kindes für Nebensachen
an und glauben, die Garantie des Erfolgs alles Unterrichts finde
sich nur in der vollendeten Ausbildung des ersteren. Alles, was
Kopf und Hand geben kann, kommt gewiss nach, wenn das
Herz eines Kinds solid gut ist."[58]

Pestalozzi recognised not only that education involved the whole
personality of the individual at one time, but also that it was a
diachronic process which began at a child's birth. Therefore the
experiences of the infant from this moment on were of vital importance. In consequence Pestalozzi laid great stress on the relationship a child had with his parents, especially his mother, and saw
in this relationship the starting point of every aspect of education.

The task of establishing the elements of every form of human
experience and learning and then organising them in such a way
as to be naturally comprehended by a child was a formidable one.
When he attempted to carry it out in practice, Pestalozzi often had
to contend with the weakness of his own character and the
indifference of his environment. However dedicated to the
"Method", even his assistants, limited in number, were bound to
develop some aspects of the system at the expense of others; and
harmony was to become even less possible when they began to
disagree amongst themselves and with Pestalozzi. Quite apart
from the administrative problems of running an increasingly large
organisation, Pestalozzi was faced with one crisis after another : the
closure of his establishments at Stans and Burgdorf, the dispute
with Fellenberg, the departure of Schmid in 1810, and the official
report of Girard in the same year, the clash with Niederer, and
finally Schmid's expulsion from the Canton of Vaud in 1824.
Pestalozzi feared that the set-backs suffered in establishing the
"Method" would tarnish the basic concept itself, and therefore
drew attention to the truth of the "Method" as something independent of time and place :

"Wie schwach ist die sinnliche Menschennatur, oder vielmehr,
wie schwach ist alles in ihr, was nicht ewig, was nicht göttlich
in reiner Erhabenheit in ihr dasteht ! Wie (schwach) ist alles
in ihr, was nicht zur Unabhängigkeit von Gegenwarth und
Abwesenheit gereifet, alles, was Zeit und Raum in uns zu
schwächen und auszulöschen vermag !"[59]

Pestalozzi continually comforted himself and reassured others by
insisting that the "Method" was an ideal. But, as such, he recognised at the same time that it was unattainable :

"Das Wissen und Können unsers Geschlechts ist in allen seinen Fächern Stückwerk, und auch das Höchste und Beste unsrer Kultur bildet und organisiert sich nur stückweise; der Mensch geht in jedem einzelnen Teil seiner sich nur stückweise bildenden Kultur bald vorwärts, bald wieder zurück. Es wird und kann kein Zustand entstehen, der den Ansprüchen dieser grossen Idee je allgemein ein Genüge leisten wird."[60]

Pestalozzi felt that all one could do was to "arbeiten im Einzelnen und traumen im Ganzen".[61] Nevertheless his worst fears were ultimately realised. The temporal failure of the Yverdon institute fragmented his efforts, obscured his ideals. Yet the need for an analysis of all educational matter and its presentation in accordance with a child's stage of development remain today requirements in the field of education; and the empirical approach allowed by the "Method" in the organisation of details as well as its insistence on total education make it a framework which can still accommodate modern trends in educational theory.

Many of the reasons for the eventual failure of his educational institutions lay with Pestalozzi himself. It has already been noted that he lacked powers of administration, and whereas in earlier days he may have more than offset these by the energy and enthusiasm of youth, it is not surprising to find that, as he moved from his sixties to his seventies and as his assistants became more self-confident and assertive, his organisation gradually disintegrated. In 1810 Pestalozzi described his feeling of powerlessness thus :

"Ich muss mich jez vast in allem meinem Thun wie ein schwachender Grossvatter mitten unter krafftvollen Söhnen, die sein Haus vast ohne sein Zuthun führen und leiten, benehmen."[62]

While he always hoped for the moment when he could safely retire, he never felt confident that his work could continue without his person providing the unifying force.

Apart from his proven, though exaggerated, lack of administrative powers, the very appearance of Pestalozzi was such as to discourage confidence. His hair was often unkempt, his face lined with smallpox scars and covered with freckles. He walked with a gait so jerky and irregular that it seemed he was liable at any moment to trip over his own feet. He himself talked of his

"grossen, wirklich sehr fehlerhaften Nachlässigkeit in allen Etiketten und überhaupt in allen Sachen, die an sich keine Wichtigkeit haben."[63]

And certainly he had little regard for social conventions, especially as far as dress was concerned—not that he pursued eccentricity for its own sake, it merely resulted from his negligence. Yet if the nature of his personality resulted in administrative weakness and lack of influential support, it was equally the cause of his remarkable achievements. One of his friends said that he would never entrust Pestalozzi with anything, not even a hen-house, but were he himself king, he would make him his first counsellor. Pestalozzi had a lively mind, a quick wit, a quiet charm, and a gentle humour. He also possessed breadth of vision and, above all, a profound love of humanity. An Yverdon teacher wrote of him :

"Ich habe wenige Menschen kennengelernt, aus deren Lebens-mitte ein so reicher Strom der Liebe floss als aus seinem Herzen. Die Liebe war recht eigentlich sein Lebenselement, der unversieg-bare göttliche Trieb, der von Jugend auf all seinem Streben und Wirken Richtung und Ziel gab."[64]

Pestalozzi received the support of many people because he demanded nothing of them except sympathy for his aims. His organisation was held together by mutual affection and a common purpose, not by a system of powers and duties directed from above. He underlined the nature of his beliefs when he contrasted his approach with that of Fellenberg :

"Fellenberg baut die Rettung der Welt auf den Anbau seines Hofs; ich habe nichts, wo ich mein Haupt hinlegen kann. Mein Herz ist mein Alles. Und was sich nicht an dieses Herz knüpfet, gegen das habe ich keine Gewalt. . . . Er ist indessen durch einen bestimmten Plan, durch bestimmte Mittel an seinen Weg gebunden; ich und die Meinigen wollen durchaus auf nichts bauen, das uns bindet und gegen die reine und freye Ausübung unserer Grundsätze bindet und beschränkt."[65]

Even if the freedom which he upheld enabled his followers to damage his cause, by how much more did it enable them to enrich it.

Nothing can have done more to attract others to Pestalozzi's cause than his own total dedication to it. From the start he had sought some way of helping the cause of mankind, especially the underprivileged. Gradually the means of attaining his aims became clear. Only through education, organised with infinite care and universally applied, could the human race better itself :

"Solange der Mensch Mensch ist, so ist das Wesen der wahren Erziehungsweise in das Herz der Menschen gegraben, und solange ich das glaube, verzweifle ich nicht an der Möglichkeit, durch Erziehung unserm Geschlechte Gutes thun zu können."[66]

To this creed Pestalozzi committed himself selflessly and totally.

NOTES

Where possible, references are given to the "Sämtliche Werke" (abbreviated W) and the "Sämtliche Briefe" (abbreviated B). In the case of writings which have not yet appeared in the "Sämtliche Werke", references are given to the "Werke in acht Bänden" published by the Rotapfel Verlag, Zürich-Erlenbach (abbreviated RW). Details of these works can be found in the Bibliography.

    1. Published under the title, *Mandat und Ordnungen Unserer Gnädigen Herren, Burgermeister Klein- und Grosser Räthen der Stadt Zürich.*

    2. One should make it one's unfailing duty to glorify the Day of the Lord by conscientiously attending the sermons proclaiming God's Word, and the catechisms. (Ibid.)

    3. "exaggerated ostentation in clothing" leading to the "great corruption and permanent detriment of our citizens". (Ibid.)

    4. And it is also our earnest desire that all new fashions, whether they be forbidden herein or not, especially as it is impossible to list everything, should be absolutely forbidden. (Ibid.)

    5. In order that our beneficial decrees and commands be obeyed more than has been the case hitherto and that thereby the chastisement of an otherwise angry God be restrained through genuine repentance, we wish to all in these matters the spirit of obedience, which God the Father may be pleased, by his loving kindness, to grant to each and every man. (Ibid.)

    6. You say these Swiss are free? These prosperous citizens in their enclosed towns free? These poor devils amongst their cliffs and rocks free? The things that one can make a person believe! Especially when one keeps such an old story in preserving spirit. Once upon a time they freed themselves from a tyrant and for a moment were able to imagine themselves free; and then from the carcass of their oppressor the dear sun created for them, by a strange rebirth, a whole swarm of little tyrants; and now they go on telling the old story again and again and one hears it until one is sick of it: how once upon a time they had set themselves free; and now they sit behind their walls imprisoned by their habits and laws, by their table-talk and their narrow-minded ideas. (J. W. Goethe, *Schweizer Reisen,* dtv Gesamtausgabe 28, München 1962, p. 11).

    7. There are certainly in Zurich ten reading and thinking people for every one in these parts. (H. Schöffler, *Das literarische Zürich 1700 bis 1750,* Leipzig 1925, p. 108).

    8. Whereas in the great Berlin one meets scarcely three or four people of genius and taste, one finds more than twenty or thirty of them in the small Zurich. (Ibid., p. 108).

9. Instruction in civics for the young people. (Emil Ermatinger, *Dichtung und Geistesleben der deutschen Schweiz*, München, 1933, p. 436).

10. The increasing corruption and spiritual decline of the country people derived largely from the town. It used to be the general complaint of pastors at that time that all evil came from the towns. (RW8, p. 431).

11. Towns are the abyss of the human race. (J. J. Rousseau, *Emile*, Classiques Garnier, Paris, 1957, p. 37).

12. Like a higher being as the turning point between the old and new worlds of education. Powerfully gripped by all-powerful nature, realising as no other the separation of his fellow-men from the strong influence of the senses and from intellectual life, he broke with Herculean strength the chains of the mind, and gave the child back to himself and education back to the child and human nature (RW7, p. 199).

13. The work was translated into English in the eighteenth century under the title, *The Rural Socrates: Or, A Description of the Oeconomical and Moral Conduct of a Country Philosopher*, London, 1770.

14. See Martin Hürlimann, *Die Aufklärung in Zürich*, Leipzig, 1924, pp. 102–3.

15. Wishes.

16. A young man who cuts such a small figure in his country as I, has no right to impart blame or suggest improvements, for that lies outside his sphere. So I am told almost every day; but I suppose that at least I may be allowed to *wish*? (W1, p. 25).

17. That someone should print a few sheets full of simple and good educational principles which would be comprehensible and useful to even the poorest citizen or farmer. (W1, p. 28).

18. Certainly no satire on our situation. (W1, p. 3).

19. Indeed I found myself in the world like a man driven from a distant continent into this one; but the more I felt thus displaced, the stronger became my partiality for my aims and for the uniqueness of my way. But the more vigorously I pursued my aims, the more serious did the consequences of my lack of talents become which I needed to achieve these aims and which I did not have. (W14, pp. 91–2).

20. Independence, self-reliance, philanthropy, dedication, and patriotism, were the key-words of our public education. But the means whereby all these qualities could be acquired and which was so finely praised to us, namely intellectual distinction, was left without an adequate and well-grounded development of the practical powers which could substantially lead us to them. (RW8, p. 438).

21. An excellent stimulant of misconceptions. (RW8, p. 440).

22. You know, Sir, that I have made it the sole occupation of my life to apply myself to farming; you may well believe that moral intention and patriotism are not entirely divorced from this. (B3, p. 29).

23. Merely to drive a wheel whose motion raises a haughty citizen. (W1, p. 159).

24. The poor man must be educated for poverty. (W1, p. 143).

25. A profound and exact knowledge of the real needs, limitations, and situations of poverty, intimate knowledge of the probable future status of the poor. (W1, p. 143).

26. Development and formation of their hearts. (W1, p. 140).

27. The industrialist must be able to be the father of his firm. (W1, p. 162).

28. A gentle human hand. (W1, p. 138).

29. I have not been trained to be a writer . . . And about everything which does not interest me as the need of mankind, I am indifferent and one of the most ignorant of men. And therefore everything which I can say as a writer must have a highly inadequate aspect. (B3, p. 83).

30. The Evening Hour of a Hermit.

31. In the inmost recess of his nature. (W1, p. 266).

32. "One-sidedness" and "the diffuse tangle of extensive knowledge". (W1, p. 268).

33. Solid objects. (W1, p. 267).

34. Artificial way of schooling. (W1, p. 267).

35. The "paternal home" became the "basis of all the genuine natural education of humanity". (W1, p. 271).

36. A fatherly attitude forms the regent, a fraternal attitude the citizen. (W1, p. 271).

37. The domestic joys of mankind are the finest on earth and the joy of parents over their children is the most sacred joy of mankind. (W2, p. 141).

38. No legislation can do that, Sir, only the fatherly heart of a ruler. (W2, p. 195).

39. But wherever I look around me, from the prince down to the nightwatchman, from the highest council in the land to the lowest village parish, everyone is seeking his own advantage and everyone puts pressure on anything which stands in his way. (W2, p. 129).

40. If it only needed work and wages to make the poor happy, everything would soon be solved. But that is not the case. With rich and poor the heart must be in order, if they are to be happy. (W2, pp. 55–6).

41. Order, objects close to hand, and the gentle development of the forces of humanity, must form the basis of popular education because undoubtedly they are the basis of genuine human truth. (W2, p. 200).

42. In the meantime, "Lienhard und Gertrud" will be a permanent memorial to the fact that I exhausted my powers to save the true aristocracy; but my efforts were rewarded with nothing but ingratitude. (B3, p. 273).

43. Such ideas cannot at first be the concern of the legislator or ruler. They must necessarily be begun on the private initiative of individuals and only after they have made their impact in the state as a totally private enterprise, only then can the state regard the extension of their clarified and well-proven principles as its concern. (B3, p. 273).

44. My Enquiries into the Course of Nature in the Development of the Human Race.

45. I can seek nothing but the truth which lies within myself. (W12, pp. 6–7).

46. I am convinced my truth is the truth of the people, my error the error of the people. (W12, p. 7).

47. Therefore it is not true that primitive man lived peacefully on earth . . . On the contrary it is true that the human race divided the earth before it became united upon it. (W12, p. 46).

48. The social state is essentially a continuation of the battle of all against all which has its beginnings in the corruption of the natural state, and, in the social, merely changes its form, but is not, for that reason, waged with less passion. (W12, p. 79).

49. See note 34.

50. Into the manifold confusion of wordy doctrines and opinions. (W1, p. 267).

51. ABC puppets. (W13, p. 190).

52. "How Gertrude teaches her children"; "On the idea of elementary education"; "Swan-song".

53. See Pestalozzi's letter to Trapp of 4–1–1805 (B4, pp. 268–9).

54. In the whole of education and instruction there is nothing positive except the child himself as an individual and the individual power which lies within him. (RW7, p. 174).

55. Psychologically arranged sequences. (W13, p. 461).

56. All three abilities, the ability to perceive, the ability to speak, and the ability to think must be recognised as forming the basic concept behind all methods of developing the intellect. (RW8, p. 297).

57. The inner dignity of human nature. (W20, p. 18).

58. We regard all the individual elements of instruction as subordinate in comparison with the totality of a child's character and believe that the success of all instruction can only be guaranteed by the full development of the heart. Everything which the head and hand can give will definitely follow if the heart of a child is good and solid. (B5, p. 63).

59. How weak is the material world of human nature, or rather how weak everything in it is which does not exist eternally, divinely, and in pure sublimity in it! How weak is everything in it which has not matured to be independent of presence or absence, everything which time and place are capable of weakening or extinguishing within us. (B7, p. 328).

60. The knowledge and ability of our race is, in all its aspects, patchy, and even the greatest and best things in our culture only form and organise themselves bit by bit; man in each aspect of his patchily established culture goes forward at one moment, back at the next. No situation will or can arise which will ever do justice generally to the demands of this great idea. (RW8, p. 278).

61. Work in parts and dream the whole. (B7, p. 61).

62. Now in almost all my activities I must act like an ageing grandfather surrounded by strong sons who direct and organise his house almost without his co-operation. (B7, p. 32).

63. Great, really very reprehensible neglect of all matters of etiquette

and indeed of all matters which are of no fundamental importance. (B1, p. 28).

64. I have known few men whose life gave forth such a rich stream of love as that which flowed from his heart. Love was indeed his element of life, the inexhaustible and divine driving force which from his youth onwards imparted a sense of direction and purpose to all his strivings and activities. (*Begegnungen mit Pestalozzi*, Basel, 1945, p. 76).

65. For Fellenberg the deliverance of the world depends on the cultivation of his property; I have nowhere to lay my head. My heart is my all. And against anything which does not unite itself with this heart, I have no power . . . Whereas he is tied to his way by a specific plan, by specific methods, I and my adherents want to build on absolutely nothing which ties us or which hampers or limits the uninhibited and free practice of our principles. (B5, p. 52).

66. As long as man remains man, the essence of true educational methods will lie buried in the heart of man, and as long as I believe that, I will never despair of the possibility of doing good to our race through education. (B7, p. 257).

SELECT BIBLIOGRAPHY

Works
Sämtliche Werke. Hsg. A. Buchenau, E. Spranger & H. Stettbacher. Berlin, Leipzig, Zürich 1927–.
Werke in acht Bänden. Gedenkausgabe zu seinem zweihundertsten Geburtstage. Hsg. P. Baumgartner. Rotapfel Verlag, Erlenbach-Zürich 1945–9 (8 vols.).

Letters
Sämtliche Briefe. Edited by the Pestalozzianum and the Zentralbibliothek, Zürich 1946–.
Ausgewählte Briefe Pestalozzis. Hsg. H. Stettbacher. Basel 1945.

Contemporary Reminiscences
Pestalozzi im Lichte zweier Zeitgenossen: Henning und Niederer. Postscript by E. Dejung. Zürich 1944.
Pestalozzi im Urteil zweier Mitarbeiter: Krüsi und Niederer 1839–40. Annotated and introduced by E. Dejung. Zürich 1961.
Begegnungen mit Pestalozzi. Ausgewählte zeitgenössische Berichte. Hsg. W. Klinke. Basel 1945.

Biographical and critical literature
In German:
Hans Ganz   *Pestalozzi, Leben und Werk.* Zürich 1946.
Adolf Haller   *Pestalozzis Leben in Briefen und Berichten.* Ebenhausen bei München 1927.

M. Lavater-Sloman *Pestalozzi, die Geschichte seines Lebens.* Zürich and
Stuttgart 1954.
Max Liedtke   *Johann Heinrich Pestalozzi in Selbstzeugnissen und
Bilddokumenten.* Reinbek bei Hamburg 1968.
Karl Müller   *Johann Heinrich Pestalozzi. Eine Einführung in seine
Gedanken.* Stuttgart 1952.
H. Schönebaum   *Pestalozzi.* 4 vols. Leipzig, Erfurt, & Langensalza
1927–42.
In English:
J. A. Green   *Life and Work of Pestalozzi.* London 1913.
M. R. Heafford   *Pestalozzi, His thought and its relevance today.*
Methuen, London 1967.
K. Silber   *Pestalozzi, the man and his work.* Routledge and
Kegan Paul, London 1960.

LIST OF AUTHORS TREATED IN VOLS. I TO VI

* Revised versions in SWISS MEN OF LETTERS.

List of Contributors

Allan Blunden, B.A., Fitzwilliam College, Cambridge.
Nicholas Boyle, B.A., Research Fellow in German, Magdalene College, Cambridge.
John Cottingham, M.A., Lecturer in Philosophy, University of Reading.
M. R. Heafford, M.A., B.Litt., Lecturer in Education, Hockerill College, Bishop's Stortford.
G. L. Jones, M.A., B.Litt., Lecturer in German, University of Wales (Cardiff).
Brian Keith-Smith, M.Phil., Lecturer in German, University of Bristol.
Prof. J. M. Ritchie, M.A., Dr. Phil., Dept. of Germanic Studies, University of Sheffield.
Paul A. Roubiczek, M.A. h.c. and M.A. (Cant.), Fellow of Clare College; Lecturer in German, University of Cambridge, retired.
David Turner, M.A., Lecturer in German, University of Hull.
Prof. H. M. Waidson, M.A., Dr.Phil., Dept. of German, University College of Swansea.
Prof. W. E. Yuill, M.A., Dept. of German, University of Nottingham.